MSU LIBRARIES
3 2109 00156 9186

D0464062

The Family
in Cross-cultural
Perspective

2 cy

The Family in Cross-cultural Perspective

WILLIAM N. STEPHENS
THE UNIVERSITY OF KANSAS

Holt, Rinehart and Winston

New York Chicago San Francisco
Toronto London

Library of Congress Catalog Card Number: 63-13942

2122059

Printed in the United States of America

89012 68 9876

Preface

This book was written for students of the family on several levels—for college undergraduates taking family courses, for interested laymen, for social scientists who wish to add to their information on family customs, and, finally, for other cross-cultural researchers. The book reports a cross-cultural survey. It is based on a review of the literature—written mainly by anthropologists—on family customs in other societies. It treats a rather wide range of topics, as indicated by the Table of Contents: plural marriage, unilineal kin groups, arranged marriage, bride price, marriage ceremonial, rules against adultery, roles of husband and wife, family deference customs, and so forth. For each topic some cross-cultural findings are reported. The following general questions are addressed:

1. What is the range of possibilities? How do they do it in other lands?
2. What is the frequency and distribution of particular types of customs? What arrangements are most common?
3. How do American family customs stand in world-wide perspective? How do we compare with the rest of the world? (We are peculiar.)

4. What goes with what? Here, I treat two different sorts of issues. In the first place, I describe various patterning effects. Certain customs seem, almost always, to combine in very limited, predetermined ways. If a man avoids his father-in-law, he must avoid his mother-in-law. If a menstruating woman observes a cooking taboo, she must also observe a sex taboo. If one has a wedding, there must be a wedding feast. Second, I deal with some questions of cause and effect, by offering correlational evidence. The autocratic state begets an autocratic family. Alimony seems to result from a weakness of extended kinship. Romantic love is, in part, a product of sex restrictions. And so forth.

This is intended to be a fairly comprehensive survey. Almost every aspect of family life is treated—*if* there are fairly decent cross-cultural data. In two respects, though, the survey does fall short of complete comprehensiveness. In the first place, it was preceded by three other books that report cross-cultural surveys on limited areas of family customs. Each of these books is, for its respective area, a bit more intensive than the present one. If, after reading this volume, you want to find out more about sex behavior, I refer you to *Patterns of Sexual Behavior* by Ford and Beach. If you want to learn more about child rearing in other societies, read Whiting and Child's *Child Training and Personality*. Finally, there is a good-sized corpus of comparative and cross-cultural studies treating various aspects of kinship, with G. P. Murdock's *Social Structure* heading the list. However, although these three books are more intensive in their respective areas, the present work reports new findings in these areas too. Also, as a *general* cross-cultural survey of family customs, this book does stand by itself. It is the only book of its kind. Many of its findings are new, hitherto unreported, and hence treated nowhere else. Other facts reported here were previously known, but only to specialized scholars within anthropology.

A second limitation to the comprehensiveness of this survey is posed by the ethnographic coverage on which it is based. Some aspects of family life, such as the content of a wedding ceremony, are relatively easy for an anthropologist to find out about and report. Other things, such as role conflict in housewives, are harder to find out about. Needless to say, the easy-to-find-out-about areas tend to be well reported; many anthropologists talk about them, many societies are well documented in regard to them. The hard-to-find-out-about areas are ill reported; anthropologists seldom discuss them, few societies are described in regard to them, and those few reports that do exist usually present special problems of validity. Therefore, any survey such as the present one must overlook many potentially interesting issues, must leave unanswered many significant questions—simply because reasonably adequate evidence is not available. This is a great shame, but it represents the facts of life in the field of cross-cultural research.

For permission to publish quotations, thanks are due to the following: to Kathleen Gough Aberle, for permission to quote from her "The Nayars and the Definition of Marriage" and "The Traditional Kinship System of the Nayars of Malabar"; to George Allen & Unwin, Ltd. for permission to quote from Raymond Firth's *We, the Tikopia* and for permission to quote from Edith Clarke's *My Mother Who Fathered Me*; to the American Anthropological Association for permission to quote from Talcott Parsons' "The Kinship System of the Contemporary United States," and for permission to quote from "Kinship Terminology and the American Kinship System" by David Schneider and George Homans; to the American Museum of Natural History for permission to quote from "The Chukchee" by Waldemar Bogoras, from "Notes on the Social Organization and Customs of the Mandan, Hidatsa, and Crow Indians" by Robert Lowie, and from "Kinship in the Admiralty Islands" by Margaret Mead; to The American Philosophical Society and to Sue W. Miles for permission to quote from her "The Sixteenth-Century Pokom-Maya; a Documentary Analysis of Social Structure and Archaeological Setting"; to The American Sociological Association for permission to quote from "Age and Sex Categories" by Ralph Linton; to the American Sociological Association and to Hugo Beigel for permission to quote from his "Romantic Love"; to Appleton-Century-Crofts for permission to quote from *Crashing Thunder* by Paul Radin, and from *The Study of Man* by Ralph Linton; to The Bernice P. Bishop Museum and to Ernest and Pearl Beaglehole for permission to quote from their "Ethnology of Pukapuka"; also to The Bernice P. Bishop Museum for permission to quote from "Social Organization of Manua" by Margaret Mead and from "Tongan Society" by Edward Winslow Homer; to Cambridge University Press for permission to quote from *Kindred and Clan in the Middle Ages and After* by Bertha Surtees Phillpotts; to Christophers, Ltd. for permission to quote from *Law and Order in Polynesia* by H. Ian Hogbin; to the Clarendon Press for permission to quote from E. E. Evans-Pritchard's *Witchcraft, Oracles and Magic among the Azande* and from Beatrice Blackwood's *Both Sides of Buka Passage*; to Elizabeth Colson for permission to quote from her "Plateau Tonga" and from *Marriage and the Family among the Plateau Tonga of Northern Rhodesia*; to Columbia University Press for permission to quote from *A Chinese Village* by Martin Yang, from *Ojibwa Sociology* by Ruth Landes, from *Social Organization of the Papago Indians* by Ruth Underhill, and from "Marquesan Culture" by Ralph Linton (the latter appearing in *The Individual and His Society* by Abram Kardiner); to Doubleday & Company, Inc. for permission to quote from *Sex and Family in the Bible and the Middle East* by Raphael Patai, copyright 1959 by Raphael Patai; to Charles Frake for permission to quote from his "Social Organization and Shifting Cultivation among the Sindangan Subanun"; to The Free Press of Glencoe for permission to quote from *Essays in Sociological Theory Pure and Applied* by Talcott Parsons and from *Premarital Sexual Standards in America* by Ira Reiss; to Hildred Geertz for permission to quote from her "Javanese Values and Family Relationships"; to Victor Gollancz, Ltd. and Harper & Row, Publishers for permission to quote from *Return to Laughter* by E. S. Bowen; to Harper & Row, Publishers for permission to quote from *A Black Civilization* by W. Lloyd Warner and from "The Family in India" by David Mandelbaum (the latter appearing in *The Family: Its Function and Destiny* by R. N. Anshen); to Harvard University Press for permission to quote from *Children of the Kibbutz* by Melford Spiro, from *Children of the People* by Dorothea Leighton and Clyde Kluckhohn, from *The Navaho* by Kluckhohn and Leighton, and from *A Solomon Island Society* by Douglas Oliver; to Jules Henry for permission to quote from his *Jungle People*; to Harcourt, Brace & World, Inc. for permission to quote from

Son of Old Man Hat by Walter Dyk; to David Higham Associates for permission to quote from *Himalayan Village* by Geoffrey Gorer; to The International African Institute for permission to quote from "Native Marriage in Buganda" by Lucy Mair; to Alfred A. Knopf, Inc. for permission to quote from *The Prophet* by Kahlil Gibran (copyright 1923 by Kahlil Gibran; renewal copyright 1951 by Administrators C. T. A. of Kahlil Gibran Estate, and Mary G. Gibran); to Collier-Macmillan, Ltd. for permission to quote from *The Kiwai Papuans of British New Guinea* by G. Landtman, from *The Lakhers* by Neal Parry, from *The Life of a South African Tribe* by H. A. Junod, and from *The Todas* by W. H. R. Rivers; to The Macmillan Company, for permission to quote from *Social Structure* by G. P. Murdock and from *When the Tree Flowered* by John G. Neihardt; to The Josiah Macy, Jr. Foundation for permission to quote from *Problems of Infancy and Childhood* by Milton Senn; to The Manchester University Press for permission to quote from Elizabeth Colson's *Marriage and the Family among the Plateau Tonga of Northern Rhodesia*; to the McGraw-Hill Book Company, Inc. for permission to quote from *Primitive Behavior* by W. I. Thomas, copyright 1937; to the David McKay Company, Inc. for permission to quote from *Himself: the Autobiography of a Hindu Lady* by Ramabai Ranade.

Special thanks are due Margaret Mead, who graciously helped me get permission to quote copiously from the following of her works: *Coming of Age in Samoa*, "Social Organization of Manua," *Growing Up in New Guinea*, "Kinship in the Admiralty Islands," and *Sex and Temperament in Three Primitive Societies*; thanks to William Morrow & Company, Inc. for permission to quote from Margaret Mead's *Coming of Age in Samoa, Growing Up in New Guinea*, and *Sex and Temperament in Three Primitive Societies*; to John Murray for permission to quote from Verrier Elwin's *The Baiga*; to W. W. Norton & Company, Inc. for permission to quote from *Life in Lesu* by Hortense Powdermaker; to *Oceania* for permission to quote from "A New Guinea Infancy: from Conception to Weaning in Wogeo" by H. Ian Hogbin; to Oxford University Press for permission to quote from *The Maria Gonds of Bastar* by W. V. Grigson and from *The Muria and*

Their Ghotul by Verrier Elwin; to F. W. Preece Ltd. for permission to quote from *The Australian Aboriginal* by Herbert Basedow; to Routledge & Kegan Paul Ltd. for permission to quote from *An African People in the Twentieth Century* by Lucy Mair, from *Growing Up in New Guinea* by Margaret Mead, from *Growing Up in an Egyptian Village* by Hamed Ammar, from *Philippine Pagans* by R. F. Barton, from *The Social Institutions of the Kipsigis* by J. G. Peristiany, and from *The Khoisan Peoples of South Africa* by I. Schapera; to The Royal Anthropological Institute of Great Britain and Ireland for permission to quote from "Women and Their Life in Central Australia" by Geza Roheim, from "The Natives of Borneo" by H. Ling Roth, from "Three Tribes of Western Australia" by A. R. Radcliffe-Browne, from "The Nayars and the Definition of Marriage" by E. Kathleen Gough, and from "The Structural Implication of Matrilateral Cross-cousin Marriage" by E. R. Leach; to Peter Smith for permission to quote from *The Irish Countryman* by C. M. Arensberg; to The Bureau of American Ethnology for permission to quote from "Chippewa Child Life and Its Cultural Background" by Inez Hilger; to The Williams & Wilkins Company for permission to quote from "Comparative Data on Division of Labor by Sex" by G. P. Murdock; to Melford Spiro for permission to quote from his *Children of the Kibbutz* and "Ifaluk: a South Sea Culture"; to The University of California Press for permission to quote from *Matrilineal Kinship* by David Schneider and Kathleen Gough, from The University of California Syllabus Series, No. 101 (selections from Herodotus), from "Clan and Moiety in Native North America" by Ronald Olson, and from "The Autobiography of a Winnebago Indian" by Paul Radin; to The University of Chicago Press for permission to quote from "Early Nineteenth-century American Literature on Child Rearing" by Robert Sunley (appearing in *Childhood in Contemporary Cultures* by Margaret Mead and Martha Wolfenstein; copyright 1955 by the University of Chicago), from "Chiricahua Apache Social Organization" by Morris Opler (appearing in *Social Anthropology of North American Tribes* by Fred Eggan; copyright 1937 by the University of Chicago), from *Suye Mura: A Japanese Village* by John Embree (copyright 1939 by the University of Chicago), from *The Tara-*

humara by Wendell Bennett and R. M. Zingg (copyright 1935 by the University of Chicago), from "A Hindu Wife" by D. N. Mitra (copyright 1946 by the University of Chicago), and from "The American Family: Consensus and Freedom" by Margaret Park Redfield (copyright 1946 by the University of Chicago); to the University of Illinois Press for permission to quote from *Life in a Mexican Village: Tepoztlan Revisited* by Oscar Lewis and from *Theory of Culture Change* by Julian Steward; to the Indiana University Press for permission to quote from *The Twice-born* by Morris Carstairs; to the University of Kentucky Press for permission to quote from *Balkan Village* by Irwin Sanders; to the University of Minnesota Press for permission to quote from *The People of Alor* (copyright 1944) by Cora DuBois; to The University of North Carolina Press for permission to quote from *Tropical Childhood* by David Landy; to The Vanguard Press, Inc. for permission to quote from *Sex in History* by G. Rattray Taylor (copyright 1954 by G. Rattray Taylor); to John Wiley & Sons, Inc. for permission to quote from "Culture and Personality Development in a Gusii Community" by Robert and Barbara LeVine and from "The Rajputs of Khalapur" by Leigh Triandis and John Hitchcock, both appearing in *Child Rearing in Six Societies* by Beatrice B. Whiting; and to the Yale University Press for permission to quote from *Becoming a Kwoma* by John Whiting, from *Sun Chief* by Leo Simmons, and from *Smoke from Their Fires* by Clellan Ford.

Appreciation is due two great ethnography collections, which were the basis for this work: The Human Relations Area Files and Harvard's Peabody Museum Library.

Finally, I must acknowledge my debt to G. P. Murdock, the pre-eminent scholar in this entire area. He, far more than anyone else, has led the way in the cross-cultural study of family and kinship. Latecomers, such as myself, are merely following paths that he has already cleared.

Lawrence, Kansas W. N. S
February 1963

Contents

1

Is the Family Universal?

The family is a social group characterized by common residence, economic cooperation, and reproduction. It includes adults of both sexes, at least two of whom maintain a socially approved sexual relationship, and one or more children, own or adopted, of the sexually cohabiting adults. The family is to be distinguished from marriage which is a complex of customs centering upon the relationship between a sexually associating pair of adults within the family. Marriage defines the manner of establishing and terminating such a relationship, the normative behavior and reciprocal obligations within it, and the locally accepted restrictions upon its personnel.

Used alone, the term "family" is ambiguous. The layman and even the social scientist often apply it undiscriminatingly to several social groups which, despite functional similarities, exhibit important points of difference. These must be laid bare by analysis before the term can be used in rigorous scientific discourse.

Three distinct types of family organization emerge from our survey of 250 representative human societies. The first and most basic, called herewith the *nuclear* family, consists typically of a married man and woman with their offspring, although in individual cases one or more additional persons may reside with them. The nuclear family will be familiar to the reader as the type of family recognized to the exclusion of all others by our own society. Among the majority of the peoples of the earth, however, nuclear families are combined, like atoms in a molecule, into larger aggregates. These composite forms of the family fall into two types, which differ in the principles by which the constituent nuclear families are affiliated. A *polygamous* family consists of two or more nuclear families affiliated by plural marriages, that is, by having one married parent in common. Under polygyny, for instance, one man plays the role of husband and father in several nuclear families and thereby unites them into a larger familial group. An *extended* family consists of two or more nuclear families affiliated through an extension of the parent-child relationship rather than of the husband-wife relationship, that is, by joining the nuclear family of a married adult to that of his parents. The patrilocal extended family, often called the patriarchal family, furnishes an excellent example. It embraces, typically, an older man, his wife or wives, his unmarried children, his married sons, and the wives and children of the latter. Three generations, including the nuclear families of father and sons, live under a single roof or in a cluster of adjacent dwellings. . . .

The nuclear family is a universal social grouping. Either as the sole prevailing form of the family or as the basic unit from which more complex familial forms are compounded, it exists as a distinct and strongly functional group in every known society. . . .

The view of Linton that the nuclear family plays 'an insignificant role in the lives of many societies' receives no support from our data. In no case have we found a reliable ethnographer denying either the existence or the importance of this elemental social group. (Murdock 1949: 1–3)

If you were to start reading a textbook on Marriage and the Family you would probably find, somewhere early in the book, some statement to the effect that the family is one of those rare human institutions that is so important, so essential, that human beings simply cannot do without it, and that, therefore, every society—no matter how strange and primitive—has the family. All societies have the family. There are no exceptions. The family is universal to all mankind.

This is a rather frequent pronouncement by textbook writers on the family. They get this notion from the experts, the anthropologists. The most eminent and respected of anthropologists, men such as Clyde Kluckhohn (1960) and George Peter Murdock, have long been saying the same thing. All societies have the family.

Most anthropologists say this—not all. Melford Spiro, for one, has his doubts. These arose as a result of field work in a kibbutz community in Israel, where children live apart from their parents and are reared in dormitories. Kathleen Gough Aberle is another anthropologist who, because of her own field work, has some reservations about the universality of the family. She studied the Nayars of southern India, among whom all women were husbandless and all children were fatherless. Both Spiro and Gough say essentially this: "Maybe the family is universal and maybe it is not. *It all depends on how you define it.*" (Spiro 1960; Gough 1959)

When I started my own cross-cultural survey of family customs, I felt that one of the things I should do was to tackle this old question: Is the family universal? So I set about doing the best I could to answer it—scanning the ethnographic literature, taking particular pains to read descriptions of all possible exceptional cases.

I quickly ran into two really difficult problems. The first was a data problem. Many societies are ill-described. Many an ethnography[1] gives a hazy, incomplete picture of family customs. There are a good many societies that may or may not have the family; we cannot be sure, because they are incompletely described.

The second problem was the one raised by Spiro and Gough. Some societies may or may not have the family, depending on how you define "family." At first glance, the universality of the family hangs on a purely arbitrary decision about choice of definition (disregarding, for the moment, the data problem). If you

---

[1] An ethnography is a written description of the customs of some other society. The ethnographer, the person who has written the ethnography, is in most cases an anthropologist. Like other cross-cultural researchers, I am completely dependent, in my studies, on these ethnographic descriptions. My "raw data" comes from ethnographies—accounts of other societies, written by others.

define the family one way—making a very broad, inclusive definition—then the family may very well be universal. However, if you define the family with a less inclusive definition, certain odd cases like the Nayars and the kibbutzim turn out to lack the family—by definition—and the family cannot be regarded as universal. In other words, at first it looked as if the question of the universality of the family was a rather pointless argument, depending on the arbitrary choice of definitions.

However, as I delved more deeply into the problem, I found it was even more hopeless than this. I was not able to give even an arbitrary answer to the question because I was unable to arrive at a clear definition of the term "family." "Family" is really terribly hard to define properly. We all use this term. Doubtless, we all have the illusion that we know what we mean by it. But when one sets about trying to separate families from nonfamilies, he begins to realize how very hard it is to say just exactly what a "family" is.

To make a long story short, I failed in my task of getting a good definition of the family, and I was never able to give a good, precise answer to the question, "Is the family universal?" Still, I decided to devote the first part of this book to a recounting of my failure. This is for two reasons. First, it should prove a good exercise in that basic problem of science—and of thought, generally—the problem of definitions. Because it is hard to define, the term "family" is an especially good case study, illustrating as it does so many of the pitfalls, difficulties, and headaches that may face a person who tries to define a concept precisely.

The second reason has to do with presentation. In trying to define "family" and answer the question of its universality, I will have to review various aspects of the family, various types and clusters of family-related customs. I will have to note some of the many cross-cultural variations in family-related customs as well as some of the many cross-cultural regularities. All of this, I think, should prove an apt and interesting introduction to our subsequent cross-cultural survey of the family.

Chapter 1 will move through the following steps. First, I will offer my definition of the concept "family." After the definition has been spelled out we will take it apart and examine its difficulties. After this critical exercise, we will move on to a consideration of borderline cases. These are a number of societies that come close to "not having the family" by almost any definition. Finally, I will remark on an apparently near-universal cluster of culture traits, of which the customs we term "family" appear to be a part; and we shall review some perfectly logical, but non-occurring, alternatives to this cluster of culture traits.

First, the job of definition. Preparatory to the definition of "family," I must say what I mean by "marriage."

Marriage Defined

Marriage is a socially legitimate sexual union, begun with a public announcement and undertaken with some idea of permanence; it is assumed with a more or less explicit marriage contract, which spells out reciprocal rights and obligations between spouses, and between the spouses and their future children.

This definition rests on four subsidiary terms which, in turn, require definitions of their own. They are "socially legitimate sexual union," "begun with a public announcement," "with some idea of permanence," and "marriage contract."

Socially legitimate sexual union. This is a sexual union which is not "against the law." The married couple will not come in conflict with some social norm, or be punished, for having sexual intercourse.

Since marriage, by definition, involves a socially legitimate sexual union, a married couple does not have to be discreet about the fact that they are having sexual intercourse. Perhaps they do not announce to the world "We have sexual intercourse," but they say "We are married," "I'd like you to meet my wife," "This is my husband," and so forth. And the terms "married," "wife" and "husband" imply—to all except little children who have not yet learned the facts of life—that they *are* having sexual intercourse, or that they may if they want to.

In short, one thing "marriage" means is a socially legitimate sexual union—a social arrangement that sanctions intercourse between the mates.

Begun with a public announcement. Nearly always, marriage begins with an elaborate ceremonial, which may include feasting, fancy dress, processionals, perhaps religious observances of some kind, and large-scale financial outlay by either the groom, the groom's parents, or the bride's parents. At the very least, bride and groom announce their marriage to "society"—to kinfolk and neighbors, perhaps to the state and law court, or to God (as in the Christian church wedding).

With some idea of permanence. Marriage, as opposed to other possible kinds of sexual unions, is not supposed to be a temporary arrangement. It is not a one-night affair, or a short-term contract (of six months, or two years, or five). It is supposed to last " 'til death do us part," or, at least " 'til death or divorce do us part."

Assumed with a marriage contract. Getting married means taking on obligations. Some of these obligations may be very specific and formalized; others are not. In some societies the marriage contract is highly legalized. If writing is known, the marriage contract may be drawn up like any other legal document. In such highly legal marriage contracts, there are usually lists of specific offenses against each spouse; any major offense is punishable by divorce, or by fine, or by some other sort of penalty. The marriage contract may state who gets what in case of divorce: who gets the children, how the property will be divided. The marriage contract often contains financial agreements; a certain amount may have to be paid to the wife's father before the marriage is fully "legal."

Aside from the specific terms of the marriage agreement, there are other implicit obligations a person assumes when he contracts for marriage. He agrees—however implicitly—to play the spouse role that his society deems appropriate. Depending on what society it is and what the particular cultural requirements are, the groom may implicitly agree to give economic support to his wife, to help his father-in-law, to teach and discipline his children, and not to philander. The bride may agree (implicitly) to cook, clean house, carry wood and water, mend, and do various other personal services for her husband, to be an acquiescent sex partner, to care for the children, to help with the farm work, and so forth. These implicit, informal, extralegal parts of the marriage contract also have "teeth" in them; breaches of the implicit marriage contract may also bring punishment, in terms of community disapproval or, at the very least, family quarreling and dissension.

I started by saying that marriage is a socially legitimate sexual union, which, because it is socially legitimate, can be and is announced to the world. One way marriage differs from extramarital sexual unions is that it imposes obligations in return for sexual gratification—the obligations of the marriage contract. In an adulterous sex encounter, or during ceremonial sexual license, or in a permissive sex relationship (see Chap. 5), people do, at times, get their sex "free." But in marriage, sexual gratification is not free—even though it may seem to be. Marriage, to which sex satisfaction may be a major inducement, is fraught with obligations—to the spouse, to children, perhaps to the spouse's relatives, and, at times, even obligations to the state or the church.

Of course, there is the reverse side of the coin. When you get married, other people become obligated to you, too—your spouse, perhaps your spouse's relatives, your future children. Perhaps the essence of social living is obligations: obligations you owe to others, and obligations other people owe to you. When a person gets married his obligations are widened and enhanced—he becomes "more social," in a sense. He assumes more social ties. There are now more people with whom he is interdependent.

Also, marriage often means a *shift* in social obligations. It adds new obligations, but it may weaken previous reciprocal obligations between the newly-married person and his parents and other blood relatives. This is usually the case in our own society, but we seem to be a bit extreme in this regard.

This concludes the background to my definition of marriage. Once more, here is the definition:

Marriage is (a) a socially legitimate sexual union, begun with (b) a public announcement, undertaken with (c) some idea of permanence, and assumed with a more or less explicit (d) marriage contract, which spells out reciprocal obligations between spouses, and between spouses and their future children.

The Family Defined

I will define the family as a social arrangement based on marriage and the marriage contract, including recognition of the rights and duties of parenthood, common residence for husband, wife, and children, and reciprocal economic obligations between husband and wife.

This definition also rests on four subsidiary terms: "marriage and the marriage contract" (already defined), plus three others that require further definition—"reciprocal economic obligations between husband and wife," "common residence," and "rights and duties of parenthood."

Reciprocal economic obligations between husband and wife. Husband and wife cooperate in their work and share in their consumption; they "fit together" within an economic unit. Perhaps they work together on the farm, the wife doing the farm wife's tasks, and the husband doing the farmer's tasks. Nearly everywhere the wife cooks, keeps house, and cares for the children. In our own society, in an urban setting, the subsistence work—"bringing home the bacon"—is the "proper" sphere of the husband. In most societies, husband and wife share the subsistence work. Husband and wife also own property in common—a house or land, livestock, and so forth—so that the family is a sort of joint property-holding unit, a little corporation. Children are also part of this economic unit, first as consumers, then perhaps as producers, and finally as heirs to the estate.

Common residence. Wife and her children live together in the same house. Husband either lives in the same house with them or lives close by—close enough for frequent, daily interaction with wife and children.

Rights and duties of parenthood. Wife lives with and cares for her children, and they are socially recognized as "hers." Husband lives with or near them, and the children are socially recognized as "his." This social recognition of parenthood may mean a variety of things. It always means incest taboos: a parent can't marry or have intercourse with his (or her) child. Parenthood also means responsibility for the care and upbringing of the children, perhaps with some form of liability if a child is neglected or commits a crime and gets into trouble. Parenthood may also mean reciprocal economic obligations, from parent to child, and from child to parent. Some examples: working for father on the family farm, paying a son's bride price, financing father's death feast, supporting a widowed mother.

Finally, the child-parent relationship is used to assign child to other sorts of social groups, especially larger kin groups. Example: because X is your father, you belong to X's clan, are allowed to use the property of X's brother, worship X's ancestral gods, observe the clan's food taboos, unite with X's clan for work-bees and during feuds (see Chap. 3). In other words, the social recognition of parenthood is integral to the complex of customs termed "kinship": it is part of an arrangement for assigning people to wider social relationships and social groups, which are explained or rationalized in terms of "blood-relatedness."

I could name other things that often characterize the family, but these are, I think, the bedrock, defining attributes: 1) marriage; 2) economic ties or cooperative work between husband and wife; 3) common residence; and 4) socially recognized parenthood.

One characteristic of the family, as contrasted with other social groupings, such as religious cults, business organizations, secret societies, or football teams, is the fact that the family involves everyone in the society. Everyone—or almost everyone—is "brought up" in a family, has a childhood "home." In some societies, everyone is expected to marry and to be a parent, and is looked at askance if he (or she) doesn't. This is less true in our society than in some others. We do have institutions, such as orphanages, for rearing children, and some people do get through life without being parents, or without even getting married. Still, by virtue of various sorts of social pressures, most of us manage to wend our way through the complete family cycle: child in a family, spouse, and parent.

Finally, I want to recapitulate one of Murdock's points. A *nuclear* family is a group composed of one husband, one wife, and their children. As Murdock said, nuclear families may combine—"like atoms in a molecule"—to form larger aggregates: extended families, and polygynous families.[2] However, when I refer to "the family" without using a qualifier ("extended family," or "polygynous family"), I will *always* mean the *nuclear* family.

This concludes my definitions of the "family" and "marriage." Let us now examine some of the problems that these definitions present.

The Definition of Marriage Attacked

The first defining attribute of marriage was a *socially legitimate sexual union.* This first point is not too difficult. However, it should be recognized that "socially legitimate" is a rather vague term. Understandably, the ethnographers usually don't say whether or not marriage involves a "socially legitimate sexual union." Perhaps we are safe in assuming that the sexual union between husband and wife *is* always "socially legitimate," but we should keep in mind the fact that often the ethnographers do not specifically *say* that it is.

Another thing we must recognize is that, in many societies, there are periods when sexual intercourse between husband and wife is *not* socially legitimate—when it is "against the law," taboo. The main taboo periods are the times before and after childbirth. The pregnancy sex taboo may begin any time after the second or third month of the wife's pregnancy and last until delivery. While the pregnancy sex taboo is in force, the pregnant wife may not have sexual intercourse. *After* the birth, the wife (in many societies) observes a *post partum* sex taboo, which may last for several years. Also, nearly all societies seem to observe a menstrual sex taboo: a woman may not have sexual intercourse while she is menstruating (Stephens 1962). In addition to the pregnancy sex taboo, the *post partum* sex taboo, and the menstrual sex taboo, there may be other sex taboos in honor of special occasions: before a hunting trip, before and after a war expedition, when the crops are harvested, or during various times of religious significance. In fact, if I might make a wild guess, I would speculate that in

---

[2] Polygynous family: one in which there is one husband and two or more wives.

the "average" primitive society (if there is such a thing), sexual intercourse between husband and wife is socially legitimate *less than half the time.*

So it is all right to say that marriage involves a "socially legitimate sexual union" if this means that it is "socially legitimate" for husband and wife to have sexual intercourse during certain specified, nontaboo periods. But we should keep in mind that most societies—nearly all, no doubt—do have taboo periods during which marital sexual intercourse is *not* permitted. In some societies, the taboo periods last longer than the nontaboo periods.

A final point on this issue of social legitimacy. In our own society, the only socially legitimate sex relationship is between husband and wife; sexual intercourse is only permissible when it occurs within marriage. In many other societies—most, in fact—this is not the case: extramarital sex, in some form, is permitted (see Chap. 5).

The next defining attribute of marriage was that it begins with a *public announcement.* There is not too much difficulty with this point either. Most societies have elaborate marriage ceremonials, which certainly qualify as very adequate and very public announcements that marriage is about to commence. There are other societies, however, without marriage ceremonials. For these cases it is a bit harder to tell whether marriage begins with a public announcement. In some cases, apparently, it does; in other cases marriage, or what passes for marriage, probably does not begin with a public announcement. But there are some doubtful borderline cases.

The third defining attribute of marriage is that it is contracted with *some idea of permanence*: it lasts until "death or divorce do us part." The problem here is judging intent. In societies with extremely high divorce rates, where divorce is easy to come by, just how serious is the intent of permanent mateship? For example, Leighton and Kluckhohn report that, in a sample of Navaho: "Only about one woman out of three and one man out of four reaches old age with the same spouse, and men who have had six or seven different wives in succession are frequently encountered." (Leighton and Kluckhohn 1948:83)

In my ethnographic notes, there are a number of cases of this sort (Aymara, Copper Eskimo, Jamaica, Kaingang, Ojibwa). Do people in such societies *really* get married with the intention of making it permanent?

The fourth and last defining attribute of marriage is that it is accompanied by a *marriage contract.* "Marriage contract" is, unfortunately, a rather vague term. Ethnographers sometimes describe some aspect of the marriage contract. But it is not the sort of thing that an ethnographer would report as being absent, even if it *were* absent. Perhaps we would be safe in assuming that a marriage contract—at the very least, some sort of implicit marriage contract (obligation to play the conventional spouse role) —is always present. But often the ethnographer says nothing about the marriage contract—whether it is present, or absent, or what it consists of.

One of the marginal cases we will soon examine, the common-law marriage pattern in Jamaica, is interesting with respect to the marriage contract; "common-law marriage" in this case seems to mean an arrangement to *evade* some of the obligations of the marriage contract and still be "married." An eat-your-cake-and-have-it-too sort of affair. At least, from the point of view of the man.

We have now reviewed the definition of marriage, and turned up a few difficulties. "Marriage contract" is a vague term, hard to match against the ethnographic data. The same is true, perhaps to a lesser extent, of "socially legitimate sexual union." Some societies have extremely high divorce rates. Do people in these places marry "with some idea of permanence"? And in regard to "begun with a public announcement," there are some doubtful borderline cases.

The Definition of the Family Attacked

We have already considered the first defining attribute of the family—marriage.

The second defining attribute of the family was *reciprocal economic obligations* between husband and wife. Here we run into a data problem. Many ethnographies tell us very little about the economic obligations between husband and wife. If a society existed in which there were no economic obligations between husband and wife we cannot be sure that it would be reported by the anthropologist.

There is a second problem here. "Reciprocal economic obligations between husband and wife" implies, or might be taken to imply, that the family is a separate economic unit. In our own society, this is very often the case: the family *is* a separate economic unit. Although the house may be in the wife's "name" and the salary checks may be made out to the husband, for all practical purposes what belongs to the husband also belongs to the wife, and will eventually be willed to the children. Husband is the "breadwinner," Wife "runs the house," and between them they manage an establishment—a family (that is, a nuclear-family household).

But in many societies, and even among certain families in our own society, the nuclear family is *not* a separate economic unit. This is particularly the case within the *extended-family household* —the household arrangement that predominates in about one fourth of the societies in Murdock's *World Ethnographic Sample.*

Let us take a hypothetical example of an extended-family household. This household is made up of husband and wife and their children, the husband's father, husband's mother, husband's brother, husband's brother's wife, and husband's brother's children. It is a farm family. The menfolk—husband, husband's father, husband's brother, and the older boys—do the work in the fields. The children all play together. The womenfolk cooperate in caring for the children, although wife will give her own children some special attention. They all eat together at one long table. The women and older girls cooperate in the cooking, serving, and dishwashing. The women also share the various tasks of house cleaning, poultry care, food processing, and other tasks of farm work regarded as "women's work."

Husband's father has nominal ownership of the house and farm, but it is understood that husband and husband's brother have implicit ownership rights and will inherit the property when the old man dies. Each of their children will also have some sort of inheritance rights.

In such a situation, one might say that husband and wife do

have "reciprocal economic obligations" because they are both expected to—and do—contribute to this extended-family enterprise. Husband helps with the "men's work," and wife helps with the "women's work." Both belong to the same economic unit. But the economic unit is the extended family; it is not the nuclear family. Husband and wife (with their children), by themselves, could not be said to make up a separate economic unit.

So often the nuclear family is not a separate economic unit but merely part of a larger economic unit—an extended family or, perhaps, a polygynous family.

There are also many societies in which husband and wife belong to *different* economic units. Each spouse belongs to a different unilineal[3] kin group, which collectively owns property and works collectively on kin-group enterprises. In such cases, the unilineal kin groups act to "split" the nuclear family; husband has economic interests within his unilineal kin group, and wife has economic interests within her own unilineal kin group, which is separate from her husband's (see Chap. 3).

Because of kin-group membership or simply due to customs of private ownership, it may occur that husband and wife *do not own property in common.* Perhaps husband owns the house, some farm land, the cows, his tools and personal possessions; wife owns other farm land, the poultry and poultry produce, the cooking pot, and her personal possessions (see Chap. 6).

Finally, in many societies the husband is not the "breadwinner." Wife works her own fields, raises her own crops, and is economically self-sufficient, or nearly so.

To summarize the various difficulties with this defining attribute of the family—reciprocal economic duties between husband and wife:

1. In some ethnographies, work of husband and wife is incompletely reported, or not reported at all.

2. The nuclear family is often not a separate economic unit, but instead a subsidiary part of some larger economic unit, most commonly an extended-family household.

---

[3] For definition and description of unilineal kin group, see Chapter 3.

3. The nuclear family may be "split," to some extent, by unilineal kin groups.

4. Because of unilineal kin groups or customs of private ownership, husband and wife may own little or no property in common.

5. In most societies wives do subsistence work and are partially or wholly self-supporting.

The statement "within the family there are reciprocal economic obligations between husband and wife" is really not very meaningful. The crucial question is, how much in the way of economic obligations or cooperative work must they share in order for the family to exist? If wife does not rely on husband for economic support—does the family exist? Does it exist if they own no property in common? If husband and wife are economically self-sufficient of each other, own separate property, and cooperate only to care for their children—does the family exist? What is the bare minimum of economic obligation between a mated pair that must be present before that mated pair (and their children) constitute a family?

The third defining attribute of the family was *common residence* for husband, wife, and children.

Here the definition runs into real trouble. In the first place, "common residence" cannot be taken to mean that they all live under the same roof. In Murdock's *World Ethnographic Sample*, 125 societies, about one fourth of the societies in the sample, are characterized by *mother-child households*. That is, in a good proportion of the societies of the world, mother and young children customarily live in one house, and father, for a good part of the time, at least, lives in another house.

Now the question is, how close must father be living to mother and children for the maintenance of a "common residence"? Must he be within fifty feet of mother and children? In the next block? Can he live a mile away?

Usually, in the mother-child household arrangements, father appears to live fairly near to his wife and children—next door, or in the same small compound, so that he sees them frequently, daily (Whiting and D'Andrade, m.s.). But occasionally he doesn't live near to them. Furthermore, in some societies there are variant patterns; a certain percentage of fathers live with or near their families, but others live far away. Also, in some societies, fathers—as a regular occurrence—wander far from home (Somali, Iban, Tepoztlan-Mexico). Finally, we face the data problem again. For some mother-child household societies, we simply do not know how near the father is; the ethnographer does not tell us.

In short, the mother-child household poses a number of difficulties for the definition of the family: there is the data problem (incomplete reports), the problem of variant patterns within the same society (some fathers living near and other fathers living far away), and the problem of where to draw the line. What is common residence? If "common residence" must mean that father, mother, and young children all live in the same house, then the family, as I defined it, is clearly *not* universal to all known societies. If, on the other hand, "common residence" can mean that father lives "close" to mother and children, we are confronted with the question: How close is "close"? How near must father be before common residence can be said to exist?

To further underline this problem, I will cite a rather extreme example of mother-child households: the Kipsigis of Kenya. The Kipsigis live in grasslands country. They occupy rather widely scattered farm-homesteads. That is, their settlement pattern is somewhat similar to that of American farmers: dispersed farmhouses, separated from each other by fields and pastures. The Kipsigis have various household arrangements, but the one that concerns us here is the *mother-child farm-homestead* (which is probably not the most common Kipsigis household arrangement . The goal of Kipsigis men is to accumulate wives and cattle. Polygyny—plural wives—serves the end of cattle accumulation: it makes possible greater herds, more cattle keepers. A young Kipsigis man marries a first wife, and lives with her on a farm-homestead. As time passes—if he is lucky—he has a son who is mature enough to manage the homestead cattle. At this point the man tries to marry again and set up a new homestead—fairly distant from the first—with a new wife. If he is fortunate and successful, and lives long enough, he will eventually preside over several farm-homesteads, each one occupied by one of his wives and her children (by him). He spends some of his time at each of his homesteads, but will probably devote more time to the homestead of his youngest wife (Peristiany 1939).

In such a situation, is there "common residence"? Does the family exist in such a case, or not?

There is another problem: the *children's* absence. It seems to be almost universally true that in societies with a high proportion of mother-child households, boys move away from home at or before puberty (Stephens 1962, Chap. 4). Since Murdock designated one fourth of the societies in his *World Ethnographic Sample as* "mother-child-household societies," and since this condition is—at least—almost universal for all mother-child-household societies, it is clear that the adolescent boy's "living out" (or at least "sleeping out") is a very common condition the world over. In a good many of these cases, apparently, the separation is not complete. The boy does not sleep at home (he has his own sleeping hut, or sleeps in a bachelors' house); but he may eat at home, he may do some work for his parents, and he may spend some time around home. However, in a few societies the separation between a boy and his family does appear to be pretty drastic. Among the Murngin and the Nyakusa, for example, adolescent boys have their own villages (Wilson 1951; Warner 1937). In some avunculocal societies,[4] such as the Trobriands, the boy moves to the village of another relative (Malinowski 1922, 1929, 1935).

So, it is hard to be specific about "common residence" as a defining attribute of the family because father and older boys often "live out," or at least "sleep out," at varying distances from home, and under varying arrangements. Finally, there are a few societies in which *young* children do not live at home either. In my ethnographic notes there are two African cases, the Hehe and the Thonga, in which the grandmother customarily takes the child away from home when it is weaned, keeps the child with her, and then returns it to its parents some years later (Brown 1935; Junod

---

[4] Societies in which, most commonly, a newly married couple lives with or near the groom's matrilineal kin—with his "mother's brothers."

1927). There are additional societies, such as Samoa, in which young children wander rather freely from one set of relatives to another, often spending little time at home (Mead 1930).

To summarize: "common residence" poses many difficulties to the definition of the family. It is true that the nuclear-family members—husband, wife, and unmarried children—often do live together, under the same roof. But "living out," by the husband, or by the children, is so common and takes so many differing forms that perhaps the definition of the family would be clearer and stronger if we forgot about "common residence" and excluded it from the definition.

The fourth and last defining attribute of the family was *the rights and duties of parenthood,* which I described as follows: "Wife lives with and cares for her children, and they are socially recognized as 'hers.' Husband lives with or near them, and the children are socially recognized as 'his.' " I further said that parenthood means, among other things, responsibility for the care and upbringing of children, and reciprocal economic obligations between children and parents. These two phrases, "responsibility for the care and upbringing of children" and "reciprocal economic obligations between children and parents," are probably a bit vague, and again confront us with the data problem: in some ethnographies, little or nothing is said about parental and filial responsibilities. Also, there are quite a few *matrilineal* societies—societies in which father and his children belong to different unilineal kin groups. In some of these matrilineal cases, the jural or formal rights, powers, and obligations of the father vis-à-vis his children are most attenuated. In societies such as the Eastern Timbira, Menangkebau, or Trobriands, it *might* be argued (for each case, the issue is in doubt) that the father does not have "rights" over his children or "duties" toward them.

We have now reviewed the various difficulties and failings inherent in my definitions of *marriage* and of *the family.* It should be fairly clear, by now, why it is so difficult to say whether or not the family is universal to all known societies. In places, the definition is vague. Many societies are not adequately described. Finally, there are various borderline areas, vexing problems of either/or, such as: how near must father live to mother in order for them to "occupy a common residence"; how much economic cooperation and sharing must there be between husband and wife in order that they can be said to have "reciprocal economic obligations"?

Borderline Cases

As far as I know, there is no known society that clearly and unequivocably "does not have the family" (by my definition). However, there is one case on record that, if it is not a clear exception, comes very close to qualifying as such—the Nayars of Malabar. Other societies are doubtful cases, particularly on the point of "common residence"—cases such as the Kipsigis, the Nyakusa, the Hehe, and the Thonga. Finally, there are other exceptions which, for various reasons, could not be considered as representing "societies." In this section we shall look at some of these borderline cases: the Nayars, the kibbutzim, the common-law and mother-child families of Jamaica, the *mut'a* marriage of the Arabs, and the *mokhthoditi* unions of the Todas.

The Nayars

The Nayars are a Hindu caste group living in southern India. Traditionally, they were a warrior subcaste; they were fairly high-status military retainers, the Malabar version of the Knights of the Round Table. In the local caste hierarchy, they ranked beneath only the Brahmins and the royal subcastes. Today their old culture has broken down. At present, there is nothing very exceptional about their family customs. However, in the old days things were different, and, apparently, most exceptional.

I say "apparently" because, to my knowledge, there is no very reliable *firsthand* account of their former "family" customs. The ethnographer is Kathleen Gough, a modern anthropologist who attempts to reconstruct the old culture by referring to documents of various kinds and by taking informants' reports of "how it was in the old days." This sort of past-tense ethnography is not unusual in anthropology. A good many ethnographies of the American Indians, for example, are of this type. However, because this is such an exceptional case, it should be kept in mind that this report is secondhand, so to speak. Gough was not actually "there." She could not check these documents and informants' reports by seeing the customs with her own eyes, because the customs no longer existed.

The best way to describe the old "family" customs is to follow a Nayar girl through part of her life cycle. At puberty, the girl was ritually married. She and her ritual husband stayed together for a few days. Then she went back home; they separated forever. After her "marriage," the girl was a woman—free to take on lovers. Apparently, Nayar women could have several lovers at one time (as could Nayar men). The lovers were of two types: 1) passing visitors, and 2) "visiting husbands":

> A husband visited his wife after supper at night and left before breakfast next morning. He placed his weapons at the door of his wife's room, and if others came later they were free to sleep on the verandah of the woman's house. Either party to a union might terminate it at any time without formality. A passing guest recompensed a woman with a small cash gift at each visit. But a more regular husband from within the neighborhood had certain customary obligations. At the start of the union, it was common although not essential for him to present the woman with a cloth of the kind worn as a skirt. Later he was expected to make small personal gifts to her at the three main festivals of the year. These gifts included a loin-cloth, betel-leaves and areca nuts for chewing, hair-oil and bathing oil, and certain vegetables. Failure on the part of a husband to make such a gift was a tacit sign that he had ended the relationship. Most important, when a woman became pregnant, it was essential for one or more men of appropriate subcaste to acknowledge probable paternity. This they did by providing a fee of cloth and some vegetables to the . . . midwife who attended the women in childbirth. . . .
>
> Although he made regular gifts to her at festivals, in no sense of the term did a man maintain his wife. Her food and regular clothing she obtained from her matrilineal group. The gifts of a woman's husbands were personal luxuries which pertained to her role as a sexual partner—extra clothing, articles of toilet, betel and areca nut—the giving of which is associated with courtship, and the expense of actual delivery—not, be it noted, of the maintenance

> of either mother or child. The gifts continued to be made at festivals only while the relationship lasted. No man had obligations to a wife of the past.
>
> In these circumstances, the exact physiological fatherhood of a child was often uncertain, although, of course, paternity was presumed to lie with the man or men who had paid the delivery expenses. But even when physiological paternity was known with reasonable certainty, the genitor had no economic, social, legal or ritual rights in, nor obligations to, his children after he had once paid the fees of their births. Their guardianship, care and discipline were entirely the concern of their matrilineal kinsfolk headed by their *karanavan.* (Gough 1959)

The woman lived in a large household with her brothers, sisters, mother, and maternal aunts and uncles (plus her own children and those of her sisters). Her "visiting husbands" were there only at nighttime. The "men of the house," the men who "lived" there, did the work, and helped discipline the children, were her brothers and maternal uncles. They, in turn, were "visiting husbands,"—nighttime visitors—in other households.

Let us review the definitions of marriage and the family and see at what points the Nayar may not have met the requirements for "having the family." First, the definition of marriage:

A socially legitimate sexual union? Yes, it was. No doubt about this.

Begun with a public announcement? In doubt. Perhaps the "husband's" gifts were a sort of announcement of mateship, but we can't be sure.

Undertaken with some idea of permanence? Doubtful.

Assumed with a marriage contract? Doubtful. Gough tells us of certain obligations that the "husband" contracts for—gifts at festival occasions and at childbirth; she gives no indication, however, that the woman enters into any sort of marriage contract.

Now the other defining attributes of the family:

Reciprocal economic obligations between husband and wife? Apparently not. The woman seems to have had no economic obligations to her visiting husband at all. Apparently, she had absolutely no work obligations to him: she didn't cook for him, keep house for him, or mind his children, and so forth. The "husband," for his part, seems only to have "paid" her for her sexual favors. In fact, the role of the Nayar "wife" looks very much like that of the American prostitute or kept woman, with one important difference: among the Nayar, this role was perfectly "proper"; it was socially legitimate.

Common residence for husband, wife, and children? Probably no. According to Gough, any particular "husband" was only an occasional nighttime visitor. He came after supper, and left before breakfast. Many nights, no doubt, he did not come; one of the woman's other "husbands" visited her. His recognized "home" was with his matrilineal kin, the household of his sisters, mother, maternal aunts, and uncles.

Rights and duties of parenthood? Doubtful. Apparently, fatherhood involved only one vestigial paternal duty: paying the midwife.

Did the Nayar "have the family" or not? According to my definition, they probably did not. However, the Nayar do confront us with several weaknesses in the definition. To wit: What constitutes "common residence"? What constitutes "economic obligations"? How do we know when a mateship is begun with some idea of permanence?

The Kibbutz

Throughout the history of Western society, there have been numerous utopian social movements—radical attempts to remold social life into a more perfect form. Often, the utopians have tried to revolutionize family life. To my knowledge, none of these utopian experiments has ever "worked" (that is, lasted a long time). Because these cases are short-lived, and because they usually occur in just one or several small communities, they cannot be considered "societies." Some of them, to be sure, don't "have the family," but none of them could be termed "societies that don't have the family."[5]

---

[5] You might ask: Why aren't they societies? What constitutes a society? Those are very good questions, which I would rather not answer. Compared with the problems inherent in properly defining "society," difficulties in the definition of "family" pale to insignificance.

I will review, here, just one such utopian experiment, the kibbutzim of Israel. There have been several kibbutz movements, as there are over 300 kibbutz communities in present-day Israel. The kibbutz community I will refer to is Kiryat Yedidim (fictitious name), as described by Melford Spiro (Spiro 1956, 1958). Kiryat Yedidim was founded by a group of young European Jews in the 1920's. It was designed to be a little communist community, a sort of self-contained collective farm. All property was to be owned in common by the entire community; all work was to be for the benefit and enrichment of the kibbutz, that is, there was to be no such thing as individual or family property. Kiryat Yedidim, as it exists today, falls a bit short of this communist goal, but it does make a serious approach toward it.

As far as marriage and family customs are concerned: in the first place, there is no wedding ceremony. When a couple decides to "marry," they merely apply to the housing committee for a common room. (Later, when the woman becomes pregnant, they are legally married according to Israeli law.) A "husband" and "wife" do live together; they have their own room. However, they take their meals at the communal dining hall, and each works for the kibbutz.

> Marriage entails few changes in the life of either spouse. The woman, whose membership in the kibbutz is legally distinct from that of her husband, changes neither her name nor her work when she marries. She is supported, not by her husband, but by the entire kibbutz to whose economic well-being she, in turn, contributes by her labor. Women, like men, work a nine-hour day, although relatively few women today work in the agricultural branches of the kibbutz economy. If the wife is economically independent of her husband, so is the husband independent of his wife for domestic services. These—meals, laundry, mending, and so forth—are provided in the various communal institutions of the

---

The term "society" raises the added problem of boundaries. At what boundary line does one society end and another society begin? When is a group sufficiently culturally distinct, or culturally homogeneous, or large, to be considered a separate society? To what society do you belong? Western society? American society? Middle-class midwestern American society? Middle-class white Protestant Peoria, Illinois society?

> kibbutz. Should either become ill, he is assured of complete and continuous economic support, not by dint of special initiative on the part of his spouse, but because the kibbutz continues to provide for his needs. Having a child poses no economic problems for the couple. The kibbutz assumes complete responsibility for its economic welfare. In brief, economic factors play no role in cementing the relationship between husband and wife. The marital bond is compounded of emotional, sexual, and social ties exclusively. The advent of children does not alter this generalization; the kibbutz family is not an economic unit. (Spiro 1958:6)

Children do not live with their parents; they are brought up in dormitories.

> The educational system of Kiryat Yedidim is known as *chinuch meshatuf*, or collective education. Its characteristic feature is the fact that the children live in communal nurseries with age peers, where they are reared by "nurses," nursery teachers, and teachers, rather than by their parents. Since parents of both sexes work in the kibbutz economy, the daily interaction between parent and child is in general restricted to the interval between the parents' return from work in the afternoon and the child's bed-time.
>
> The children do not live in one immense institution-like dwelling. They are organized into small peer groups—the number of children in a group varying and increasing with age—which occupy scattered dwellings or "cottages" within the kibbutz. . . .
>
> An infant enters the kibbutz educational system when he returns with his mother from the hospital at the age of four or five days. . . . Thus, the responsibility for the kibbutz child is assumed immediately by some one or more persons other than his parents. . . .
>
> The adult with whom the young child has most frequent contact and who is directly responsible for his well-being and his education is his "nurse." (Spiro 1958:8–25)

So, in Kiryat Yedidim, there are no "parents" in the ordinary sense of the term. A child may visit with his mother and father for an hour or two per day; but he does not live with them, they do not take care of him, they are not responsible for him.

On what grounds, by the definition, may we say that the family is not present in Kiryat Yedidim?

Is marriage a socially legitimate sexual union? Yes, it is.

Is it begun with a public announcement? Probably. The request to the housing committee no doubt constitutes a public announcement.

Is marriage undertaken with some idea of permanence? Probably it is.

Is there a marriage contract? We can't say. There may be some sort of implicit marriage—or mateship—contract.

Are there economic obligations between husband and wife? Clearly, husband and wife are not a workteam. Neither are they a property-owning unit. So perhaps the answer is "no." Yet, both husband and wife work for the greater glory of the kibbutz, which in turn supplies them with food, clothing, and so forth. The kibbutz community is the economic unit. Perhaps, as cooperating members of the kibbutz, they do have "economic obligations" to each other, in the same way as do a husband and wife in an extended-family farm-homestead.

Is there common residence for husband, wife, and children? No. Husband and wife reside together, but their children do not live with them.

Are there rights and duties of parenthood? Doubtful. About the only "right" of parenthood appears to be the right to visit with the child.

In short, the kibbutz of Kiryat Yedidim clearly does not have the family. However, this little kibbutz cannot be considered a "society." It is a social experiment, and, from all indications, a rather short-lived social experiment. Spiro says there are serious strains and considerable dissatisfaction—not the least of which stem from the attempt to "emancipate" women from motherhood. By all signs, this experiment in family customs is not long for this world.

Jamaica

In various Christian countries *common-law marriage* exists as a variant form of mateship. By "common-law," I mean a union which is not "legal," and which is not sanctioned by the church. In Mexico, according to the 1950 census, 20 percent of all unions were common-law (Lewis 1959:17). Common-law marriage is prevalent among certain groups of New World Negroes. Frazier has described it among Negroes in the United States (Frazier 1949), and various writers have documented its occurrence in the Caribbean (Clarke 1957; Cohen 1956; Henriques 1953; Smith 1956). Where common-law marriage occurs, it may give rise to a number of different patterns of mateship, which, for one reason or another, fail the requirements of being classified as "marriage" and "family."

I will review, here, three such patterns, which occur in Jamaica and have been described by Edith Clarke. They are permanent concubinage, temporary concubinage, and the fatherless family.

Marriage in Jamaica, according to one of Clarke's informants, "is not for the poor man" (Clarke 1957:77). To be "properly" married is expensive; it involves an elaborate church wedding, a wedding feast, special clothes, and other expenses. Those Jamaicans who can afford it are, usually, "properly married" (often after a period of trial-marriage). Those who can't afford it turn to illegal, common-law unions (or "concubinage," as Clarke calls it).

One form of concubinage is a permanent union, or at least a union that is undertaken with some intention of permanence. The couple are not legally married; there is no marriage ceremony; the man has no legal liability in the case of separation. There is some doubt as to whether or not permanent concubinage is begun with a "public announcement." Aside from this, it seems to satisfy the requirements of being a true "marriage."

Some of the poorer Jamaicans are itinerant sugar-cane workers; they move from town to town, following seasonal work. ("In *tempo moto* I ping-pong around, one week on, one week off.") A good many of these people practice short-term "housekeeper" arrangements, that is, temporary concubinage.

> Both in the huts and in the barrack rooms, men, and in many cases men and women, shared sleeping accommodations. This often led to temporary quasi-conjugal relationships which relieved some of the immediate economic needs of the partners. They pooled their resources and shared living expenses. The man got someone to do

his marketing, cook his food and wash his clothes for considerably less than it would cost him to pay for these services. . . . The woman was assured of her keep and a roof over her head. She continued her normal activities but could now spend whatever she earned on clothes and other necessities and send money to assist in the maintenance of any children she might have left at home. Although these "housekeeper" arrangements, as they are called, may not be formed primarily for sexual reasons, it is normal for the parties to have sexual relations and for children to be born. . . . these relationships are entered into almost haphazardly, with no implication of permanence and are inevitably highly unstable. If the woman becomes pregnant the association invariably breaks up either immediately or after the child is born. (Clarke 1957:93–101)

Temporary concubinage, like permanent concubinage, does not seem to begin with a public announcement. It further fails the requirements of the definition of the family on two other counts: apparently, it is not undertaken with the intention of permanence; and children are absent. If the woman has had previous children, they are cared for by her mother or some other relative. If the woman becomes pregnant, the union dissolves.

A third pattern, associated with common-law marriage, is the fatherless family. A woman lives with her children (and perhaps with her parents). She has a succession of lovers. Sometimes these men stay with her for a while, in her home. Sometimes they don't even do that (Clarke 1957:103). Depending on what form it takes, the fatherless family may fail various requirements of the definition: common residence of husband, wife, and child; economic obligations between husband and wife; rights and duties of parenthood (fatherhood); and so forth.

Of course, fatherless families or "broken homes" occur everywhere, as the result of death, desertion, or divorce. In many primitive societies broken homes are automatically "mended," by means of the sororate and levirate (see Chap. 4); that is, when one loses a spouse, the spouse is automatically and immediately replaced. But in most "civilized" parts of the world, such as Europe, the United States, or Jamaica, this is not the case.

Mut'a Marriage

This is a variant form of mateship, found in parts of the Moslem Middle East. This is definitely not "marriage" according to the definition, because it is undertaken for a specified, short-term period—for instance, during the time a man is on a pilgrimage, or while he is on a protracted business trip. To paraphrase the definition: this is a socially legitimate sexual union, begun with the idea of *im*permanence. A *mut'a* marriage contract is drawn up, specifying the length of time the union is to last. When the time period ends, "husband" and "wife" part forever. The man pays his *mut'a* "wife" for services rendered; there are no further obligations. However, any children born of the union are considered the legitimate children of the *mut'a* "husband" and may inherit from him. In addition to the *mut'a* marriage, these people also have lifelong marriages. *Mut'a* marriage is undoubtedly less common than marriages of the more conventional type (Jeffery 1949:60).

Mokhthoditi Marriage

This is another variant form of mateship, practiced by the Todas of India. *Mokhthoditi* is clearly not "marriage" either; it is undertaken by people who are already married (that is, have other spouses).

> The *mokhthoditi* (man) has no rights over any children who might be supposed to be his; they are regarded as the children of the (woman's) regular marriage. . . .
>
> There are two forms of *mokhthoditi* union. In one the woman lives with the man just as if she were his real wife, almost the only difference being that any children would be legally the children of the legal husband of the woman . . . In the other and more usual form the man visits the woman at the house of her husband. (Rivers 1906:526–527)

Rivers does not tell us enough about *mokhthoditi* to allow us to judge just how far it diverges from "the family" (as defined).

At the very least, it does not seem to include the "rights and duties of parenthood" (fatherhood); also, in its more common form, it does not include common residence. *Mokhthoditi* is a variant pattern among the Toda; everyone has a "real" marriage, and then some people—in addition—also have *mokhthoditi* unions.

Logical Alternatives to the Family

It is probably too much to say that the family, as defined, is universally found in all known societies.[6] However, if it is not universal, it is probably almost universal. There are no clear, undoubted exceptions; there is no society which, without a doubt, clearly "does not have the family." (The Nayar come closest.) There exist, to be sure, certain forms of mateship that fail the requirements of being "marriage" or "family"; but these represent either variant patterns within societies that also have more conventional family arrangements (Toda, Arabs, Jamaica), or small, short-term social experiments (Kibbutz). In addition, there are certain borderline cases—societies that may or may not "have the family," depending on the definition. The Kipsigis, Hehe, and Nyakusa are examples of this sort. Finally, of course, many ethnographies are incomplete; if the data were better, we might find a few exceptions.

Still, as compared with this handful of borderline cases and possible exceptions, there are hundreds of societies that apparently *aren't* exceptions. Consider the fact that G. P. Murdock, with his encyclopedic knowledge of ethnographic literature, *could* conclude that the family *is* universal. Even if he was overly bold in coming to this conclusion, he never would have reached it if the societies that seem to have the family were not legion, and the societies that appear not to have the family were not few and inconspicuous.

I think we can tentatively conclude that, although the family may not be universal to all known societies, it is almost universal. Furthermore, in my opinion, the family is only part of a larger pattern or custom-complex which is also almost universal. This

---

[6] The imprecision of the definition, alone, prevents such a statement.

larger pattern includes at least three elements: 1) the family (including marriage); 2) extended kinship (the reckoning of affinal- and blood-relatedness beyond the nuclear family); and 3) incest taboos, which apply not only to nuclear family members but also to various extended kin.

This large pattern—family, extended kinship, incest taboos—is found in nearly all societies. In its essentials, the pattern is almost always the same. There are incidental variations, to be sure. We have already reviewed many variations in the family—in household arrangements, economic ties, and so forth. Extended kinship also takes many forms—different kinds of unilineal and residential kin groups, varieties of patterned kin behavior, and so forth (Chap. 3). Incest taboos—which kin are sexually taboo and which are not—also have their local variations. But everywhere, or almost everywhere, these three elements—nuclear family, extended kinship, and incest taboos—run through human societies like a scarlet thread, giving some degree of sameness, everywhere, to the conditions of mating, child rearing, and social placement.

People get married, live in families, observe incest taboos, and have ties with kinfolk. The details—of marriage and family customs, incest taboos, and extended kin groupings—show great intercultural variation; the essentials show little, if any, variation. Considering the many ways in which human life does differ from culture to culture, this is rather astonishing. It is anything but "natural" and self-evident that all (or almost all) societies should have the family, incest taboos, and extended kinship, because there are other, perfectly logical, alternative arrangements.

One logical alternative to the family/incest taboo/kinship pattern is the *freely cohabiting band.* In this hypothetical case, there are no incest taboos, no prohibitions against adultery, not even any concept of adultery. All persons of the opposite sex are "fair game." Each woman nurses and cares for her own children, with some help from other women. As there would be great doubt about who is the "real" father of any particular child, there is a sort of collective fatherhood. All men of the band have certain paternal or avuncular-type ties to all the children. Needless to say, there is no marriage and no marriage contract. For economic purposes, the entire band is one big "family," one cooperating social unit.

What could be more simple, more natural? There would be no need for wife exchange with other bands. Sex life would be truly spontaneous and unshackled. Yet, this condition of "natural man" has never been found. As far as we know, it has never occurred.

Another logical alternative is a *society without incest taboos.* This hypothetical society has marriage, marriage contracts, and rules against adultery. But there is no concept of incest. Father can marry daughter, and mother can marry son; but most marriages take place within the same generation—between brother and sister, or between cousins. Family groups—large extended families, particularly—can perpetuate themselves indefinitely. They can be sexually self-sufficient, with no need to turn to other family groups in search of wives.

To appreciate the relative simplicity and efficiency of such an arrangement, one must have some understanding of the terrific burden and complication that incest rules impose on many primitive tribes. In some of these societies, incest taboos are so widely extended that a girl must actually leave her home village, band, or district in order to find a husband. Also, marriage usually involves burdensome marriage payments, which must be passed between the families of bride and groom. Without incest taboos, these difficulties could be eliminated. Life might be much simpler and easier for many peoples. Yet, as far as we know, this hypothetical society without incest taboos has never occurred; if it ever did occur, it did not survive to be recorded by anthropologists.

A third logical alternative is the *mother-child family.* Mother and children live together, but there is no father. Mother's sexual relations are with casual lovers, who do not live with her, and are not—socially—fathers to her children. The mother's brothers and uncles act as father substitutes; they are the "men of the house." They, in turn, are casual lovers to *other* mothers, who live with *their* brothers and uncles.

As we have seen, the Nayar seem to have fit this case. Mother-child families occur as a variant pattern in many societies, such as Jamaica, and the United States. Sometimes the mother lives with other adult kin; sometimes she does not. Sometimes she has lovers; in other cases, she remains continent after losing her husband. However, with the possible exception of the Nayar, the mother-child family is never found as the dominant, most usual, arrangement. It seems that fathers, that is, *social* fathers, are necessary.

A final logical alternative is represented by the kibbutz experiment. Children live in dormitories, are cared for and trained by nurses and teachers, and are not "raised" by their parents. This is never found, either, as a lasting social arrangement. Apparently, it is simply not feasible to separate young children from their mothers, or at least from their female kinfolk (making allowance for the Hehe and Thonga grandmothers).

There are, no doubt, other possible arrangements, which—although they never occur—might "logically" replace the family-incest taboos-kinship pattern. But no matter how simple and efficient such alternatives appear, they are apparently not practical, because they are never found as the dominant arrangement for any society (with the possible exception of the Nayar).

Why is it that alternatives are impossible? Why is the family/incest taboos/kinship pattern so inevitable? Here the answer must be disappointing. We don't know.

To be sure, various people have proposed reasons. Murdock, for example, gives numerous reasons for the strength, the utility, hence the universality of the family (Murdock 1949:3–11). In Chapter 5 we shall review no less than eight reasons given by Lowie, Westermarck, Freud, Murdock, Tylor, Kluckhohn, Kingsley Davis, and others, for the universality of incest taboos. But clever and interesting as many of these "reasons" are, they are merely after-the-fact speculations—interesting possibilities. They are guesses, not knowledge. Why does human society seem to require this knit-together package of family/incest taboos/kinship? This must remain one of the many mysteries of nature.

2

Plural Marriage

Kowtow
To the great Yen How
And wish him the best of lives,
With his one little two little three little four little
five little six little
Wives.

There are four possible forms of marriage; monogamy, one husband and one wife; polygyny, one husband and two or more wives; polyandry, one wife and two or more husbands; and group marriage, two or more husbands and two or more wives. This chapter will deal with the last three forms: polygyny, polyandry, and group marriage, the forms of plural marriage.

Most societies permit polygyny, and are characterized by a mixture of polygyny and monogamy. That is, in most societies, a certain percentage of marriages are polygynous, while some marriages are monogamous. In Murdock's *World Ethnographic Sample,* only about 20 percent of the societies are designated as strictly monogamous.

If strict monogamy is uncommon, polyandry and group marriage are positively rare. The *World Ethnographic Sample* lists four societies in which polyandry is the dominant marriage form: Toda, Marquesas, Nayar, and Tibet. There is no known society in which group marriage is clearly the dominant, or most frequent, marriage form, but, as we shall see, there are a number of doubtful borderline cases. In a handful of additional societies, polyandry and group marriage appear infrequently as variant marriage-forms.

So, the mixture of polygyny and monogamy seems to characterize about four fifths of the world's societies. About one fifth are strictly monogamous. And polyandry or group marriage appear occasionally, as very rare, exotic marriage forms. Let us start with polyandry and group marriage.

Polyandry and Group Marriage

We are considering these two marriage forms together because they often go together. That is, where you find polyandry you often find group marriage, and vice versa. It appears that polygyny—one man's having several wives—is a very usual, "natural" human condition. Polyandry—several men sharing one wife—appears to be very unusual, very "unnatural." So, it looks as if wherever men could bring themselves to share a common wife, they have done the "natural" thing and added more wives. Polyandry begets group marriage. At least, so it appears.

We shall first go over the few ethnographic accounts (known to the author) of polyandry and group marriage. We will start with cases in which polyandry/group marriage appears to be the dominant marriage form, and conclude with other cases in which it is apparently variant, or infrequent. As we consider these ethnographic accounts, we will look for several points: 1) How is the jealousy problem handled, and are the co-husbands jealous of each other? 2) What are the economic inducements, if any, to plural husbanding? 3) Why is there not a wife surplus and husband shortage where polyandry is the dominant pattern? 4) How is fatherhood decided?

The first case is the Todas, a non-Hindu tribe in India, described by W. H. R. Rivers:

> The Todas have a completely organized and definite system of polyandry. When a woman marries a man, it is understood that she becomes the wife of his brothers at the same time. When a

boy is married to a girl, not only are his brothers usually regarded as also the husbands of the girl, but any brother born later will similarly be regarded as sharing his older brother's rights.

In the vast majority of polyandrous marriages at the present time, the husbands are own brothers. . . . In the few cases in which the husbands are not own brothers, they are clan-brothers, that is, they belong to the same clan and are of the same generation.

THE JEALOUSY PROBLEM

. . . it seems that there is never any difficulty, and that disputes never arise. The brothers live together, and my informants seemed to regard it as a ridiculous idea that there should ever be disputes or jealousies of the kind that might be expected in such a household. . . .

From the foregoing account it appears that a woman may have one or more lovers as well as several husbands. From the account given of the dairy ritual, it appears that she may also have sexual relations with dairymen of various grades. . . . Further, there seems to be no doubt that there is little restriction of any kind on sexual intercourse. I was assured by several Todas not only that adultery was no motive for divorce, but that it was in no way regarded wrong. . . .

Instead of adultery being regarded immoral, I rather suspected, though I could not satisfy myself on the point, that, according to the Toda idea, immorality attaches rather to the man who grudges his wife to another. One group of those who experience difficulty in getting to the next world after death are the *kashtvainol,* or grudging people, and I believe this term includes those who would in a more civilized community be plaintiffs in the divorce court.

PATERNITY

. . . the brothers are all equally regarded as the fathers of the child. . . .

In most of the genealogies, the descent is traced from some one man, but there can be no doubt whatever that this man was usually only one of several brothers, and the probable reason why one name only is remembered is that this name was that of an important member of the community, or of the last surviving of the brother-husbands.

SEX RATIO

There is no doubt whatever as to the close association of the polyandry of the Todas with female infanticide.

GROUP MARRIAGE

. . . a study of the genealogies shows that often each brother has his own wife, or that several brothers have more than one wife between them . . . there is a tendency for the polyandry of the Todas to become combined with polygyny. (Rivers 1906:515–530)

So the Todas had fraternal polyandry, which occasionally slipped into group marriage. They practiced female infanticide. The question of paternity is a bit hazy; Rivers first says that all husbands are equally the fathers of the child; then he speaks of genealogical descent being traced from one father. He says that the co-husbands appear not to be jealous; indeed, the Todas appeared to feel it was "bad form" to show sexual jealousy.

The next case is the Polynesian inhabitants of the Marquesas Islands in the South Pacific; the ethnographer is Ralph Linton. Like the Nayar, this is another past-tense ethnography. Linton arrived there after the culture was greatly changed and (I believe) polyandry had vanished. His account is based on informants' reports of "how it was in the old days."

The Marquesan household was polyandrous, there being usually two or three men to one woman, while in the household of the chief there might be eleven or twelve men to three or four women, one head wife and subsidiary wives. . . . Well-to-do households would usually add one or even two wives to the establishment some years after the initial marriage of the household head. All members of such a group had sexual rights in each other, the arrangement constituting a sort of group marriage.

ECONOMIC INDUCEMENT TO CO-HUSBANDING

A chief or head of a rich family would sometimes arrange a marriage with a young woman because she had three or four lovers whom he wished to attach. The men would follow the woman; in this way the family head could build up the manpower of his household. Only the poorest households at the lower social levels were monogamous, and there was much envy of rich households by poor ones.

Households were graded in prestige. The basis of the grading rested primarily on man power; the more active adult males the household had, the more wealth it could accumulate.

SEX RATIO

The household consisted of the main husband, the wife or wives, and a series of subsidiary husbands. Even with plural wives the men in a household far outnumbered the women. The numerical disparity of the sexes on these islands was puzzling. The Marquesans swore they did not practice infanticide, yet the ratio of males to females was about two and a half males to one female. It is probable that they did away with the younger girls but kept the practice from cultural notice.

ORGANIZATION OF THE HOUSEHOLD

The average household consisted then of a household head, a group of other men, and a single wife. The second husband outranked the other subsidiary husbands and took charge of the household in the absence of the head. He also exercised preferential sexual rights with the wife, either with the first husband's permission or during his absence. In the chief's establishment all the husbands would have certain sexual rights with the chief's wife, but when there were a good many husbands, they lived in another house and were called over at the will of either the chief or the wife and rewarded for good service by a night's pleasures. In theory, all members of the household had sexual rights; even servants had access to the head wife if she so wished; actually, the first husband ran things and distributed favors, although it was to his advantage to see that his underlings were sexually satisfied, so that they would work for his house and not wander off with other women.

PATERNITY

Questioned about his parentage, a native would say, "So-and-so is my real father, but the head of my household was Such-and-such, son of. . . ."

JEALOUSY

> The idea of exclusive sexual possession was almost lacking in the Marquesas, and was certainly socially disapproved. . . .
>
> After marriage there was little if any overt expression of jealousy on the part of the men. . . . Jealousy between plural husbands or even between married men over some woman ouside their households was considered very bad manners. (Linton 1939:152–175)

Apparently, Marquesan co-husbands were not brothers. As for the Todas, the paternity picture is a bit hazy; possibly, for genealogical purposes, the household head was "father" of all children in the house, but we can't be sure. There is an economic inducement to co-husbanding: a man tries to recruit co-husbands so that they will work for him and help him become a "big man." Like the Todas, the Marquesans disapproved of expressions of sexual jealousy. There is one more aspect of the Marquesans that may be connected with their apparent lack, or, at least, low intensity of sexual jealousy: they were characterized by extraordinary sexual freedom outside of marriage. I will have more to say about this later.

For the third case of polyandry, Tibet, I will quote from Linton's *Study of Man*:

> In most polyandrous societies the plural husbands are usually a group of actual or socially ascribed brothers. Tibetan polyandry is one of the classic examples. In Tibet all arable land has long since passed into family holdings. Many of these holdings have become so small that they barely suffice to support a conjugal group and could not do so if they were further subdivided. It has become customary for one son from each family to go into religious life, thus relinquishing his claim on the family land. The other sons marry a single wife, work the family holding for the support of this woman and her children, and pass the holding on to the children intact. In spite of female infanticide, the position of women is high. The wife usually takes charge of the finances of

the family and may dominate her spouses. That Tibetan polyandry is primarily due to hard economic conditions seems to be proved by the fact that it is characteristic only of the lower classes. Tibetans of higher economic status tend to be monogamous, while rich nobles are sometimes polygynous. (Linton 1936:183)

To summarize: Linton mentions female infanticide, and thinks that Tibetan polyandry is an answer to the land shortage. He does not mention the jealousy problem, or the problem of deciding paternity, or group marriage.

The fourth "polyandrous" case in the *World Ethnographic Sample* is the Nayar. We have already seen that they might be better designated as having no marriage form at all.

These are the only cases in Murdock's *World Ethnographic Sample* in which polyandry is said to be the dominant, preferred marriage form: Toda, Marquesas, Tibet, and Nayar. There are scattered mentions of other "polyandrous tribes," but we do not know *how* polyandrous they were. W. I. Thomas mentions additional polyandrous cases in India: "Polyandry, or the custom of a woman having more husbands than one at one time, is peculiar to the Himalayas. It exists in the Kulu subdivision, the Bashahr state (Simla Hill States) and to a smaller extent in the Nahan, Mandi, and Suket states. The custom is common among the Kanets of the higher hills, but the lower castes also practice it. . . ." (Thomas 1937:118–119) And Julius Caesar, in his *Gallic Wars*, reports group marriage in ancient Britain: "'Ten and twelve have wives common among them, especially brothers and brothers and parents with children; if any children are born they are considered as belonging to those men to whom the maid was first married.'" (Goodsell 1915:181)

We are now going to consider some societies that could not be called "polyandrous," but which do evince a few polyandrous and group marriages.

The first of these is the Kaingang, wandering hunters of the Brazilian jungles. This is another past-tense ethnography. When Jules Henry, the ethnographer, visited them, they were no longer wandering hunters. They had been pacified and put on reservation, and like many of our North American "Indians," had traded hunting for farming. Henry's ethnography is apparently based largely on Kaingang informants' accounts of "how it was in the old days." By the time he visited them, they no longer practiced polyandry (Henry 1941:xv).

> The Kaingang are not only monogamous and polygynous; but they were polyandrous too and they also established what I shall call "joint marriages" in which several men lived together with several women in mutual cohabitation. . . .
>
> Even before marriage a girl's sexual interests are beneficial to her family, for her lovers come with presents of food, and they are welcome at her parents' fireside. The food a lover brings is not payment for favors he has received but a gift in expectation of favors still to come. Even after her marriage a woman's amorous intrigues are of considerable advantage to those around her—even to her own husband, for every time she attracts a man she has added a hunter to the band. Wherever his mistress is, there the lover stays, and unless her husband gets wind of the affair and flies into a rage the lover may very likely follow the camp almost indefinitely. His presence is welcome, of course, for another gun or bow and another knife and axe mean so much more meat and honey. Thus even adultery plays a constructive role in Kaingang society, for it keeps within the band men who might otherwise go elsewhere in search of satisfaction, and it often culminated in polyandrous marriage, which has been one of the strongest integrating forces in Kaingang society.
>
> The story is told of Kuven who was the lover of both Kangga and her mother. Now as Kangga's father grew old and it became difficult for him to get meat, he felt more and more the necessity of having someone to help him hunt for his large family. As long as Kuven remained he could depend on him, but when it seemed that the young man was becoming interested in Yemai, a woman who was no relative of his and whom, therefore, Kuven might follow far away to her relatives, Kangga's father said to his wife and daughter: "Call Kuven; if he marries Yemai he will leave me and go away. Let him get food for your children when I die. If he marries another woman he will throw your children away." So Kangga's mother called Kuven and said to her daughter: "Marry him. I am going to live with you and him." So Kuven married both mother and daughter, and when Kangga's father died Kuven took care of the latter's children. . . .

As in the case of Kangga and her mother, the women often became the nuclei of polyandrous and also of joint marriages, which often changed their male composition frequently. Thus by her mere existence the woman held together a complex household, which disintegrated when she died. A general lack of formal rules for marriage permitted the easy building up of large *menages* by gradual additions of men and women. A household might begin with either a monogamous or polygynous marriage; as time passed another man might be added to the household and become the co-husband; perhaps another wife was added and then another man. Through the years the family would expand and contract or simply change as the wives or husbands died or were killed off in feuds or the raids of the *burgreiros*.

The Indians told me of the marriages of Wanyeki. Together with his wife Tendo, his sister and his hunting companion Chu, he wandered about, far away from other members of the tribe. This was nothing unusual for the Kaingang, who sometimes did not see one another for years. When Chu's wife died Wanyeki's wife cooked and made a sleeping-place for him, simply, as the Kaingang put it, "because he had no wife," and he became her co-husband. So Chu was saved for Wanyeki and his little isolated band and did not wander away in search of another wife. But as time passed Tendo, the wife, died, and Wanyeki and Chu were left alone. Until his nieces, his sister's daughters, grew to adolescence, Wanyeki had no wife. Then one day his sister said to him: "Wanyeki, live with them. There are no other women. They are in the same position as you–there are no men. So go around with them. There is no one else for you to marry. So marry them." Chu had died in the meanwhile, so Wanyeki, who already had had two wives married these three girls, who were much younger than he. This kind of relationship is not difficult for a Kaingang girl, for far from wishing to retain her hold on the recreations of her childhood she looks forward to the sexual experience that she has been urged to seek ever since she was a baby in arms.

Wanyeki lived alone with his three wives, his sister's daughters, until they each bore him a child. Then he joined forces with two men whom he had left long ago, and he once more became monogamous, for two of his wives left him to live with these men. Wanyeki did not object. Even though his wives took their sons with them the children remained attached to their father and were frequently in his camp. If Wanyeki had objected there would have been two courses open to him. He could have beaten his wives, in which case they would have left him anyway, or he could have quarreled with the men. In the latter case he would have lost the companionship of the angry men, who would certainly have left him. Actually Wanyeki lived for many years on friendly terms with them, and they continued to make love to his remaining wife Amendo even though they now had wives of their own.

Soon after this Wanyeki was joined by two other men, who became the co-husbands of Amendo, and when Wanyeki's son Veye by his first and now long-dead wife grew to manhood he too shared his father's wife. So father and son, instead of glowering at each other across the fire out of their jealous desire for the same woman, cohabited with her in peace, strengthening the precarious bonds of Kaingang society. The solution would not be the same in every case, for in another such household Kangndadn beat his son and drove him out for daring to copulate with his second wife. But Wanyeki and Veye shot game for each other and for their robust wife while she bore her four husbands nine lusty children and one weakling who died.

Judging from her numerous love affairs it would never be said that Amendo was unable to cope with the sexual demands of her husbands, but, as the Kaingang put it, she had a great deal of work to do cooking and fetching water for four hungry men and her children; so she called Nggeven, one of her husband's nieces, to be her co-wife. Amendo had nothing to fear from the younger woman, for they had four husbands to share between them and Amendo was active in seeking enjoyment outside the bonds of matrimony. So without jealousy or disruption Nggeven moved into this household. She did not have the ignominious position of the second wife that is so common in primitive societies, nor did Amendo ever attempt to drive her out. This closely-knit cooperating unit held together through the years until Nggeven had borne the four husbands ten children. Then Wanyeki and one of his co-husbands died. But although two of the older members of the household were dead, although Wanyeki, the husband of Amendo's youth, was dead, the remaining husbands stayed by her and hunted for her. But soon only Veye was left, for the Brazilians killed Amendo and the other husbands and Nggeven married her young son-in-law and went away. . . .

The motive that led a man to accept a co-husband was always

> the same, his own and his family's security. The more independent and the more possessive avoided it as long as they could. Many could avoid it all their lives, but others, driven by old age and the lack of young sons to take care of them or forced by a crippling injury, at last accepted co-husbands. And it was generally only because there were no marriageable women around that a man consented to become a co-husband. (Henry 1941:33–38)

Later on, Henry states that less than one quarter of the men did participate in polyandrous or group marriage. He says that while some Kaingang men did not seem prone to jealousy, others did get jealous of a lover or of a potential co-husband.

To summarize the above quotation: the motive for co-husbanding was apparently a desire for the security of numbers; Wanyeki's marital history ran the gamut of all the possible marriage forms—monogamy, polygymy, polyandry, and group marriage. Henry does not mention female infanticide, and he does not say how paternity was decided in polyandrous marriages.

The second case of polyandry as a variant marriage form is the Lepchas of Sikkim, in the foothills of the Himalayas; the ethnographer is Geoffrey Gorer. The third case is the Lesu of New Ireland, as described by Hortense Powdermaker.

LEPCHAS OF SIKKIM

> It is permissible for a man who feels himself unable to cope with his field-work, either on account of physical weakness or because he has other work which takes him a great deal from the neighborhood, to invite an unmarried younger brother to live with him and to share his fields and wife . . . The co-husbands sleep with their common wife on alternative nights, but all the children are presumed to be begotten by the first husband. (Gorer 1938:171)

LESU, NEW IRELAND, MELANESIA

> A woman may also have two husbands, known as husband number one (*tamuth towanmaga,* man first time) and number two (*tamuth inil,* man later), in the order in which she has acquired them. She calls both of them *nunga mali,* my husband. There is no evidence of a woman ever having more than two husbands at one

time. Number one makes the marriage payment to his wife's maternal relatives in the traditional manner. Number two, however, pays the *tsera* to number one and not to his wife's clan relatives. . . .

Both husbands bring the woman fish, pig, and so forth, and she cooks for each one. The three eat together, the two men with the bundle of taro between them, and the woman close by. Sometimes the three sleep in the same house, three beds in a row, and the woman between the two men. At other times husband number two will sleep in the men's house, and the woman will sleep with her husbands alternately. There appears to be no quarrelling between the two men. The children of the woman call both men *mum* (father). In the past these polyandrous marriages were the exception rather than the rule, and there is only one such marriage in Lesu now. . . .

Some men are jealous (of their wives' lovers), and some are not. (Powdermaker 1933:227, 248)

What generalizations can one make about these cases of polyandry and group marriage? In the first place, as noted earlier, the two marriage forms tend to go together. At least, this is the situation in three of the societies—Kaingang, Toda, and Marquesas. In the other three descriptions—those of the Lepcha, Lesu, and Tibet—there is an account of polyandry but no mention of group marriage; we don't know whether or not it occurred.

A second fact about co-husbanding is that it is often fraternal. This is customary among the Todas, Tibetans, and Lepchas: two or more real or classificatory brothers share their wife or wives. In the three other cases described, co-husbanding is not necessarily fraternal; this is true of the Marquesas, the Kaingang, and (I assume) of the Lesu.

Third, an economic inducement is often mentioned. The Marquesan senior husband recruits junior husbands so that they will work for him. The Kaingang practice co-husbandry for economic security. The Tibetan peasants are said to turn to polyandry as an answer to the land shortage. Among the Lepcha, a younger brother may be invited to co-husband in return for help with the farmwork. The Lesu senior husband receives the bride price from his junior husband. For one case, the Toda, no economic incentive is mentioned.

Two of the three societies in which polyandry apparently is really frequent definitely practice female infanticide. This seems clearly true of the Todas and Tibetans; there is some doubt about the Marquesans. Female infanticide seems to answer the problem of husband shortage and wife surplus, which we might expect polyandry to produce. This seems a perfectly logical, "functional" solution to the sex-ratio problem, but it is a curious anomaly that polygynous societies do not choose the same sort of "logical" solution. That is, *male* infanticide (without female infanticide) does not seem to be common in polygynous societies. I have never made a cross-cultural study of infanticide; there may be a few societies that kill some of their male infants and save all the females. But, in my ethnographic readings, I have never run across a case of this sort. Therefore, because most societies are polygynous and not polyandrous, I must conclude that this practice is not very common. In other words, polyandrous societies resort to infanticide to "correct" the ratio of husbands to wives; polygynous societies apparently do so rarely, if at all.

Finally, we have the jealousy problem. What sort of person would be willing to share his spouse? How can they stand it?

For one thing, polyandry is often fraternal. As we shall see later, there is some indirect evidence that siblings, two brothers or two sisters, are better able to tolerate sexual sharing than are unrelated persons. Siblings presumably have already lived through jealousy crises in relation to their parents, and have therefore made various adjustments.

The question remains, what sort of person, or personality, is it that can tolerate this sexual sharing? What occurs in personality development to produce the tendency to sexual jealousy; and, conversely, what produces the absence, or low intensity, of sexual jealousy?

As is true of so many basic questions of cause and effect, we don't know the answer. There is a hint of individual differences within the polyandrous societies. Among the Kaingang and Lesu, some men show sexual jealousy and other men do not. Among the Toda and Marquesans there was no mention of sexual jealousy, but in each case there was, apparently, a social sanction against the expression of jealousy.

One striking characteristic of the polyandrous societies is general sexual freedom. The Marquesans are probably the most extreme case of sexual freedom on anthropological record. They allowed children and adolescents free access to sex, allowed adults various sorts of extramarital sex liaisons, observed periods of orgiastic-sounding sexual license, and sometimes even performed sexual intercourse in public (the only report of this, to my knowledge). The Lepchas and Kaingang run the Marquesans a close second in respect to sexual freedom. The Lesu permit an open, institutionalized form of adultery, and you have read Rivers' account of sexual freedom among the Toda. (I do not know about the sex restrictions for the final case, Tibet.)

One gets the impression that in these polyandrous societies there is a laissez-faire attitude toward sex. Sex is "cheap." Sex partners, too, are "cheap" and easy to find. I would guess that there is some sort of causal nexus between co-husbanding, a mild intensity of sexual jealousy, and great sexual freedom. But what the exact causal connection is, I do not know.

A passing note: this touches on one of the recurring themes of this book—the age-old social inequality between men and women. We have seen that polyandry is rare, but that polygyny is very common. We have observed that polyandry seems to occur only in societies in which sex restrictions are generally quite loose, and that polyandrous husbands seem to be bothered little by jealousy. Polygyny, on the other hand, occurs in all sorts of societies; it occurs in many places where sex restrictions are anything but loose, where sex does not seem to be "cheap," and where many of the women do seem to suffer intensely from sexual jealousy. In other words, relatively high jealousy-potential may, in many places, prohibit polyandry, but it does not seem to prohibit polygyny. Men's feelings are spared, but women's aren't.

To conclude these generalizations about polyandry and group marriage: we have seen that co-husbanding is often accompanied by some sort of economic inducement, and that it seems to occur among peoples of low jealousy-potential. We should understand, however, that the occurrence and distribution of co-husbanding has certainly not been "explained." There are, no doubt, many other societies of rather low jealousy-potential, where some sort of economic inducement to co-husbanding could have been worked out, but where polyandry and group marriage are, in fact, completely absent. As I said, polyandry and group marriage are quite rare.

Before passing on to polygyny, we will look at two more cases that are "marginal": the Siriono, who allow permissive sex relationships between nonspouses, and the Reindeer Chukchee of Siberia, who have a sort of sexual-hospitality-by-contract. Both cases might, perhaps, be best designated as having group marriage. In other words, they pose problems of definition.

The ethnographer for the Reindeer Chukchee, Waldemar Bogoras, actually speaks of their arrangement as "group marriage."

REINDEER CHUKCHEE

Group-Marriage.—Marriage among the Chukchee does not deal with one couple only, but extends over an entire group. The Chukchee group-marriage includes sometimes up to ten married couples. The men belonging to such a marriage-union are called "companions in wives" . . . Each "companion" has a right to all the wives of his "companion," but takes advantage of his right comparatively seldom, namely, only when he visits for some reason the camp of one of the "companions." Then the host cedes him his place in the sleeping-room. If possible, he leaves the house for the night; goes to his herd, for instance. After such a call, the companion visited generally looks for an occasion to return the visit, in order, in his turn, to exercise his rights.

The union, in group-marriages, is mostly formed between persons who are well acquainted . . . , "looking (on each other) companions" . . . , especially between neighbors and relatives. Second and third cousins are almost invariably united by ties of group-marriage; brothers, however, do not enter into such unions.

The inmates of one and the same camp are seldom willing to enter into a group-marriage, the reason obviously being that the reciprocal use of wives, which in group-marriage is practiced very seldom, is liable to degenerate into complete promiscuity if the members of the group live too close together. However, many exceptions occur to both rules.

At the present time the unions through group-marriage . . . embrace practically all Chukchee families. Not to be connected with such a union, means to have no friends and good-wishers, and no protectors in case of need; for the members of a marriage-group stand nearer to one another than even relations in the male line.

At present group-marriages are often concluded without any rite. One man simply says to another, "Let us be companions in wives! . . ." After this they both exercise their rights.

Union through group-marriage is considered equal to a blood tie. The children born in the families of a marriage-union are regarded as cousins, or even as brothers and sisters. They cannot marry each other, which is natural, for they might easily have a common father. (Bogoras 1909:602–605)

I finally decided to view this as an arrangement that provides sexual hospitality for the comfort of the occasional visitor. Why did I not agree with Bogoras and call the Chukchee a case of group marriage? According to two points in the definition of marriage—a public announcement and a marriage contract between the spouses—it seemed dubious. And, of course, this so-called group marriage does not lead to "group families"; the "companions in wives" do not, usually, live near one another. Still, this is a borderline case; by the terms of my definition of marriage, Bogoras might marshal a fair argument that the Reindeer Chukchee practice "group marriage."

The second marginal case is represented by the Siriono, wandering hunters of the Bolivian jungles. The ethnographer is Allan Holmberg:

SIRIONO, BOLIVIA

Generally speaking, great freedom is allowed in matters of sex. A man is permitted to have intercourse not only with his own wife or wives but also with her (their) sisters, real and classificatory. Conversely, a woman is allowed to have intercourse not only with her husband but also with his brothers, real and classificatory, and with the husbands and potential husbands of her own and classificatory sisters. Thus apart from one's real spouse, there may be as many as eight or ten potential spouses with whom one may have relations. . . . In actual practice, relations between a man and

> his own brothers' wives, and between a woman and her own sisters' husbands, occur frequently and without censure, but those with potential spouses more distantly related occur less often and are apt to result in quarrels or lead to divorce. (Holmberg 1950:64)

This is a case of permissive sex relationships: an individual is allowed to have intercourse with persons other than his own spouse—in this case, with his spouse's siblings. Why is this not group marriage? For one thing, the "real" Siriono marriage is begun with a public announcement, whereas there is no mention of a public announcement for the sex relationships with the spouse's siblings. Still, this is a marginal case, and perhaps could be considered group marriage.[1]

Polygyny

> "We married Two Bits when he was seventeen. . . ." (Underhill 1939:62) (Papago, Northern Mexico.)

> Still more important than the foregoing was the institution of monogamy, by which, from its earliest days, the Greek civilization proclaimed its superiority to the Asiatic civilization that had preceded it. We may regard monogamy either in the light of our intuitive moral sentiment on the subject of chastity, or in the light of the interests of society. By the first, I understand that universal perception or conviction which I believe to be an ultimate fact in human nature, that the sensual side of our being is the lower side, and that some degree of shame may be appropriately attached to it. In its Oriental or polygamous stage, marriage is regarded almost exclusively in its sensual aspect, as a gratification of the animal passions, while in European marriages the mutual attachment and respect of the contracting parties, the formation of a household, and the long train of domestic feelings and duties that accompany it, have all their distinguished place among the motives of the contract, and the lower element has comparatively little prominence. In this way it may be intelligibly said, without any reference to utilitarian considerations, that monogamy is a higher state than

[1] There are many other accounts in anthropological literature of permissive sex relationships.

> polygamy. The utilitarian arguments in its defense are also extremely powerful, and may be summed up in three sentences. Nature, by making the number of males and females nearly equal, indicates it as natural. In no other form of marriage can the government of the family, which is one of the chief ends of marriage, be so happily sustained, and in no other does woman assume the position of the equal of man. (Lecky 1869:294)

So did a nineteenth-century British historian, William Edward Hartpole Lecky, view polygyny. Needless to say, he was either clearly wrong or at least open to argument on every point. For a contrasting view, let us turn to a twentieth-century American anthropologist, Ralph Linton:

> Polygyny, that is, plurality of wives, is considered the most desirable form of marriage in a very large part of the world's societies. It does not seem to be directly correlated with any particular set of economic conditions or even with the primary dependence of the society on the labor of either men or women. It exists alike in societies in which women do most of the work and every wife is an added asset to the conjugal group and in those in which men carry the economic burden and each wife is an added liability. Although such factors do not seem to influence the ideal pattern, they naturally limit its exercise. Where wives are an asset, even a poor man can be polygynous unless the bride-price is prohibitive, and actual plurality of wives tends to be common. Where wives are a liability, few men can afford the luxury of an extra wife. Thus, although the Greenland Eskimo permit polygyny, only a very good hunter can support more than one woman, and only about one man in twenty has a second wife. The same holds for most Mohammedan communities. Although a man is allowed four wives and an unlimited number of concubines by Koranic law, poor families are nearly always monogamous and only the rich can take the full number of wives permitted.
>
> . . . it seems probable that the widespread occurrence of polygyny derives more from the general primate tendency for males to collect females than from anything else. The other factors involved are only contributory causes. At the same time, polygyny does not necessarily imply a high degree of male dominance in the marriage relationship or even a low position of women in the society. Po-

> lygynous societies are as variable in this respect as are monogamous ones. While there are a few cases in which the wives are completely dependent upon the husband, in most instances their rights are well guarded. When the plural wives are congenial, the women of a polygynous household may form a block, presenting a solid front against the husband and even dominating him.
>
> . . . there are few polygynous systems in which the position of the male is really better than it is under monogamy. If the plural wives are not congenial, the family will be torn by feuds in which the husband must take the thankless role of umpire, while if they are congenial he is likely to be confronted by an organized female opposition. Among the sub-human primates the male can dominate a group of females because these females are unable to organize among themselves. He can deal with them in detail. The human male cannot dominate his wives in the same degree, since they can and do organize for both defense and offense. If all a man's wives want a particular thing, they can work on him in shifts and are fairly certain to get what they want. (Linton 1936:183–187)

At several points, Linton's statement is also open to some argument. But I would agree with at least three of his remarks: polygyny is, as Murdock has shown, very widespread; it is not clearly correlated with any sort of economic "need"; neither is it correlated with low status for women.

One fact about polygyny, then, is that it is very common. Most of the world's societies are characterized by a mixture of polygyny with monogamy. With the exceptions of Europe and (recently) North America, it occurs in all parts of the world, including the more "civilized" parts. The "great civilizations" in India and China permitted polygyny; so do the Islamic countries of North Africa and the Middle East (Linton 1936:187; Patai 1959:39-41). The Old Testament Hebrews were polygynous:

> Gideon, the Israelite judge, had many wives who bore him seventy sons (Judg. 8:30). Judging from the number of sons, Jair with thirty sons (Judg. 10:4), Ibzan with thirty sons and thirty daughters (Judg. 12:9), Abdon with forty sons (Judg. 12:14), all judges in Israel must have had several wives each. King David had several wives (I Sam. 25:39f, 43; II Sam. 3:2ff.; 5:13), and King Solomon,

> of course, had a huge number of them (I Ki. 9:16; 11:3; cf. S. of Sol. 6:8). Also of King Rehoboam, Solomon's son, it is stated that he had eighteen wives and sixty concubines (2 Chron. 11:21). Each of Rehoboam's twenty-eight sons also had many wives (2 Chron. 11:23). The frequency of marriage with two women necessitated legislation with reference to the rights of their children. (Deut. 21:15) (Patai 1959:41)

Polygyny occurred among the pre-Christian tribes of Europe. It was found in ancient Britain (Taylor 1954:28–59). Tacitus, writing of the Teutons, noted:

> The matrimonial bond is . . . strict and severe among them; nor is there anything in their manners more commendable than this. Almost singly among the barbarians they content themselves with one wife; a very few of them excepted, who, not through incontinence, but because their alliance is solicited on account of their rank, practice polygyny. (Quoted by Goodsell 1915:181)

One of the ways in which the Christian Church stamped Western Society as distinctive was by outlawing polygyny. (Taylor 1954:59).

In most of the more "civilized" societies—China, India, and the Mohammedan countries, for example—polygyny does not seem to be terribly common. It is the privilege of the wealthy few. The common man must content himself with one wife (Linton 1936:187). But in many primitive societies it is fairly common. This raises the sex ratio problem again: where polygyny is common, there must not be enough wives to go around. How is this handled? Murdock thinks that this problem is usually solved by means of early marriage for girls and late marriage for men:

> With the proportion of the sexes approximately equal, extensive polygyny means that a good many men have no wives or only one. While some women get married almost immediately after puberty, the men usually do not get their first wife until some time in their twenties; it is not until they get relatively old that they obtain more than one wife. The result is that a typical polygamous society will have a number of young women married to one old man. (Murdock and Whiting 1951:25)

So, you find cases like the Azande of the African Sudan, where "The older men had a monopoly of wives, and . . . it was difficult for a young man to marry." (Evans-Pritchard 1937:17)

In polygynous societies, having plural wives usually seems to be a mark of prestige, a status distinction. In nonstratified societies, like the Azande, it is the prerogative of older men who have "arrived," economically and politically. In societies which are socially stratified, it is one of the privileges of kings and aristocrats, the rich, the "better families." I know of eleven societies in which polygyny seems to be a mark of prestige, and two cases (Arapesh and Muria) where it is not.

Of the eleven societies where polygyny is said to be prestigeful, the first case is the Azande, and the second case is the Greenland Eskimo, already mentioned by Linton. Third are the Siriono: "On the whole, plural marriages tend to occur among the chiefs and the better hunters, who are people of the highest status." (Holmberg 1950:83) Among the Mundugumor, another New Guinea tribe, Mead speaks of ". . . the situation within the compound of the successful man, the man who has succeeded in getting the largest number of wives. A large number of wives means wealth and power." (Mead 1935) Among the Subanum of the Philippines, "The reasons for taking a second wife are diverse, but are generally based on one or more of three factors: a need to facilitate procreation, the desire to gain prestige, and obligations of preferential levirate marriage." (Frake 1955:178) And there are two more African tribes, the Hehe, where "most men of standing have several wives" (Brown 1935:84) and the Gusii, where "Plurality of wives and offspring is a major ambition of Gusii men." (LeVine)

All the above cases are small tribes, with little in the way of social stratification. There are a few more cases of highly stratified societies where, as I said, the "better families" are polygynous. Among the Trobriand Islanders, ". . . the privilege of polygyny . . . is denied to all but the highest ranking members of Trobriand society." (Fathauer 1954:2) Among the Tanala of Madagascar commoners may be polygynous, but chiefs are even *more* polygynous: "Chiefs . . . are the only men who collect large numbers of wives. Very few commoners have more than three." (Linton 1936: 185) And Patai has this to say of the peoples of North Africa and the Middle East:

> To have more than one wife was (and remained in traditional circles) a mark of high status, of prestige, and of wealth. . . . Polygyny continued to be practiced in Israel throughout the Biblical period, but it seems to have been restricted to men who occupied leading positions, who were rich, or had some other claim to distinction. . . . This is the general rule in the Middle East to this day, while the simple people, both in Biblical times and today, had (and have) to be satisfied with one wife, or at least with one at a time. (Patai 1959:39–40)

At times, polygyny is apparently more than a status *symbol*: it is a means toward the end of greater status, which accrues to the polygynous husband because of various economic or political advantages that plural wives bring him. Here are two examples of prestige and power advantages resulting from polygyny—Siwai, and Trobriands:

The Siwai have a rather complicated prestige system, which revolves around feast-giving. The way to impress people, and to obligate people to you, is to give extravagant feasts—the more the better. The featured delicacy in these feasts is pork. The Siwai, like so many Melanesians, are enthusiastic pig-raisers. But pigs are more than potential food. They are symbols of prestige; and they are valued in their own right. The Siwai are not only pig-raisers; they are also pig-*lovers:*

> . . . pig-ownership is considered essential for adult socio-economic status. To shout at a person "You have no pigs" is to offer him an insult. . . .
>
> Then there is another side to all this. When Siwai natives call their pigs by name, grin with pleasure as the beasts troop in squealing, carefully set out food for them in baskets and discuss their merit with noticeable pride, it becomes apparent to an observer that these people look upon their pigs as pets. . . .
>
> . . . even granted that a man must occasionally butcher a pig to celebrate an event, he rarely ever uses a pig which he, himself, has

raised. After years of looking after a beast, a native becomes fond of it. For example, Sinu of Jeku village invited a number of friends to help him build a house and promised them a pork banquet as a reward. When time came for killing his pig, he said he couldn't bring himself to do it. Then someone suggested that he do what was ordinarily done; exchange his pig for that of someone else; he again demurred. Finally, he bought another pig and butchered it. (Oliver 1955:348–349)

The way Siwai society is organized, women are needed to raise pigs. The more women in your establishment, the more workers you have in your gardens, the more pig food, and hence the more pigs:

> It is by no mere accident that polygynous households average more pigs than monogamous ones. Informants stated explicitly that some men married second and third wives in order to enlarge their gardens and increase their herds. They laughed at the writer's suggestion that a man might become polygynous in order to increase his sexual enjoyment. ("Why pay bride price when for a handful of tobacco you can copulate with other women as often as you like!") Opisa of Turunom did not even trouble to move his second wife from her village to his own. She, a woman twenty years his senior, simply remained at her own home and tended two of his pigs.
>
> Some of the wealthiest, most influential men had several wives; but when it was suggested to informants that polygyny was a sign of renown, they vigorously denied it, stating that the main reason for the custom is to increase herds. (Oliver 1955:352–353)

So, in order to have more of these delightful pets, which can be translated into feasts and social honor, some Siwai men are thus willing to make the sacrifice of taking a second wife. And sacrifice it is, too, because the co-wives commonly fight bitterly and often turn on their husbands; life for the Siwai polygynist is complicated, to say the least.[2]

In the second case, the Trobriands, polygyny brings *political*

---

[2] A second advantage of polygyny in Siwai is that a man with two wives has twice as many in-laws, and hence more allies in his various enterprises (Oliver 1954:223–225).

advantages. The Trobrianders' rather unique political system rests heavily on their system of marriage payments. When a Trobriand man marries, he gets, annually, large food gifts—*urigubu*—from his wife's kinsmen. To the Trobriander, marriage is a golden goose, laying perpetual golden eggs in the form of *urigubu* from his in-laws. The common man in the Trobriands may only have one wife; while he is receiving *urigubu* from his wife's relatives he is giving *urigubu* to the husbands of his female kin. But Trobriand chiefs *are* polygynous; they customarily take a wife from each of the villages in their respective districts. This means a great influx of *urigubu*; they take in much more than they give out. The *urigubu*, paid in the form of perishable foodstuffs, is used by the chiefs to consolidate their political power. They use it to pay subordinates. Chiefs also use the *urigubu* to give great feasts, hence creating many social obligations that must, sooner or later, be repaid (Fathauer 1954; Silas 1926:149; Malinowski 1922:64).

Jealousy among Co-wives

> The polygynist's lot is not a happy one. (Hogbin 1935:323) (Wogeo, Melanesia)

> "A thousand moustaches can live together, but not four breasts." (Mandelbaum 1949:102) (Proverb, Hindu India)

> "Never let your husband rest with one wife." (Bowen 1954:114) (Tiv, West Africa)

In considering polyandry I observed that, in the polyandrous societies, co-husbands seemed little bothered by sexual jealousy. There are no doubt several reasons for this (if it is true), one possible reason being generally low jealousy-potential in the polyandrous societies. Another reason is probably that, with the exception of the Toda, the men had some freedom to choose whether or not they would be co-husbands. In most polygynous societies this seems not to be the case for co-wives. They usually do not marry; they "are married." They have little choice in the matter. Often, it seems, polygynous women *are* jealous. In many societies polygyny does look like a rather cruel arrangement.

For nineteen cases in my ethnographic notes, there is some mention of jealousy or "quarreling" (which I assume means jealousy) between co-wives. In five of these societies, jealousy is said to be very frequent.[3] In seven of these cases, individual differences are reported: some wives "quarrel" and others don't.[4] For three cases, the presence of jealousy is merely mentioned, without assessment of its frequency.[5] Finally, there are four societies for which the only mention of jealousy between co-wives is some remark about its absence.[6]

Let us look at some descriptions of the jealousy of co-wives.

GUSII, KENYA

> Despite their desire for polygyny, Gusii men recognize that it brings them trouble. Dissensions among co-wives is one of the most common themes of Gusii folklore.
>
> Many a first wife is extremely opposed to her husband's taking another wife, and this is a frequent cause of quarrelling.
>
> Each wife tends to be the husband's darling when she is the latest, and to maintain that position until he marries again. . . . This tendency in itself causes jealousy among the wives. In addition, any inequality in the distribution of gifts or money, or in the number of children born and died, or the amount of education received by the children, adds to the jealousy and hatred. A woman who becomes barren or whose children die almost always believes that her co-wife has achieved this through witchcraft or poisoning. She may then attempt retaliation.
>
> In spite of the tendency for bitter hatred to develop between co-wives, there are a few Nyosia families in which they get on very well, and cooperate closely. Sometimes it is because the husband has deliberately fostered good relations; in other cases the younger

---

[3] Arabs (Patai), Gusii, Hindu India, Siwai, Wogeo.

[4] Alor, Baiga, Crow, Reindeer Chukchee, Muria, Murngin, Plateau Tonga.

[5] Kaingang, Mundugumor, Navaho.

[6] Arapesh, Tchambuli, Tanala, Tiv.

wife has submissively accepted domination by the older. In either event such harmony is exceptional. (LeVine)

SIWAI, SOLOMON ISLANDS

. . . there is hardly a Siwai who will not admit that polygyny is a deplorable institution. Sinu describes it as follows:

> There is never peace for long in a polygynous family. If the husband sleeps in the house of one wife the other one sulks all the next day. If the man is so stupid as to sleep two consecutive nights in the house of one wife, the other one will refuse to cook for him, saying: "So-and-so is your wife; go to her for food. Since I am not good enough for you to sleep with, then my food is not good enough for you to eat." Frequently the co-wives will quarrel and fight. Kanku (Sinu's maternal uncle) formerly had five wives at one time and the youngest one was always raging and fighting the others. Once she knocked an older wife senseless and then ran away and had to be forcibly returned. Since then all but one of those wives had died, and there is peace in Jeku—not a single polygynous family. Formerly there was no sleeping at night; the co-wives were continually shouting and throwing things at one another. Kanku had absolutely no control over them.
>
> Some husbands who intervene in their wives' quarrels, or persist in showing favoritism, do so at the risk of poisoning or sorcery. Wives have ample opportunity to murder or frighten their husbands by feeding them poison or by collecting some of their exuviae for dirt sorcery. A few such women were pointed out to me as having actually killed their husbands. Nor were they censured generally for their deeds; other natives agreed that the murdered husbands bring upon themselves such trouble by having more than one wife. (Oliver 1955:223-224)

MOSLEMS OF THE MIDDLE EAST

The pain and the anguish of a first wife upon having to share her beloved husband with a second new and younger wife are expressed in many proverbs, sayings, and songs. The first wife complains: "In the night of the co-wife I was embittered." Or: "The co-wife is bitter, even if she were honey in a jar." She knows only too well that the husband can "subdue a woman with another woman." As against these feelings of the first wife, the husband says (according to the woman):

"Sleeping by the old wife is to me like an oven filled with dung. Sleeping by the new wife is to me like the night of Allah's feast." (Patai 1959:40)

MURNGIN, AUSTRALIA

The wives live in a fair degree of amiability, but there is sometimes jealousy over their husband.

Dorng, a man past middle age, but still very active, had three wives, of whom Opossum was the youngest. He complained one day:

> "My wives growl at each other all the time. The two old ones are good friends, but they are jealous of Opossum. They say to her, 'Why don't you get another man? This man is our husband. He made our children come. He belongs to us. He doesn't belong to you.' Opossum says, 'Where am I to go? My other *due* are too old; I'd be the same as dead if I lived with one of them.' The two old ones say, 'Your first man is dead already.' [Dorng's brother died and he got Opossum through the levirate.] His old wives were very pleasant and kind to him, but Opossum was a scold. "When I want to sleep with one of the old sisters at night," he said, "Opossum won't go to sleep as she should. I wait and wait; sometimes morning comes, and that woman watches and won't go to sleep. All right, I wait no longer. I play with her. When I do, Opossum growls at me. The old sisters go to sleep, but sometimes they laugh at me when I play with Opossum." (Warner 1937:91)

As well as spontaneous enmity between co-wives, there are several reports of ritualized jealousy:

ALOR, EASTERN INDONESIA

When a man takes a second wife, for example, it is considered good form for the first one to quarrel about it. . . .

After a few reproaches of this sort the first wife seeks out the second. They exchange insults for a time and then begin pulling, tugging, and beating at each other. Immediately all the women of the village become involved. Each wife has a certain number of belligerent allies, and in addition there is always a large group of women who try to separate the combatants but who manage in their role of peacemakers to land some very effective blows. A whole village may be in a turmoil of struggling women waging a shifting warfare in the mud or dust of the dance place for as long as from two to four hours.

Men at such times are inclined to stand out of range and watch the tide of battle with mixed amusement and contempt. . . . . . even a wife who has urged her husband to buy another woman will go through the forms of a quarrel. (DuBois 1944:110–111)

BAIGA, INDIA

When a man takes a second—or third—wife, the marriage, if the girl is unmarried, is as expensive and elaborate as any other. A wise husband carefully prepares his *badki* (senior wife) for the coming of the *chhotki*. "You of course are the queen of my house," he says, "and you always will be. But there is too much work for you. Let me bring you a servant. We cannot afford to pay a servant, but I will keep her as a woman of the house. Then you can sit all day talking with your friends, and I'll take her to fetch wood, and send her to fetch water, and abuse her if she fails to husk the *kodon*." Sometimes the elder wife says, "Very well!" But sometimes she says, "O the work is very light; I can easily do it all myself." Sometimes she loses her temper, and makes trouble; she breaks her bangles and pretends she is a widow; she sits in a corner and refuses to speak to anyone; she cracks her fingers at her husband and abuses him. "If possible," says Dhan Singh, "it should be done with her permission: if not, it must be done without it. But then there are many quarrels afterwards, and you have to be careful, lest while you are sleeping with your *chhotki*, the *badki* doesn't come and empty the *gursi* full of burning coals all over you!" . . .

If the *chhotki*, however, has been married before, then only the *haldipani* ceremony is performed. The three sit on a bit of sack, and the yellow water is poured over them.

It is correct for a *badki*, whether she approves of the new attachment or not, to make a great deal of fuss at the *chhotki's* marriage. "He doesn't love me any more," she screams. "He'll drive me out into the jungle; he'll be always beating me; I'll get nothing to eat. Everything will be given to this new girl. Look at these presents; when I was married he never gave me anything like that," and so on. Then her friends come to her and say, "Don't weep, the girl is your sister. She is going to live with you and sleep with you; she will always be with you; what is the use of being angry with her? She will be your servant. Don't be jealous of her.

If they sleep in one bed together, if they go to the jungle together, if they go to the well together, don't be angry with them. It is the way of men."

Then the *badki* slowly allows herself to be calmed, and her husband, if he is wise, brings out a new cloth and a few bangles: such gifts make all the difference in the world. Indeed the best husbands give equal presents to the two wives at this time. (Elwin 1939:285–286)

There are a good many reports, of course, of at least some wives being able to tolerate polygyny without apparent jealousy. Most of the reported cases give the impression of considerable individual differences between co-wives with respect to jealousy-potential. For five societies—Alor, Chukchee, Muria, Tanala, and Tiv—the ethnographer says that some women urge their husbands to take on more wives. For three cases—Plateau Tonga, Tanala, and Tiv—there are accounts of co-wives forming a united front *against* their husband, ganging up on him. As Linton says, "If all a man's wives want a particular thing, they can work on him in shifts and are fairly certain to get what they want . . ." (Linton 1936:187). As an example of adjustment to polygyny, here is the case of Ava, the model co-wife:

TIV, WEST AFRICA

Everyone knew Ava and her wives. They were the model household of the community, one every husband cited when his wives disagreed. Ava was a tall, rather light-skinned woman who was one of the leading dancers and song leaders at all successful wedding parties. She was also the senior of five wives who lived with their husband and children alone in a homestead not very far from Kako's. The women were fast friends. Indeed, it was Ava who had picked out all the others. She saved up forty or fifty shillings every few years, searched out an industrious girl of congenial character, then brought her home and presented her to her husband: "Here is your new wife."

Ava's husband always welcomed her additions to his household and he always set to work to pay the rest of the bridewealth, for he knew perfectly well that Ava always picked hard-working, healthy, handsome, steady women who wouldn't run away. Many men envied him. Thanks to Ava he had peace and quiet in his home and did not, like so many others, have to spend time and money chasing truant wives. My feelings were more mixed. If, before I came out here, I had expected to feel sorry for anyone in a polygamous household, it was for the women. But these women did very well. It was their husband I felt sorry for. We tend to think of the henpecked husband as a rather weak character. But what man can stand up against five united women? If Ava's husband raised his voice to any one of his wives, all of them refused to cook for him. If he bought one of them a cloth, he had to buy four other identical cloths. Discipline of the wives was in Ava's hands, and stayed there. When the poor man got drunk one day and struck one wife for nagging—well, until he had given many and expensive presents to all his wives, the five of them slept barricaded in one hut. Yes, I knew Ava. . . .

"Never," said Ava, "let your husband rest with one wife. Men are lazy. If they have one woman to cook for them, they are content. If you leave it to your husband, you'll never get another wife to help you carry the firewood and the water and to look after you when you are ill. And if you do nag him into it, he'll pick up the first good-looking wench he sees. You can't trust a man to inquire into a woman's character and industry. Let a man pick his own mistresses; he knows what he wants there. But they're all bunglers when it comes to choosing wives."

"That," Udama interpolated, "is why a man's father selects his first wife."

"And the first wife," Ava continued, "should get the rest herself, like me."

I replied mildly that men in our country generally couldn't afford more than one wife at a time. "Earn the money yourself by going to market," Ava advised. "It only takes a small chicken to start with, if you're a good trader." I explained that we had a law against it as well. Udama stopped Ava's incredulity. "Indeed, I think it must be so. Rogo told Ihugh that very few Europeans have even one wife because the bridewealth is very high and anyhow they don't have enough women to go around." (Bowen 1954:118–121)

To summarize the jealousy of co-wives: some co-wives are jealous and others apparently aren't. There appear to be great differences between societies as well as between individual co-wives within the same society. In most known cases at least some co-wives seem to suffer rather intensely from jealousy, and a good many of the polygynous families are strife-torn.

Organization of Polygynous Families

Polygynous families evince three organizational features: 1) in certain matters, sex particularly, co-wives have clearly defined equal rights; 2) each wife is set up in a separate establishment; and 3) the senior wife is given special powers and privileges. These might be thought of as fairly conscious attempts to deal with the problem of conflict between co-wives, but, of course, we cannot be sure about this. The following two examples illustrate these organizational features and also show that, if they *are* designed to solve the problem of conflict, they fall somewhat short of their goal:

PLATEAU TONGA, AFRICA

In polygynous families as in all others, each wife is entitled from the time of marriage to her own hut. When her separate household is established, she becomes entitled to her own kitchen, her own field, and her own granary. She can be required to work only in her own field or in the separate field of the husband. Neither she nor her children can be required to work in the field of a co-wife. The produce from her field is reserved for the use of her own household, and if she shares it with a co-wife in distress this is on her own initiative. If her crop fails, her husband must provide for her household from his own field, or he must purchase grain for her household. Each wife has equal rights to maintenance and should fare the same as far as sharing in items of food provided by the husband, obtaining equivalent clothing for themselves and their children and having an equal share of the husband's attention. He should divide his personal possessions among the huts of his wives, or move them with him as he alternates his time among them. Each is entitled to his company for an equal number of nights, and this incidentally means the whole night. If he comes to her only for intercourse, and then leaves to spend the rest of the night at the house of another wife, he is treating her like a mistress and she is entitled to a divorce.

The first wife to be married has the status of chief wife. . . . Her house is placed on the right hand, and is known as the house of "the father." A subsequent wife has the status of small wife, and her house is placed to the left and is known as the house of the *mukoa,* the matrilineal group. Any further wives have the same status and their houses too are identified with the matrilineal group. The chief wife has for certain purposes higher ritual status. The husband should sleep in her house before he departs on a journey and immediately after his return. She also should be consulted in advance of the other wives, and her voice should carry the greatest weight with the husband. But any attempt by her to subordinate the other wives after they have established their own households is an attack upon their positions which would be countered by the claim that they too are free women and not slaves to do her bidding. . . .

So long as the man who forms their common bond lives and the marriages are maintained, the polygynous households are closely united in many of their activities. The wives may form a common work team for many purposes. If they are on friendly terms, they assist in common household duties, look after each other's children, and give assistance and comfort in times of illness. Their children play together and eat together. The boys share a common sleeping hut. . . .

Polygyny, despite the rules which seek to regulate it, is considered a delicate affair, difficult for a man to manage comfortably. It is made the more difficult because Tonga women have an ideal of companionship within marriage which is incompatible with polygyny, where if one wife succeeds in her aim it is only at the expense of others. Men expect their wives to be jealous of each other and to quarrel over the husband's favours. It is commonly believed that co-wives resort to various love medicines in an attempt to gain first place with the husband, and they may use sorcery against each other or each other's children to eliminate them from the scene. Sometimes the tension explodes into open accusations of dealings with sorcery, which may end in the divorce of the accused or a demand that she pay damages to her co-wife. Sometimes, however, the wives form a common front against the husband, abetting each other in their love affairs, going off in companionable couples to beer drinks and funerals while he is left at home to shift for himself, siding with each other in any quarrels which may arise. In one notable instance, they clubbed together to finance the purchase of a powerful poison with which to dispose of the husband under the expectation that they would then be free to marry their lovers. (Colson 1954:44–47)

TANALA, MADAGASCAR

. . . the first wife ranks all subsequent wives and is the unquestioned head of the woman half of the conjugal group. . . .

When a man has three wives, each wife will have a separate house for herself and her children. The first wife usually keeps the original dwelling, and the husband considers her house as his real home and keeps most of his belongings there.

However, he is required to spend one day with each wife in succession. If he spends one wife's day with another wife, it constitutes adultery under native law and entitles the slighted wife to a divorce with alimony amounting to one third of the husband's property other than land. Such an offense is considered more serious than misconduct with a woman outside the conjugal group, and the husband will be lucky if he escapes with a liberal gift to the offended wife. . . .

For purposes of cultivation, the husband's land is divided among the wives as equally as possible. Each wife works her section and can claim the husband's assistance on her day. This economic claim over the husband goes so far that if he hunts or fishes on that day the wife has a right to half his take or to half the money received from the sale of any surplus. From the produce of her section of land each woman feeds herself and her children, also the husband on the day he is with her. If there is a surplus to be sold, one-half of the proceeds go to the husband as ground rent. The other half is the property of the wife, and she usually banks it with her own family. In a well-organized conjugal group the women usually take turns working on the land while one of them remains at home to cook and tend the children. The whole family will eat first at one house and then at another, so that, if there are three wives, cooking and dishwashing will fall to the portion of any one of them only on every third day. . . . Wives will not infrequently carry on love affairs with the full knowledge of their fellow-wives without fear of betrayal. The female half of the family is thus able to control family policies to a considerable degree, and henpecked husbands are by no means unknown. If the husband tries to coerce one wife, the rest will resent it and make his life miserable by those unofficial methods with which all women are familiar. The wives receive

> added power from the fact that the husband is theoretically in complete control and cannot appeal for outside help without making himself ridiculous. (Linton 1936:184–187)

In my ethnographic notes, there are nine societies in which the elder wife is said to have special powers and privileges (Azande, Chukchee, Kipsigis, Lakher, Lesu, Murngin, Tanala, Tiv, and Plateau Tonga) and one society in which she does not (Siwai). In seven societies, the co-wives take regular turns sleeping with the husband (Dahomey, Ancient Hebrews, Lesu, Rwala Bedouin, Siwai, Tanala, and Plateau Tonga); in one society they do not (Gusii).

For five societies, it is reported that each co-wife works her own farmlands (Kipsigis, Chagga, Lesu, Tanala, and Plateau Tonga). For five societies, it is said that the polygynist must take meticulous care to distribute equally among his wives all special aid, attention, gifts, and so forth (Alor, Gusii, Lesu, Tanala, and Plateau Tonga).

Finally, each wife usually has her own separate house; this is particularly true when the co-wives are not sisters—in cases of nonsororal polygyny. In Murdock's *World Ethnographic Sample*, of forty-seven societies with nonsororal polygyny (polygyny is fairly frequent, and co-wives are customarily not sisters), all but three are characterized by "mother-child households," in which each wife has her own house (Murdock 1957).

When co-wives are also sisters, however, the situation is different. Here is what Murdock has to say about sororal polygyny:

> I discovered in my work that by and large in societies that practice sororal polygyny all the co-wives live together in the same house, or where it is a large multifamily house, in one apartment within that large house. Of the societies practicing exclusive sororal polygyny on which I have data, in eighteen of them all the wives live together in one house or apartment and only three in separate huts. Where polygamy is preferentially sororal, although nonsororal also occurs, the preponderance is still in favor of all the wives living together in one hut—sixteen against eight where each wife has a separate hut. In a number of societies allowing both sororal

> and nonsororal polygyny, the rule is different, depending upon whether the wives are sisters or not. Among the Crow Indians, for example, all the wives lived in one tepee if they were sisters, but where they were not related each wife had a tepee of her own and the husband visited them in rotation. When we come to nonsororal polygamy, the situation changes. In a majority of the fifty-five nonsororal societies of my sample, each wife is set up in her own hut, tepee, or tent. Thus there is a fairly sharp distinction in the data. The reason for this is quite obvious. A group of sisters raised in the same household as little girls—and the same is true of cousins raised in the same clan or in neighboring households—have had an opportunity to work out their personal adjustments with one another in their father's home. They can move either seriatim or as a group into the husband's home, carrying over the adjustive habits that they have learned in early childhood and therefore living together in one house or one apartment with a minimum of friction. But if you assemble women from different origins, from different communities, as is common in nonsororal polygamous societies, the co-wives have not had this adjustive experience, and a situation of conflict is set up. Sexual rivalry and competition for positions of prestige are almost inevitable among such wives. In adjustment to this, the societies practicing nonsororal polygamy tend to establish the wives in different huts where the husband visits one after another in rotation, and where he plays the part of father in several households, in each of which he is the husband of the resident women. (Murdock and Whiting 1951:20–21)

Murdock has made an extremely interesting discovery here: if co-wives are sisters, they usually live in the same house; if co-wives are not sisters, they usually live in separate houses. The deduction follows: for some reason, siblings can better tolerate, suppress, and live with a situation of sexual rivalry than can non-siblings.

To conclude this chapter, I want to make a few remarks about the *consequences* of polygyny. Various people have commented on how "basic" and "fundamental" the family is, to "society" and to "the development of the individual." If this is so, then polygynous societies and individuals raised in polygynous families should be different, in rather fundamental ways, from monogamous societies and monogamous individuals. Is this true? I think I can show that it *is* true. Or, in the language of the cautious researcher, I think I "can give indications" of a "trend in that direction."

In the first place, *nonsororal* polygyny scatters the family spatially. As Murdock has shown, when co-wives are not sisters they usually live in separate houses. In other words, the nonsororal polygynous society is characterized by mother-child households: an arrangement in which the wife, with her young children, lives in a separate house, and the husband either occupies another house of his own or "rotates" between the houses of his various wives. Mother-child households, in turn, call for a *change of residence for adolescent or prepubertal boys* (Stephens 1962: Chap. 4). When a boy is somewhere between the ages of eight and fourteen, he begins sleeping in his own house, or in a bachelor's hut. Nonsororal polygyny consequently causes a rather basic change in living arrangements: family members start moving away from each other.

Now for some general characteristics of polygynous societies, whether sororal or nonsororal. In the first place, they have a strong tendency to be sorcery-ridden. Where the percentage of polygyny in a society is fairly high, the likelihood is great that people will be extremely fearful of magical murder; that sorcery will figure importantly as an explanation for illness, death, and other misfortune; and that people will continually suspect each other of trying to "hex" them (Whiting 1959; Stephens 1962).

Another characteristic of societies with a high percentage of polygyny is that they are taboo-ridden. They are more likely to have the sex taboos mentioned in Chapter 1: the *post partum* sex taboo, the pregnancy sex taboo, and the menstrual sex taboo. These sex taboos are apt to be very long, barring, for much of the time, intercourse between husband and wife. Kin avoidances, other menstrual taboos, and taboos connected with totemism and initiations—these also tend to be more elaborate and more numerous in polygynous societies (Stephens 1962).

Finally, I think polygyny—via an indirect process—causes Oedipal problems of a certain type. Individuals—men, at least—in polygynous societies are more likely to have strong Oedipal fears. This last claim, of course, requires a lot of documenting—too much to be attempted here. (See Stephens 1962.)

The discussion of polygyny began with the quotation from Lecky, which called monogamy "a higher state than polygyny." I commented that Lecky was either wrong or open to argument on every point he made. Naively moralistic—yes. But wrong? Perhaps, in retrospect, we might concede that Lecky was half-right. Polygyny, despite its popularity and prestige value among so many of the world's societies, does seem to carry certain penalties. When the early Catholic bishops, in their general repugnance at sexual pleasure, outlawed polygyny, they seem to have influenced in a very basic way the future character of Western society. Perhaps it was for the better.

3 Kinship

> Kinship is fundamentally a re-interpretation in social terms of the facts of procreation and regularized sex union. The complex series of social relationships formed on this basis comprises activity of a residential, an economic, a political, a juridical, and a linguistic order, and constitutes a system of primary integration in the society. A scientific definition of a kinship tie between individuals means not only a specification of the genealogical bond between them and the linguistic term used to denote that bond, but a classification of their behaviors in many aspects of their life.
>
> The fact that there is no society without a kinship system of some kind means that in the first place there is overt allowance made for sentiments generated by parturition, sex union and common residence (to put it at the lowest, even where male procreation is not understood); in the second place that these physical phenomena provide a simple base, easily recognizable and usually unchallengeable, on which other necessary social relationships may be erected. Moreover, the kinship tie is permanent until death—unless diverted by the fiction of adoption. In small societies such as Tikopia, then, it can be readily grasped why kinship is at the root of much of the social structure. (Firth 1936:577)

In concluding Chapter 1, I spoke of the nuclear family and kinship as interrelated "things." Actually, the nuclear family could be considered as just one part of the kinship system, as a particularly small kin group, interlocked with other kin groups in a vast "web of kinship," as Fortes has called it. To try to visualize this web of kinship, we might start with a genealogical chart.

To explain this genealogical chart or "family tree." Each box in the chart represents a person. Each person is numbered, for future reference in the discussion; for example, Ego, whose family tree this is, is number 5 (bottom row). The boxes marked with an "M" are males; the "F's" are females. Each row represents a separate generation. The bottom row, marked "O," is Ego's own generation, including Ego (5), his brother and sister (6 and 7), and Ego's cousins (1, 2, 3, 4, 8, and 9). Row I, the first ascending generation, includes Ego's father (14), mother (15), aunts (13 and 17) and uncles (12 and 16). Row II, the second ascending generation, includes Ego's grandparents (24, 25, 26, and 27), his great-aunts (21, 23, and 29) and great-uncles (20, 22, and 28). Row III, the third ascending generation, comprises Ego's great-grandparents.

Pairs of persons, joined together by lines that describe half a box, are married to each other. Examples: 14 and 15 (Ego's father and mother), 24 and 25 (Ego's paternal grandfather and grandmother), 10 and 11, 12 and 13, 16 and 17, 30 and 31, and so forth. Persons who are joined to a married couple by a descending line are their children. Examples: 5, 6, and 7 are the children of 14 and 15; 15 and 16 are the children of 26 and 27; and so forth.

As a small exercise in the use of this chart, let us see from whom Ego got his surname, which happens to be Smith. Ego (5) got the name Smith from his father (14), who in turn got it from *his* father (24), who in turn got it from *his* father (30).

Genealogical ties are of two types, consanguineal and affinal. Most of the persons on the chart are Ego's consanguineal—or "blood"—relatives: Ego's father, his mother, his brother, his sister, his father's sister, his father's parents, his mother's brother, mother's parents, mother's mother's sister, and so on. A few remaining relatives are Ego's affinal kin or "in-laws," that is, relatives who are not in Ego's "blood line": Ego's father's sister's husband, for example.

You will note that all the persons to the left of the dotted line—Ego's father with his kin—are affinal kin or in-laws to all the persons to the right of the dotted line, that is, to Ego's mother and her kin.

When Ego's parents got married, not only did they become "related to each other," but they "related" each other's kinfolk.

Figure 1. Genealogical Chart

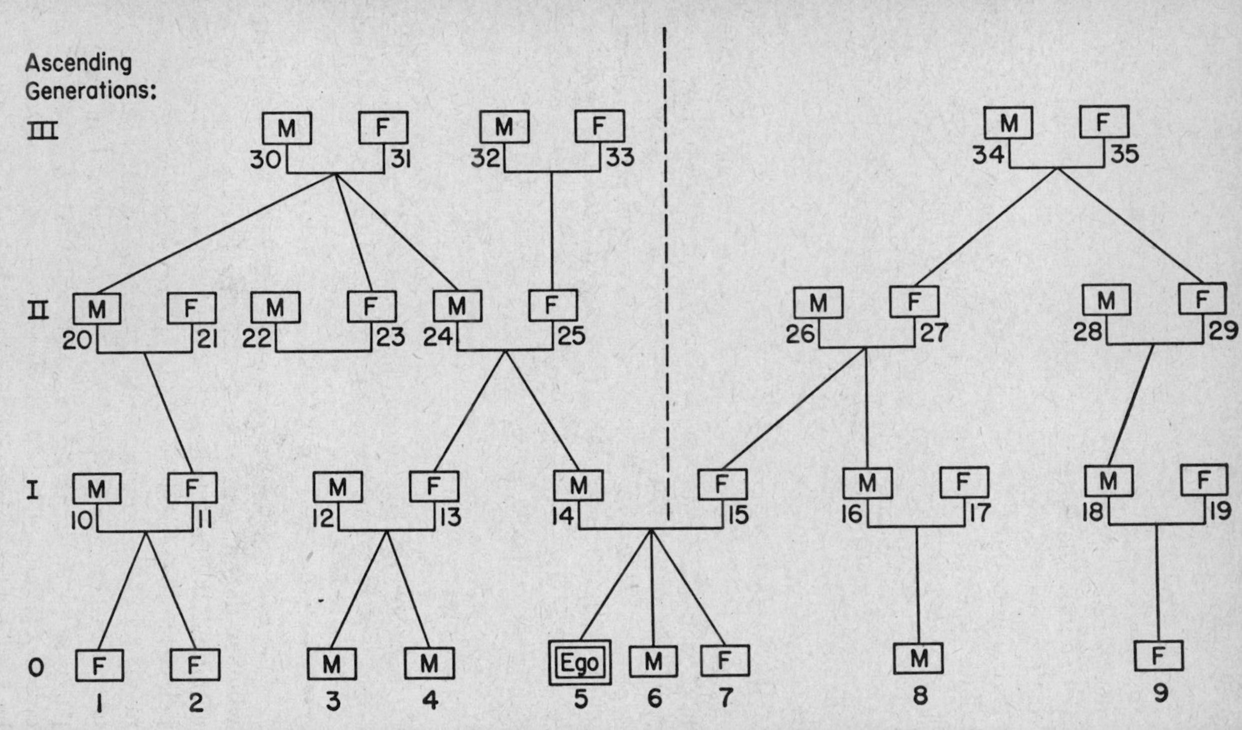

People who probably had no previous genealogical ties became "in-laws" to each other. All the persons on the left of the dotted line became affinal kin to all the persons on the right of the dotted line. The marriage of Ego's parents formed a link between their respective kinfolk; the birth of Ego added another genealogical link—this time, linking many persons on both sides of the dotted line as Ego's consanguineal kin.

As you may have noticed, this genealogical chart is incomplete. For one thing, the parents of many of the persons on this chart are not shown (10, 12, 17, 19, 21, 22, 26, 28, and so forth). Also, the really distant genealogical relationships are not represented. For instance, Ego happens to have a father's father's father's father's father's brother's son's son's son's son's son. If I had given Ego's true, complete genealogy, the chart would have been so involved, so cluttered, as to have been nearly undecipherable; besides, there simply is not room.

Genealogical ties, if they can only be traced, quickly become enormously ramified and far-reaching. Peoples with a flair for genealogy, like the Polynesians, can trace kin ties between everyone in a village, in a district, or even in an entire small society:

> . . . in Tikopia . . . every person of ordinary competency can ultimately trace connection with every other person in the community of over twelve hundred souls. As it is said, "the whole land is a single body of kinsfolk." (Firth 1936:234)

One basis for the "web of kinship" is, then, genealogical ties, which in themselves form a sort of web. Each person, throughout a normal lifetime, belongs to two nuclear families. First, he belongs to the nuclear family composed of himself, his father and mother, and his brothers and sisters (the family of orientation); later, when he marries, he also belongs to the nuclear family composed of himself, his wife, and his children (the family of procreation). Through his memberships in these two nuclear families he is joined, genealogically, with other persons in other nuclear families.[1] By acknowledging and activating his genealogical ties, a person can establish kin relationships with many other persons who, although outside his two nuclear families, are linked to them genealogically. In other words, extended kinship results from recognizing and activating various genealogical ties. Genealogical ties are recognized by means of *kin terms*; they are activated by means of *patterned kin behavior.* In a moment we will deal with patterned kin behavior. First, I must say something about kin terms.

If each sort of genealogical tie were labeled with a specially descriptive kin term, our everyday kinship vocabulary would be enormous. We would have a special kin term for each sort of relative. We would be calling people "my father's father's mother," "my mother's brother's wife's sister's son," "my father's mother's sister's son's daughter," and so forth. We don't do this, of course. We have two descriptive kin terms ("father" and "mother") and a few more *classificatory* kin terms ("grandfather," "grandmother," "aunt," "uncle," "cousin," "nephew," "niece," "brother" and "sister"), which cover all categories of kin (in conjunction with a few compounds of the classificatory terms, such as "great-grandfather," "great-aunt," "second cousin"). Each classificatory term describes several actual categories of relatives. "Grandfather" denotes both the father's father and the mother's father. "Aunt" denotes the mother's sister and the father's sister. "Cousin" denotes all consanguineal kin of Ego's generation, with the exception of his own brothers and sisters. And so forth.

The virtue of classificatory kin terms is simplicity. They spare us mental effort. Perhaps we, in our society, could manage without classificatory kin terms; most of us interact with rather few of our kinsmen anyway. But in many of the societies we shall be exam-

---

1 How does a person trace his genealogy when he is an adopted or illegitimate child? I think (although I am not sure, as I have scanty data on this point) that genealogy is usually determined by *social* parenthood, rather than by "real" or "blood" parenthood. That is, it is my impression that in most societies an adopted child traces his genealogy through his adopted parents, and not from his "real" parents; an illegitimate child traces his male "ancestry" through his mother's husband, if she marries after he is born.

ining, everyone Ego meets is—as in Tikopia—a relative of some kind; furthermore, different relatives elicit strikingly different types of patterned kin behavior. If there were no classificatory kin terms there would be too many types of relatives, too many labels assigned to people, too many decisions to make about appropriate kin behavior. In an everyone-a-relative society, such as Tikopia, classificatory kin terms, which group the innumerable possible genealogical ties into a few large classes of kin relationship, do seem to be a necessity. They do more than relieve mental strain; they must prevent great confusion.

Other societies, like our own, have classificatory kin terms, but usually the terms do not "classify" in the same way. For instance, there may be two terms for "brother": "my elder brother" and "my younger brother." The various relatives we call "cousins" might be designated by four kin terms, meaning: "male relatives of my generation descended from my father's kin," "female relatives of my generation descended from my father's kin," "male relatives of my generation descended from my mother's kin," and "female relatives of my generation descended from my mother's kin." These examples show terms that subdivide *our* classificatory kin terms "brother" and "cousin."

Further classificatory terms may embrace several of our terms, or cut across them. For example, the term "father" may apply to Ego's real father and to his father's brothers; it may even apply to all men who are of Ego's father's generation, and are members of Ego's clan. Each society groups all genealogical ties into a few classes of kin relationship by recognizing a few of the distinctions between kin but ignoring most possible distinctions. Some of the main distinctions on which classificatory kin terms are based are: 1) generation ("cousin" versus "uncle" or "nephew"); 2) sex ("uncle" versus "aunt"); 3) consanguinity versus affinity ("cousin" versus "brother-in-law"); and 4) lineality (mother's kin versus father's kin). In addition, in societies with unilineal kin groups, kin-group membership may be a further criterion for classifying relatives. For a more detailed discussion of classificatory kin terms, I refer you to Chapters 6 and 7 of Murdock's *Social Structure.*

To conclude this discussion of classificatory kin terms with some illustration, we will now look at a quotation from W. I. Thomas' *Primitive Behavior.* The quotation shows the confusion a strange classificatory system may cause a foreign visitor (Gold Coast), the variety of relatives that may be subsumed under one kin term (Shilluk, Andaman Islanders), and the fact that sometimes classificatory terms fall short of their goal of simplicity (Hidatsa).

GOLD COAST

As missionary on the African Gold Coast Father Gallaud was much puzzled by the replies he received when inquiring about parentage and kinship:

> If you wish to know of anyone who is his father and who is his mother you must put the question to him in these terms: 'Who is the father that begot you? Who is the mother that bore you?' If you ask simply, 'What is the name of your father? What is the name of your mother?' It may be that he will give you successively four or five fathers and as many mothers without including the authors of his being in the number. Those whom he will give you as his fathers will be his uncles and his old male cousins who live in the same house with him, and his mothers will similarly be his aunts and his old female cousins. . . . If you understand also that every old person is called 'my father' or 'my mother'[2] you will have an idea of the extension of these terms.

SHILLUK

Any one of the classes bearing the same name may therefore present an unexpected assortment of individuals, and the acquisition and feeling of identity are evidently, as was noted for the language systems, dependent to some extent on habit formation. Thus, among the Nilotic Shilluk the term *ora* (man speaking) is applied to the following persons:

Wife's father, wife's father's brother, wife's mother, wife's mother's sister, wife's brother, daughter's husband, wife's brother's wife, sister's husband; also the husband of all cousins, the wife's

---

[2] Apparently, these are courtesy kin terms.

mother's mother, the mother of any *uwa* (*uwa* = brother or classificatory "father's" brother's son).

ANDAMANS

Among the South Andamanese the term *dia chanola* includes father's sister, mother's sister, father's brother's wife, mother's brother's wife, grandmother, grandaunt, father's father's sister's daughter, mother's mother's sister's daughter, husband's grandmother, wife's grandmother, husband's sister (if senior and a mother), elder brother's wife (if a mother).

HIDATSA

An individual may be classified and cross-classified from various standpoints, as kin, classificatory kin, kin of classificatory kin, as member of the mother's line, as member of the father's line, as member of a hereditary sib and as member of a parallel totemic group, and so forth, with the result that from the classificatory standpoint, as Lowie points out below for the Hidatsa Indians, a man may be the "grandchild" of a woman and at the same time her "father," or the son and at the same time the "father" of his father, or a woman may be at the same time the daughter and the "mother" of a man:

> One of the most interesting features of the Hidatsa kinship system is the fact that the same individuals may stand to each other in two or more relationships. . . .
>
> "Hairy-coat is Buffalo-bird-woman's "grandchild." But he is also a member of the same clan as Buffalo-bird-woman's father, hence he is her "father". . . . Packs-wolf is Goodbird's mother's father's sister's son's daughter's husband = mother's father's daughter's husband = mother's sister's husband = father. On the other hand Packs-wolf's father was a member of Goodbird's clan, whence the relationship would be reversed, Goodbird becoming Packs-wolf's father. But this is not all. Mrs. Goodbird's sister adopted Packswolf's brother, Grow-not-knowing, as her brother, whence Mrs. Goodbird likewise became sister to Grow-not-knowing, all his brothers simultaneously becoming her brothers as well. Thus, Packs-wolf is a brother of Goodbird's wife and accordingly Goodbird's brother-in-law. . . .
>
> Son-of-star was Goodbird's own father. On the other hand,

> Goodbird was Son-of-star's father because Goodbird is of the Prairie-chicken clan to which Son-of-star's own father belonged. . . .
>
> Poor-wolf belonged to the same clan as Buffalo-bird-woman's father, and she belongs to Poor-wolf's father's clan. Accordingly, he was both her clan father and also her clan son. Actually, she only called him "father." (From R. H. Lowie, "Notes on the Social Customs of the Mandan, Hidatsa, and Crow Indians," *American Museum of Natural History, Anthropological Papers,* Vol. 21.) (Thomas 1937:100–102)

To summarize: classificatory kin terms reduce the innumerable welter of possible genealogical relationships to a few standard categories: uncles, cousins, nephews, (classificatory) "fathers," and so forth. By so doing, they simplify the business of labelling kinsmen—notwithstanding the "I'm-my-own-grandpa" problems of the Hidatsa. We, in our society, might be able to manage without classificatory kin terms, since most of us deal with rather few relatives and our kin relations are not strikingly patterned. But in many other societies the ordinary person does deal, daily, with great numbers of kinsmen, representing many sorts of genealogical ties, and kin relations *are* strikingly patterned. Hence the apparent necessity, in such places, of classificatory kin terms.

It is now time to consider patterned kin behavior.

Patterned Kin Behavior

I have divided patterned kin behavior into two general classes: 1) patterned rights and obligations between kinsmen; 2) patterned comportment between kinsmen. I have further divided patterned comportment into the following subclasses: a) deference; b) avoidance; c) joking; and d) informality, or lack of obvious patterning.[3] Before discussing exactly what is meant by "patterned kin behavior," I will give a few examples, illustrating each class and subclass.

---

[3] This division into classes is to some extent arbitrary, a matter of taste. Another writer might choose to make a different sort of division, or he might choose to assign different terms. Also, there are some individual borderline cases that are open to argument as to whether they should be termed "avoidance" or "deference," "joking" or "informality."

Deference

SILWA, EGYPT

. . . the father avoids excessive intimacy in order to be respected and obeyed. . . . Through his curt and abrupt admonitions he controls both his sons and his daughters. . . .

A mature son is not expected to sit beside his father in the same gathering; and if his presence is required he should play a very subordinate role, usually evidenced by the fact that he speaks as little as possible, and withdraws at the earliest possible opportunity. If it happens that the father is sitting on a bench at a funeral, for example, the son should sit on the ground, and if he has to sit on a bench, he should not sit on the same bench as his father, or on one opposite to him in order to avoid the face to face position. If the son is lying on the ground, he should sit upon seeing his father passing by; and he should never be sitting while his father is standing. Of course, he cannot smoke in his father's presence, or do anything that might imply that he is not giving full attention to his father. . . .

Moreover, certain manners must be observed, such as walking behind the father or an elder and not abreast of him, standing up or at least sitting properly on the ground on his approach, dismounting from donkey-back on seeing the father in a formal gathering, and so on. (Ammar 1954:52, 130)

Avoidance

GANDA, AFRICA

The husband and his wife's mother, as well as all women whom she calls mother, call one another *muko.* The rules of behavior between persons who stand in this relationship are all such as to prevent their coming into close contact. . . . They may not take one another by the hand, pass one another in a doorway, look one another straight in the face (the woman should cover her head or fix her eyes upon the ground, and if they meet in the road would turn aside), or be left alone to speak together. They may not eat together, nor may one eat food which the other has left. . . . I also remember a conversation in which real horror was expressed at my statement that in Europe a man could touch his mother-in-law. (Mair 1934:92–23)

Joking

TARAHUMARA, NORTHERN MEXICO

The term *mucimuli* refers to a "joking" relationship with a brother-in-law or a sister-in-law. . . . The relationship is a humorous one and consists of rather obscene play and speech between the parties concerned. . . . The play consists of obscene jokes, attempts to lift the woman's skirts, touching of private parts, pulling off clothes, wrestling, and numerous other tricks which would never be tolerated in other relationships, even that of man and wife. When men and women, or men and men, are playing with each other at a party, and the watchers are enjoying the fun a great deal, it is almost a certainty that the entertainers are *mucimuli*. (Bennett and Zingg 1935:222)

Informality, or Lack of Obvious Patterning

UNITED STATES

An informant with three uncles would call one "John," one "Uncle Bill," and the other "Jim." When pressed to explain why he called the first uncle just plain "John," he would reply by saying that the person was a dirty so-and-so and that he would not dignify the man by calling him uncle. . . . The next question would be "Well, how about your other uncle, Jim? Why don't you call him Uncle Jim?" And the explanation would be, "Jim is a wonderful guy! He and I have always been the closest friends. When I was a kid we would . . ." and out would come a picture of an idyllic relationship. The final question, of course, would be, "What about Uncle Bill?" And Uncle Bill would usually prove to be liked—a nice guy—"He's O.K.," or some such mildly positive or mildly negative sentiment.

The pattern seemed to be that wherever there was strong affect either positive *or* negative, the "uncle" form would be dropped and the first name alone used. (Schneider and Homans 1955:1199–1200)

Patterned Rights and Obligations

KWOMA, NEW GUINEA

A *maternal uncle* holds a unique position with respect to property rights. A child has the right to take any food that he wishes from this relative and need only announce the fact to him. In so doing, however, he incurs the responsibility of paying a considerable amount of shell money at the time of the age-grading ceremonies. (Whiting 1941:42)

TONGA, POLYNESIA

The sister's children are *fahu* to their mother's brother. They have the privilege of taking their uncle's goods, also the goods of his children, either during his life or after his death. Even one of the uncle's wives might be appropriated. At the wedding of a man's child, his sister's children may help themselves to the presents. The brother's children must show respect (fakaapaapa) to the sister's children. The institution of *fahu* is a one-sided, nonreciprocal affair. The victims never have a chance to retaliate, but they exercise a similar privilege towards their own mother's brother and his offspring. Toward one's *fahu* only respect and acquiescence must be shown. . . .

One chiefly informant remarked to me that he was lucky in having no closely related *fahu,* as he had no sister. He had, however, female cousins, whose children were *fahu* to him to a certain extent, but not like a real or great *fahu.* One such remote *fahu* visited this chief while I was with him, his father's brother's daughter's daughter. She did not have the privilege of a near *fahu* but must ask his permission before taking his property. . . .

Modern Tongan dictionaries describe the *fahu* as "one that is above the law," and the verb *fakafahufahu* as "to act as an outlaw." In actual practice the *fahu* (or *ilamutu,* to use the term of relationship) often did appropriate the property of his mother's brother *(tuasina),* who as a rule did not protest. At the kava ceremony the *fahu* ate the relish presented to his mother's brother. The grandchildren, also referred to as *fahu*, had the same privilege. (E. W. Gifford, "Tongan Society," *Bernice P. Bishop Museum, Bulletin* 61, pp. 22–25) (Quoted by W. I. Thomas 1937:124)

SAMOA, POLYNESIA

A relative is regarded as someone upon whom one has a multitude of claims and to whom one owes a multitude of obligations. From a relative one may demand food, clothing, and shelter, or assistance in a feud. Refusal of such a demand brands one as stingy and lacking in human kindness, the virtue most esteemed among the Samoans. No definite repayment is made at the time such services are given except in the case of the distribution of food to all those who share in a family enterprise. But careful count of the value of the property given and of the service rendered is kept and a return gift demanded at the earliest opportunity. Nevertheless, in native theory the two acts are separate, each one in turn becoming a "beggar," a pensioner upon another's bounty. In olden times, the beggar sometimes wore a special girdle which delicately hinted at the cause of his visit. One old chief gave me a graphic description of the behavior of someone who had come to ask a favour of a relative. "He will come early in the morning and enter quietly, sitting down in the very back of the house, in the place of least honour. You will say to him, 'So you have come, be welcome!' and he will answer, 'I have come indeed, saving your noble presence.' Then you will say, 'Are you thirsty? Alas for your coming, there is little that is good within the house.' And he will answer, 'Let it rest, thank you, for indeed I am not hungry nor would I drink.' And he will sit and you will sit all day long and no mention is made of the purpose of his coming. All day he will sit and brush the ashes out of the hearth, performing this menial and dirty task with very great care and attention. If someone must go inland to the plantation to fetch food, he is the first to offer to go. If someone must go fishing to fill out the crew of a canoe, surely he is delighted to go, even though the sun is hot and his journey hither has been long. And all day you sit and wonder, 'What can it be that he has come for? Is it that largest pig that he wants, or has he heard perhaps that my daughter has just finished a large and beautiful piece of tapa? Would it perhaps be well to send that tapa, as I had perhaps planned, as a present to my talking chief, to send it now, so that I may refuse him with all good faith?' And he sits and studies your countenance and wonders if you will be favourable to his request. He plays with the children but refuses the necklace of flowers which they have woven for him and gives it instead to your daughter. Finally night comes. It is time to sleep and still he has not spoken. So finally you say to him, 'Lo, I would sleep. Will you sleep also or will you be returning whence you have come?' And only then will he speak and tell you the desire in his heart." (Mead 1928)

I said that the genealogical chart represents one basis of kinship. But genealogy is not, in itself, kinship. A genealogical tie does not guarantee a kin relationship. We all have countless genealogical "relatives" whom we don't know, have never met, whom we don't even know exist. For all practical purposes, these people are not kin. An unknown or unrecognized genealogical tie does not, in itself, constitute kinship. We may have other genealogical "relatives" who are so distantly related—a mother's father's father's sister's husband's son's wife's son, for example—as not to be considered "real" kin. If a genealogical tie is known but not "activated," it still does not constitute "real" kinship. As I further said, genealogical ties are activated by means of patterned kin behavior.

What do I mean by *patterned* kin behavior? One thing I mean by "patterned" is that behavior between a pair of kinsmen is fairly predictable and stable. One kinsman knows—in some details, at least—how another kinsman will act toward him. He can predict his behavior, or some aspects of it, in advance. The second thing I mean by "patterned" is that the kin behavior is not stable and predictable merely because of the known individual traits of the persons involved, as in a nonkin friendship relationship. Instead, the behavior is predictable because it is *culturally standardized.* Custom dictates a "proper way" to act toward father, mother's brother, wife's mother, and relatives in general, and people carry out the customs. This customary "proper way," this set of rules for behavior toward various categories of kin, dictates patterned kin behavior. And patterned kin behavior, I think, could fairly be called the essence of kinship.

Some patterned kin behavior seems to apply equally to all categories of kinsmen. In the Samoa example just given, it seems that any sort of kinsman can evoke the mutual aid obligation that

Margaret Mead describes. Likewise, in our society, it is my impression that there is a general hospitality obligation that attaches to any sort of kin relationship. Other patterned kin behavior may attach to particular *groupings* of kin; for example, you may have particular obligations to everyone in your unilineal kin group. (I will have more to say presently about unilineal kin groups.) Finally, patterned kin behavior may attach to a particular kin relationship: Ego to father, or Ego to mother's brother, or Ego to father's sister's son, and so on. In the Kwoma example, Ego has special property-taking rights vis-à-vis his mother's brother. In our own society, forms of address are patterned according to particular kin relationships. Thus, you address your father as "father" or "dad" and your mother as "mother" or "mom," for example. It is the rare American who will address his father as "Pete" (the father's given name) or his mother as "Flossie." Likewise, no one calls his grandfather "George" or his grandmother "Molly"; again, relationship terms are used. On the other hand, you do *not* use the relationship term when addressing a brother, sister, or cousin. You say "Mac," not "brother" or "brother Mac" (Schneider and Homans 1955).

Often, it seems, patterned kin behavior "goes with" classificatory kin terms. Thus, everyone you call by a given classificatory kin term—"grandfather," "father" (real and classificatory), "uncle," and so forth—will receive about the same sort of patterned kin behavior. In the Tonga example, a person is *fahu* to everyone he calls by the classificatory kin term *tuasina*. With his most closely related *tuasina* (his real mother's brother) he has rather extreme-sounding property-taking rights. With less closely related *tuasina* he has similar property-taking rights, but of diminished "intensity"; he may not "go as far" with them as he can with his real mother's brother.

To summarize: patterned kin behavior is behavior between kinsmen that is stable, predictable, or standardized, by custom, that is, by various rules or norms inherent in a culture. Some kinds of patterned kin behavior may apply fairly equally to all persons recognized as kin. (Example: the general mutual-aid-hospitality ethic in Samoa or, in diminished force, in the United States.) On the other hand, patterned kin behavior may apply to all persons within a unilineal kin group. Finally, certain kinds of patterned kin behavior are specific to a particular kin relationship. (Example: you must call your grandfather "grandfather," but you may call your brother by his proper name.) Apparently, patterned kin behavior often "goes with" classificatory kin terms: with all persons whom you call by a particular classificatory kin term, such as "grandfather," you will observe rather similar patterned kin behavior.

I divided patterned kin behavior into two general classes: rights and obligations, and comportment. The meaning of "rights and obligations" is self-evident. Rights are privileges, "things you have coming from" various kinsmen. Obligations are the reverse: duties, "things they have coming from" you. Sometimes the balance of rights and duties between two kinsmen is reciprocal, "fair." In other cases, it is very nonreciprocal and seems (to the outsider) very unfair; the Tongan *fahu* is a case in point.

I divided comportment into four subtypes: deference, avoidance, joking, and informality. We will now examine each of these subtypes, one by one.

Deference

Deference involves the general posture of respect, submissiveness, and obedience. It characterizes unequal relationships. The inferior, submissive person shows deference to the dominant, superior, privileged person. In the Egyptian example of deference, the son (the inferior person) showed deference to his father (the superior, dominant person). Ammar lists these deference customs in his Egyptian village: the son apparently obeys his father's "curt and abrupt admonitions"; in a gathering, the son observes various kinds of sitting etiquette and lets his father do the talking; the son does not smoke in his father's presence; when they are walking together, the son walks behind his father. Other societies have other deference customs: bowing, kneeling, hand-kissing; speech etiquette, such as speaking in a low voice, not joking, not arguing or contradicting; mealtime etiquette, such as giving the deferred-to person the seat of honor, giving him the best food, letting him eat first; and body-elevation rules, such as not being higher than the deferred-to person, or standing upon greeting the deferred-to person, or sitting on the ground while the deferred-to person sits on a chair.

Rather extreme deference customs characterize the preindustrial civilizations of the world: old Japan, China, Hindu India, Egypt and the Middle East generally, most of Latin America, and the more "civilized" parts of Africa and Southeast Asia. Deference customs appear to be much less marked in most primitive tribes, and, of course, they are virtually absent in the United States. During feudal times, Europe was probably characterized by extreme deference customs, but now Western Europe, at least, seems to have become liberalized in this respect. (There is one notable exception: Spain.) There is a very strong correlation between deferential (or autocratic) kin relationships and autocratic state. Where the state is democratic (as in the United States and most of Western Europe) or nonexistent (as in most primitive tribes), kin relationships are fairly nondeferential and "democratic"; where the state has been autocratic for a long period of time (with, perhaps, a very recent change to democracy), kin relationships tend to be autocratic too.

Extreme deference thus characterizes a certain type of society —the autocratic agrarian state. It also characterizes only certain types of kin relationships. Deference is shown to men by women, and to older men by younger men. Marked deference is rarely shown to female kin either by men or by other women.[4] Also, I suspect that deference toward men by older-generation women—mother, aunt, grandmother—is rare. In the ethnographic literature, the most frequently mentioned deferential relationships are wife-to-husband, and Ego to older male consanguineal relatives—to father, elder brother, uncles, and grandfathers. Furthermore, in these kin relationships deference goes only one way. Husband never, or almost never, shows deference to wife; and father, elder brother, uncles never show deference to Ego.

---

[4] The remnants of "chivalry" toward women in Europe and parts of America—such customs as offering a woman your seat on the bus, opening the door for your wife, seating mother first at the dinner table—represent a possible borderline case.

In Chapter 7 I will have much more to say about deference relationships; there I will, among other things, document the generalizations about deference that I have just made.

Now let us consider avoidance relationships.

Avoidance

Like deference, avoidance implies "formality," a restriction on intimacy and spontaneous expression of emotion. However, avoidance is different in two respects. For one thing, deference is a sort of ritual expression of social inequality; the deference customs seem to say, "You are strong, I am weak; you are noble, I am base; you are privileged, I am unprivileged." Also, deference customs are one-way, nonreciprocal; son gives deference to father, but father is not, in turn, deferential to son. Avoidance customs, on the other hand, are neither one-way nor a demonstration of social inequality. People in an avoidance relationship avoid *each other*; the avoidance customs you observe toward your mother-in-law, she also observes toward you. Also, avoiding your mother-in-law does not necessarily mean that she is inferior to you, or that you are inferior to her. It merely seems to mean that you should not be intimate with each other, that you should "keep your distance."

In the avoidance quotation given for the Baganda of Africa, a man and his mother-in-law observed these avoidance rules: can't touch each other, can't look eye-to-eye, can't eat together, can't converse alone, can't eat each other's leavings.

Other fairly widespread avoidance customs, found in other societies, are: can't talk about sex, can't sleep in the same house, can't talk directly (must converse through an intermediary, or at a distance), can't see or touch some part of the avoided person's body (for example, head, face, breasts).

Rather extreme-sounding avoidance relationships, similar to the Baganda's, are fairly common in primitive societies. Avoidance is correlated with at least two other social conditions. One is the presence of unilineal kin groups. The other is the long *post partum* sex taboo, which, as noted in Chapter 2, tends in turn to occur in polygynous societies.

Like deference, avoidance is specific to particular kin relationships. Men seldom avoid other men, and women rarely avoid women. Avoidance is, first of all, characteristic of cross-sex kin relationships. Men avoid women, and vice versa.[5] Second, very few consanguineal or "blood" kin relationships are characterized by avoidance. Men rarely or never avoid a daughter, mother, aunt, grandmother, or niece; women rarely if ever avoid their sons, fathers, uncles, grandfathers, or nephews. Between blood-kin, avoidance does often occur between same-generation cross-sex kin. A man avoids his sisters and his female cousins. Most avoidance relationships, however, are between in-laws. The classic avoidance relationship is between a man and his mother-in-law. Another common avoidance relationship is between a man and his daughter-in-law.

The picture that emerges is one of three common "focal" avoidance relationships: brother-sister, man to mother-in-law, and man to son's wife. Each of these focal avoidance relationships carries a number of "extensions." For example, in a society where a man must avoid his sister, he must also avoid female cousins. Where he avoids his mother-in-law, he also avoids others of his wife's blood kin. Where a woman avoids her father-in-law, she also avoids others of her husband's blood kin. Thus, usually, if you avoid any kinsman you will avoid a great many kinsmen. But, if you do not avoid the "focal" person (say, your mother-in-law), neither will you avoid her "extensions" (others of the wife's kin).

I tried to find out whether, and to what extent, the extensions are determined by classificatory kin terms. That is, are the "extensions" of mother-in-law, for example, merely all the persons Ego calls by the same classification kin term as he calls his mother-in-law, which might include his wife's aunts, sisters, and grandmothers? As it turned out, the ethnographic data did not provide any decisive answers. In some societies, like the Ganda, classificatory kin terms apparently *do* determine the extensions of an avoidance relationship: in other societies they do not.

---

5 Avoidance between same-sex persons, when it occurs, is nearly always an extension of the mother-in-law avoidance or of the man-to-son's-wife avoidance.

The most obvious consequence of extreme avoidances is that they make life difficult. As I said, if a society has any avoidance relationships at all, it usually has a great number of them. And the extreme avoidance customs, as you can imagine, require a great deal of vigilance. You must watch what you say, be careful where your eyes look, be watchful about who is present in a social gathering, even run and hide at times. Before saying more about avoidances, I will give two examples to illustrate the grotesque amount of inconvenience they cause. The first example is represented by the Chiricahua Apache, hunting nomads of northern Mexico and southwestern United States. As you read about their avoidances, keep in mind that the Chiricahua lived in tiny camps.

BROTHER-SISTER AVOIDANCE

"In the old days those who had the same father and mother hardly spoke to each other. They would sit there and wouldn't say anything. They talked to the father and mother in each other's presence but not to each other. If joking (risqué) goes on when they are both there, one of them has to go away to show respect.

"If you come where your sister is alone, you put disgrace on the whole family. If the mother and father aren't at home and the sister is alone, you must leave the camp. You must stay somewhere else. You must go to the sunny side of the hill or in the shade and sleep until your parents come home. . . ."

Informants have described to me how they have come home from the hunt, tired and hungry, and have not thought of entering the home because a sister was there alone.

EXTENSIONS OF BROTHER-SISTER AVOIDANCE

"A Chiricahua man and woman related in this way hardly speak to one another. Two cousins who call each other *cilah* hardly speak. Cousins . . . could not even go out walking with each other. They can't joke much. Something holds them apart, so that they can't get too familiar."

MOTHER-IN-LAW AVOIDANCE, AND ITS EXTENSIONS

It is obligatory for the husband to avoid his mother-in-law, his father-in-law, his mother-in-law's mother, and his father-in-law's mother. With these individuals there is no choice or alternative. . . .

There are others with whom an avoidance relationship is usually established, though this is not strictly necessary, and the polite form of speech may take its place. . . . These persons include the sisters and brothers of the mother-in-law and the father-in-law.

AVOIDANCE BEHAVIOR (IN THE MORE EXTREME AVOIDANCE RELATIONSHIPS)

. . . the principals are prevented from ever meeting face to face. All negotiations between them must be carried on through a third person, usually the wife of the married man; for, of a married couple, only the man avoids any of his mate's relatives. There is a general term, reciprocally used, which can be translated "that one whom I avoid." It is employed in speaking of any person with whom an avoidance relationship has been established.

The avoidance relationship necessitates some manner of warning from others to those in an avoidance relationship who are inadvertently about to come into each other's view. Bystanders are most obliging in this respect, and the usual warning, "Do not walk there," is constantly heard. (Opler 1937)

The next example is represented by the Manus, a Melanesian people of the Admiralty Islands. The Manus do not have brother-sister avoidance, but they do go in for in-law avoidances on a large scale. A man avoids his son's wife, his younger brother's wife, his wife's brother's wife, his mother-in-law, and *all* of his wife's consanguineal relatives, male and female. Apparently, few or none of these avoidance relationships last a lifetime, but there always seem to be plenty of people to avoid:

Women are aided in their avoidance outside the home by a calico cloak which has superseded the characteristic peaked rain mat of aboriginal days. . . . In a canoe gathering at which her *kaleals*[6] are present she sits huddled up on the canoe platform, her head bowed between her knees, her knees hunched, and her whole form wrapped in the cloak. . . .

The women who labor under the greatest disadvantage are young women in their husbands' villages, and older women whose daughters have married into their own villages. A young wife in

---

[6] Persons to be avoided.

> her husband's village may have to avoid half a dozen older men. An older woman may have several sons-in-law from whom she must hide or run away. Hiding her face is only acceptable in lieu of running away when running away is impossible, as in a canoe, or when a woman is surprised in a group. If a man appears on the edge of a group, the women who are his *kaleals* hastily cover their faces and drift away into the back of the house or out of the house altogether, or off the *arakeu* on to a canoe platform.
>
> Technically, for purposes of observing *kaleals*, a house is divided into two parts by one or more mats hung from the ceiling. Such a house can accommodate two households in which live a man and a woman whom he calls daughter-in-law and who must therefore avoid him, and never raise her voice so that he can hear it at the other end of a house. Nor can she ever go into his section of the house except when he is absent. This division of the house is designed to accommodate *kaleals* of the father-in-law–daughter-in-law type which are felt to be less drastic than those of the mother-in-law–son-in-law type. The occupation of a house by two brothers, in which case the younger wife must avoid the older brother, as titular "father-in-law," is a common situation. . . .
>
> For a woman . . . as the weight of the "father-in-law" taboo drops from her shoulders, the weight of taboos based on her position as "mother-in-law" must be assumed. There is no respite for her with increasing age. She has had to avoid her "fathers-in-law" and now she must avoid her "sons-in-law." Her response to anyone naming a *kaleal*, or bringing a *kaleal* into the conversation is one of angry embarrassment. (Mead 1934: 266–269)

To summarize: avoidance customs prevent intimacy and close contact between certain categories of kin; avoidance is usually between cross-sex persons. There are three focal avoidance relationships: male Ego to mother-in-law, male Ego to sister, and male Ego to son's wife; each carries a number of extensions, so that if you avoid one of these focal relatives you will also avoid a certain number of other relatives. If a society has one avoidance relationship, it usually has many. Avoidance customs are frequently so extreme as to cause a fantastic amount of inconvenience and hardship.

The question naturally arises: What is the origin of—the reason for—such apparently senseless and dysfunctional customs?

A partial answer to that question is as follows: kin avoidances express, among other things, a phobic attitude toward incest, which has its origins in Oedipal problems. A discussion of the evidence supporting this Freudian interpretation of kin avoidances is given in one of the sources listed in the Bibliography (Stephens 1962).

Joking

The example of the joking relationship was the *mucimuli* of the Tarahumara: rough-housing, genital snatching, and other sorts of sexual horseplay. At first glance, this seems the exact opposite of avoidance and deference. In a way it is. Both avoidance and deference involve "formality," an inhibition on spontaneous action. Joking certainly seems the opposite of formality. Generally, a "joking relationship" (described in an ethnography) seems to mean sexual joking.[7] Also, it frequently means aggressive joking: belittling, sarcasm, and mild physical violence.

Like deference and avoidance relationships, joking relationships are patterned. They involve behavior that is culturally standardized, predictable, and specified as "proper behavior" between a given pair of relatives. The form the joking takes often seems quite stereotyped. Margaret Mead has this to say of an obligatory joking relationship:

MUNDUGUMOR, NEW GUINEA

> A joking relative is not a person with whom one may joke if one wishes, but rather a relative towards whom joking is the correct behaviour, a kind of behaviour that is as culturally fixed as shaking hands.
>
> Perhaps it will make the matter clearer to imagine what it would be like if one were taught in America to shake hands with one's uncles and kiss the hands of one's aunts, while when one met a

[7] I know numerous cases where a "joking relationship" is said to include sexual joking, and of only one case—the milder of the Navahos' joking relationships—where "joking" is said not to involve sexual jokes (Aberle 1954: 42–43). In addition, there are a number of accounts of "joking relationships" in which it is not specified whether "joking" includes sexual joking.

grandparent, one took off one's hat, threw away one's cigarette or pipe, and stood rigidly at attention, and upon meeting a cousin the correct behaviour was to thumb one's nose. Imagine further that in a small, inbred rural community, relationships were traced a very long way in every genealogical line, and so not only one's mother's sisters and one's father's but all of their first and even second cousins of the female sex were called "aunt," until there were some twenty or thirty relatives of varying ages in the community, all of whom had to have their hands kissed, and an equal number at whom one thumbed one's nose. It will be seen also that in such a large group, one's "aunts" and "uncles" and "cousins" would be of all ages, and would occur in the same school or the same playground. This approximates the normal condition in a primitive society that insists upon different treatment for different classes of relatives. In Mundugumor everyone must be continually on the alert and ready to respond with the appropriate behaviour. A failure to joke is more serious than a failure of an American to greet properly an acquaintance upon the street. It may easily be as serious as a failure to salute a superior officer, or to acknowledge a possible employer's friendly greeting. And whereas the American can walk down the street only watchful to distinguish between those whom he knows and those whom he does not, and only sufficiently attentive to the form that his greeting takes to regulate its boisterousness or its familiarity, in many primitive societies much more elaborate behaviour is demanded.

So a Mundugumor child is taught that everyone who is related to it as mother's brother, father's sister, sister's child of a male, brother's child of a female, and their spouses, is a joking relative with whom one engages in rough-house, accusations of unusual and inappropriate conduct, threats, mock bullying, and the like. If a man meets his father's sister—and this applies not only to his father's own sister but to all the women whom his father calls sister, and whom we should call first, second, sometimes third cousin to his father—he slaps her on the back, tells her she is getting old, will probably die soon, has a frightful-looking bone ornament in her nose, and he tries to pull some areca-nut out of her carrying-basket. Similarly when a man meets a brother-in-law, any man whom his wife calls brother or any man married to a woman whom he calls sister, he must be shy and circumspect, not ask him for an areca-nut or offer to share food with him, but greet him with great coolness tinged with embarrassment. The world is early presented to the

> child as one in which there are a large number of such fixed relationships, with a separate behaviour-pattern appropriate to some and highly inappropriate and insulting to others, a world in which one must always be upon one's guard, and always ready to respond correctly and with apparent spontaneity to these highly formal demands. . . . Even gaiety is not in any sense a relaxation for a Mundugumor; he must always be gay on the right occasions and addressing the right persons, he must always be watchful that none of the persons toward whom, or in the presence of whom, such behaviour would be incorrect are anywhere about. This gives a tightrope quality to all jest and laughter. (Mead 1935)

One thing Mead describes here is the complication involved in simultaneously observing avoidance relationships and joking relationships. It is true that joking is correlated with avoidance. There is a tendency for joking relationships to occur in societies that also have rather extreme avoidance relationships (Stephens 1962). The Manus, for example, have a joking relationship.[8] Mead paints a rather grim picture of joking among the Mundugumor; perhaps we should not generalize this to apply to all joking societies. But when obligatory joking relationships occur in a society that also has avoidance relationships, they must demand a certain amount of vigilance and social dexterity, and, as Mead describes the total effect (to the outsider) must be one of extremely stereotyped, "artificial" social interaction.

I have never made a large-scale cross-cultural study of joking relationships, as I have of avoidance and deference relationships, and therefore cannot generalize about their distribution among the world's societies, or their distribution among the possible kin relationships. My impression, from what ethnographic notes I have, is that extreme-sounding, obligatory joking relationships are fairly common in societies that also observe extreme avoidance relationships. Avoidance and joking tend to go together in a "package." In a "joking/avoiding society," you may avoid your mother-in-law, joke with your brother-in-law, avoid your sisters

---

[8] When Mead asked a Manus wife if she allowed her husband to touch her breasts, the woman indignantly replied: "Of course not; that (privilege) belongs to my cross-cousin (joking relative) only" (Mead 1931).

and female cousins, joke with your father's sisters, and so forth. But this point could have better documentation than it has now.

Which relatives may be involved in a joking relationship? It is my impression that anyone except parents or children are "fair game." There are mentions of joking relationships with siblings, aunts and uncles, grandparents, and in-laws. In my own ethnographic notes, most cases of joking are between cross-sex kin—brother and sister, a man and his father's sister, a man and his brother's wife, and so forth.

To conclude this discussion of joking, I will turn to a long description of a joking relationship among the Hopi of the Southwest United States. The account was given by the Hopi autobiographer, Don Talayesva ("Sun Chief"):

HOPI, ARIZONA

There was another "grandfather," Talasweoma, the husband of another of my father's clan sisters, who was pretty rough to me. . . . This man was terrible. He was always accusing me of some mischief, grabbing for my penis, and saying that he would cut it off. One day in the month of May he and his uncle, who was a very old man and my father's ceremonial father, corralled their sheep near the village on the southwest edge of the mesa. We children went out before breakfast to watch them castrate the rams and billy goats. Some of us were sitting on a rock nearby. Talasweoma's son tied up and held the legs of the animals while he did the cutting. When breakfast time drew near he jumped up quickly, turned around, caught hold of my arm, pulled me into the corral, and said, "This is a boy I want to cut. He is naughty. I caught him in my house trying to make love to my wife. I am going to castrate him. Then if he wants to live he cannot eat or drink for a number of days."

He fastened my hands together and drew up my legs in the way they tied the billy goats. While I lay on the ground greatly frightened, he sharpened his knife carefully on a stone, watching me. He said, "Now after your balls are cut out, you will grow to be a nice-looking boy." The other children stood staring at me. I was crying. He got down over me, felt about my private parts, and tied a string around them, just as he had done with the goats to check the bleeding. Then he took up his knife, rubbed it on a stone again, eyed me closely, and said, "Now your time has come." Seizing my privates, he rubbed his knife across them smooth with my body, as though he were cutting off everything. I struggled and yelled. But he was using the blunt edge of the knife. One of his grown sons took my side, saying, "Turn him loose: you will learn your lesson yet." That son unbound me and said, "Now, Chuka, when you get to be a big boy it will be your turn to do that to him."

That old man was laughing loudly when I started up the mesa in a fast run. I went crying to my mother. She said that he was my "grandfather" and that she could do nothing about it; but that when I became a big boy I could get even with him. She said that he had a right to tease me and that it showed how much he cared for me. His wife, who was my aunt, took my side, comforted me, and warned the terrible man that some day I would treat him the same way.

After I was four or five nearly all my grandfathers, father's sisters' and clan sisters' husbands, played very rough jokes on me, snatched at my penis, and threatened to castrate me, charging that I had been caught making love to their wives, who were my aunts. All these women took my part, called me their sweetheart, fondled my penis, and pretended to want it badly. They would say, "Throw it to me," reach out their hands as if catching it, and smack their lips. I liked to play with them but I was afraid of their rough husbands and thought they would castrate me. It was a long time before I could be sure that they meant only to tease.

(*When Don grows older*)

I had more fun in clown work than anything else, but I did get some satisfaction out of teasing my "grandfathers," especially the old fellows who had joked me so terribly as a boy. I threatened to sleep with their wives, rolled them in the snow, and even threw them in mud puddles and spoiled their clothes. One day in 1919 we were building a warehouse at Hubbell's store. I was mixing cement in a large trough when my old "grandfather," Talasweoma, who had pretended to castrate me, came up with a small bag on his back. He said, "Well, Talayesva, I am old and quite ugly now, but I am sorry to see that you look even worse." I looked up and smiled, for he *was* ugly with a bent, bony frame, wrinkled hide, tangled hair, and little dim, squint eyes. I stepped over to him quickly, picked him up, and threw him into the sloppy mortar. As he scrambled out, he was pushed in again. He cried, "Please don't throw me back, I have learned my lesson, and I'll be good." The

Hopi were laughing, but Mr. Hubbell, the trader, stepped up, looked cross, and scolded me for being too rough on the old man. He hobbled into the store, scraping mortar off himself. Later I I walked in and said, "What is the matter, have you been crying?" "No," he replied, "I am very happy." Then I bought him fifty cents' worth of sugar and a pound of coffee. I had already begun to tease my own "grandchildren" and treat them pretty rough.

(*Don grows still older*)

. . . as I passed the Buffalo shrine, a car overtook me and the driver stopped about ten steps ahead. Whenever I ran, he started up again and kept just out of my reach. There were five people in the car watching me and laughing. At last I caught on and climbed in. The driver was Irene's uncle's son, Perry, whom I had teased for years. When I got off at Bakabi, he looked around and laughed as if to say, "I am squaring accounts for what I have suffered from you." (Simmons 1942:39–40, 280, 368)

Informality, or Lack of Obvious Patterning

One question about patterned kin behavior is: just how important are the cultural rules, in the face of human emotions and individual differences? Does everyone always do just as his culture demands? In a kin-relationship demanding formality, are people always formal? Are there never any slips into intimacy or informality? In a joking relationship, do people always joke? Are the prescribed customs of patterned kin behavior always followed? Does no Baganda *ever* touch his mother-in-law? Does no son in Silwa *ever* walk abreast of his father? Or, are there individual variations, "violations" of the kinship rules?

The approach of most ethnographers is to summarize the cultural rules, and not to look closely for individual differences. So the impression one gets from many ethnographies is that people are most faithful to the kinship rules, that their kin behavior is stereotyped—similar to Mead's description of the Mundugumor. Sometimes patterned kin behavior (as described by the ethnographer) seems so strict, so all-embracing, that social interaction appears to be quite standardized; people seem to behave like the social insects, like ants or bees. Since people are not insects, patterned kin behavior is probably never as "effective," as faithfully followed, as some ethnographies imply.

Still, every kin relationship must fall somewhere on a continuum of degree-of-patterning. Kin relationships that are "high" on this continuum are very "patterned." In these "high" cases, the rules of proper kin behavior are all-embracing, giving little or no leeway for individual variation; furthermore, these rules are followed rather faithfully. The Mundugumor seem to have kin relationships of this sort. In the "middle" of this continuum would be kin relationships that are less enclosed in a straight jacket of custom; they allow some leeway for individual variation, or their rules of "proper" kin behavior are violated more frequently. Perhaps the Hopi joking relationship would be a case of this sort; they seem to have some individual variation in style and "intensity" of joking. At the very bottom of the continuum would be—theoretically—kin relationships characterized by absolutely no patterned kin behavior at all. Strictly speaking, such cases of absolutely no patterned kin behavior would not be kin relationships at all, but merely genealogical relationships.

The category *Informality, or lack of obvious patterning,* applies to cases *near the bottom* of this continuum. When an ethnographer describes a kin relationship of this sort, there is no obvious rule of comportment—no conspicuous custom of deference, avoidance, or joking—that he can refer to. Neither are there any conspicuous rights or obligations (like the Tongan *fahu*). Usually there is some implicit, inconspicuous patterning in the kin relationship; for example, some implicit obligation of hospitality and mutual aid. When an ethnographer describes a kin relationship of this sort there is nothing much he can "hang his hat on," and he usually falls back on vague descriptive terms such as "informal," "friendly," "casual," or "warm."

As you probably have already concluded, American culture is generally characterized by kin relationships of this kind. The patterning—if it is there—is implicit, inconspicuous, and generally "weak." (See Parsons 1943:31–32.) This is one of the many instances in which American family and kinship customs, seen in world-wide perspective, are deviant, unusual, and rather peculiar. We may view the joking/avoidance societies as odd, but it is actually we who are the odd ones (if "odd" means unusual). If an ethnographer were to study us for patterned kin behavior, about the only clear and conspicuous patterning custom he could find would be the use of kin terms in addressing older-generation relatives (which is an extremely common custom of patterned kin behavior, and seems to characterize nearly all societies). And, as Schneider and Homans have demonstrated, even this custom is violated. Some of Schneider and Homans' informants called their uncles by their given names ("Jim" instead of "Uncle Jim"). A few even called their parents by their first names. Apparently, in America only grandparents are sacrosanct; in Schneider and Homans' sample, only grandparents were always addressed by the relationship term (Schneider and Homans 1955).

This concludes my review of categories of patterned kin behavior: rights and obligations, and patterned comportment—deference, avoidance, joking, and informality.[9] Some kin relationships are often highly patterned; others are less so. The mother-child relationship, for example, seems never to have marked deference, avoidance, or joking. Some societies are characterized —generally—by highly patterned kin behavior. The Mundugumor are a case in point. Other societies have less patterning in their kin relationships, with our own society representing the extreme example of this type. When kin behavior is highly patterned, kinship has great over-all importance in shaping and directing social life. We shall now look at accounts of three societies in which patterned kin behavior appears to have great general importance.

NAVAHO, ARIZONA-NEW MEXICO

. . . there is a definite way to behave towards all persons addressed by the same kinship term. The limited set of patterns for social life,

---

[9] Reference to the *sanctions* that enforce patterned kin behavior is conspicuous by its absence in ethnographic literature. I know of no mention of legal sanctions—fines, banishment, and so forth—for failing to comply with the customs of patterned comportment between kin; and I know of only two cases of supernatural sanctions. Apparently, patterned kin behavior requires only the more subtle of social pressures for its enforcement, such as the threat of embarrassment, unspoken anger, diffuse social disapproval.

acquired in childhood, is later used to bridge excursions into the wider social environment. The ways in which a Navaho adult deals with all individuals who come into his life tend to represent modifications of these master designs for interpersonal relations. He wants to classify each new acquaintance with one or another of these relatives and to treat him accordingly. One of his difficulties in adjusting to white men is that they do not fit into this system. (Leighton & Kluckhohn 1948:45)

HOPI, ARIZONA

Whenever two or more individuals meet in Hopi society, the first act is to establish the relationship of each to the other, and from there on behavior usually follows a customary and almost ritualized course. (Simmons 1942:15)

KARIERA, AUSTRALIA

. . . the relationship system . . . is based on actual relations of consanguinity and affinity that can be traced by means of the genealogical knowledge preserved by old men and women. The recognition of relationships is so extended that everyone with whom an individual comes in contact in the ordinary course of social life is his relative. It is impossible for a man to have any social relations with anyone who is not his relative because there is no standard by which two persons in this position can regulate their conduct towards one another. I am compelled to treat a person differently according as he is my "brother," "brother-in-law," "father," or "uncle." If I do not know which of these he is, all intercourse is impossible. . . .

When (for example) a stranger comes to a camp that he has never visited before, he does not enter the camp, but remains at some distance. A few of the older men, after a while, approach him, and the first thing they proceed to do is to find out who the stranger is. The commonest question that is put to him is "Who is your *maeli*?" (father's father). The discussion proceeds on genealogical lines until all parties are satisfied of the exact relation of the stranger to each of the natives present in the camp. When this point is reached, the stranger can be admitted to the camp, and the different men and women are pointed out to him and their relation to him defined. I watched two or three of these discussions in West

> Australia. I took with me on my journey a native of the Talainji tribe, and at each native camp we came to, the same process had to be gone through. In one case, after a long discussion, they were still unable to discover any traceable relationship between my servant and the men of the camp. That night my "boy" refused to sleep in the native camp, as was his usual custom, and on talking to him, I found that he was frightened. These men were not his relatives, and they were therefore his enemies. This represents the real feelings of the natives on the matter. If I am a blackfellow and meet another blackfellow that other must be either my relative or my enemy. If he is my enemy I shall take the first opportunity of killing him, for fear he will kill me. (A. R. Radcliffe-Brown, "Three Tribes of Western Australia," *Journal of the Anthropological Institute*, Vol. 43. Quoted in Thomas 1937:99)

By this time, you should have some idea of what Fortes meant by the "web of kinship." Patterned kin relations give "structure" to society: they "hold things together," make social relations regular, predictable, and to some extent uniform. If you are an ethnographer in a society with highly patterned kin relations and you can describe the patterning of each kin relationship, then you have described a fairly large and significant segment of the entire "social system," that is, you have described many of the regularities of social behavior. With this hope in mind, many an ethnographer does try to describe his tribe's entire "relationship system"; he takes each kin relationship, one by one, gives the kin terms, and then describes the more obvious of the patterned kin behavior within that kin relationship. I would like to give an example of this kind of description, but such summaries of relationship are too long to be quoted. The ethnographic literature is full of them; here, I must refer you to other sources. These are some particularly good examples: Oliver on the Siwai; Aberle on the Navaho; Blackwood on Kurtachi; Laura Thompson on Fiji; Colson on the Plateau Tonga; Firth on Tikopia; Opler on the Chiricahua; Warner on the Murngin; and Titiev on the Hopi. (See the Ethnographic Bibliography.)

Kinship, then, by means of patterned kin behavior, gives structure to society. Kinship also provides structure by grouping people together. In other words, "the web of kinship" has two facets or aspects: one is patterned kin behavior; the other is kin groups. Let us now consider kin groups.

Unilineal Kin Groups

A kin group is, as the name implies, a group of kinsmen. Murdock divides all kin groups into two general classes: residential kin groups, and consanguineal kin groups (Murdock 1949:41). Residential kin groups include the nuclear family and its composite forms—polygynous families, and extended families. Consanguineal kin groups are composed exclusively of blood relatives (thereby excluding the family, since husband and wife are not blood relatives). There are three general ways of determining membership in a consanguineal kin group: you may belong to your father's kin group (patrilineal descent), your mother's kin group (matrilineal descent), or you may include blood relatives on both your father's side and your mother's side in your consanguineal kin group (bilateral descent).

Most of the societies of the world (over 60 percent of the societies in Murdock's *World Ethnographic Sample*) have unilineal descent—either patrilineal or matrilineal—and, hence, have unilineal consanguineal kin groups. With patrilineal descent, Ego, his siblings, his father, father's siblings, father's father, and more distant relatives in the male line, all belong to the same unilineal kin group; Ego's mother belongs to a different unilineal kin group. With matrilineal descent the situation is reversed: Ego and his siblings, Ego's mother and her siblings, Ego's mother's mother and her siblings, and more distant relatives in the female line, all belong to the same unilineal kin group; Ego's father belongs to a different unilineal kin group. Patrilineal descent appears to be the most common. In the *World Ethnographic Sample*, 238 societies are designated patrilineal, 77 societies are matrilineal, and 30 have double descent. In a society with double descent, Ego belongs to two separate unilineal kin groups: one kin group composed of his father and relatives in the male line, the other kin group composed of his mother and relatives in the female line. In other words, double descent is simply a combination of patrilineal and matrilineal descent.

Other ways of assigning people to unilineal kin groups do occur, but they are quite rare. The Mundugumor have what they call "ropes": a boy belongs to his mother's kin group (and not to his father's), and a girl belongs to her father's kin group (and not to her mother's) (Mead 1935). Among the Apinaye of Brazil, a boy belongs to his father's kin group and a girl belongs to her mother's kin group. Among the Buginese and Macassar of Celebes, odd-numbered children belong to their mother's unilineal kin group, and even-numbered children belong to their father's unilineal kin group (Murdock 1949:45).

"Bilateral descent"—which characterizes the United States and Europe—means, simply, that unilineal kin groups are absent (Murdock 1960:2). Instead of belonging to your father's unilineal kin group or your mother's unlineal kin group, you recognize a certain number of blood relatives on both "sides of the family" as your "kinfolk" or kindred. Murdock has this to say about the bilaterally-reckoned kindred:

> The most distinctive structural fact about the (bilateral) kindred is that, save through accident, it can never be the same for any two individuals with the exception of own siblings. For any given person, its membership ramifies out through diverse kinship connections until it is terminated at some degree of relationship—frequently with second cousins, although the limits are often drawn somewhat closer or farther away than this and may be rather indefinite. The kindreds of different persons overlap or intersect rather than coincide. Those, for example, of first cousins, the sons of two brothers, have part of their membership in common —the near relatives through their respective fathers—and the rest distinct; the kinsmen of either cousin through his mother do not belong to the kindred of the other.
>
> Since kindreds interlace and overlap, they do not and cannot form discrete or separate segments of the entire society. Neither a tribe nor a community can be subdivided into constituent kindreds. This intersecting or non-exclusive characteristic is found only with bilateral descent. Every other rule of descent[10] produces only clearly differentiated, isolable, discrete kin groups, which never overlap with others of their kind. (Murdock 1949:60–61)

[10] That is, unilineal descent.

In other words, bilateral descent is "messy"; unilineal descent is "neat." With bilateral descent, no two people (aside from brothers and sisters) belong to the same consanguineal kin group. Your kin group is different from your father's, your mother's, your children's, or anyone else's (aside from that of your brother and sister). Also, the boundaries of bilateral kin groups are often rather vague. Who belongs to your bilateral kin group? Which of your relatives are so distantly related to you as to not belong to your kin group; where do you draw the line?

By contrast, unilineal kin groups, as Murdock says, divide the society into discrete, separate *segments.* Each segment usually has a name. Ask a Navaho what is his unilineal kin group, and he will say: "I am a Bitter Water," or "I am a Many Goats" (I belong to the Bitter Water clan; I belong to the Many Goats clan). Ask a Siwai, and he may say: "I am a Belly Fat," or "I am a Legs Apart," or "I am a Left Behind." If you belong to a unilineal kin group, you know exactly where you belong. The boundaries of the unilineal kin group are clearly marked; you know exactly who is your unilineal kinsman, and who isn't. The unilineal kin groups do not "interlace and overlap," like the bilaterally-reckoned kindreds. Some Navaho are of the Bitter Water clan, other Navaho are of the Many Goats clan; but *no* Navaho belongs to both clans. A unilineal kin group, as Geertz says, "is seen as a sort of single person by all the nonmembers of it, in the same way that a corporation is seen as a single person under American commercial law. For those who stand outside the segment, but within the tribal society generally, the segment forms a simple unity. . . ."(Geertz "Cultural Ecology" m.s.). The analogy with a corporation is apt: the unilineal kin group has a name (like General Motors), it often corporately owns property, and it may have legal liability—it may be fined, or "prosecuted" by feud. I will have more to say, in a moment, on the various attributes of unilineal kin groups.

So, unilineal kin groups are corporate entities; they are discrete, separate, and named, like General Motors, or the New York Yankees. They are formed by means of unilineal descent: you are *either* a member of your mother's kin group *or* a member of your father's kin group, but not (except in the infrequent cases of double descent) a member of both parents' kin groups.

In a way, the unilineal kin group splits the family. One member of the nuclear family, either father or mother, must be an outsider. With patrilineal descent, for instance, mother is an outsider; father and children belong to one kin group, while she belongs to another. Does this mean that mother is not even "related" to her children, that they do not even recognize her as kin? The answer is no. Apparently, unilineal descent never goes this far. In a patrilineal society, genealogical ties—and real kinship—are still traced to the mother and her kin; in a matrilineal society, the father and his kin are still recognized as relatives (Murdock 1949:42). Unilineal kin groups might best be viewed as "a something extra" in the way of kinship, which our society lacks but which most societies have. Unilineal societies, like bilateral societies, trace genealogical ties on both "sides of the family," and observe various sorts of patterned kin behavior with both "the father's people" and "the mother's people." But, in *addition* to this bilaterally-reckoned kinship, they have special *groups* of kin. These special groups are the unilineal kin groups—in some societies patrilineal (with membership inherited from father to children) and in other societies matrilineal (with membership inherited from mother to children). Often, as we shall see, these unilineal groups are quite important in dictating further patterned kin behavior (mainly rights and obligations) and in regulating social life.

Unilineal kin groups were described as discrete "segments." Actually, they in turn are composed of still smaller segments. In a unilineal society there are often kin groups within kin groups. In a typical unilineal society, the segmenting might look something like this. First of all, Ego belongs to a fairly small, fairly localized unilineal kin group, small enough so that the members of the kin group can actually trace genealogical ties with each other. The ethnographer would usually call this smaller segment a lineage (Beaglehole and Beaglehole 1938:221; Steward 1955: 153; Geertz). Ego's lineage, plus several other lineages, combine to form a larger unilineal kin group; in other words, each of the lineages is a segment of this larger kin group. Anthropologists have used various terms for this supralineage kin group: clan, phratry, gens, sib, sept. For the time being, let us call it a clan. The clan is so big that often, it seems, some clan members cannot actually trace genealogical ties with each other. But they all "know" they are fellow clansmen, because they have all inherited the same clan membership—they are all Belly Fats, say, or Bitter Waters; usually, too, some myth of common ancestry accompanies clan membership (Steward 1955:154; Titiev 1943:527). Finally, Ego belongs to a still larger unilineal kin group—a moiety. Ego's clan forms a segment of a moiety. The moiety is the largest, most far reaching, of the unilineal kin groups in Ego's society; other kin groups are all segments or subsegments of it. The entire society is composed of two moieties. Each moiety is segmented into a number of clans, and each clan is segmented into a number of lineages. In this sense, in Ego's society there are kin groups within kin groups.

In the above example there was a threefold segmentation: lineage to clan to moiety. Actually, of course, there is no standard number of steps to segmenting. In one society there may be three, in another society two (lineage and clan), in another society five (lineage, sub-sub-sib, sub-sib, sib, moiety), and in another society no segmenting at all. Sometimes the segmenting climaxes in a moiety, and at other times it doesn't; for instance, a society may be ultimately divided into four large, dispersed phratries. Segmenting probably results from the growth and dispersal—over a period of time—of a unilineal kin group. For example, if a localized lineage gets so large that half of it moves away—you have segmenting right there. The anthropologist, who comes along later, will call the old dispersed lineage a "clan" or "sib," and call each of its two new parts a "lineage."

Finally, segmented unilineal kin groups are not quite as "neat" as I made them out to be. For one thing, the process of segmentation tends to be uneven: in a given society, one clan may have four lineages and another "clan" may have only one lineage. More important, the boundary lines between the various segments are rather vaguely drawn, at least in most ethnographies. Let us return to the example of Ego, who belongs to a lineage, which is part of a clan, which is part of a moiety. Ego's life is, in great measure, shaped by his membership in this segmented kin group. It determines whom he will marry, what farm land he will work, who will pay his fines when he gets in trouble, what gods he will worship, where he will live, and with whom he will cooperate in various ceremonials marking births, initiations, marriages, funerals, and various annual festival occasions. The question is, *which* segment determines which of these things? Is the farm land Ego works owned by his lineage, his moiety, or his clan? Does he worship clan gods or moiety gods? What body of kin arranges his marriage and raises the bride price—his lineage, or some other group? Does each segment have a name?

This aspect of unilineal kin groups—which segment does what—is not neat; in most ethnographies (with some notable exceptions) it is not clearly described. This will limit me, somewhat, when I try to describe the attributes of unilineal kin groups.

Attributes of Unilineal Kin Groups

A Name

In the first place, unilineal kin groups usually are named (Murdock 1949:50). Because a unilineal kin group is a corporate entity, it seems helpful for it to have some sort of label or symbol of its corporateness. Linton says:

> Wherever the clan is recognized there are mechanisms for keeping this fact of relationship before the mind of the individual and stressing its importance. The clan unit will usually have a name and very frequently a symbol of some sort, such as a particular animal or object, which its members treat with respect. Its members will often have distinctive details of dress or ornament, so that clan affiliations can be recognized at a glance. (Linton 1936:198)

By "symbol," Linton is evidently referring to totemism, which will be discussed in a moment. As far as "distinctive details of dress and ornament" is concerned, there is actually very little mention of this sort of thing in the ethnographic literature. Often, however (although not always), the unilineal kin group is named.

In my ethnographic notes, there is no society in which all unilineal kin-group segments are said to be unnamed. In three societies, Murngin, Siwai, and Tchambuli, all unilineal kin-group segments apparently bear names. In three other societies, Hopi, Navaho, and Plateau Tonga, some segments are named, and other segments are not named. For thirteen societies, the ethnographer mentions kin-group names, but it is not clear whether all or only some segments are named (Alor, China, Gusii, Kipsigis, Kurtachi, Muria, Ojibwa, Papago, Tiv, Toda, Trobriands, Tikopia, Wogeo).[11] There are, however, a good many descriptions of unilineal societies that have no mention of kin-group names.

As I said, members of a unilineal kin group consider themselves kinsmen, although often, in fact, it may not be possible to trace genealogical ties. When genealogical ties cannot be traced, a kin group name must be of great help in maintaining the boundaries of the kin group, and in assuring its members that they are, in fact, kinsmen. Imagine, for example, that your name is Smith and that you belong to the Smith clan (that is, to a clan composed of all people named Smith). Wherever you went, you could determine your kinsmen with ease. You would merely have to ask, "Are you a Smith?" When someone answered "Yes," you would "know" he was a kinsman.

Kin group names are often taken from plants, animals, or natural phenomena, as in the following moiety names: Red Ants and White Ants (Pima), Buzzard and Coyote (Papago), Bat and Hawk (Wogeo), Sun and Mother (!) (Tchambuli). The Muria phratry names are Serpent, Tortoise, Goat, Tiger, and Fish. Some American Indian tribes had nicknames as well as "proper" names for their unilineal kin groups:

> . . . among the Delaware the Wolf phratry is nicknamed "Round-foot," the Turkey phratry "Don't chew," the Turtle phratry "crawling." Delaware clan nicknames are even more suggestive than those of the Plains: one clan is called "Snapping-ears" from the supposed fondness of its members for going into the fields of neighbors and

---

[11] In some of these societies, unilineal kin groups are probably not segmented at all; in other cases they undoubtedly are.

snapping off roasting ears. Other clans go by such names as "Beggars," "Rubbing-the-eye," and "Cranky." Among the Iroquois the nicknames are used more commonly than the animal appellations. The Bear clan is referred to as "Broken-off-tail," the Hawk as "Boards" (an allusion to the large sticks in the hawk's nest), and the Deer as "Cloven-foot" or "Those-whose-nostrils-are-large-and-fine-looking." (Olson 1934:356–357)

Here are some Navaho kin group names: Many Goats, Red Clay, Walk Around You, Along the Stream, Bitahni, Bitter Water, and Poles Sprung Out in Water (Dyk: 1938). Finally, here are some kin groups of the pig-loving Siwai, whom I mentioned in Chapter 2: Tree-rats, What-is-it-calleds, Belly-fats, Left-behinds, Eagles, Kingfishers, Eye-rollers, Legs-apart, Pot-likes, Whistlers, Cockatoo-people, Nose-blowers, If-I'd-been-here, Cranes (Oliver 1955:108–120).

Exogamy

A second attribute of unilineal kin groups is exogamy; incest taboos are extended far beyond close blood ties, to include unilineal kin group members. As I said, it often seems as though some members of a unilineal kin group are so distantly related that they cannot even trace their genealogical connection. But they "know" they are blood kin because they belong to the same kin group; hence, usually, they cannot marry. In *Social Structure*, Murdock reports that only 10 of 178 unilineal societies "reveal a complete absence of (unilineal kin group) exogamy. In half of these instances the kin groups appear to be emergent and not fully elaborated." (Murdock 1949:48) In my smaller sample, there are only two unilineal societies that might possibly (the picture is unclear) be without any exogamous unilineal kin groups: the Papago, who seem to have very "weak" unilineal kin groups, and the Pukapuka who, it could be argued, have no unilineal kin groups at all (Murdock 1960). I have notes on twenty-three other unilineal societies that do mention exogamous unilineal kin groups: Ashanti, China, Fiji, Gusii, Hopi, Ifaluk, Kaska, Kipsigis, Kurtachi, Lepcha, Muria, Murngin, Navaho, Nayar, Ojibwa, Rajput, Siwai, Tiv, Toda, Plateau Tonga, Trobriands, Tchambuli, and Wogeo.

Usually, it seems, exogamy extends to the largest kin group. For example, if you have a threefold segmentation—lineage, clan, and moiety—the moiety will be exogamous, and the clan and lineage will be exogamous simply because they are smaller parts of the moiety. Olson says that this was "frequently" the case for the American Indians (Olson 1934:355). For nine cases in my notes, exogamy is said to extend to the largest possible unilineal kin group—to the moiety, phratry, or "linked clan group" (Hopi, Kaska, Muria, Murngin, Navaho, Siwai, Trobriands, Tchambuli, and Wogeo). In two other cases, exogamy "cuts off" before it reaches the largest kin group. Among the Todas, clans are exogamous but moieties are not (Rivers 1906:504). Among the Kipsigis, exogamy extends only to a "subdivision" of the clan (Peristiany 1939:108).

Common Religious Obligations

A unilineal kin group may have its own "religion." The kin group will have its own supernaturals, which are generally ancestors of some sort. Kin-group members will have common religious obligations; they will observe certain taboos, and cooperate in religious ceremonials. Finally, the religion will be rationalized by a body of mythology, which will often include an account of its (and the kin group's) origin. An apparent function of the kin-group religion is that its various features—common ancestral spirits, commonly observed taboos and cooperative ceremonials, mythology—tend to draw the kin group's members together, and give them a feeling of oneness (Linton 1936:198).

It is hard to generalize about the frequency of occurrence of kin-group religions. In many ethnographies they are unmentioned, but I know of only one unilineal society that clearly does not have any kin-group religion (Navaho). It is even harder to say how kin-group religion relates to the segmenting of kin groups. In a unilineal society, does each segment—say, lineage, clan, and phratry—have its own separate deities and religious observances? This sort of question is rarely answered in an ethnography. Among the Kipsigis and Siwai, larger kin groups have their religions, but their smaller kin-group segments apparently do not. For the Murngin, the reverse seems to be true. The other cases in my ethnographic notes are unreported on this point.

The kin-group religion may take various forms. For example, every Manus household has its Sir Ghost, a recently dead ancestor whose skull is kept in the house, who is communed with during seances, and who seems to keep a fairly close check on the doings of his living kinsmen (Mead 1931). The Hopi have their *kivas*, little clan-temples that house the various ritual objects of the Hopi clan-religion. Chinese clans maintain ancestor halls for the memory and worship of clan ancestors. Among the Muria of India:

> In each *bhum* (clan area) there was a spiritual capitol called the *pen-rawar* or *pen-kara*. Here lived the clan-god or Anga with the clan-priest to tend him and mediate between him and his kinsmen. Here they came for the chief festivals of the Anga; here they brought their dead and erected their *menhirs*; here they gathered for the special *panchayat* that discussed offenses against the clan laws. (Elwin 1947:59)

In other kin-group religions there are no shrines, and every man is his own priest.

Often the ancestral spirits are nonhuman; they are animals, plants, or various natural phenomena. This sort of kin-group religion is called totemism, and is very common. John Fischer, surveying a large sample of primitive societies, found that about half of them were characterized by totemism (Fischer m.s.). Richard Wyndham describes below his encounter with the totemic religion:

AFRICAN SUDAN

> As we approached Wun Rog, the giraffes, which I had thought tame farther south, did not even trouble to get out of the way of our car, for in this district they share with other animals the security of being the tribe's totem. That evening, while we were talking to an old chief outside his hut, I saw a snake slither from the door towards us. It was a beautiful creature—in colour pure Veronese

> green. The old man pointed to it. It came nearer and, in spite of its beauty, I instinctively looked for a stick. Aginejok stopped me: "For God's sake, don't kill it; he says it's his grandfather!" Later, I saw a bowl of milk put out for grandpa's supper. (Wyndham 1936:119)

Totemism rests on the belief that all members of a unilineal kin group have descended from a common nonhuman ancestor. If the ancestor is an animal, a sort of kinship bond may be maintained with its living representatives (as with the snake grandfather). The kin-group name is frequently taken from the totem ancestor. Thus, the Bears, Tree-rats, Cockatoo People, would be unilineal kin groups whose totem ancestors were, respectively, a bear, a tree-rat, and a cockatoo. Totemism is often accompanied by food taboos; this usually means that members of a unilineal kin group are not allowed to kill or eat their totem. For example, the Raccoons (members of a kin group whose totem ancestor is the raccoon) may not kill or eat raccoons. Fischer, in his cross-cultural survey, found that thirty-one of the totemic societies in his sample observed totemic food taboos; only seven did not, and eight were unreported for food taboos (Fischer m.s.). Here is a description of some of the Muria's food taboos:

MURIA, INDIA

> None of the members of the Bakravans or Goat phratry may eat goat's meat. We have seen that there is an added reason for this among the Maravi because, in the story of their origin, the Marar from whose house the tortoise emigrated offered it a goat. When a goat dies the Maravi perform funerary rites for it; they will not even touch the water from which a goat has drunk. This rule is taken very seriously. Twenty years ago in Palari one Bhaira Maravi ate goat's flesh by mistake and died of it, his throat swelling and choking him. Baghunath Maravi also ate it by accident, but he sacrificed a pig to Mati Pen and a buffalo to Bara Pen and was saved, though his brother died. In Kondagaon a man of the Partabi sept ate a goat and was very ill. He was excommunicated and only readmitted to the tribe after paying a heavy fine.
>
> The members of the Kachhimvans or Tortoise phratry avoid eating the tortoise and worship it. The Naitami clan in addition to honouring the tortoise revere the dog, which they regard as their

elder brother. Members of the Sori or Tiger phratry, however, have a buffalo totem, since members of the clan consider that they were betrayed by the tiger who ate the original member of their clan. But they still refuse to kill a tiger, and when one is killed they perform funerary rites for it.

Members of the Nagvans or Serpent phratry are supposed to be immune to the bite of the cobra, but some of the members of this phratry also honour other animals. . . .

Members of the Usendi clan . . . do not eat the *usi* bird. The Kaudo sept has to avoid the horse: its members may not ride a horse or touch it. If a horse is tied in front of a Kaudo house, it goes mad or dies. The Komra sept never cut down a *kassi* tree, nor do they eat its leaves as vegetables. They must not cook *roti* with oil. (Elwin 1947:66)

In addition to food taboos, the totemic religion may include a certain amount of religious paraphernalia—ritual objects, sacred places, ceremonials, and so forth. To illustrate this and to conclude the discussion of totemism, here is W. Lloyd Warner's description of totemism among the Murngin.

MURNGIN, AUSTRALIA

The Murngin clan . . . possesses one or more sacred totemic water holes, formed by a creator totem, in which the whole of tribal life is focused; all members of the clan are born from this water hole and all go back to it at death; in it the totem's spirits live with the mythological ancestor, the souls of the dead, and the unborn children. The male members of the clan who can be the permanent occupants of the group's land possess totemic emblems in common. . . .

A child inherits its totem from its father. When the totemic emblem is shown to the boy for the first time the father or clan leader says, "This is your father," or "your grandfather." The boy will always call it by one of these terms. Most men call their totem "father." . . . [See in this connection Freud 1950:127–132.]

If women look at a totemic emblem they are killed by their own group, with the help of any other group that has been offended by their actions. The clan to which they belong is not held responsible except in a minor way. Some years ago the Liagaomir clan was holding a totemic ceremony, using its carpet snake totemic emblems (painted wooden trumpets). Two women stole up to the ceremonial ground and watched the men blowing the trumpet, went back to the women's camp and told them what they had seen. When the men came back to camp and heard of their behavior, Yanindja, the leader, said, "When will we kill them?"

Everyone replied, "Immediately." (Warner 1937:16, 106, 160)

Corporate Property-ownership

A unilineal kin group, being a corporate group, will frequently own property. There will be certain properties that are not clearly owned by any individual; instead, the entire kin group owns them, acting like a corporation. As you might imagine, the properties may take various forms, including the following:

Shrines, temples, and sacred places (Muria, Murngin, Nayar, Hopi, China, Siwai),
Personal names, crests, songs (Haida, and other North American tribes),
Servants (Nayar),
Canoes (Tikopia),
Shell money (Siwai),
Club houses (Tchambuli),
Houses and house sites (Fiji, Ifaluk, Menangkabau, Nayar, Tikopia, Trobriands),

and, especially, economically valuable land—usually farm land (Fiji, Ifaluk, Menangkabau, Nayar, Pukapuka, Siwai, Somali, Tikopia, Trobriands, Wogeo).

Often you find a complicated system of residual rights. An individual or family may "own" some farm land; but the farm land cannot be sold, since the kin group (and perhaps other agencies) also has ownership rights. This seems to be the case for Ashanti, Ifaluk, Menangkabau, Pukapuka, Siwai, Tikopia, and Wogeo. Firth describes such a situation:

TIKOPIA, WESTERN POLYNESIA

Inquiries as to land ownership in Tikopia elicit a description in one of four different ways. An orchard is described as being the land of a certain clan, the land of the chief of the clan, the land of one of the component houses, or the land of an individual in it. Each attribute is correct and it depends on the point of view of the questioner and informant what reply is given. . . . as elsewhere the puzzle is to be solved only after consideration of the respective privileges and claims of each party to the situation. (Firth 1936: 375)

How frequent is it that the unilineal kin group does corporately own property? This seems to be fairly common, but it is hard to be sure. In my ethnographic notes, there are sixteen societies in which unilineal kin groups own property, and three societies in which they apparently do not own property (Navaho, Ojibwa, and Plateau Tonga); and, of course, the usual additional cases of no information.

Which of the kin-group segments tend to be the property owners: the smaller segments (lineages and the like), the larger segments (phratry, moiety), or both? In my ethnographic notes, there are only seven societies for which kin group segments are discussed vis-á-vis property ownership. Two of the cases are the Navaho and Plateau Tonga, listed above, in which none of the segments own property. In the other five cases, the smaller segments are said to be the land-holding groups, and the larger segments are not; for the Nayar, Trobriands and Pukapukans, it is the sublineage; for the Siwai, it is the lineage; in Fiji, it is the clan. Here is what Oliver has to say about the Siwai:

> A factor of great importance is the link between matrilineage (the smallest segment) and land. Shrines and rights of access to them are shared by members of any sib, sub-sib, and sub-sub-sib but none of these aggregates owns economically valuable land as does the matrilineage group. Every Tree-rat matrilineage corporately owns full or residual title to tracts of arable land, and most matrilineages can also claim such title to forest hunting grounds, sago swamps, and fishing streams. (Oliver 1955: 112)

Corporate Enterprise

The unilineal kin group may undertake corporate enterprise. Its members may cooperate for economic or ceremonial purposes.

Here are some examples. The Fijian clan was a tribute-paying unit. A Navaho kin group (the "local clan element") would pay damages for a member who got in trouble, or finance a "sing" (curing rite) for a sick member. The kin group may corporately give food for a large, interclan feast (Fiji, Pukapuka, Trobriands). Kin-group members may join together in work-bees (Fiji, Gusii, Trobriands). Unilineal kin groups may assemble on certain get-together occasions, such as funerals (Ashanti, Nayar, Siwai, Tikopia, Plateau Tonga), or initiations (Nayar and Tikopia). The Muria have great clan festivals; the Murngin also have their clan ceremonies. Kaska moieties (local segments of them, no doubt) gave potlatches for each other. To cite a further example, here is Oliver's description of the get-together activities of a Siwai lineage:

> In few cases do all members of any one Tree-rat matrilineage reside in the same hamlet or village—some usually move to other settlements upon marriage—yet they all assemble on occasions to celebrate a *maru* ritual for one of them, or to gossip together, or mourn. Whenever one of them, or the spouse or offspring of one of them, is seriously ill, other members are sure to be present. (Oliver 1955:111)

Usually it is not clear whether all or only some kin-group members join in this corporate enterprise. In some cases, all members clearly do not join in. In Tikopia, according to Firth, the number of kinsmen participating depends on the type of occasion:

> The general principle is that the immediacy of the occasion determines how far the branches of a house (kin group) shall assemble and whether all the constituent individual families shall be present. . . . At marriage, initiation or death the bonds of kinship become effective over a much wider range and the several branches of the parent stem [that is, the clan] unite in virtue of their common ancestor for the economic and ritual services to be performed. . . . Frequently when all the members of the house do not come to participate in the transaction of their group, each branch of a family sends representatives. (Firth 1936:354)

On the issue of segmentation, there is the usual scarcity of ethnographic data. Probably the smaller, more localized kin-group segments are dominant, vis-à-vis corporate enterprise. The smaller segments may generally be the more important cooperative units, as appears to be the case among the Plateau Tonga, Siwai, Trobrianders, Tikopians, and Pukapukans; while the larger unilineal segments convene and act jointly only for special ceremonial get-togethers (Ashanti, Nayar, Somali), or not at all (Ifaluk, Papago, Plateau Tonga).

Government

The unilineal kin group may have a government of sorts: an executive, a code of laws, and power to punish infractions of those laws. In my ethnographic notes, there are fourteen cases in which a kin-group headman or chief is mentioned: Ashanti, Fiji, Ifaluk, Kurtachi, Menangkabau, Murngin, Nayar, Pukapuka, Silwa, Somali, Tikopia, Toda, Tonga, and Wogeo. For two more cases, kin groups are said to be without an executive: Kipsigis (clans) and Tiv (all kin-group segments). And in two societies, the Navaho and Trobriands, smaller segments have executives but the larger kin-groupings do not. In some cases, chiefship in a kin group is determined by seniority: it goes to the eldest living male (Ifaluk, Kurtachi, Pukapuka, Tikopia, Tonga, Trobriands). At other times this is not the case; the chief or headman seems to be chosen on his merits (Silwa, Toda). As well as a headman, a kin group may also have a judicial and executive council (Hopi, Muria, Somali).

The kin group may act as a unit of social control, enforcing its rules and punishing infractions (China, Muria, Nayar, Pukapuka, Silwa, Somali, Tiv). Also, the kin group may be held accountable—by some larger political grouping—for the conduct of each of its members:

NAYAR, INDIA

If some member of a lineage broke a caste law, for example by dining or fornicating with a low caste person or failing to pay

> dues to the temple, his whole lineage was temporarily ostracized by the (caste) assemby until it called him to book. His property-group must then pay a fine . . . to the assembly and he must go through a rite of purification before his lineage could be readmitted to caste. (Gough 1954:41)

There is scant information on the degree of power the kin-group executive may wield. In Ifaluk and Wogeo he is said to act as a judge, settling disputes between kin-group members. In Ifaluk, Fiji and Tikopia, he "controls" the kin-group's lands and properties. Among the Wogeo, he can summon people to work for him. One gets the impression that usually the headman does not have autocratic powers; but, as I said, this issue is seldom discussed.

Obligations of Mutual Aid and Hospitality

Members of a unilineal kin group may be obligated to help one another. Among the Ashanti, Ifaluk, and Kurtachi, a traveler can stop in a strange village, find out who his distantly-related clansmen are, and receive hospitality from them. Among the Rajputs (Hindu India) and in Silwa (Egypt), lineage members have a special right to ask each other for financial assistance. The Chinese clans have various social-welfare functions, taking care of indigent members and financing higher education for poor but promising members (Yang 1945:135, 137). In other places, a general mutual-aid ethic seems to prevail within the unilineal kin group (Kipsigis, Kwoma, Lepcha, Navaho, Siwai, Trobriands, Wogeo).

How strong is this obligation of mutual aid? Sometimes, the feeling of interdependence appears to be pretty strong. Citing, once more, the Siwai matrilineages:

SIWAI, SOLOMON ISLANDS

> They usually assist one another in economic and political enterprises, and seldom compete for renown. Matrilineage mates are considered responsible for each other's welfare in this life and in the

> next, and it is they who try to compel the family survivors of a deceased member to provide an adequate funeral. . . . The intimate relations among matrilineage mates is symbolized in the belief that if a sorcerer attacks one of them, all the rest will die; in the days of feuding, vengeance wreaked upon the matrilineage mate of an enemy was often as satisfactory as death of the enemy himself. (Oliver 1955:111)

In other cases, the mere fact of common kin-group membership does not guarantee mutual aid; to be a "real" kin tie, carrying mutual obligations, common kin-group membership must be reinforced by a history of face-to-face contact and cooperation. The Plateau Tonga, for example, usually do *not* trust unknown clansmen to take care of them when they are away from home, and apparently "recognize" only those clansmen who "act like" clansmen:

PLATEAU TONGA, AFRICA

> "This David is not my own relative. He is only of my clan. . . . I can say this because he does not help me with any work in the field or anywhere else. He just lives at every village. He has no wife and he knows he has no wife. But when he comes to live with me, he does not help with the work, and that is why I say he is not my relative. He who does not help me is not my relative." (Colson 1954:87)

Among the Lepcha and Kipsigis, help may be claimed from a known clan member, but rarely if ever from a distant, unknown clan member; the hospitality ethic, cited for the Ashanti, Ifaluk, and Kurtachi, apparently does not apply in these cases. Among the Navaho, both the clan and its segment (the "local clan element") is characterized by a mutual aid ethic, but the obligation seems to be a good deal stronger within the smaller segment (Aberle 1954:15–19). And for the Gusii, the largest hospitality unit is a relatively small segment, the "*riiga* lineage"; common membership in the larger segments, clan, subclan, or sub-subclan, does not carry an obligation to hospitality (LeVine).

Feuding

The unilineal kin group, being, at times, a political unit, may also be a military unit. The kin group, acting as a body, fights other kin groups. The "military history" of a unilineal kin group seems usually to consist of blood feuds (Gusii, Navaho, Nayar, Silwa, Siwai, Somali, Tiv, Trobriands, Murngin). A member is killed by someone in another kin group. Vengeance is taken on the other kin group. The other kin group in turn retaliates. Their retaliation is reavenged. And so on. For example, among the Murngin:

> An important activity of the clan is war, the clan being the war-making group. Within this group no violent conflict ever takes place, no matter how much cause is given. Members may quarrel, but for clansmen to fight one another would be considered an unnatural act in Murngin society and it never occurs. When the clan is at war the ceremonial leader almost always acts as the war leader. A clan seldom goes to battle as a group against another one, but usually has an eternal feud with certain others which results in occasional ambushes in which a man or two is killed, . . .
>
> Of the seventy-two recorded battles in the last twenty years in which members of Murngin factions were killed, fifty were for blood revenge—the desire to avenge the killing of a relative, usually a clansman, by members of another clan. (Warner 1937:17, 159)

Once started, a feud may go on indefinitely in the absence of some mechanism for patching up differences. Such a mechanism —the payment of blood money—is mentioned for a few societies (Kipsigis, Navaho, Silwa, Somali); when the first murder is committed, the kin group of the murderer pays an indemnity to the kin group of the murdered man, thus giving them their "vengeance" and forestalling a feud.

It looks as if the largest kin grouping usually does not act collectively in feuds; rather, the feud group is more likely to be a small or intermediate-size segment. Among the Gusii, for example, the lineage was the feud group; lineages of the same clan would feud with each other, and then, at times, unite to fight members of another clan (LeVine). Among the Tiv of West Africa:

> The greater the distance, genealogically, between two lineages inhabiting adjoining *utar* the more likely they are to think of each other as potential enemies. Thus people of two minimal segments with an immediate common ancestor act towards each other as brothers and allies and deny the possibility of fighting between them, though in fact they may fight fairly often with clubs or stones. Between segments of a slightly greater depth, bows and arrows may be used, but no poison. Tiv say they shoot into the air trying only to scare their opponents. Tiv admit the possibility of fighting between such segments, but deny war and often speak of the desirability of good relations. . . . Between segments of the very large order . . . there is no hesitation in speaking in terms of enmity and warfare. . . . Individual fighting and homicide follow the same scale of values. To strike a close agnate is a moral offence for which one's agnates may justifiably bewitch one. To get into a fight with a non-Tiv is sometimes foolhardy, but certainly not immoral. (Bohannan and Bohannan 1953:25–26)

In my ethnographic notes, there is one case in which the largest unilineal group is apparently the feuding unit (Silwa, Egypt), and seven societies in which the feuding unit is a small or intermediate-size segment (Gusii, Navaho, Nayar, Somali, Murngin, Tiv, Trobriands).

Groupings of bilateral kindred may also carry on feuds, as we know from our folk tradition of those reckless mountain boys, the Hatfields and McCoys. Kindreds may also arrange to pay blood money in order to stave off feuding. The tribes of ancient Germany and Scandinavia had an elaborate blood-money code, called *wergild.* Bertha Surtees Phillpotts describes the *wergild* arrangement in Iceland:

> Each class pays to the corresponding class of the opposite side, thus the father, son and brother of the slayer pay to the corresponding kinsmen of the slain. It is to be observed that the slayer pays nothing, the assumption being that he was exiled and his goods forfeited. (Phillpotts 1913:13)

Wergild was still current in 16th-century Denmark. In 1537 King Christian III decided to ban it, because it made murder too easy:

> "It is a general plague in the kingdom that the one seeks the life of the other on trivial grounds, and the only cause is that money is taken for manslaughter, and the slayer's innocent kindred and friends, yea the very babe that lies in the cradle, must collect money and help to compensate for the dead, whereon many rely, and commit such deeds, which they would not do if they knew that a death-punishment awaited them in their turn." (Phillpotts 1913: 82)

To conclude, here is the record of a *trygde-ed* or oath of peace, sworn by two kindreds after a *wergild* payment (Denmark):

> "Then in God's name came forward the aforesaid Morthen Perssen, acting on his own behalf and for the said son of his deceased brother and for other common kinsmen on the paternal and maternal side who were not present, (and) Jens Krogermager, Frands Perssen, Christoffer Jorgenssen and Lass Kieldssen (came forward also) . . . and all together now this day here at the *Thing*, before God and the people, with mouth and hand, all holding (the) sword, gave and promised . . . peace to the aforesaid Michill Lauessen . . . and all their common kindred." (Phillpotts 1913:225)

Summary of the Attributes of the Unilineal Kin Group

This, I think, is a fairly comprehensive list of the characteristics of a unilineal kin group: a name; exogamy; a kin-group religion, often totemic, and frequently rationalized by means of origin myths; corporate property-ownership; corporate enterprise, either in daily work or in occasional ceremonial get-togethers; some sort of apparatus for government, usually pretty rudimentary, it seems; obligations of mutual help and hospitality; and military unity in inter-kin group feuds. Also, as I mentioned when discussing kin terms, classificatory kin terms may be extended to unilineal kin group members. Linton says:

Lastly, it is common for clan members to use the same terms of relationship toward each other that they use toward members of their immediate family groups. Thus a man will frequently call all clan members of his own generation brother and sister, all males in his father's generation father, if the group is patrilineal, all women in his father's generation father's sister, and so forth. This usage does not imply that the individual is in any doubt as to who is his real brother or father or aunt. It is merely a technique for emphasizing the fact that the whole clan is, in theory, one big family.

In spite of such attempts to emphasize the unity of the clan and its likeness to the consanguine family group, it can never actually replace this group as a functional unit. In the normal course of events any clan soon becomes too large for all its members to have direct personal contacts with each other. In the clan the mutual attitudes which give the close consanguine group strong solidarity and high capacity for cooperation become weakened and diffused. . . .

The patterns governing the behavior of clan members toward one another are nearly always modeled on those governing the reciprocal behavior of actual family members, but in the absence of genuine attitudes these patterns undergo a gradual attenuation. Thus the theoretical rights and duties of the clan head, if it has one, are nearly always a repetition of those of the family head. However, the clan head will never have as much real power over his clansmen as the family head has over his family. Even when he is absolute in theory, he will be limited in practice by a series of checks and balances. Similarly, the individual will not behave in the same way toward a clan brother or father that he will toward an actual brother or father. If there is a general pattern of respect and obedience toward fathers, the individual will accord these to his own father in the highest degree, will give somewhat less to a classificatory father who is closely related and well known to him and still less to a "father" who is a remote relative with whom he has had little contact. He may be in duty bound to help any man who he calls brother, but he certainly will not help all "brothers" to the same extent. (Linton 1936:198–199)[12]

---

[12] This statement by Linton is a series of interesting but undocumented —not properly documented, anyway—generalizations. On two points, which touch on my previous discussion, I should give special warning. In the first

Finally, as I said before, unilineal kin groups are frequently segmented, kin groups within kin groups; and one becomes a member of a unilineal kin group either by tracing descent through his father (patrilineal kin group) or by tracing descent through his mother (matrilineal kin group).

How common are these various attributes of unilineal kin groups? We don't know. Unilineal descent—tracing kin-group membership through either the father or mother, but not through both parents—would have to be a universal attribute. If you did not have unilineal descent, you would not have a unilineal kin group; this is the bedrock, defining attribute. Each of the other attributes, we know, are *not* universal. Unilineal kin groups can be found which are unnamed, or not exogamous, or not property-owning groups, and so forth. Murdock thinks that exogamy is almost universal to unilineal kin groups (Murdock 1949:48). A name, too, may be very common, but we have less information on that. Perhaps exogamy and names are the most common characteristics of unilineal kin groups (along with unilineal descent), and the other attributes are less common. But since ethnographies are generally rather incomplete (particularly, in citing some customs as present but in neglecting to say what other customs are *absent*), we can't say.

If we had better data, we could say more about this. We might even be able to make a cumulative scale—similar to the menstrual taboo, avoidance and deference scales, discussed in Chapter 9—to measure the "strength" of a unilineal kin group. For example, it may be that nearly all kin groups, weak as well as strong, have certain attributes, such as a name, and a rule of exogamy. Kin groups of intermediate strength may have additional, slightly

---

place, he says it is "common" for classificatory kin terms to be extended to unilineal kin group (or "clan") members. Perhaps it is common, but we do not know; a study has never been done. Second, Linton says that classificatory kin terms, when extended to distant relatives, carry similar but "diminished" patterned kin behavior. For example, a classificatory "father" is treated somewhat like the real father, but less so: with less respect, less in the way of mutual obligations, and so forth. This may also be generally true, and it would be interesting to find out if it is; at present, we simply do not know.

less common, attributes, such as a kin-group religion, perhaps, or unity during feuds. And the very strong unilineal kin groups may have all these attributes, plus others—maybe corporate landownership, or corporate enterprise in daily work. However, with the present incompleteness of the data, we cannot say exactly how such a scale would look, or even whether such a cumulative scale of kin-group strength is possible.

In a summary of unilineal kin-group attributes, perhaps I should say something about the relationships *between* kin groups. In the first place, they may feud with each other, as we have seen. Also, they may express their mutual antagonism in more ritualized ways, such as in lacrosse games, fishing contests, or competitive feast-giving. At times, kin groups are ranked, with some groups being more "noble" and "aristocratic" than others; but it is my impression that frequently unilineal kin groups are not ranked in relation to each other. Finally, since unilineal kin groups are usually exogamous, they must exchange wives with each other. I will have more to say about this later.

A Final Word on Segments

In a society with segmented unilineal kin groups, it must usually be true that the members of the smaller segments are "closer" to each other. The smaller segments stand a better chance of being localized: their members, or a good many of them at least, live near each other. Living close together, they must have more face-to-face interaction, know each other better, and establish stronger ties with each other. What fragments of ethnographic data I could collect do indicate that the smaller segments are more likely to be the property-owning groups, the groups for continuous corporate enterprise, and the feuding units.

Murdock divides kin groups into three categories: corporate kin groups, occasional kin groups, and circumscriptive kin groups. A corporate kin group, by Murdock's definition, is one that owns property. An occasional kin group is one that does not own property, and only convenes on special get-together occasions, such as special clan festivals. A circumscriptive kin group is one that owns no property and whose members never gather or act as a unit—for example, a large, dispersed moiety, which is only a group in the sense that its members bear a moiety name ("Red Ants"), and may not marry one another (observe the "circumscription" of exogamy) (Murdock 1960:4–5).

It looks as if the larger, more dispersed kin groups are more likely to be "occasional" (getting together only for special occasions) or "circumscriptive" (never gathering together), whereas the smaller, more localized kin-group segments are more apt to be corporate groups, characterized by corporate ownership of property and continuous corporate enterprise. But evidence on this point is inadequate.

As a final benediction on the subject of unilineal segments, let us return once more to Douglas Oliver and his Siwai:

> Exemplifying the first explanation is the fact that Hornbills should not intermarry with Tree-rats, Eye-rollers, or Cranes. . . .
>
> It will be recalled that the Cockatoo segment of the Eye-rollers (Kingfisher sib) are said to have acquired the Cockatoo as their secondary totem through a Cockatoo's aid to a *kupuna* ancestress. . . .
>
> The entire *Mi'kahnanai* matrilineage (a subdivision of the Rukaruinai sub-sub-sib, Belly-fats sub-sib) is *nokihoro* with a Matuku matrilineage centered in Hinna and with a Kingfisher matrilineage centered in Ku'hinna. (Oliver 1955:117–120)

The Origin of Unilineal Kin Groups

How did unilineal descent—and, hence, unilineal kin groups—ever get started? Since origins of this sort are lost in unrecorded history, we can do little more than speculate about this. A number of anthropologists believe that the first step is unilocal residence. First you get unilocal residence, either patrilocal, in which wives move to their husbands' home territory, or matrilocal, where husbands move to join their wives in their wives' home territory. As a result of unilocal residence you eventually get unilineal descent. The fact that patrilineal societies are usually patrilocal, and matrilineal societies are often matrilocal, adds a bit of support to this view[13] (Aberle 1961:661; Titiev 1943; Lowie 1940:264; Murdock 1949:75).

How, then, does a unilocal rule of residence come about, and why does this lead to unilineal kin groups? There may be a number of ways, but one possible way was suggested by Julian Steward, when he pointed out that if a community or band is small enough, it is—because of incest taboos between close blood relatives—necessarily exogamous (Steward 1955:136).

Take a tiny, nomadic band of hunters. Such a band will frequently be quite small, due to the sparse food supply. Often, it will be a "family band"—father and son, or two brothers, each with their wives and children. In such a case, there are no new wives to be had within the band, because of incest taboos.[14] When children grow up, they must find spouses in other similar hunting bands. So this band is exogamous: it must exchange wives with other bands.

The question now is, who is going to join whom? Will the men leave home to join their wives in other bands (matrilocal residence)? Or will wives be brought in from other bands, while the men stick together in their natal band (patrilocal residence)? Or, will they do it both ways: some men going away in search of wives, while other men stay at home and let their wives come to them (bilocal residence)? In fact, in such hunting societies any of these arrangements may occur; in the *World Ethnographic Sample*, slightly less than half of the hunting and gathering societies are bilocal; the rest are either patrilocal or matrilocal.

So, about half the time there is no strong predisposition toward

---

[13] This is usually, but not always, the case. Murdock, in *Social Structure*, reports fifty-two societies that do have unilocal rules of residence (patrilocal or matrilocal), but do *not* have unilineal descent—either matrilineal or patrilineal (Murdock 1949:59).

A society may also be unilineal, and not have the corresponding rule of residence. In the *World Ethnographic Sample*, 208 of 238 patrilineal societies are also patrilocal; 38 of 77 matrilineal societies are matrilocal (Murdock 1957).

[14] This is excluding the levirate and sororate, which will be discussed in the next chapter.

either patrilocality or matrilocality. But often there is such a predisposition, and then you get a unilocal residence. How, then, would unilocal residence lead to unilineal descent?

Let us take, as a hypothetical example, a family band that is patrilocal. The men in the group are "permanent": they were born there and, under ordinary circumstances, they will live in the same band until they die. They are not only close kinsmen: they are lifelong companions. They form the permanent "core" of the group. The women, on the other hand, are all "temporary." Female children will leave the band when they marry, never to return—except, perhaps, for visits. Wives are, to a certain extent, "outsiders": they were brought in from other bands.

The band is very much a corporate group; its members live together under rather intimate conditions, share their food, cooperate in the food quest, and so forth. And yet the core of men is permanent, the women are transients.

Such a situation might be fertile ground for the idea of patrilineal descent—the notion of a special group, composed of the permanent men and their children, but excluding their "transient" wives. When female children grew up and married outside the band, they would never be considered full members of their new bands; they would be, to a degree, "outsiders." In a sense they would still belong to their old, parental band (or kin group).

In the same way, a matrilocal rule of residence might lead to matrilineal descent. In this case, the women would be the permanent core of the group, the "insiders"; the men, who married into the band, would be the "transients," the nonkinsmen.

So you have a very small, partly localized unilineal kin group composed of the "permanent" members of the band, plus its out-marrying members—in the patrilocal/patrilineal case, its mature women who move away to become wives in other bands; in the matrilineal/matrilocal case, the men who marry into other bands. This little group already has some of the unilineal kin-group attributes I have discussed: it recognizes a unilineal rule of descent, it is exogamous, and (with the exception of its out-marrying members), it forms a unit for corporate enterprise. Then other kin-group attributes might accrue: a name perhaps, or a kin-group religion (totemism or an ancestor cult), or unity in feuds.

The next step is growth and segmentation. If the hunting band happened to be a particularly "successful" one, so that for several generations it had more births than deaths, it would soon be too big for its territory; it would have to split up. This would be the first step in segmentation. You would now have a larger kin group (a "clan" or "sib"), with a common name, exogamy, and so forth, made up of two "lineages"—two widely separate unilineal bands, together with their out-marrying members. Then, of course, the growth and segmentation could continue more or less indefinitely. If conditions were right, this unilineal organization would persist through time, so that when this tribe eventually "evolved" culturally and abandoned hunting for farming, the old system of unilineal kin groups would continue.

This is just speculation, of course. If it does, sometimes, happen this way, it may happen other ways, too. For example, it may be that some of the larger kin groups, such as moieties or phratries, do not result from the "fission process" I just described. Instead, they may be simple unions of previously separate kin groups. Also, the origin of unilineal kin groups may not always be at the simple band level; sometimes, no doubt, they originate among people who are already farmers or herders. Finally, rules of descent may change. Not only may bilateral descent become patrilineal or matrilineal; patrilineal (or matrilineal) descent may later change back to bilateral descent. A matrilineal society, over time, may even change to a patrilineal society. (But, according to Murdock, the reverse never happens.) (Murdock 1949:59)

If a unilocal rule of residence does lead to the corresponding unilineal rule of descent, what causes the unilocal rule of residence? Again, we can only guess about this. Murdock's guesses are as follows: either important subsistence work performed by women, or generally high status for women, or a low level of political integration, predispose toward matrilocal residence; unimportance of women in the subsistence economy, polygyny, property ownership in the hands of men, or frequent warfare—all of these predispose toward patrilocal residence (Murdock 1949:204–206). My favorite guesses are a bit different, and apply only to unilocal residence among hunting bands (as discussed above). They are male dominance, poor hunting, and bride service.

The poor hunting argument was first advanced by A. R. Radcliffe-Brown to explain patrilocality among some Australian tribes. These people wander about in semidesert country, hunting and gathering plant food. Securing the next meal or finding water in time is often touch-and-go. In such a situation, survival depends on detailed knowledge of the countryside: the movements and habits of game, the times of fruition of various plants, how to locate submerged water and recognize water-carrying plants, and so forth. Radcliffe-Brown says that this knowledge is precious and takes years to come by; that it is, to some extent, nontransferable to strange territories; and that the men are the main possessors of this knowledge. This he offers as the reason for patrilocality among the Australians: it would be too great an extravagance to move a man out of his home territory, after he had spent years learning it (Radcliffe-Brown 1930).

So in some hunting bands, if the subsistence situation were precarious, knowledge of the land valuable, and men were the main carriers of this knowledge, these circumstances might predispose toward patrilocal residence.

Bride service, on the other hand, would predispose toward matrilocal residence. In most societies, as we shall see in the next chapter, wives are not to be had "for free." They must be paid for. In a society with capital goods, they will be paid for in whatever the local currency happens to be—baskets of yams, or dogs' teeth, or cows, or sea-shells, or gongs. But most bands of hunting nomads cannot accumulate capital goods, so these people frequently barter their own labor and hunting skill in return for wives. When a man in such a tribe picks out a wife (or has her picked out for him) he moves in with her family, hunts and works for them, and spends a sort of probationary period, which may last anywhere from a few months to several years. In this way he "pays" for his wife, and a father gets some "value" out of his daughters (their suitors' labors) before they marry and, perhaps, leave him.

Jules Henry, discussing polyandry among the Kaingang, described how old men would use their women to lure new, young hunters into the band—as a sort of social security measure:

KAINGANG, BRAZIL

> Whoever lived alone with his wife or wives . . . was really without any man on whom he could absolutely depend to keep him from starvation at all times. . . .
>
> The story is told of Kuven who was the lover of both Kangga and her mother. Now as Kangga's father grew old and it became difficult for him to get meat, he felt more and more the necessity of having someone to help him hunt for his large family. As long as Kuven remained he could depend on him, but when it seemed that the young man was becoming interested in Yemai, a woman who was no relative of his and whom, therefore, Kuven might follow far away to her relatives, Kangga's father said to his wife and daughter: "Call Kuven: if he marries Yemai he will leave me and go away. Let him get food for your children when I die. If he marries another woman he will throw your children away." So Kangga's mother called Kuven and said to her daughter: "Marry him. I am going to live with you and him." So Kuven married both mother and daughter, and when Kangga's father died Kuven took care of the latter's children. (Henry 1941:46, 36)

In this case, the old man employed "bride-service psychology." Using his women as a lure, he brought in a new hunter. Wishing to make the "bride service" permanent, he not only gave Kuven his daughter, but also gave him his own wife, thereby tying him to his own band. If the Kaingang had had a rule of matrilocal residence, this would have been unnecessary, because matrilocal residence is, in a way, a sort of permanent bride service.

So, in some hunting bands, matrilocal residence perhaps developed as a special variant of bride service. Its women lured new hunters into the band; and father set the condition that daughter was not to leave home. By its daughters' sex appeal, a band was able to attract and keep new hunters.

To summarize: patrilocal residence may, at times, be encouraged by the premium on men's knowledge of their local territory; and matrilocal residence may, at times, develop as a sort of permanent bride-service arrangement.

Finally, as we shall see in Chapters 6 and 7, in nearly all societies men appear to be a bit more powerful, dominant, and privileged than women are. It often seems that men, to some extent, make the "rules" of the culture to suit their own convenience. This male dominance might be an added reason for patrilocal residence; men would rather not marry into their wives' strange bands. Thus, since they tend to make the rules, they usually have their wives brought to them. Matrilocal residence is much less prevalent than patrilocal residence; this might be partly due to male dominance, which appears to be very common.

Rules of Residence

Before going on, I want to say a bit more about rules of residence. When a young couple marries, they must live somewhere, and there are a limited number of possibilities. They may live near the boy's parents (patrilocal residence), they may live near the girl's parents (matrilocal residence), or they may move away from both sets of parents (neolocal residence). Similarly, a society may have a "rule" of residence—a general custom, pattern, or trend—dictating where people will live. A society may be generally patrilocal, matrilocal, or neolocal. Or, the society may have no such "rule" of residence, in which case it will usually be called "bilocal." Our society, if it has a pattern or trend vis-à-vis marital residence, would probably be designated neolocal; frequently, among ourselves, a young couple makes a new home, fairly distant from all parents and in-laws (Glick 1941:515).

As you might expect, we are rather unusual in this regard. In the *World Ethnographic Sample*, only twenty-seven societies are designated "neolocal," and only thirty-one societies are designated "bilocal." Most societies do have a "rule"[15] of residence, and the

[15] A "rule of residence" is really a statistical trend; it is rarely, if ever, a hard-and-fast rule that admits no exceptions. I know of no society in which a rule of residence is said to apply to 100 percent of the population. On the other hand, in my notes are 13 societies that do have a "rule" of residence which is, in fact, a mere trend (Fiji, Hehe, Iban, Kurtachi, Navaho, Papago, Pukapuka, Siwai, Plateau Tonga, Barranquitas, San Pedro la Laguna, Tarong, Tepoztlan). For example, the "patrilocal" Siwai are really about 65 percent patrilocal; some Siwai marriages are matrilocal or neolocal.

"rule" is rarely neolocal. In the *World Ethnographic Sample*, 314 societies are patrilocal, 84 societies are matrilocal, 18 societies are avunculocal (the young couple lives with the man's male matrilineal kin—his "mother's brothers"), and 86 societies have various rules of temporary post-marital residence.[16]

In most parts of the world, when a young couple marries, one spouse is "marrying-in" (staying with his or her parents), and the other spouse is "marrying-out" (leaving his or her parents to join the spouse's parents). In a moment I want to say something about out-marrying. First, a few words about the in-marrying spouse—the spouse that stays with his (or her) parents.

In the first place, there are different "degrees" or "intensities" of in-marrying. "Patrilocality," for example, may simply mean that the young couple resides in the same neighborhood, district, or village as the man's parents. Or, it may mean that they move next door to the man's parents. In many societies, particularly in Africa, we find a patrilocal extended-family *compound*: a cluster of huts in which live the old man, his wife or wives, and the old man's sons, with their wives. Finally, you may have a *patrilocal extended-family household*: the young couple simply moves in with the man's parents, living in the same house with them. In the *World Ethnographic Sample*, 151 societies are characterized by extended-family households, either matrilocal or patrilocal.[17]

When in-marrying is fairly "close"—that is, when a married man continues to live in his father's house or compound (or a married woman in her mother's house or compound, in the matrilocal case)—the new family tends to merge with the old, parental family. In this case, marriage does not create a new, independent,

---

[16] Here are some examples. Uxoripatrilocal: the young couple lives with the girl's parents for a few years; then they move to join the boy's parents. Virivunculocal: first they live with the boy's parents; then they join the boy's mother's brother.

[17] A society's "household type," like a society's "rule of residence," must nearly always be a matter of statistical trend. Thus, a society "characterized by extended-family households" will show, as infrequent, variant patterns, other household types as well. And societies, like our own, in which the extended-family household is not the dominant, most common form will still have a certain number of extended-family households.

economic and residential unit. In a patrilocal extended-family household or compound, the young couple lives with the man's parents, the man continues to work for his father, and the old man usually continues to boss the family enterprise (China, Dahomey, Ireland, Gusii, Iban, Lepcha, Mende, Papago, Samoa, Serbia, Silwa, Suye Mura, Tepoztlan, Ukrainians; exception–Tarong). In such a case, the new nuclear family is seldom a separate property-owning unit; fields, livestock, house, and so forth, belong to the extended family (or to the old man) (Gusii, Iban, Lepcha, Silwa. Aymara, China, Ireland, Mende, Samoa, Suye Mura, Tepoztlan, Ukraine; exceptions–Tallensi, Tarong). For example, Koenig says that in the Ukrainian extended family, "clothing alone is privately owned; everything else is considered common property" (Koenig 1937:317). In China (village of Taitou), Yang says:

> Except for personal belongings, everything in a farm family is owned in common, or by the family as a whole. A member who earns more for the family is honored by the others and he may even enjoy some prestige which does not accrue to them, but he cannot claim ownership of the family's property any more than they can. . . .
>
> At the time of the New Year Festival, or when there is a fair in the market town or an opera in a neighboring village, the father or the family head will give to everyone a small sum which becomes his individual property. (Yang 1945:78, 79)

Here is what Margaret Mead has to say about the (bilocal) extended family household in Samoa:

> All important property is the property of the descent group. The implements and utensils of daily use . . . pigs and chickens and small pieces of *tapa*. . . . Personal property is practically non-existent. (Mead 1930:73)
>
> In most marriages there is no sense of setting up a new and separate establishment. The change is felt in the change of residence for either husband or wife and in the reciprocal relations which spring up between the two families. But the young couple live in the main household, simply receiving a bamboo pillow, a mosquito net and a pile of mats for their bed. Only for the chief or

> the chief's son is a new house built. The wife works with all the women of the household and waits upon all the men. The husband shares the enterprises of the other men and boys. Neither in personal service given nor received are the two marked off as a unit. . . . For even in the care of the young children and in the decisions as to their future, the uncles and aunts and grandparents participate as fully as the parents. It is only when a man is *matai* (household-head) as well as father, that he has control over his own children; and when this is so, the relationship is blurred in opposite fashion, for he has the same control over many other young people who are less closely related to him. (Mead 1928)

So, in-marriage into an extended-family household or compound means that the new family merges into the old, parental family, as a mere subsidiary part of it. The new husband, in the patrilocal case, is hardly the "man of the house"; his father usually runs things. And, usually, the new family cannot accumulate its own property and become independent; corporate enterprise and property ownership are on the extended family level. So, the young people bide their time. Eventually, when the old man dies or retires, *they* will own the homestead, they will run things. When their son grows up and marries, he will create a new subsidiary family, to live with them, work for the greater glory of *their* extended-family homestead, and wait for them to die.

An extended-family unit like this is continuous in a way that a neolocal, nuclear family is not. A single extended-family homestead may be occupied for an indefinite series of generations, all by the same "family line." An extended-family household has the same sort of permanence as a town, or a unilineal kin group.

To summarize, there are varying degrees of in-marrying: in the same neighborhood, next door to, or in the same house as the parents. When in-marrying is "close," one's new family becomes merged with one's old (natal) family, and an extended-family unit results.

Out-marrying, on the other hand, may be either "near" (to a different neighborhood of the same village) or "far" (to a distant village). In the *World Ethnographic Sample,* 158 societies have "exogamous communities"; in these societies the out-marrying spouse must leave town (or leave the band or hamlet). In such a society, everyone in the community is ordinarily either a kinsman (covered by exogamous rules) or the spouse of a kinsman; hence, wives or husbands must be found in other communities. The out-marrying spouse must therefore often leave her home town, and, not infrequently, she must go really far away from her parental family and friends. I say "she" because this is not uncommon with patrilocal residence, but rare with matrilocal residence. When the out-marrying spouse is a man, he will rarely move far from home—another example, perhaps, of the age-old social inequality between the sexes (Whiting and D'Andrade).

Often, it seems, out-marrying involves a certain amount of hardship. At this point I am going to give some illustrations of the trials of the out-marrying spouse.

COPPER ESKIMO

> If the bride is to be taken to another settlement the bridegroom makes a small payment to her parents; they then give a farewell feast in her honour, and she is led away, weeping because she is leaving her familiar surroundings and going out into a new and unknown world. (Jenness 1922:159)

KURTACHI, SOLOMON ISLANDS

> The time when the girl is handed over to her husband is, in every case, judging both from what I have seen and what the girls themselves have told me, a period of strain. It not infrequently happens that the young wife, whether from actual fear or merely from shyness, runs away before the marriage can be consummated, and takes refuge with her mother. Her mother is supposed to bring her back, together with an offering of ceremonial pudding, but sometimes much persuasion, or even force, is necessary before she can be induced to return. (Blackwood 1935:102)

GUSII, KENYA

> A month after the transfer of cattle, the bride must be taken from her father's homestead to the home of the groom. Among the adjacent Luo and other East African tribes, it is customary for kinsmen of the bride to fight with kinsmen of the groom and attempt to prevent her departure. With the Gusii, however, it is the bride herself who resists, or who hides herself underneath the roof of a

nearby house . . . and her father, having received the bridewealth cattle by this time, may even help persuade her to go if her reluctance appears to be sincere. Five young clansmen of the groom come to take the bride and two immediately post themselves at her side to prevent her escape, while the others receive the final permission of her parents. When it has been granted the bride holds onto the house posts and must be dragged outside by the young men. Finally she goes along with them, crying and with her hands on her head. This traditional resistance is usually token and not really intended to break off the marriage. (LeVine)

RAJPUT CASTE GROUP, KHALAPUR, INDIA

During the ceremony which marks the sending of a letter to the groom's house to set the date of the wedding, the girl, hidden in some dark corner of the house, weeps, by herself. This weeping is not a ritual mourning but a genuine expression of grief.

When a new bride enters her husband's house, she is put "on display" every afternoon for several days. All the women of the family's lineage are invited to see her and her dowry. The bride, her sari pulled over her head and face, sits huddled on the courtyard floor. One by one the visiting women lift her veil and peer at her face, while the bride, with lowered eyelids, struggles to turn away. Having seen the bride and perhaps commented on her looks, the visitor turns to an inspection of the dowry. The mother-in-law displays the various items and tells her visitors how many utensils and pieces of clothing the bride has brought to the house. Each woman is comparing the dowry to those of other families, and the older women may verbalize these comparisons and make slighting remarks about the quantity and quality of the goods, or they may praise the dowry to the detriment of some other family who has recently acquired a bride. By the middle of the afternoon the courtyard is full of women, busily talking to each other and catching up on the latest news. No one speaks to the bride, and it would be shameless for her to join the conversation. She must not even be caught looking at any of the visitors. Although she may peek through her sari while it is over her face, she does not lift it and she must keep her eyes lowered when anyone lifts her veil to look at her. The children, both those of the family and those who have come with their mothers, view the proceedings and occasionally a little girl with a troubled expression on her young face, stands thoughtfully viewing the silent figure huddled in the midst of the chattering women. (Triandis and Hitchcock)

HINDU INDIA

We met each other for the first time on the night of our marriage. . . .

The bride stayed in our family on this occasion for about a week or so, as is the general custom. As a *bow* (bride) she had to be very cautious about her movements, her conversation with others, and even about her own comforts and conveniences. She was required to wear a veil almost all day. In every respect she was supposed to act according to the instructions of the elder women of the family. And she had not even the freedom to talk to her own people when they visited her, without the sanction of the authorities. She was escorted everywhere—even from one room to another. In a word, a *bow* had to undergo a "jail" life during this period.

I had practically no opportunity of meeting her during the day because, according to agelong custom, that would have been regarded as shameful behavior both on her part and on mine. I had to wait until about midnight, when she would stealthily come to my room, avoiding the eyes of all then awake. Similarly she had to leave the room very early in the morning, before anybody else was awake.

. . . a *bow* is always and everywhere a *bow* and she has to behave accordingly, complying with the restrictions of each family. She cannot be so free as she is while staying with her husband outside the family. The restrictions were not very rigid in our family—probably due to the absence of my mother. My wife was clever enough to please the members of my family by not committing such actions as were not liked by them. For example, she would not wear shoes in the presence of the elders, though she did not stir without them while staying with me. (away from Husband's relatives) She used to bathe early in the morning and then enter the storeroom in the kitchen. She would not take any food before the elders had partaken of it. (Mitra 1949:102, 104)

. . . there is a tendency to institutionalize mother-in-law strictness, so that mothers-in-law are expected to be harsh in order the better to inculcate the respect and awe which a good daughter-in-law is supposed to display toward them. Such strictness may be rather

> willingly enforced by the mother-in-law, for her reception of the newcomer is often not untinged with hostility. A Kannada (Kanarese) folksong puts it as follows:
>
> "Joy at the prospect of her coming
> But when from you your son she's stealing
> Gape your dismayed mouth at the heavens."
>
> Nor does the new wife generally have an easy time of it with the other women of the household. Her sisters-in-law tend to regard her as a competitor and are apt to carry tales about her shortcomings to the mother-in-law. (Mandelbaum 1949:101–102)

So, as I said, patrilocal residence may involve hardship for the girl who marries out of her own village. She may leave her family and friends and go among strangers—who seem a bit hostile at times. Because of her out-marrying status, she may observe various taboos such as the public prudery between husband and wife in the Indian example. And, she may face interpersonal complications attendant on life in an extended-family unit—such as the jealousy of her husband's mother. Matrilocal residence, on the other hand, seems never to be as hard on the out-marrying man; for one thing, he rarely moves very far away from his own kin.

From the viewpoint of either spouse, extended-family living must have its strains. If the out-marrying spouse faces hardships, the in-marrying spouse is, to some extent, "held back," still treated somewhat like a child, and denied the full privileges of adulthood. Then, of course, there is the morbid business of waiting for father to die, so that the husband can finally become "man of the house."

A possible virtue of the extended family is that it offers more security than the isolated nuclear family. In most societies, the nuclear family is to some degree merged with larger kinship units—unilineal kin groups, or more or less concentrated sorts of residential kin groups (with the extended-family household being the most concentrated type of large residential kin group). As we have seen, a unilineal kin group can take on various functions that are normally considered, in our society, the job of the nuclear family: it may own the property, be the unit for mutual aid and corporate enterprise, be an authority unit with a clan "father," and so forth. The extended-family unit may do the same sort of thing. In such a situation the "family" is enlarged, so to speak. There are many people to mind the children, take in the crops, nurse the ill, and offer emotional support (as well as interpersonal conflict) to each other. For one thing, this means a measure of "social security": if husband dies or runs away, there will still be a provider, the children will not starve; if wife is ill, the housekeeping will still be done, the meals cooked, and the children looked after. This social-security aspect alone is probably of great importance, since in most "backward" societies, and in tropical lands, the death rate is very high; one simply cannot count on a loved one (wife, or husband, or father) living very long. In addition to social security, the larger kinship unit probably offers emotional security as well. People do not have "all their eggs in one basket." There is not the necessity of focusing emotional dependence on a single person, who may be taken away by death or desertion. Also, the extended family, being larger, is not as "tight" an interaction unit as the isolated nuclear family; nurturance, dependence, aggression, and love are "diffused" to a greater degree. Finally, the kinfolk may offer a "way out" of interpersonal difficulties within the nuclear family:

> It is possible to classify the different households open to her (a Samoan girl) as those with hardest work, least chaperonage, least scolding, largest or least number of contemporaries, fewest babies, best food, and so forth. Few children live continuously in one household, but are always testing out other possible residences. And this can be done under the guise of visits and with no suggestion of truancy. But the minute that the mildest annoyance grows up at home, the possibility of flight moderates the discipline and alleviates the child's sense of dependency. No Samoan child, except the *taupo*, or the thoroughly delinquent, ever has to deal with a feeling of being trapped. There are always relatives to whom one can flee. This is the invariable answer which a Samoan gives when some familial impasse is laid before him. "But she will go to some *other* relative." And theoretically the supply of relatives is inexhaustible. Unless the vagrant has committed some very serious offense like incest, it is only necessary formally to depart from the bosom of one's household. A girl whose father has beaten her overseverely in the morn-

ing will be found living in haughty sanctuary, two hundred feet away, in a different household. (Mead 1928) (Samoa)

Most societies do have these larger kin groupings—unilineal kin groups, and/or extended-family households, compounds, or neighborhood clusters—which, to some extent, "take on the functions of" and supplement the nuclear family. In this respect our own society is fundamentally different from most others. Our nuclear family is truly isolated: there are no unilineal kin groups, extended-family households are uncommon (Glick 1941), and marriage is normally neolocal—the young couple moves away and becomes "independent" of parents and in-laws.

As Talcott Parsons says:

> For young people not to break away from their parental families at the proper time is a failure to live up to expectations, an unwarranted expression of dependency. But just as they have a duty to break away, they also have a right to independence. Hence for an older couple—or a widow or widower—to join the household of a married child is not, in terms of the kinship structure, a "natural" arrangement. This is proved by the fact that it is seldom done at all except under pressure, either for economic support or to mitigate extreme loneliness and social isolation. (Parsons 1943:37)

Or, as a "working girl" says:

> "You got to love your fella enough to leave your family for him, although you had to love them enough to stay with them until he came along. Then you got to love your babies enough to leave everyone (including your husband if necessary) to raise 'em. But don't go and expect much in return, for they are just getting ready to go off and leave you with somebody *they* meet at a picnic or dance. (Redfield 1946:177)

Kinship and Social Structure

In the early part of this chapter I described patterned kin behavior—deference, avoidance, joking, and patterned rights and obligations between kin—and commented that patterned kin behavior tends to give regularity, predictability, and "structure" to social relationships. I said that in a society where kinship is important, and where kin relations tend to be highly patterned, an ethnographer can account for a significant portion of the regularities of social life merely by describing the patterned kin behavior within the various kin relationships.

Kin groups also provide structure, in a somewhat different way. Whereas patterned kin behavior gives regularity and predictability, kin groups provide *integration*; they group people together, create social ties. Thus, unilineal kin groups form social units that often corporately own property, have their own governments, and so forth. Residential kin groups, especially the extended family (whether it is an extended-family household, compound, or neighborhood cluster), have similar integrative functions. They also may have a government of sorts; as the unilineal kin group may have its headman, the extended family has its patriarch. The extended family is frequently a property-owning unit, a unit of corporate enterprise, and so on. So, while patterned kin behavior gives structure to society by making social relationships regular, predictable, and to some extent uniform, kin groups give further structure by providing numerous ties between people—grouping people together, making them interdependent.

Actually, of course, it is not as simple as this. Kin groups also have their regularizing functions. And patterned kin behavior has integrative functions. Patterned comportment (deference, avoidance, and joking), it is true, seems largely concerned with making social behavior "regular," even stereotyped. But patterned rights and obligations, like the mutual aid obligation in Samoa, must tend to tie people to each other.

The various attributes of unilineal kin groups, such as exogamy, totemism with food taboos, loyalty in feuds, and corporate property-ownership, stem from cultural rules. A person who belongs to a unilineal kin group is bound by its rules; a member of the Raccoon clan may not fornicate with clan members, may not eat raccoons, must give hospitality to visiting clan members, must obey his headman, may make his gardens on the clan lands, can count on help from his fellow Raccoons at harvest time, will contribute to a clan feast four times a year, and so forth. In other words, the clan rules dictate patterned kin behavior. They regularize and standardize, to some extent, the behavior of clan members. Kin groups have more than an integrative function; they have a standardizing function, too.

As I further said, our society is unusual; kinship, among ourselves, is relatively unimportant. We have a minimum of patterned kin behavior. We do not have unilineal kin groups. We even have little in the way of extended-family groupings. The rules that dictate much of our social behavior—how we interact with the boss, the teacher, the policeman, the grocery clerk, the next-door neighbor—do not derive from kinship. Our society has other integrative agencies that are much more important than kinship; we have government, business, large corporations, voluntary associations, and so forth.

Our society is extreme in this respect. In many other societies, there *is* no "government" or "business," and kinship does a great deal more to structure and organize social life. As Freeman says:

> Imagine a society without specialists in various occupations, without schools or teachers, without churches or clergymen, without jails or police, without courts or judges. This is a society in which there are no governmental bureaucrats, no physicians or nurses, no farmers or merchants, one in which the only division of labor is made along age and sex lines. In such a society everyone would be pretty much like everyone else. Within age and sex groups all would do the same things and have the same rights and the same duties. But how would such a society be organized? Without teachers, who would educate the children? Without clergymen, who would guide the religious life of the community? Without police, who would apprehend criminals, and without judges, who would determine their guilt or innocence? Who would run the society, cure the ill, grow the food, sell the basic necessities? (Freeman 1958:26)

Freeman's answer is "the family." My answer would be: kin groups—including the nuclear and extended family, plus unilineal kin groups. In other words, various functions that are performed by economic specialization and government in our society are performed by groupings of kin in tribal, stateless societies.

The same idea is voiced by an old Pomo Indian:

> "In the white ways of doing things the family is not so important. The police and soldiers take care of protecting you, the courts give you justice, the post office carries messages for you, the school teaches you. Everything is taken care of, even your children, if you die; but with us the family (that is, kin) must do all of that." (Aginsky 1940)

Here are some of the functions of kinship in Tikopia:

> In Tikopia the following are some of the spheres into which kinship enters as an articulating principle. It is the basis of association in the small residential units, the households; it is the acknowledged bond between the members of the major named groups of the society; it provides the link with elders and in part with chiefs, who exercise political and religious functions for these groups and for the society as a whole; it is the overt principle regulating the ownership and suzerainty of land. Kinship provides the terms of address and reference, thus giving a linguistic bridge between individuals; it is the common basis of assistance in cooking and primary economic cooperation; it stands behind a great series of duties, privileges, taboos, and avoidances; it prescribes certain types of sex union and marriage; it is the basis for the assemblage of members of the society of the birth, initiation, sickness or death of anyone. Enshrined in tradition, it bulks largely in accounts of the origins of present-day social groups and the distribution of territory among them; projected into the realm of the spirit-heavens it gives the basis for approach to ancestors and gods. (Firth 1936: 577)

So, in some societies (like Tikopia), kinship is highly developed, and in other societies (such as the United States), it is not. Some societies have a lot of "kinship-structuring"—avoidance relationships, joking relationships, deference customs, unilineal kin groups; other societies have relatively little kinship-structuring.

For some reason, at least some aspects of kinship-structuring tend to occur together in the same societies. Earlier, I mentioned the positive correlation between avoidance relationships and joking relationships. Avoidance and joking appear to "go together," in a "package." From what evidence I have, a society with rather extreme avoidance relationships will also frequently have joking relationships too. Unilineal kin groups, likewise, appear to be part of this package; they are strongly correlated with the presence of avoidance relationships, and also seem to go with joking relationships. (The data on joking is not good.) The societies of the world tend to gravitate toward two poles: 1) kinship-structured societies, characterized by avoidance, joking, and unilineal kin groups; and 2) nonkinship-structured societies, which have neither joking nor kin avoidance, and do not have unilineal kin groups[18] (Stephens 1962).

The Web of Kinship

In many societies there is no state—no apparatus of "government," as we know it.[19] Territorial integration is fairly limited; each little community and each kin group is to some extent a separate principality; "civil war" in the form of feuds seems often to be fairly common. Still, stateless societies are more integrated than one might expect. A widely scattered population, tied together by no government, may still share a common language and culture, may consider itself a single "tribe" or "nation," and may even be able to unite for war against other tribes.

How can a large, scattered tribe like this continue as a single tribe? Why is it not six, or twenty, or a hundred different tribes? Why does not each village have its own distinctive culture and its own language? The answer, or part of the answer, at least—is kinship. In the absence of a state, kinship can still serve to tie together a scattered population. It seems to do this by the following means:

Dispersed kin groups. Unilineal kin groups, as we have seen, are frequently segmented; the smaller segments tend to be localized, and the larger kin groupings, the "moieties" and "phratries," are usually dispersed. Dispersed kin groups can give some unity

---

[18] This is only a correlation, of course; there are exceptions.

Deference, on the other hand, does *not* seem to be correlated with avoidance, joking, or unilineal kin groups.

[19] In *Social Structure,* Murdock reports that of 212 societies 108 had no state, each community being politically independent (Murdock 1949:85).

to a scattered population. If distant clansmen, residing in scattered communities, are bound by clan rules to give each other hospitality, this must encourage traveling, visiting, and "mixing." If a dispersed clan or phratry has occasional ceremonial get-togethers, these should also serve to tie together people from different localities.

Kin-group exogamy. Because kinsmen usually may not marry each other, kin groups are bound to exchange spouses with each other.

Community exogamy. Because kin groups are ordinarily exogamous, no single kin group can ever have a monopoly on a single community. There are two possibilities: either the community is composed of several kin groups, who exchange wives with each other; or, the community is composed of the in-married "core" of only one kin group (with its "transient" spouses), and must necessarily get its spouses from some other community. The first possibility is the endogamous community; its members do not have to establish marriage ties with other communities. The second possibility is the exogamous community; in such a community there are no available spouses, so ties of marriage are necessarily established with other communities.

At this point I am going to give three examples illustrating how kinship—by means of kin-group exogamy, community exogamy, and dispersed unilineal kin groups—can tie together a scattered population.

The first example is the Shoshone. These people lived in the semiarid Great Basin and Plateau region of Utah, Nevada, Idaho, and Montana. They did relatively little hunting; they maintained a precarious existence by gathering plant food, largely seeds. They wandered in tiny family bands over the semidesert wastes, living from hand to mouth. The Shoshone had a minimum of formal social structure: no "state," no "tribe," no unilineal kin groups. Still, with minor local variations, the Shoshone had one culture, one language. The reason for this, apparently, was band exogamy. Because the Shoshone lived in family bands, the bands were constantly exchanging spouses with each other. Due to band exogamy, a certain amount of population-mixing was always going on. The band territories seem to have been large (since the food supply was scarce) and rather fluid, so that this population-mixing embraced great areas. Because of band exogamy the family bands were not socially isolated; if you wandered upon another band, it was fairly certain to contain relatives as a result of previous intermarriages. At certain harvest times, several of these "related" bands might even join together for a while, although they would split up again when food became scarce. Julian Steward says that Shoshone "society" "may be likened to a net in that each family had occasional associations with families on all sides of it and these latter with families farther away and these with still others so that there were no social, economic or political frontiers. The entire area consisted of interlocking associations of family with family . . . marriage bonds were fairly enduring, and they created a strong fabric of close relationships, which extended from one locality to the next." (Steward 1955:117)

The next example of the web of kinship is the Trobriand Islanders. Compared with the Shoshone, Trobriand society is highly structured; it has matrilineal kin groups, a rule of residence (avunculocal), and even a state of a rather rudimentary and peculiar sort. The Trobrianders are agriculturists, raising yams and other vegetables in their tropical gardens. Compared with the Shoshone, the population is dense; people live in hamlets, and the hamlets seem to be fairly close to each other. The web of kinship in the Trobriands is extremely complicated and ramified; so much so that I probably will not be able to do it justice in a short description. However, its cardinal points appear to be the matrilineal subclan, avunculocal residence, and *urigubu.*

The Trobriand clan is large and dispersed, with its members living in widely scattered hamlets. Its localized segment we shall call the subclan; it is made up of a group of matrilineally-related men who live together with their wives and children (with the mature women of the subclan, its out-married members, apparently living in other communities). When Ego is a boy he lives with his mother and father, in their village. When he reaches adolescence, he moves to the village of his mother's subclan: he begins living with his "mother's brothers." When he marries he continues to stay in the village of his mother's brothers, but his wife is brought in from still another village. When his son reaches adolescence, the son will move to still another village—the one occupied by his wife's subclan "brothers." Thus, every Trobriander has ties with a number of different villages, due to outmarrying and avunculocal residence. He lives with his matrilineage mates. He maintains ties with his own parents. His wife and children have ties with the wife's parents and, especially,

Figure 2

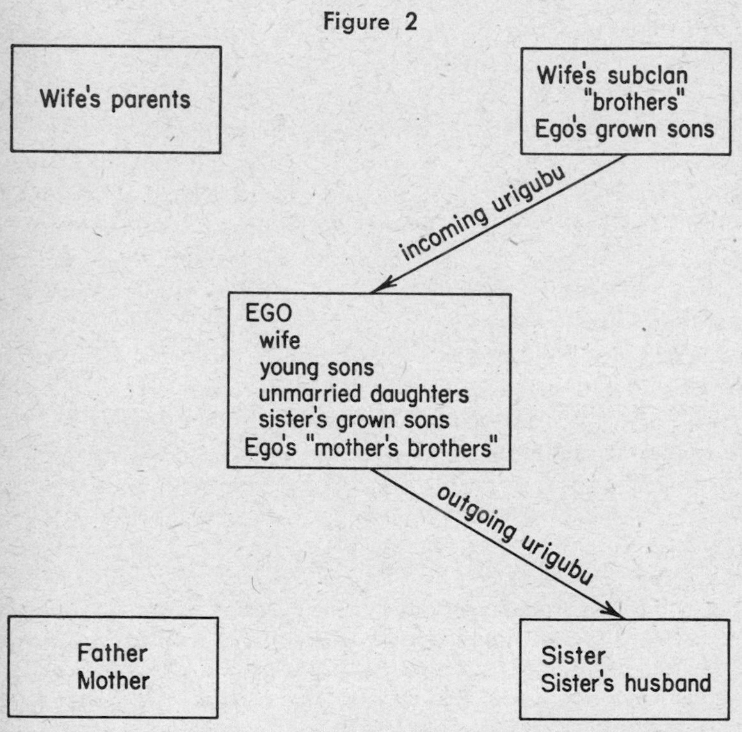

with the wife's subclan. And so does he. About half of Ego's food will come as presents from his wife's subclan "brothers." This is the *urigubu,* a sort of perpetual dowry payment. Furthermore, Ego will give about half of his crops, as *urigubu* payments, to the husbands of his sisters.

All of this is represented in Figure 2, in which each box is a separate village. In a way, this chart may exaggerate the web of kinship; some of the people shown in separate boxes may, at times, actually live in the same village. But other aspects of the Trobriand web of kinship are not even shown in the chart; for example, Ego may have various ties with his father's matrilineage mates. And there remains, of course, the dispersed Trobriand clan, with its representatives in many different villages.

The last example is the Navaho, farmers and sheepherders of the American Southwest. The Navaho live either in scattered farm homesteads or in migratory sheep camps. They have dispersed matrilineal clans. They have no strong residence pattern, but there is some trend toward matrilocal extended families. When a Navaho man marries—if he adopts matrilocal residence—he will leave his parents and move into the homestead or sheep camp of his wife's parents. There he will live with them and, to some extent, work under the direction of his wife's father. But his life is by no means confined to his wife's homestead. He continues to visit his mother and father, and even does some work for them. He does the same for his brothers and sisters. Also, from time to time he meets with the local members of his matrilineal clan. In other words, he spends a great deal of his time visiting, and a great deal of his labor is for the benefit of other homesteads and other relatives: his mother, his sister, a clan "brother," even his father's matrilineal clansmen. Likewise, his own homestead will also have frequent visitors: his wife's brothers, and various other relatives. Aberle says:

> The residential unit, either as a day-to-day affair or viewed over a longer span of time, appears to the outsider to be in a state of considerable flux. On any given day a man might be absent from his wife's family unit for any of several reasons: a half-day or full-day trip to the trading post; visiting matrilineal kin or father's kin; several hours chasing horses; taking out the sheep if need be; farming on a plot of his wife's family a half-mile or a mile away; working for his mother and her family on a plot near her place; looking after his own sheep, left with his sister. (Aberle 1961:144)

Such visits home by married men seem to be a common feature of matrilineal-matrilocal societies. As I said when discussing outmarrying, women sometimes marry far from home, but men in matrilocal societies rarely do. When they move in with their wives' parents, men still tend to stay near enough to their parental homes for frequent visits. Their allegiance is split between "home" and wife's home. (The matrilocal Menangkabau call the husband a "borrowed man.") In matrilineal-matrilocal societies, the men are the out-married members of their local matrilineages; one reason they may visit "home" is to participate in their matrilineage activities. The out-married men may actually run things there. The "patriarch" of a matrilineal extended family, or the head man of a localized matrilineage, may be a married man who lives elsewhere, with his wife and his wife's family.

So in matrilineal-matrilocal societies like the Navaho, there tends to be a high degree of integration of neighboring communities as a result of the split allegiances of the out-married men. In patrilineal-patrilocal societies, on the other hand, it is the women who marry out. At times they marry really far from home—too far for frequent visiting. In such patrilineal-patrilocal cases, particularly where there is fairly distant out-marrying, it is doubtful whether the "split allegiances" of the out-married women has the same effect in tying together different communities.

There is another way in which localities may be tied together: by continuous marriage arrangements. Small kin-groupings, in two or more communities, may—as a fairly permanent arrangement—supply each other with brides. The simplest, most direct type of continuous marriage arrangement is exchange marriage. Extended Family A gives a bride to Extended Family B, and in return Extended Family B gives a bride to Extended Family A. (The trading units, of course, don't have to be extended families; they may be localized lineages, or nuclear families, or even nonlocalized clans.)

A more roundabout but, apparently, more common type of marriage deal results from cross-cousin marriage. If you are a male your cross-cousins are your mother's brother's daughters and your father's sister's daughters—females who, although they may be fairly close "blood kin," can never be members of your unilineal kin group. Of course, in a unilineal society, your classificatory "cross-cousins" may include females who are not related to you at all. For example, your classificatory "mother's brother's daughters" may include all same-generation women in your mother's unilineal kin group.

Where cross-cousin marriage prevails, it does not seem to be a hard-and-fast rule, but merely a statistical trend;[20] many people will marry their cross-cousins, but not all people will. Instead of being a strict marriage rule, cross-cousin marriage seems rather to be encouraged by some special inducement: the bride price will be less, or in-laws will be well-known and reliable, or someone will be angry if you *don't* marry your cross-cousin.

Cross-cousin marriage is of two types: symmetrical, and asymmetrical. With symmetrical cross-cousin marriage you may marry either your mother's brother's daughters or your father's sister's daughters. This means that two or more groups can actually trade brides back and forth. Over the long run, the exchange of spouses should come out fairly evenly. Still, with such an arrangement, bride price will frequently also be paid. So, as a result of symmetrical cross-cousin marriage, a small number of localized kin-groupings become locked together in a continuous financial-legal arrangement—with an interminable series of betrothal arrangements, bride-price negotiations, wedding feasts, and so forth.

With asymmetrical cross-cousin marriage, on the other hand, you are expected to marry one category of cross-cousin, but not the other. In some societies the mother's brother's daughter is the preferred mate; in other societies it is the father's sister's daughter. This often means that two groups may not trade brides. Group A may give brides to Group B. Group B will probably pay for them with bride price, but it will not give brides to Group A. It will give its brides to still another group, Group C (Leach 1951).

Asymmetrical cross-cousin marriage may lead to marriage circles, embracing a number of localized groups; Group A gives most of its brides to Group B; Group B gives most of its brides to Group C; Group C gives to Group D; and Group D gives

---

[20] In my ethnographic notes, there are no cases in which cross-cousin marriage is said to be a strict rule. For nine societies, cross-cousin marriage is said to be "preferred," but not always followed: Fiji, Siwai, Toda, Plateau Tonga, Trobriands, Wogeo, Murngin, Muria, and Siriono.

brides back to Group A. Or, it may lead to a marriage chain: A gives to B gives to C gives to D, and so on, but Group A never gets brides in return (Salisbury 1956:639).

Richard Salisbury gives an example of a marriage chain he discovered among the Siane of New Guinea. The chain embraces a series of communities, beginning in the inland, highland territory and ending near the coast. Among the Siane, the main bride price currency is shell money, which is imported from neighboring coastal peoples and is, hence, first obtained by the Siane communities at the "end" of the marriage chain—nearest the coast. As a result of marriage payments, the shell money gradually "flows up" the marriage chain, until it reaches the communities farthest inland. Wives, on the other hand, "flow down" the marriage chain. Each localized group in the chain (except those at the very beginning and very end) tends to get its wives from its inland neighbors and give wives to its neighbors in the direction of the coast. This is just a tendency, not a strict rule.[21] Apparently, the tendency, in this case, does not even stem from asymmetrical cross-cousin marriage; it seems to have resulted simply from people selling wives to the highest bidders: the neighboring communities with the most shell money, the communities nearer the coast. Thus we have a continuous marriage arrangement between a series of localized groups, resulting in the group at the end of the chain being rich in wives, and the group at the beginning of the chain being poor in wives (but rich in shell money) (Salisbury 1956).

Exogamy, then, can establish ties of a sort between different kin groups and different localities. At times we find continuous, self-reinforcing marriage arrangements that establish multiple ties—many marriages—between groups. This can result from exchange marriage, or from cross-cousin marriage, or from some more subtle cause such as the distribution of wealth among the Siane. In other societies there are no continuous marriage arrangements, and the marriage ties between groups are more haphazard and diffused.

---

[21] If it were a strict rule, of course, the "first" group in the chain would be left with no wives at all.

How much can the mere business of buying and selling brides tie groups to each other? Among the Somali, apparently, a marriage can stop a feud (Lewis 1955:111). But among the Gusii, it cannot; the Gusii say, "Those whom we marry are those whom we fight." (LeVine) At times, bride exchange results in a rather legalistic relationship governed by a detailed marriage contract. If a Somali husband, for example, has legally proper grounds for divorce, he may "dispose of" his wife, and "her family will be held responsible for making good the loss, either by giving another daughter in her place or by repaying the bride-price." (Lewis 1955:138)

The terms of marriage finance may obligate, fairly permanently, one group to the other. One example of this is the Trobrianders' *urigubu*, the continuing dowry payments that husband receives from wife's brothers. In other societies the obligations are reciprocal; in Alor, affines are continually giving each other gongs, pots, pigs, and other valuables:

ALOR, EASTERN INDONESIA

> Marriage has as one of its major functions the establishment of a series of exchanges between groups of extended affinal kin which will continue as long as the marriage lasts. (DuBois 1944:84)

SAMOA, POLYNESIA

> There are constant economic regroupings of the members of descent groups in relation to other descent groups, as the result of marriages. Each descent group constitutes an *itu* (literally "side"), an economic and ceremonial unit in the transactions relating to marriage and birth. The bride's *itu* always contributes *toga,* the bridegroom's *itu, oloa.* This relationship continues as long as the marriage endures. The gift-giving obligations recur whenever either husband or wife visit the other's relatives, at the birth of each child, and the death of either husband or wife. If the marriage is severed after children are born, the two sides of the house retain their obligations in regard to the child. In a society where divorce and remarriage are exceedingly common, it will be seen how exceedingly complex such relationships may become. (Mead 1930:75)

Here is an example that is a bit more complicated: the *waku* (sister's son) to *gawel* (mother's brother) kinship-reciprocal, among the Murngin. The Murngin have matrilateral cross-cousin marriage, so that a man will usually marry the daughter of his real or classificatory *gawel*. In this case, it looks as if the ties resulting from patterned kin behavior are reinforced by marriage ties:

MURNGIN, AUSTRALIA

As soon as a boy is old enough to comprehend, his parents point *gawel* out to him, or a *gawel* may tell his boy that he is his potential father-in-law and as such must receive special attention. This means that throughout *waku's* life he is always giving presents to *gawel*. The latter at times returns them. All the articles of the daily diet and material culture are included in this gift-making. When a *waku* has been initiated into the tribal secrets to the point where he knows and has seen his *ranga*,[22] he often gives the string from it to his *gawel*. This is the finest gift one man could make to another, unless it were the *ranga* itself or a hair belt made from a dead clansman's hair. In a way, any of these presents would give an important part of the social personality of the *waku* to his *gawel*. The gifts are always more numerous from the younger man to the older; but when a *gawel* receives *ranga* string, a *ranga*, or the hair belt, he must reciprocate by giving a return present to show his appreciation, or he would offend his *waku*.

When a *gawel* gives his daughter to his sister's son, this is not merely a gift, for the *waku* by tribal law has a right to her and would fight for her if the *gawel* tried to give her to someone else. He would also feel that he had the right to *gawel's* wife's second daughter and the privilege of declining the offer of a third. There would be an obligation, too, on *gawel* to give his *waku* another wife if the first were barren or died before giving birth to a child. If a *waku's* wife runs away from him, his *gawel* would under almost any circumstances do everything possible to get her back for the husband. If he did not, he would feel obligated to give the *waku* another daughter in her place. . . .

The *waku-gawel* reciprocal is utilized for . . . trading. All men try to have as many distant *waku* as they can. Presents are con-

---

22 The *ranga* seems to be some sort of ritual object that represents the boy's totem.

stantly being exchanged between the two, not to acquire material wealth so much as to extend a man's sphere of influence beyond the nearby clans. It pleases a Murngin to have a present sent from a distant people and adds greatly to his social prestige. It also gives him a greater feeling of safety when traveling, to know that he has a *waku* or *gawel* with whom he has this trading relationship. *Waku* and *gawel* visit each other and their behavior demonstrates real friendship when they meet. (Warner 1937:93–95)

Finally, here is Margaret Mead's description of the web of intermarriage among the gentle Arapesh.

ARAPESH, NEW GUINEA

When a father selects a wife for his son, he is moved by many considerations. First, there is the problem whether to choose a wife close to home, from the next village, from a clan with which his own clan has already intermarried. This is very good. It is good that brother and sister should marry brother and sister, that if one clan gives two of its girls to the other, the other clan should reciprocate with two of its daughters. This is no hard and fast rule. The Arapesh construct their marriages to last, and are not bound to any fixed system that might dictate marriages in which the young people are the wrong ages. But still the marriage nearer home is a desirable one. The men folk of the two clans, already bound together by several ties, will urge a further tie. Against these considerations, there are the advantages of a marriage in a far-away place. This kind of marriage widens the circle of friendliness within which the next generation will walk about safely, sure of a welcome after a hard, cold journey. A tie set up by a marriage between distant places will bind those two places together for a long time to come, perhaps, with good luck, forever. The descendants of the marriage will remember it, calling all the people from their mother's village "grandfather," and welcoming them respectfully when they come to feasts. Furthermore, if the new bride comes from a village towards the beach she may bring some special skill with her, which she will teach to her daughters and her daughters-in-law. It was thus that the secret of making the *wulus,* a *soigne* braided grass skirt, was brought to the people of Suabibis five generations ago, by a bride from Daguar. But against this choice there is the fear of sorcery. If one chooses a wife from the strangers, if one permits one's daughter to go among strangers, fear, the compulsive resort to sorcery when angered and frightened, may destroy the marriage. So the fathers and uncles balance the matter in their minds.

In the girl herself they look for various definite attributes. She should have the right kind of relatives, many male kindred, men who are good hunters, successful gardeners, slow to anger and wise in making choices. The father who chooses a wife for his son is choosing also, and as importantly, his son's brothers-in-law, and his grandchildren's maternal uncles. Instead of regarding marriage as a necessary evil, as so many people do, as an unfortunate compromise which makes it inevitable that a stranger be allowed to enter the house and sit down familiarly within it, the Arapesh regard marriage as primarily an opportunity to increase the warm family circle within which one's descendants may then live even more safely than one has lived oneself. This attitude is brought out very clearly in their comment on incest. I had the greatest difficulty in getting any comment upon it at all. The only formulation on the subject that I obtained is contained in a series of rather esoteric aphorisms:

"Your own mother,
Your own sister,
Your own pigs,
Your own yams that you have piled up,
You may not eat.
Other people's mothers,
Other people's sisters,
Other people's pigs,
Other people's yams that they have piled up,
You may eat."

To questions about incest I did not receive the answers that I had received in all other native societies in which I had worked, violent condemnation of the practice combined with scandalous revelations of a case of incest in a neighbouring house or a neighbouring village. Instead both the emphatic condemnation and the accusations were lacking: "No, we don't sleep with our sisters. We give our sisters to other men and other men give us their sisters." Obviously, it was simple as that. Why did I press the point? And had they not heard of a single case of incest? I queried. Yes, finally, one man said that he had. He had gone on a long journey, toward Aitape, and there in the village of a strange people he had heard a quarrel; a man was angry because his wife refused to live with him, but instead kept returning to her brother, with whom she cohabited. Was that what I meant? That, in effect, was what I meant. No, we don't do that. What would the old men say to a young man who wished to take his sister to wife? They didn't know. No one knew. The old men never discussed the matter. So I set them to asking the old men, one at a time. And the answers were the same. They came to this: "What, you would like to marry your sister! What is the matter with you anyway? Don't you want a brother-in-law? Don't you realize that if you marry another man's sister and another man marries your sister, you will have at least two brothers-in-law, while if you marry your own sister you will have none? With whom will you hunt, with whom will you garden, whom will you go to visit?" Thus incest is regarded among the Arapesh not with horror and repulsion towards a temptation that they feel their flesh is heir to, but as a stupid negation of the joys of increasing, through marriage, the number of people whom one can love and trust.

So the father, in choosing his son's wife, considers her brothers and her cousins, who will be his son's friends in the years to come. It is well if there are many of them. (Mead 1935)

Wandering with Relatives

To conclude the chapter, I am going to give a series of quotes from *Son of Old Man Hat.* This is the autobiography of the Navaho Indian, Left Handed, who lived with his adopted father (Old Man Hat) and mother in a migratory sheep camp. The quotations illustrate and give human detail to some of the topics of this chapter, namely, classificatory kin terms, patterned rights and obligations between kin, and the manner in which extended kinship may "take on the functions of" the nuclear family.

"I was born when the cottonwood leaves were about the size of my thumbnail, but the date was not due yet for my birth. It should have been another month. Something had happened to my mother, she'd hurt herself, that was why I was born before my time. I was just a tiny little baby, and my feet and fingers weren't strong, they were like water. My mother thought I wasn't going to live.

"She was very sick when I was born and had no milk, so her older sister picked me up and started to take care of me. She didn't have any milk either, but she went among the women who had babies and begged them for some. She had many necklaces of different-colored beads, and when she brought the women and their babies home with her she'd pick me up and hand me over to one of them. That's where I got my milk. After a while she didn't have to go around among the women any more, because four of them lived right close by. All four had babies, and every day they came to our place. Whenever they wanted to nurse me one of them would come and give me my feed. They helped me out until I was able to eat. All four were still feeding me while we were moving back to the reservation from Fort Sumner, as far as Chinlee. There they quit, and I was able to eat anything from there on. My mother (mother's older sister) and her husband were the only ones who took care of me.

"When we returned from Fort Sumner we settled at Chinlee. My mother's husband had another wife in a hogan close by, and he left to visit her. While he was gone my mother's former husband came. She had been married to him before the Indians went to Fort Sumner, but he'd stayed behind on the reservation by himself for four years. When he heard we were back he started to hunt for my mother, and at Chinlee he found her. From then on he lived with his wife again. His clan was Many Goats, his name was Old Man Hat.

"My mother (adopted mother) decided to go with him to Black Mountain where some of his relatives were living. She took me to a hogan where an older clan sister of mine lived and said, 'I'm going away, and I'm leaving my baby here with you. Please be sure and take good care of my baby, your younger brother, just as though he were your own child.' My sister said, 'You can go. Don't worry, I'll surely take good care of him. . . .' A year after she left me my mother came back. . . .

"In winter we lived on Black Mountain, but in the summer we moved down to the foot of the mountain, to a place called Another Canyon. In this canyon, where there were many lakes, my father, Old Man Hat, and my uncle, Bitahni, planted corn. . . .

"At that time my father was also married to Bitahni's Sister. She was a clan mother of mine and my mother's clan sister. We were all living together in one hogan. I don't know how he came to be married to her. Maybe my mother told him to marry her, or it may be my father asked my mother, saying he wanted to marry her. Anyway my father had two wives, but it wasn't long before my mother and her sister quarreled.

"One afternoon my father and mother began fighting. I was sitting outside watching them. Finally my father threw my mother down and sat on her. Then my uncle's sister dragged Old Man Hat off my mother, and my mother got up and went after my father again. . . . My mother sure did swear and cuss my father and her sister. It was all due to jealousy. . . .

"Friend of Who Has Children came to our house one day while my father was away. He was a Red Clay. My mother and I were just starting to eat, and she told him to eat with us. There was only one spoon, and we all used it. Once, as the man was using the spoon, my mother asked for it. He handed it to her, and she reached over and took it. After we'd eaten my mother went out with the herd, and he went away.

"When my father came home he asked me. 'Was anyone here today?' I said, 'Yes.' 'How many people came today?' I said, 'Only one.' He asked me who it was. I knew the man very well, and I said, 'Friend of Who Has Children. He came, and we ate with him.' 'Where'd your mother sit?' 'On the west side, close to this man.' 'Where'd you sit?' 'I was sitting on the south side.' And I added, 'We ate with the spoon. The man had the spoon, and my mother took it away from him.' My father got up, picked up the spoon and handed it to me. 'Now you hand it to me just as the man handed it to your mother.' I handed it to him, 'Just like this,' I said. He took the spoon. 'Now,' he said, 'I'm the man, and you're your mother. How'd she take hold of the spoon?' 'This way,' I said, and I did just as my mother had done. After I told him all this he got on his horse and rode away. While my mother was herding he got after her and whipped her. That was for my story. . . .

"One winter we lived on Black Mountain at Willows Coming Out. In the spring, all at once, I discovered we were moving. We moved down from the mountain to the flat, to a place called Bush Sitting Up. There we located late that spring. From there we moved across the valley to Lukachukai Mountain, to a place called Green

Valleys Coming Together. Not far from there, right on top of the point, we stopped and located. We took all our stuff off the horses, and they said, 'We won't move any further. This is a good place to locate.'

"Then Quiver's sister, Moving On, and her husband, Landi, who was of the Walk Around You Clan, came to where we camped. They were driving some sheep and goats which they put in with our bunch. After that Slim Man and his wife arrived, and not long after Slim Man's mother. He'd been raised by this woman; she was his mother's sister. She and her husband and her daughter and her son and her son-in-law came with a herd also. They felled two pine trees right close together and used that for a sheep corral. They made a partition between them, and one corral belonged to us, and the other belonged to Slim Man's outfit. . . .

"The day after all those who lived around us gathered at our place and began to talk of moving. My father said, 'We'll move back to our place. We'll go with my little one.' He meant my sister, Moving On; he wanted to take her along back to our country. 'What do you think about it?' he asked her. 'Do you want to go back with us, my little one?' She said, 'Yes, I'm willing to go.' Then Mexican's mother's outfit and Slim Man and his mother's outfit all said, 'We want to move and go to where our relatives are living at Bay In The Mountain. We'll be living over there with them.' . . .

"One day they wanted to move again, down to Coyote Water. They said, 'They're going to have a Night Chant at Chinlee. It's coming up soon, so we'll move closer.' We started for that place, and Ruins and Tunes To His Voice and three women who didn't have any husbands moved with us. These women belonged to the Bitter Water Clan. They were full sisters, and when we got to Coyote Water they settled down close by us.

"There one of the women got after my sister's husband, or he went after her; anyway my sister saw him with this woman. She came to our place, and she was awfully mad. When her husband came after her she said, 'Don't bother with me any more; I don't want you to touch me again. And I don't want to bother with you, or touch you again. Go back to your wife, Big Comanche Woman. Go back to her. You think she's a beautiful woman, but she's not, she hasn't any nose. So you just go back to your beautiful wife, that old, big, fat thing. You think she's pretty, so go back to her and lie over there.' . . .

"One day a man and his wife stopped at our hogan. His name was Slave Of The Texan; he was an Along The Stream. His wife was Bitahni. They were going to Cheek to visit a man called Bunch Of Whiskers who was a relative of Slave Of The Texan. They stayed at our place that day and all night. In the morning my mother killed a sheep for them. They were so thankful for the meat. 'This meat tastes a whole lot different than ours,' said the woman. . . .

"One spring we moved off the mountain to a place called Tree On Hill. We stopped and camped there and began shearing our sheep. At that time there weren't any shears; we used old cans or any kind of tin for knives. Tin used to be scarce, it was hard to get. . . . A little above us were some hogans. That was Tunes To His Voice's and Ruins' outfits, and Old Man Thankful, who was my clan grandfather, and his wife, who was a Many Goats, and Red Wife Beater, who'd married Tunes To His Voice's sister not long before. They came to our place when we were about to start shearing. The old man said, 'I'm glad you people came. I want you all to help us. I'd like to have this shearing done as soon as possible. I've heard a store has been put up at Fort Defiance, and the trader wants skins and wool. I'd like to take my wool there, so you all help me, my nephews, my children,' he said to them. 'I'd like to get through with the shearing as soon as I can and go to that place with my wool.' . . .

"We went back, past the hogan, and over to the place where they were cooking. Ruins' wife came over too, with a crowd of people right behind her. They were her relatives, Mexican People and Two Streams Running To Each Other. They were after her for presents. She had a lot of robes and blanket-skirts, two buckskins, a red belt and a big bundle of red flannel with which they used to weave blankets, and which they put on the decorated-stick. Ruins' wife's mother began giving out these things to her close relatives. She gave the robes and skirts away and tore the red flannel in pieces and gave that out. A skirt and the red belt she put aside for herself. . . .

"The first spring that they took the herd to the store to shear the sheep I stayed with my father, Slim Man and his wife. Slim Man and I went out every day, herding the sheep and goats that were left. While we were out herding he used to kill the bugs in my hair. I had a lot of them. He said, 'If it wasn't for me these bugs would kill you.' . . .

"A few days after Blue Goat left a man and his wife came to our place. They said they started from Ganado and went down to visit Ruins. Next they went and visited Who Has Mules, then Choclays Kinsman and some other people on the west side of Black Mountain. From there they came to our place. The woman was a Bitter Water; her husband was a Many Goats. He was my father's nephew. He'd been with Old Man Hat when he was young. That's why they came and visited us also. He was an oldish sort of man, but his wife was young and slim. They were driving a bunch of sheep they'd gotten from their relatives, and when they arrived at our place toward evening they drove them in to our herd. . . .

"Around in shearing season my father and mother took part of our herd to Keams Canyon. They were gone for a long time, and I was all alone at home. They worried about me while they were at Keams Canyon shearing the sheep, and so they sent me my younger brother. My real mother had another husband, his name was Yishi, and this man's nephew came with my brother. He stayed with us one night and went right back the next day.

"The day after my brother arrived we started herding together, and from there on we both went out with the sheep every day. He surprised me. Even though he was a small boy he knew a lot of songs. I didn't know any kind of song. . . .

"There wasn't any rain at all, or any cloud. It was hot and getting worse every day. Even at that we stayed at this one place for many days. Nobody did anything or went any place, and I did nothing but herd. Then we heard that my father, Choclays Kinsman, had moved down to the flat and was living at Hawohi Water. They wanted to move to where he was living, and so we started for that place. . . .

"We stayed at this place many days. Then all at once they said, 'We'll move again.' We moved, passing Many Streams, and on past The Lake, past Anything Falls In to Flowing From Tassel Rock. From the mouth of that little canyon out into the valley where the water spreads was a nice level place all sandy. There my father, Slim Man, lived. He had a farm in the valley, and the corn was ripe. My mother went over to the hogan where he lived and brought back some corn. She used to call his wife, my daughter. She said, 'My daughter said to me, "You can come and get corn and make yourself corn-bread whenever you want to. When you come just go into the field and help yourself. Take all the corn you want." That's what my daughter said, so I must go and make us some corn-bread. Slim Man wasn't at home. I asked for him, I said to my daughter, "Where has my son gone to?" She said, "He's staying with another woman." ' He'd married another woman, who was a Red Clay, and from there on he had two wives.

"There we located all during the fall and had corn right along. When fall came we helped them take it in off the field and lay it out to dry. About then my father, His Horse Is Slow, came to our place. . . .

"While I'd been walking around out in the salt-weed a man had come to our place. He was a Bitahni. My mother said, 'A man came to our camp, your grandfather, Old Man Won't Do As He's Told. He took his horse to where he wants to hobble it.' After we'd turned the wether into the herd we went back to camp, and he was back from where he'd hobbled his horse. . . .

"A few days after we'd moved back to above The Middle Wash, where some of our hogans were standing, a man and his wife came to visit us. His name was Walk Up In Anger. He was a Bitahni. His wife was the niece of Giving Out Anger. She was a Red Clay. We started shearing, and His Horse Is Slow and his wife came also and helped us shear for many days. . . .

"I used to hold the heads of the sheep for this woman while she was shearing. While I was holding a sheep's head for her my uncle, Walk Up In Anger, said, 'My nephew, you ought to get yourself a woman. You'd better get one, so you can have a good time with her. When you get yourself a woman she'll help us around too.' His wife said, 'If you want your nephew to get married why don't you get a woman for him?' 'I'll get a woman for him,' he said, 'so he'll have a good time.' She said, 'Your nephew doesn't know anything about women. He doesn't know how to get one, and he doesn't know how to work at one.' Then he said to his wife, 'Well, you're staying with him right now close together, and you'll be the one to show him how the thing has to be done.' She said, 'If I tried to teach him you wouldn't like it. You'd sure be mad.' But he said, 'Even if you start to teach him, even if I see you teaching him, I won't say anything. I won't do anything, because I don't care. All I want is for my nephew to learn. That's all I care about. I want him to learn about women. So you can go right ahead and teach him how.' They were talking to each other that way for a while, and my uncle said, 'Now, my nephew, you can go ahead. You mustn't be bashful, and my wife will teach you how to get at a woman. She'll teach you everything.' That's what he said, and I was afraid of her. I thought she'd get after me. I thought they really meant it, but he was only joshing. When they were through shearing they gave them some wool and a sheep too, and they went back to their home. . . .

"I got there, and we started playing the moccasin game. While we were playing two women arrived. They were from Little Wife Beater's place. They said to me, 'We came over to tell you the old folks got into a quarrel. They fought, and the old woman is lying there crying. It looks like she's been hurt badly, and the old man's gone away.' Right away I went back, and the two women came after me. When I got home my mother was lying there; it sounded as though she had quite a pain. The old man had gone away. 'What's the matter with you?' I asked her. She said, 'I don't know. It's your father. I don't know what he's done to me. I fought with your father, and he's left and gone away. So I don't know what he's done to me, and I don't know where he's gone to.' I went out, and on the other side of the sheep I saw a light. He'd made a fire and was lying there. The two women went over to him. When they came back they said, 'The old man wants his herd separated for him. He said he wants to leave.' . . . I asked my mother, 'Who's that man who came here on horseback?' She said, 'That was my older brother.' She meant Smooth Man's Son. His clan was Walk Around You. His father and my mother's father had been brothers. Their clan was Salt. She said, 'He came and scolded me about your father. He said he met your father and asked him where he was going. He said your father said, "I'm going home. I've left the old woman." So that's why he came, and he gave me a good scolding. He asked me "Are you having a good time now by yourself? Do you think from here on you'll have a good life? And do you think from here on you'll have everything you didn't have before? I know you're acting now as if you're suffering from a very bad pain, but I know you're just making believe. I know you haven't got a bit of of pain. Maybe you have a little, but that's nothing, because everything is all your own fault. It's not the old man's fault, and I'm not blaming the old man. I'm sorry for him. I'm sorry for him for your sake. You may not be sorry for him, but I am, because soon you won't be like you were before." This is the way my brother spoke to me, and a lot of other things besides. What do you think about it?' I said, 'I'm thinking about my father. I've been thinking about him and looking for him all day, and I'm sorry for him, because there's no one around here I can call my father.' . . . I went after my father. . . . I got off my horse and walked up to him just about the time he had the fire going. He sat back and told me to come over. I walked up and sat right by him, and he put his arm around me, and I put an arm around him. 'Where do you think you're going, my baby?' he said to me. I said, 'I've come for you.' 'What do you think? Are you sorry for me, my baby?' I said, 'Yes, I'm sorry for you.' When I said this I almost cried. He said, 'I'm the same, I'm sorry for you, my baby. . . .'

"The next day I was out with the herd all day. In the evening after we'd eaten supper my father came. He walked right in and sat by me, a little way from my mother. My mother was lying against a great big pillow and started to groan, making believe she had an awful pain. 'What did you come here for?' she said. 'I thought you'd left for good.' My father said, 'I thought you wanted me back. And that groaning, you're just making it, making believe you've got an awful pain.' She said, 'Yes, you killed me. But now you can kill me right now. Kill me instantly. Then you can go wherever you want to go and wherever you wish to. So kill me right now. From there on you'll enjoy life.' . . .

"I was herding the next day, and when I came back in the and inside the hogan a man was sitting by my mother. He had his evening a horse was hobbled out in the valley. I didn't recognize it, medicine-outfit with him. He was a singer named Red Hair. My father had gone after him that day and brought him back. He sang over my mother three days and three nights; by that time she was good and well. Then the man went home. From there on they were good to each other. They didn't have another quarrel. But before that they used to get mad every once in a while. . . .

". . . a man came to my father and said, 'They want you to come to Quiver's place. He and his brothers and nephews are there. On the other side is Giving Out Anger and his clansmen. They are after one another. They want to fight. They all have bows and arrows. So they want you to go over.' . . . On one side were Quiver and his brothers, Small Bitahni, Big Bitahni, and Walk Up In Anger. On Giving Out Anger's side were Old Man Black, Old Man Gentle, No Sense, Wounded Smith and Big Red Clay. They were all brothers of the Red Clay Clan. They were all saying the same thing, they wanted to fight, they wanted to kill one another, they didn't care to live. Between the two parties were Old Man Hat, Choclays Kinsman, Who Has Mules, Slim Man and Pounding House. They were Many Goats. They were on Quiver's side. On the side of the Red Clay was a man named Whiskers, he was an Along The Stream, and a fellow named Big Chancres, he was a Bitter Water, and some others. They didn't want to let them fight. . . .

(Old Man Hat talking)

"As soon as I got on my horse all the fellows got on theirs and came right after me. They were all after my tobacco. Old Man Gentle was the first one to ride up to me. He said, 'My older brother, my old older brother, please give me a piece of your tobacco.' I turned around—I had it tied on the back of the saddle —I untied it and got out the tobacco and cut him off a piece. Then everybody wanted some. They all said, 'Give me a piece too, my grandfather, my uncle, my brother. Give me some too.' I got mad at them. I said, 'I didn't get this tobacco for all of you. I asked for it only for myself. If you wanted tobacco why didn't you ask the headman for it?' Then I just started cutting pieces off, giving a piece to each one. . . .

"Old Man White Horse and his older brother, Stutterer, had come to our place. They were Many Goats. White Horse said, 'We were just going to start the Nda. . . .'

"My father rode out from where they'd camped . . . and as he started riding back to us some people came after him. That was Who Has Mules and his wife and some others with him. Then some more started towards us; that was Choclays Kinsman and his wife and some people with them. And some more came. They were all from Cheek. That was Wounded Smith and Big Red Clay and others that were with them. Then some more started towards us. They were all Mexican People. There was a bunch of them. One fellow's name was He Crosses His Legs. As soon as he rode up he said to my father, 'Well, my grandfather, we're all hungry. We didn't have anything to eat all day yesterday and last night. We're about starved now.' They were all saying the same, calling him my old father, my grandfather, 'We want something to eat.' My father said, 'I've nothing to eat for you. There's nothing to eat.' He Crosses His Legs said, 'Nothing to eat! How about all those sheep? You've got lots of sheep all over under the trees. A man like you having so many sheep and saying he's got nothing to eat.' My father smiled and said, 'If you're not lazy you can go ahead and help yourselves. I give you all those sheep. If you can eat them all go ahead.' . . .

"Who Has Mules (whose wife just died) said, 'Yes, I'm in sorrow, but still I'm taking care of myself. I'm not thinking badly of myself, and I'm thinking about all my things. I'm not letting everything go. I'm still holding onto everything.' Then he said, 'That's why I'm going around among you, my clansmen. When I get lonely, when I can't stand the sorrow, I get on my horse and go and visit you, my clansmen. Then, when I go around, I forget a little about it. . . .'

(Death of Old Man Hat)

"That morning we went on to Where The Mexican Fixed The

Spring. Some people were living there. There was Old Man Little Yellow, who was a Poles Sprung Out In Water, and a man called Anger. He was a Bitter Water. He was Old Man Little Yellow's son-in-law. Then there was Old Man Blue Goat, my father's nephew, and another man named Always Spitting, who was an older brother of Blue Goat. There were also two of Old Man Blue Goat's nephews. They were my father's grandsons and sons of the old woman, my father's niece. She lived there and her daughter and grand-daughter. They were Many Goats. Those were the people my father wanted to have put up a Feather Chant for him. That's why we moved there.

"When we entered the hogan my father walked up to the old woman and sat down beside her, and she put her arms around his shoulders and began to cry, saying, 'Alas, my son, alas.' They held each other quite a while, and the others did the same. Everyone walked up and put his arms around him.

"One evening, about five days later, my mother came back from those people's place. That's where my father was. She stayed over there with him every day, and in the evening she returned to where we were living. This evening she came back and said, 'They're going to put up a chant. They've got everything ready. They've got enough baskets, enough of everything, so they're going to give a chant for your father. They're going to get a singer named One Birth After Another. He's the one who knows the Feather Rite.'

"The old man was getting worse all the time, but still he just kept quiet by himself. . . .

"Every morning while they were singing and treating my father I went out with the herd. . . . People were coming in every day. In the evening after the fourth fire my father, Choclays Kinsman, arrived. . . .

"In the morning—it was the last day—I tied up four sheep to be butchered. While they were butchering I went out with the herd and was herding all day. When I returned in the evening I saw more people, more men and more women. Many of them were Red House, and some were Standing House, and a lot were Many Goats. It was a big crowd that evening. As soon as it got real dark they started singing. Red Woman's Grandson was beating the basket. He was the leader. The singer was lying down, taking it easy. . . .

"He was lying still, just breathing a little all that night, and just as morning came, just as you saw a little white and blue sky coming over the mountain, he passed away. He died that morning and all his relatives and friends began to cry. As soon as he died they told me to go and round up the horses, and while his relatives and friends were holding him and crying I started out, and while I was running I was crying too. I caught my father's race horse and rounded up the others and drove them back. . . .

". . . all the sheep and horses were there, and there was a crowd, all my father's relatives and a lot of people from different places, talking about how they'd divide the things up. My father's brother, Choclay's Kinsman, got on his horse and rode over where the sheep were, and everybody moved there after him. He said, 'I'll give sheep to every one of you. Some will get twenty head, some fifty, and some of you will get a hundred. In that way every one of you will get some sheep. I'll do the same with the horses. I'll give each of you a horse or two. I don't want any sheep or horses for myself, because I've got enough. But it's up to you, my relatives and friends, if you want to give me a sheep or a horse it'll be all right. I'll be thankful for it. But before I start giving them out to you I want my boy to have his first. We'll all help separate my boy's sheep and horses, and then I'll start giving you some.'

"They separated the sheep for us, and my mother and I had a little over five hundred head. And they separated fourteen horses of mine. My father (Choclays Kinsman) came up to me and said, 'Get two more out of that bunch. Any two you like.' So I went over and got me a young mare and a three-year-old stallion. I didn't get any of his sheep. He'd close to nine hundred head, but his clan relatives got them all. They got all his cattle too. But the cattle were up on Black Mountain, so all the people who were related to him went up there and rounded them up and gave one or two heads to each other. There was only one steer in the bunch, and my father's brother kept that for himself." (Dyk 1938)

4

Mate Choice, Marriage, and Divorce

THE MARRIAGE OF CRASHING THUNDER

"One fall I did not go and instead I stayed with my grandfather. He told me to get married. I was about twenty-three years old then. I had courted women ever since I was old enough. Every time I did anything I always thought of women in connection with it. I tried to court as many women as I could. I wanted badly to be a beau for I considered it a great thing. I wanted to be a ladies' man.

"My grandfather had asked me to marry a certain girl, so I went over to the place where she was staying. When I arrived there I tried to meet the girl secretly, which I succeeded in doing. I told her of my intention and asked her to go home with me. Then she went home for I had met her some distance from her home.

"After a while she came back all dressed up and ready. She had on a waist covered with silver buckles and a beautifully colored hair ornament and she wore many strings of beads around her neck, and bracelets around her wrists. Her fingers were covered with rings and she wore a pair of ornamented leggings. She wore a wide-flap ornamented moccasin and in each ear she had about half a dozen ear holes and they were full of small silver pieces made into ear ornaments. She was painted also. She had painted her cheeks red and the parting of her hair red. She was all dressed up.

"I went on horseback. We rode the horse together. We were not going that night to the place from which I had come, because I had previously been asked to sing at a medicine feast by my band (at a place) which was on our way home. I would therefore not go home until the next morning. So on my way there I had the girl hide near the place we were to have the feast, for we were eloping and that was the custom.

"The girl had a red blanket which she was wearing so I had her hide under a small oak bush. It rained all night and the next day. When we were through in the morning, I went to the place (where I had put her) and she was still there, but she was soaked through and through from the rain and her paint was smeared over her face in such a way that one could hardly recognize her. Then we went home. When we arrived home, my grandfather's wife came out to meet us and she helped the girl down from the horse and led her into the lodge. Then we ate. When we were through, the girl took off her clothing and gave it to them and they gave her other clothing to wear. After the girl had stayed there three nights, she had her menses, so she had to camp by herself, and there she had to sleep at night. Then a horse was given to this girl that I had married.

"After a while my grandfather had a private talk with me, and he said: 'Grandson, it is said that this girl you have married is not a maiden but really a widow, and I am not pleased with it, as this is your first marriage and you are a young man. I suppose you know whether it is true or not, whether she is a maiden or not?' 'Yes,' I answered. 'You can stop living with her, if you wish,' he said. So I went away on a visit and from there I went away for good. After some time I learned that the woman had gone home. Then I went home. He (my grandfather) was glad that I had not stayed with her. 'You can marry another and a better one,' said he to me, 'one that I shall choose for you, you shall marry.' Thus he spoke to me. However I said to him, 'Grandfather, you have begged women for me often enough. Don't ever ask for anyone for me again, as I do not care to marry a woman that is begged for.' Thus I spoke to him. He was not at all pleased at this for he said I was not allowing him to command me." (Radin 1920:405) (Winnebago, Wisconsin)

THE COURTSHIP OF HIGH HORSE

"There was a band of Shyelas (Cheyennes) camped up the creek that time. High Horse and I would go up there to play throwing-them-off-their-horses or maybe hoop-and-spear with the boys our age; for the Shyelas were friends and almost like our own people come to visit us.

"One day when we were up there having a good time, I noticed that High Horse was not with us any more, and I wondered if he had gone home. So afterwhile I rode off down the creek towards the Miniconjou village. There was some brush around a spring, and High Horse was in there. He was talking to a Shyela girl, and he did not see me. First I thought I would yell at him; but I did not, for all at once I felt sad and ashamed. So I turned back and rode home another way.

"The next time I saw him, I thought he was sick because he was queer with me, but he said he was not sick. Afterwhile he began talking without looking at me, and he said that maybe when we were great warriors we would have women too just like other men. Crazy Horse had a woman, didn't he? And all the great warriors had too, didn't they? And so maybe it would be the same way with us. And I said we were not great warriors yet, and we did not have to think about that now. And he said, 'I know you talk to Tashina, because I have seen you doing it. Maybe you will have her for your woman sometime; and maybe I will see a girl I want too.'

"Then I laughed and said I talked to Tashina because I used to be her horse, and she wasn't like other girls anyway. I was just telling her about the things we were going to do. And he *yah-yahed,* making forked fingers at me. Then I was angry, and I said, 'You have been sneaking around in the brush after that Shyela girl again, haven't you?' Then he was angry too, and left, and rode home.

"All the rest of that day I was angry at High Horse; but when I awoke in the morning, I thought of him first thing, and I was not angry any more at all. I was sad, and I got sadder and sadder all that day. So I rode out on a high hill and sat there thinking about how we had said we were twins, and we had found each other at last and we would never be apart again, and we would be brother-friends and do great deeds and everybody would praise us. And when I looked around at the sky and the prairie, it was big and empty, and I was all alone in it and nothing cared about me. So I sat there and wept a long time.

"Next day I was sadder than the day before, and I thought I would go and see High Horse again. Maybe he was sad too and would not be angry at me any more. So I started towards the Miniconjou village, riding slowly because my mind was still forked; and all at once there was a horseback coming slowly out of the brush up there. When I saw it was High Horse, my heart drummed; but when he came close I could see that it was bad with him. 'How, Kola,' he said; and his voice was low and weak, as though he might be getting ready to die pretty soon. And I said, 'What is wrong with you, brother-friend? Are you sick in your belly?' And he groaned and said, 'I am sick all over, brother-friend, and you must help me, for if nobody helps me I think I shall die.' Then he groaned some more; and I said, 'You know I will help you, for we are twins and brother-friends, and if you die then I must die too.'

"So we got off our horses and sat together in a clump of brush where nobody would see us, and High Horse said, 'My brother, it is true. I have been talking to a Shyela girl and her name is Wacin Hin Washtay Win (Good Plume).' When he had said that he muttered the name to himself for a while—like singing to yourself under your breath. Then the sickness went out of his face, and it was all shining when he looked at me and began telling me about Good Plume and how beautiful she was. It made me sad again to hear him, for I thought he was going crazy the way he told it, all out of breath. Then all at once the sickness came back in his face again, and he said, 'Brother-friend, I want her so much that I cannot eat and I cannot sleep, and if I do not get her, maybe I shall just starve to death.' 'I will think,' I said, 'and we shall see what we can do.'

"Then I thought awhile. If my brother was about to die, would I not have to go and help him even if I died too? If he was going crazy, then would I not have to help him, even if I had to go crazy too? So I said, 'You must take some horses to her father and tell him how much you want the girl. Maybe then he will give her to you.' But High Horse shook his head and groaned. 'Her father is a man of many horses,' he said, 'and I have only my buffalo-runner and the old horse we got from the Nez Perces and Absorakas.' And I said: 'If you are not man enough to try, how can I help you?' 'You will see that I am man enough to try anything,' he said, 'and I will do just what you tell me.' When he said that, he looked like a warrior charging. Then he jumped on his horse and galloped away toward his village.

"I waited and waited, and after that I still waited a long time. It was getting dark when High Horse came riding back slowly with his chin on his chest. When he had got off his horse and sat down beside me, he just held his head in his hands for a while. Then he said, 'The old man just laughed at me. He just laughed and waved his hand for me to go away from there.'

"After I had thought awhile, I said, 'Brother-friend, it is harder than I thought. This is something that will take a little more time. You will sleep with me tonight, and tomorrow I shall have a better plan.'

"So after we had slept, and it was morning, I said: 'Hold fast to your pipe, brother-friend, and do not lose courage. I have a plan. The old man will not take two horses. You will offer him four horses, for I will give you Whirlwind and the horse I got from the Nez Perces and Absorakas. You will go to the old man with these. You will say how much you want the girl and that you have two good buffalo-runners, also a horse just beginning to get old and another one hardly old at all. Maybe he will not laugh at you this time. If he takes the horses, you will have the girl and we shall have only our legs to ride. But that will be good, for we will go on the war-path *maka mani* (earth-walking, on foot), and when we get back we shall have many, many ponies and be great warriors, and everybody will praise us and the old man will be proud of you.'

"So High Horse did as I told him. But before the sun was overhead, he came back looking even sicker than ever, and he had to groan awhile before he could tell me how the old man laughed harder than before and waved his hand to say go away and quit talking foolishness.

"So I thought awhile, and then I said: 'The old man will not take four good horses for the girl, and that is all we have. Maybe she will run away with you, and then when you come back she will be your woman and you will have your horses too.' But that was no good either, because High Horse said he asked her when they were talking under the blanket, and she did not want to run away. She wanted to be bought like a fine woman.

"So I thought awhile, and then I said: 'I have the right plan at last, brother-friend; and if you quit groaning and have a strong heart, you will get her this time.' And High Horse said, 'My heart is strong enough to do anything anybody can think up, if I can only have Good Plume.' Then I said: 'The old man will not take two horses. He will not take four horses either. The girl will not run away with you. Then you will just steal her, and I will tell you how to do it. Maybe she wants you to steal her anyway. This is going to be the biggest thing we ever did.'

"So this is how it was.

"When it was dark High Horse and I rode up the creek to the Shyela village and hid in the brush until we thought everyone was asleep. Then I tied my horse and we sneaked up to the old man's tepee, leading the other horse and being very careful not to make any noise. Once a dog barked and a man came out of a tepee and looked around in the starlight. We were flat on our bellies by then, and when the man saw it was only a horse grazing, he kicked the dog and went back into his tepee.

"I would be holding the horse outside until High Horse could pull up a couple of stakes, crawl inside, gag the girl and drag her out. Then we would put her on the horse in front of him and he would get away from there fast and be happy all his life. The old people might start yelling, but everybody would be too excited to do anything, and I could run to my horse and get away. When High Horse came back, Good Plume would be his woman, and the old man would get used to it.

"When High Horse pulled the first stake, he waited awhile to see if the snoring would stop inside. It did not stop, so he pulled another stake, and still the snoring went on. Then I could see him crawling under. The snoring still went on, and that is all I would hear for a while. Pretty soon something popped, and the old man snorted.

"This is how it was. The old people had only this one girl, and they liked her so much that they had made a fine bed out of rawhide thongs for her to sleep on. Then when they saw how pretty she was getting to be, they were afraid some foolish young man might steal her in the night; so they always tied her with thongs to this bed.

"High Horse was in there feeling around for a good way to grab the girl, and when he knew she was tied, he took his knife and began cutting thongs. When the first one popped and the old man snorted, he was so scared that he dropped on his belly and quit breathing for awhile. Then he began cutting thongs again. His heart drummed so hard that he was afraid it would waken the girl; but she just went right on breathing quietly until he got down around her thighs. Of course he was getting more and more excited by now, and all at once the knife slipped and stuck the girl . . .

"Grandson, it was bad. It was very bad. The girl shrieked, the old man began yelling, the old woman began screaming, and High Horse was getting out of there so fast he nearly knocked the tepee down. By the time we were both on the horse, people were rushing out of their tepees shouting to each other and all the dogs were barking. It was dim starlight, and everybody was so excited that nobody knew what anybody was yelling about; so we got away.

"Next day High Horse was feeling sicker than ever, and even I was feeling a little sick. But I said, 'Brother, we nearly got her that time, and if you are man enough and your knife does not slip, next time we will get her, for I will think up a better plan.' And High Horse groaned and said, 'Maybe they will kill me next time, but I am going to die anyway if I don't get Good Plume, and I am man enough to fight the whole Shyela village if they catch me.' 'Then quit groaning,' I said, 'and have a strong heart, for I have a plan already; only we must wait until the people up there are not excited any more.'

"So we counted ten days and waited; and while we waited we talked about my plan. . . .

"So this is the way it was. When we had counted ten days, we rode far around the Shyela village and came to the creek above it when the sun was low. Then High Horse stripped naked and I began painting him with mud all over. When I was through, he was all crooked stripes and spots, and he looked like some animal nobody ever saw. When he saw himself in the water he said, 'I look so terrible that I scare myself.' And I said, 'You look so terrible you scare even me a little, and I made you. If you get caught, people will think you are some bad spirit and they will run away; so you must not be afraid of anything; and don't let your knife slip this time.'

"When the night was getting old and no dogs barked, we crawled into the Shyela village leading the horse. We did this so slowly that no dog noticed us. There was snoring in the girl's tepee. So High Horse pulled a stake. The snoring went on. Then he crawled in. Pretty soon a thong popped and I heard the old woman say, 'Wake up! Wake up! There is somebody in this tepee!' And the old man said, 'Of course there is somebody in this tepee. I am in this tepee. Go to sleep and don't bother me.' Pretty soon there was snoring again.

"I listened hard for another pop, but there was only snoring—more than before, like two men snoring back and forth at each other. And this is how it was in there.

"When the old woman and old man talked, High Horse lay flat on his belly and stopped breathing for a while. But he was very tired and very weak because he had not slept or eaten much for a long time, he was so sick about the girl. So all at once he was snoring as hard as the old man was.

"I waited and waited. The morning star came up. I waited and waited. There was a thin streak of day. I could not call to High Horse, so I waited. The hills were beginning to stare. Then I got out of there with the horse and hid up the creek in the brush where I had tied Whirlwind.

"Pretty soon all at once there was a big noise—screaming and yelling and barking down there in the village. It was even worse than the other time. Then I could hear somebody running hard, and it was High Horse, coming like an antelope. He was coming up the creek towards me, and he surely looked terrible in the daylight. All at once he dodged into a big hollow tree by the creek, and I could not go to him or call to him because I could hear people coming. It was a party of men with axes and knives and spears and guns. They were looking here and looking there and being very careful because of the terrible thing they had seen running. They stopped close to the hollow tree, and when they could not see any tracks, one said, 'It was a bad spirit that has gone back into the water.' Then they went away, for I think they were glad not to catch what they had chased.

"This is how it happened in the tepee. When the day began to come in through the flap, the girl awoke and looked around. The first thing she saw was that terrible animal sleeping there beside her bed. And that was when the big noise began and High Horse started running.

"I was lying there in the brush now listening, and afterwhile the big noise stopped and I could hear tepee poles coming down. The people were moving camp because of the bad spirit in that place; and when I had waited some more, there was no sound to hear at all, and I knew the people were all gone. So I went to High Horse; and when he came out of his tree he looked so sick and sad and terrible all at once that I had to laugh. Anyway, they had not caught us, and that was good. But High Horse did not laugh any, he just groaned. So I quit laughing, and said, 'Have a strong heart, brother-friend, and when I have washed the mud off, I will think up a better plan.'" (Neihardt 1951:772-783) (Dakota, Wyoming-Nebraska-South Dakota)

THE MARRIAGE OF LEFT HANDED

"My mother was always going out and visiting our relatives, and every time she'd go to where this woman lived. She wanted to get her for me. But I never thought of her. I didn't care for her at all. One day, when she went over there, she saw the woman weaving a nice blanket. She had all different kinds of colored yarn which she'd bought at the store, and that's what she was using. It had a lot of pretty designs. My mother saw the blanket and thought it was very nice, and she found out the woman was a good weaver. . . .

"Sometime after that she went over there again and began talking with the woman. 'I'd like to get you to stay with me. I'm thinking if you'd like to have my son. I'd like to know right now. If you like my son I want you to stay with him. If you do, from there on we'll help each other, and we'll live together. I know all your works and all your weavings. I know you're a good worker and a good weaver. I've been looking for a woman like you, who knows about weaving, but I can't find one. That's what I'm thinking. What do you think about that?'

"The woman said, 'It's all right with me, but I don't think your son cares about me.' . . .

"My mother said, 'Well, what do you think about it? If you say, all right, I'll surely let you have my son.' The woman laughed and said, 'Well, it's up to him. If he likes me I'd like to have him.' Then my mother told her all about me, that I was alone and a single man. She said, 'My son is a good worker. He never goes out for nothing, and he doesn't know anything about gambling, and he never goes around to the singings. He only knows about the sheep, horses and cattle. And he takes good care of himself. He's not like these other men, who don't know anything.'

"She was away all day, over there with this woman. She said to her, 'I want you to stay with my son. Now you go around among your relatives and tell them what I said.' But the woman said, 'My relatives won't say anything about it. It's up to me. I want him very much. And my mother there, she doesn't care, she won't say anything. So now you just go home and bring your son over here.' 'Well,' my mother said, 'that's nice. I'll give you two horses and one bull.' The woman said, 'All right, I'm satisfied.' Then my mother set a date, she said, 'I'll be here in a couple of days.'

"Around evening I came back, and she was home too . . . she said, 'My son, I was over there where that woman lives. I've been staying with her all day. I think she's a good woman. I know she's a good weaver, and she knows a lot of things besides. I asked her if she wanted you, and she said all right. She said she's been wishing for you all this time, and I said to her, "We'll be together. So I want you to stay with my son." I promised her two horses and one bull, and she was satisfied with that, and so I said, "I'll be here with my son in two days." What do you think about it?' But I didn't say anything. She said, 'I think it'll be nice, having this woman here with us, because she's a good worker and a good weaver, and she's got three children. She'll help us a lot. So I want you to stay with her.' I thought, 'What's the matter with my mother? She must be crazy, telling that woman all those things without letting me know. But I didn't say a word. She was talking to herself for a long time, but I didn't bother her at all.

"When she was through talking I said, 'Well, mother, you don't know what you're talking about. You must be getting crazy. You must be a little off, because that woman, whom you want me to have, that woman, I think, is older than I am, and she already has children. And I know she's got a husband too. I've never seen her husband, but I know she's got one.' 'No, my son, I know what I'm talking about. I asked her a lot of questions, and I asked about her husband. She said, "I haven't got a husband. I had one, but I didn't like him, so I let him go. And now I'm all alone, just with my children and my mother." Now, my son, don't say anything, just go and take this woman, because I know they'll help us a lot. You know I'm getting old. I can't do all the work around the home. I can't stand it all. And you're just by yourself, doing all these tasks, and need a lot of help, and so do I.' . . .

"After breakfast the next morning wc turned out the sheep and I went herding. That day my mother went among our relatives and told them what she wanted. They all said, 'That's nice. We'll have a wedding. We'll all be there.' "

(Left Handed marries the woman, lives with her a short time, and

—after meeting a man whom he thinks is her previous husband—leaves her and returns to his mother.)

"A woman and two children came to our place one day. One of the children was her granddaughter. The woman knew all about my wife. She said, 'She's just like a dog. I've known her for a long time. She began going around with men when she was a little girl. She went with Navaho, Whites, Mexicans, Hopi and all the others. That's the kind of woman she is.' She told me all about her. When I heard these things I was so sorry for myself and so ashamed. I felt very badly. Even though I'd left her I didn't want to hear about her, I didn't care to listen. But she kept talking, first about the woman and then about her husband. 'Sure enough, that was her husband. Before she married him he never had a wife at all. He used to go among the horses. So when they found him with the horses they gave him a name. His name is Horse's Ass. You've been with Horse's Ass's Wife.' When I heard this it almost killed me. The rest I hadn't paid any attention to, though I felt badly about it, but this last was the worst. . . .

"Then she (his mother) began to tell me about the woman who was staying with us. She said, 'This woman said she'll leave her granddaughter here with us.' She was a pretty girl about eleven years of age, but I didn't let her say much about it. 'I don't care to hear about those things,' I said. 'The girl is too young, and she might be worse than the other one. So I don't like to hear about it.' She quit talking about it then and let it go. . . .

" 'It's no use for me to get married, because I've got so much to do for myself and my mother, and I've got to tend to my sheep, horses and cattle. So I don't want to monkey with a woman. It's nothing to me. They're good for nothing. That's the way I'm thinking about them. If I get a woman she'll be holding me tight, and everything I've got now will all have disappeared, and I won't ever know where it's gone. So I'd like to be alone. I like to be single. Then I can go anywhere I want to. And I don't want to leave my mother, and I don't want to leave all my stock. That's the way I am. So don't talk to me about it. . . .' " (Dyk 1938:299-332) (Navaho, Arizona-New Mexico)

THE MARRIAGE OF SUN CHIEF

"One day when I had returned from the surveyors' camp and was eating supper, my old pal Louis came from Moenkopi. We welcomed each other heartily, and he said that he had missed me sorely and was determined to find me, even though I hid myself in the ground like a prairie dog. That evening he was as eager to go out among the girls as ever and asked me to suggest one. I told him that I was not familiar with any girls in Oraibi and did not like it so well for that reason. Louis said, 'I have made love with Iola of the Fire Clan before, but now she does not like me very well.' I knew that she was staying with her clan sister, Irene, whose parents had gone to the field house at Loloma Spring. Since we could think of no other available lovers, Louis said, 'Let's take these girls by force.' I discouraged it and told him that I had never used force on any girl, that I had never been familiar with Irene, and that I might get into trouble. I knew that Irene was marriageable for me but I did not know whether she wanted me or not. I argued that since Louis had had Iola before, he could get away with it, but that it was too risky for me to try forcing Irene. But Louis urged until I finally agreed.

"We found the girls grinding corn and decided to sneak into Irene's house and wait in the dark. Finally, as the two entered, Louis grabbed Iola and blew out the light. I caught hold of Irene and quickly assured her that she had nothing to fear. She remained still and quiet; but Iola struggled with Louis for a while, then stopped, and became very friendly. They went off into a corner. I put my arms around Irene, drew her to me, and said, 'What is in your mind?' 'Have you asked your parents about this?' she inquired. 'No, but I will shortly,' I answered. We talked softly for a while and when we heard Louis and Iola at lovemaking, I begged Irene urgently with words of love and promises of marriage. Finally she said, 'It is up to you.' Then I led her, with a sheepskin, to another corner of the room where she remained passive but very sweet. After some time she said, 'Now you must ask your parents about our marrying. Let's go and leave this terrible man, Louis.' I told her to be a good girl, gave her a nice bracelet, slipped out, went to the roof of my mother's house, and lay down to sleep out under the stars.

"The next day was Sunday. And since I was working for the government, I went down to the store at New Oraibi, hung around, and 'kept the Sabbath Day holy.' I had a good job now, and I thought some of marriage. When I returned from the surveyors' camp Monday evening, Irene's parents were home. After supper I went to their house. They offered me food, and the father later asked if there was anything he could do for me. Then I asked for the hand of Irene. He replied: 'My daughter is not a good-looking girl. If your relatives are willing, you may have her.' I told him that I had my parents' consent and that they were well pleased. This was a lie, but a necessary one in order to spend the night with Irene. They agreed and arranged for us to have the next room. We had a very good time. I reminded her of our train ride and how she later teased me about Polehongsie and asked her whether she wanted me as a lover then. She laughed and said that she did, but that I had another girl and, after all, it was my business to ask her first. She asked, 'What would you have done if I had proposed to you?' I told her that I would have clapped my hands for joy. Then we kissed without limit. All our talk was sweet and I thought there could never be an argument between us. At cockcrow I went home for a nap on the old roof.

"At breakfast I raised the subject of marriage. 'I spent the night at Huminquima's,' I said. 'And now I want to marry his daughter, Irene.' 'What did they say?' asked my mother. I assured her that Irene's parents had already agreed. My brother Ira smiled. He was engaged to Blanche, Irene's clan sister, and expected to be married in the fall. My father spoke: 'Well, I won't object, for then you would think I am against you. You are not a good-looking man, and she is not a beautiful woman, so I think you will stay together and treat each other fairly. A good-looking woman neglects her husband, because it is so easy to get another.' My spirit was high when I left for work. Riding down the mesa, I waved to Irene, let out a war whoop, beat my horse into a gallop, and thought that I would always be happy. . . .

"One day the news circulated that Ira was getting married in November, and that my turn would follow four days later, making a double wedding. Both our girls belonged to the Masau'u or Fire Clan, and their people made this plan. My brother was worried and complained, 'Our father is poor and cannot afford a double wedding. What shall we do?' Then he remembered that our great-uncle, Talasquaptewa, had approved of our marriages and said, 'Perhaps he will buy a buckskin for one of us or give us some sheep for the wedding feast.' I replied, 'If he doesn't, we will refuse to herd for him.' My father took $30 or $40 of my money to help buy the buckskins.

"One evening after the crops were harvested, Ira's girl, Blanche, was brought to our house by her mother. She ground corn meal on her knees for three days, remaining in the house most of the time, but Ira was not permitted to sleep with her. I herded and was told to keep away from Irene because she was grinding white corn meal at her house for our family.

"On the evening of the third day the female relatives of Blanche's clan came to our house and spent the night. I stayed away, sleeping with Dennis. Early in the morning these women washed Ira's head, and our female relatives washed the bride's head, placed the bride's and groom's hair together in one bowl of yucca suds, and twisted it into one strand, believing that this would cause them to cleave to each other like the meat on a clingstone peach. Our women bathed the girl's arms and legs, and her female relatives removed all Ira's clothes except his loin-cloth, and bathed him thoroughly. Then Ira and Blanche went to the east edge of the mesa to pray at sunrise. The new bride spent the day grinding corn and baking *piki*. That night Ira slept with her in our house.

"On the following morning Iola, the sister of Dennis, called me, 'Get up and go see what is in your house. I hear you have a pet eagle.' I found Irene grinding corn with all her might. She had been brought there by her mother the night before. As I stood in the door and watched her, I felt as though I were dreaming and scratched my head, seeking for words. My mother smiled and said, 'Talayevsa, don't be foolish.' I went out sheepishly, returned to my sleeping place, yanked the cover from Dennis, who was still asleep, and said, 'Get up, lazybones, it is your turn next. I am now a man with a wife.' Iola teased me, claiming that I ran around with other women so much that my relatives had to marry me off. I did not show up again at my mother's house all day. Later Irene told me that she was worried about this.

"The aunts of my father's clan, and of my ceremonial and doctor father's clans, ganged up and staged a big mud fight with the men of my family. They caught my grandfather, Homikniwa, and plastered him with mud from head to foot. They also poured mud and water all over my father and tried to cut his hair for letting me marry into the Fire Clan. They made all manner of fun of Irene, calling her crosseyed, lazy, dirty, and a poor cook, and praised me highly, asserting that they would like to have me for a husband. Dear old Masenimka, my godmother, threw mud on my father and uncles and said that she wanted me for her lover. This mud fight was to show that they were very fond of me, and that they thought Irene was making a good choice.

"On the third day I began worrying about my coming bath, for I was very ticklish and did not know whether I could stand still under the hands of so many women. A little after sundown my mother told Irene to stop grinding the blue corn and sit by the fire on a soft seat. I had not seen much of her since she came to our house, and when we had spoken it was usually in a whisper. Soon her relatives came to spend the night—the same women who had stripped and bathed Ira. I thought I had never seen so many women and even those whom I had known all my life seemed a little strange to me. I had little to say all evening, and at bedtime I took my blanket and started out. My father said, 'Wait a minute, Talayesva. Where are you sleeping? I want to be able to find you in the morning.' When I told him that I was sleeping with Dennis, he replied, 'Be sure to leave the door unlocked so that I can wake you early.' I was worried. When I reached my sleeping place, Iola looked at me and laughed. Dennis offered encouragement by telling me that he was in the same trap and had to get married soon. We discussed this problem until midnight. I reconciled myself by saying, 'Well, we have to stand and take it. If we run off, the people will call us Kahopi.'

"My father struck a match and said, 'Get up, son, and come quickly. They are preparing the yucca suds.' Then he woke Dennis and asked him to see that I started. As I dressed to go, Dennis said, 'You are now on your way to the happy life, you old married man.' When I entered the house, I saw many eyes staring at me. There were Irene's mother and her sisters, Blanche's mother and her relatives, in fact all the women of the Fire Clan, also the women of the Coyote and Water-Coyote clans, and most of my real and ceremonial aunts. They had assembled to give me a bath. My mother was assisting Irene's mother with the yucca suds. I was so timid that I took steps not more than an inch long. My mother said, 'Hurry up.' I laid back my shirt collar and knelt with Irene before a bowl of yucca suds. My relatives washed Irene's head and her relatives washed mine. Then they poured all the suds into one bowl, put our heads together, mixed our hair and twisted it into one strand to unite us for life. Many women rinsed our hair by pouring cold water over it. When it was completed, Irene's mother told me to take off my clothes. I felt so uncertain about my loincloth that I made an excuse to go out, ran behind the house, and checked it carefully. When I had returned and undressed, Irene's mother led me outside. My real aunts tried to bathe me first in fun, and scuffled with Irene's relatives. Then Irene's mother bathed me from tip to toe. All the women took their turn bathing me, while I stood shivering in the cold. I had to appear gentle and kindhearted and say to each of them, 'I thank you very much.' They assured me that they had washed away all remaining traces of youth and had prepared my flesh for married manhood.

"I hurried into the house, wrapped myself in a blanket, and stood until Irene's relatives told me to sit down near the fire. Irene's hair was arranged in the married woman's style, and her mother advised her to be a good housewife. Irene and I took a pinch of sacred corn meal, went to the east edge of the mesa, held the meal to our lips, prayed silently, and sprinkled it toward the rising sun. We returned to the house in silence and my mother and sister prepared our breakfast. Before Irene's mother left, she built a fire under the *piki* stone. After breakfast Irene made batter and began baking *piki*.

"I returned to Dennis' house for a few minutes. He shouted our football yell, felt my wet head, and said, 'Now you are a married man, stay on your side.' 'Yes,' I replied, 'all our pleasures are over.' . . .

"One day I went to the post office with Chief Tewaquiaptewa and received five letters. . . . The fifth letter was from my old girl Mettie, which said:

'My dear Friend:

'I am heartbroken to hear of your marriage. I cry myself to sleep every night and wish that I could leave school. You were my lover first, and when I return home, I shall have you again in spite of your wife and all the gossip in the village. You will never get away from me.

Your loving friend,
Mettie.'

"When I read that, I raised my head for a long breath. The Chief asked, 'What is the matter, Don?' 'In this letter,' I replied, 'Mettie says that I will always be hers.' I read it to him. He smiled and said, 'I think she means just that. When she comes home, I would go to see her and cheer her up.' I think I would have been more excited over my wedding if she had been the bride. . . .

"The brides and their relatives prepared food to bring to our house in the evening. About sunset they came with their mothers, bringing a large tub filled with food. When they returned to their houses, our own relatives were invited to come and eat. That was the occasion for giving us advice. Our great-uncle, Talasquaptewa, spoke first: 'Thank you, my nephews. You are not very good-looking, and I thought you were never going to marry. I am glad that you have chosen such fine wives. You know every woman hates a lazy man, so you must work hard and assist your new fathers in the field and with the herding. When they find that you are good helpers, they will be pleased and treat you like real sons. When you kill game, or find spinach or other food plants in the fields, bring them to your wives. They will receive them gladly. Make believe that your wife is your real mother. Take good care of her, treat her fairly, and never scold her. If you love your wife, she will love you, give you joy, and feed you well. Even when you are worried and unhappy, it will pay you to show a shining face to her. If your married life is a failure, it will be your own fault. Please prove yourselves to be men worthy of your clan.'

"The next day my parents killed two more sheep, made a stew, and took a large tub of food to our wives' homes. Irene and Blanche invited all their relatives to come and eat, and it was then that their uncles advised them on their family duties.

"After the feast in the brides' houses, it was time for them and their relatives to prepare corn-meal gifts in exchange for the wedding costumes. The brides and their relatives ground corn for many days. Little girls seven and eight years old helped with the grinding. Many heaping plaques of fine corn meal were taken to our house—perhaps twenty bushels—to be distributed among the relatives who had assisted us. This completed the wedding obligations.

"It is customary for the groom to decide when he will move into his wife's house.[1] I remained at my house for about two weeks, visiting Irene every night. Ira stayed three weeks longer. It was necessary for me to go live with Irene early, because her father, Huminquima, was not a very good worker. Before I went, I hauled wood for them like a dutiful son-in-law. I also took part in the Soyal ceremony, observing the rules of continence. After the Soyal I borrowed Frank's team and wagon and went for an extra large load of wood without telling Irene. I returned late in the afternoon, stopped the wagon at my wife's door, and unhitched. Irene's mother shelled corn for my horses while I unloaded the wood. Irene came to the door and asked me how I would like my eggs. I thought of sneaking home, but, knowing that would never do, I

[1] The Hopi are matrilineal and matrilocal.

timidly entered the house and ate a little of the scrambled eggs. I soon remarked that I was not very hungry, and hurried out with the shelled corn, feeling that the Fire Clan were very high-tone people. Taking the wagon to my home, I asked my mother for a square meal, which caused her to laugh. About sunset, as I returned from hobbling the horses, Irene came to our house calling, 'Come and eat.' She invited all my family—according to custom—but they properly declined. I meekly followed my wife to her home and sat down with the family to a dish of hot tamales wrapped in corn-husks and tied with yucca stems. But I ate so slowly that Irene's mother unwrapped tamales and placed them in a row before me. I thought, 'This old lady is very kindhearted, perhaps she will do this for me always.' But I was mistaken; at breakfast I had to unwrap my own tamales, and was put to work for my wife's people." (Simmons 1942:212-222) (Hopi, Arizona)

Mate Choice

Why do people marry? Some are smitten by love, like High Horse. Others, like Don Talayesva, drift into marriage. Still others, like Left Handed or Crashing Thunder, are pushed into marriage.

The reasons for marriage depend, to some extent, on who chooses the spouse. If people are free to choose their own spouses, then individual motives come into play: romantic love, sexual desire, loneliness, desire for children and full adult status, or more exotic motives. (One motive for marriage among the Siwai is the desire to raise one's own pigs.) In many societies, people are often *not* free to decide whom they will marry; marriages are "arranged" by their parents and kinsmen. In these cases you find other incentives and criteria for choice, such as the size of the bride price, the reputation of the potential spouse's kin group, levirate and sororate obligations, and traditions of continuous marriage arrangements.

Where there is free mate choice, it is usually preceded by courtship. When marriage is "arranged," on the other hand, the only preliminaries are the negotiations between the two kin groups; sometimes bride and groom do not even meet until the day of their marriage (China, Hindu India, Japan).

Before I begin to discuss arranged marriage, I will give two examples of courtship in other societies. In the first example—the town of Tepoztlan in Mexico—courtship is very stilted and formal. In the second example—the Iban of Borneo—courtship is informal and intimate.

TEPOZTLAN, MEXICO

The first step in courting is to send the girl a letter declaring love. . . .[2]

Young people who are unable to write well ask a friend with more education to do it for them. Girls and boys who have been to secondary school are particularly sought out as letter writers, and they derive a great deal of prestige in this way. The letters are written in flowery style and are usually copied out of a book of etiquette. A typical letter is the following:

"Adored Senorita:

"The impulses of my heart are such that they encourage even the most cautious man to commit indiscretion which sooner or later he will regret. Perhaps this will not happen to me in taking the liberty of writing this letter. My feelings are such that I am taking the liberty in order to ascertain my coming fate, pending the day when you honor me with your affirmative or negative response.

"My soul is carried to the extreme in manifesting in exaggerated phrases, which are lacking in substance and sound, the love that you inspire. But do not think that because of this I do not feel a true passion for your incomparable beauty and goodness. The proof is that, despite the fear that my petition will be denied, I tremulously write this declaration and anxiously await the result, hoping that my love will be requited.

"Favour me, Senorita, and attend my entreaty; and if, unutterable words, you feel a little sympathy toward one so audacious as to love you tenderly, communicate with me quickly and in all sincerity.

"With all the sentiment which invades the heart of your respectful and constant adorer.

"Your devoted servant,"

A boy may send two or three such letters anonymously before he has the courage to affix his name. If a favourable reply is re-

[2] Apparently, this is done before the boy ever meets the girl or talks to her.

ceived, the boy arranges for a meeting. Any answer but an outright refusal is taken to be favourable. (Lewis 1951:401)

In contrast, here is courtship among the Iban or "Dyak":

IBAN, BORNEO

The mode of courtship among the Dyaks is peculiar. No courting goes on by day, but at night, when all is quiet, a young lover creeps to the side of the curtain of his ladylove, and awakes her. The girls sleep apart from their parents—sometimes in the same room, but more often in the loft. He presents her with a roll of *sireh* leaf, in which is wrapped the betel-nut ingredients the Dyaks love to chew.

If, when awakened, the girl accepts the betel-nut roll which the young man presents her, and puts it in her mouth, it is a sign that his visit is acceptable, and that he may stay and speak to her. If, on the other hand, she says, "Please blow up the fire," or "Be good enough to light the lamp" (which is usually bamboo filled with resin), it shows that she will have nothing to say to him, and he recognizes the usual form of dismissal and goes away.

If the lover's visit be acceptable to her, they chew *sireh* and betel-nut, a plentiful supply of which the man brings with him, and make arrangements about the future. This nocturnal visiting goes on for some weeks. If the parents of the girl think the match a suitable one, the young people are permitted to see each other very often. On the other hand, if the young man does not find favour with them, they soon let him know that his visits are not desired. They do not allow their daughter to see him alone, and the matter goes no farther.

This nightly courtship is, in fact, the only way a man and woman can become acquainted with each other, for such a thing as privacy during the day is quite unknown in a Dyak house. If the girl be pleased with her lover, he remains with her until close upon daybreak, when he leaves with her some article as a pledge of his honour, such as a bead necklace, or ring, or a headkerchief, or anything else which he may have about him. This act of leaving some gift with the girl is considered as a betrothal between the two parties, and the man who refuses to marry the girl after doing so is considered guilty of breach of promise of marriage, and liable, according to Dyak law, to a fine.

I have often spoken to older Dyaks about the matter, and have been told by them that these nocturnal visits very seldom result in immorality. The girl who is not careful how she behaves very soon gets a bad name among the young men, and all her chances of securing a husband are lost. And it is a fact that, considering the population, there are not many illegitimate children among the Dyaks.

When the young couple have decided the question of the future to their mutual satisfaction, the next step in the proceedings is for the man to make known his wishes to his own parents, and then a visit is paid by the man's relatives and friends to the girl's parents to request formally the hand of their daughter in marriage. This consent is seldom refused, because as a rule the parents of the girl approve her choice, or they would not have allowed her to receive visits from the man. (Gomes 1911:120–121)

Arranged Marriage

Many people, in a good many societies, have little if anything to say about whom they will marry. Women, more than men, are particularly likely to be helpless pawns in the marriage plans of their parents and kin (Kipsigis, Kurtachi, Tibet, Papago, Pukapuka, Lepcha, Ancient Anglo-Saxons). Young, previously unmarried men are also apt to have little choice, although if they marry again later in life, when they are financially independent, they stand a better chance of choosing their own wives (Kipsigis, Lepcha, Chukchee, Tibet, Pukapuka). Here are some quotations illustrating marriage-by-coercion:

KWAKIUTL, VANCOUVER ISLAND

"When I was old enough to get a wife—I was about twenty-five—my brother looked for a girl in the same position that I and my brothers had. Without my consent, they picked a wife for me—Lagius' daughter. The one I wanted was prettier than the one they chose for me, but she was in a lower position than me, so they wouldn't let me marry her. I argued about it and was very angry with my brother, but I couldn't do anything . . . Anyway, my older brother made arrangements for my marriage. He gave Lagius, the head chief of the Nimkis, two hundred blankets to keep Lagius from letting others have his daughter." (Ford 1941:149)

BAIGA, INDIA

"In Dadargaon I was forcibly married to Marru. None of us wanted the marriage. I was too young, only ten years old, and my father didn't like Marru. But my brother Chaitu had run away with Marru's wife, and Marru said that he must have a girl in return. So I was married to him, but I never went to him or even touched him." (Elwin 1939:136)

TEPOZTLAN, MEXICO

"I was eleven years old when a boy came from Gabriel Mariaca to ask for my hand. He came with his parents and a jar of silver money. But my grandmother became angry and told them I was still a child, and she didn't want to see me going about carrying babies yet. When I was twelve my mother took me home again. Then a boy of sixteen came to ask for me, and my mother said yes. She told me that she wanted me to marry before something bad happened to me. I did not want to marry, especially because I did not know who the boy was. My mother said that if I did not say yes to the priest in the church she would throw me from the top of the church. I was afraid and did what my mother told me." (Lewis 1955:399)[3]

LEPCHA, SIKKIM

It sometimes happens that after *asek* has been performed the boy and girl feel a really strong repulsion for one another. In many cases a girl will simulate repulsion and will refuse to let her groom sleep with her; but this is thought to be chiefly due to shame and to dislike of having to leave her parents' home; and therefore the young people are cajoled and bribed and threatened and even sometimes beaten to make them like one another. (Gorer 1938:157)

PUKAPUKA, POLYNESIA

A man set on marrying a girl who at first refuses him makes frequent and regular presents of fish, nuts, taro, even fishhooks, to her parents, and helps them at every opportunity in house build-

---

[3] In Tepoztlan courtship is a recent innovation. Arranged marriage was the old custom.

ing, canoe making, etc. The parents soon realize his object. They talk to their daughter, telling her she ought to marry the man. If the girl refuses, they give her a thrashing, saying that as they have accepted all the presents, they will be shamed before the whole island if she does not pay this indebtedness. Willing or unwilling, the girl is thus taken to the man. If she later runs away, she is dragged back to her husband. If she remains recalcitrant, girl, husband, and parents fight it out until one or the other decides to give in. (Beaglehole and Beaglehole 1938:296)

Who arranges these "arranged marriages"? Who has the power to decide whom a person will marry? Leach says:

. . . the social groups which "arrange" such a marriage between themselves are, in almost all societies, of essentially the same kind. The core of such a group is composed of the adult males of a kin group all resident in one place. By this I do not mean to argue that women have no part to play in the arrangement of a marriage or that remotely situated kinsfolk are wholly ignored; I merely mean that the corporate group of persons who have the most decisive say in bringing about an arranged marriage is always a group of co-resident males representing, as a rule, three genealogical generations, namely: the old men or grandfathers, the normal adults or fathers, and the young adults or sons. (Leach 1951:24)

The ethnographic literature does not contain very specific information on this issue. For six cases in my ethnographic notes, the "father" is said to arrange the marriage: Ancient Anglo-Saxons, Ancient Hebrews, Ashanti, Ireland (County Clare), Kipsigis, and Ojibwa. For two cases, it is "the parents": Muria and Tepoztlan. For three cases, it is "the parents" with the help of a matchmaker or go-between: China (Taitou), Japan, and Subanum. For the Cheyenne, it is the parents and the girl's brother. For two cases, it is the parents and elder male relatives: Lepcha and Hindu India (Rajputs of Khalapur and Deoli). Finally, for the Navaho it is "parents and other relatives."

In arranged marriage, what are the criteria for choice? As far as I can gather, a family or kin group may choose a spouse for its child for any one of four main reasons. The first reason is bridewealth considerations. As we shall see presently, bride-price finance is a really major affair in many societies, and a great economic crisis for many families—comparable to buying or selling a house in our own society. Bride price means heavy expense for the boy's people; for the girl's people, it means one of life's main chances for economic gain. (With dowry payments, the situation is reversed.) Also, bridewealth payments are often continuous, stretching over many years, and involve various social and work obligations that are not directly financial. Although I know of no ethnography in which this is specifically discussed, I imagine these considerations may enter into mate choice. The "selling group" (usually the bride's family and kin, but not always) wants to get as much as it can, and the "buying group" wants to avoid too extreme economic burdens.

A second criterion for mate choice in arranged marriage may be the reputation of the potential spouse's parents and/or kin group. This may be in terms of social status. For example, in the Kwakiutl illustration just given, Charley (the informant) says, "They picked a wife for me—Lagius' daughter. The one I wanted was prettier than the one they chose for me, but she was in a lower position than me, so they wouldn't let me marry her." (Ford 1941: 149) Or, the reputation may be in terms of other human qualities, which should lead to pleasant affinal ties. Among the Arapesh, Mead says, the bride ". . . should have the right kind of relatives, many male kindred, men who are good hunters, successful gardeners, slow to anger and wise in making choices." (Mead 1935)

A third determinant of mate choice in cases of arranged marriage is continuous marriage arrangements, particularly those resulting from cross-cousin marriage. We saw an example of this in the last chapter, in the quotation describing the mother's brother (*gawel*) = sister's son (*waku*) reciprocal among the Murngin of Australia:

> When a *gawel* gives his daughter to his sister's son, this is not merely a gift, for the *waku* by tribal law has a right to her and would fight for her if the *gawel* tried to give her to someone else. He would also feel that he had the right to *gawel's* second daughter and the privilege of declining the offer of a third. There would

be an obligation, too, on *gawel* to give his *waku* another wife if the first were barren or died before giving birth to a child. If a *waku's* wife runs away from him his *gawel* would under almost any circumstances do everything possible to get her back for the husband. If he did not, he would feel obligated to give the *waku* another daughter in her place. (Warner 1937:95)

A final determinant for mate choice is sororate and levirate arrangements. These are a sort of extension of bride-price legality. The idea usually seems to be that the bride has been purchased; therefore, if she dies prematurely, runs away, or perhaps—as in the Murngin example above—is barren, she must be replaced by the family or kin group which received the bride price.[4] Also, since the wife has been purchased, she may be inherited like any other property. (From the bride's point of view, this means that *her* husband will also be automatically replaced when he dies.) As Frake says: "In essence, the levirate and sororate custom means that the families of orientation of new spouses assume the obligation of guaranteeing the longevity of their married child by agreeing to substitute a sibling, or, if necessary, another person, if their child dies." (Frake 1955:180) *Sororate* is the replacement of a defunct wife by her sister or other female kin. *Levirate* is the inheritance of a dead man's wife by his brother or other male kin. Both the sororate and levirate are common in primitive societies. In Murdock's sample (1949), the levirate was reported present for 127 societies and absent for 58 societies; the sororate was reported present for 100 cases, and absent for 59 (Murdock 1949:29). We have already seen an example of the sororate, in the Murngin illustration just given. Here are some descriptions of the levirate:

LEPCHA, SIKKIM

In Lepcha theory the husband's group purchases the wife, as is explicitly recognized in the term "price of the bride"; . . . therefore if the husband dies the wife is still the property of his group, and can be married to another member of the same group

---

[4] Apparently, the Murngin equivalent of bride price is the presents that *waku* gives to *gawel* throughout his lifetime.

without further reference to her parents, though on such occasions the wife's parents are actually given small courtesy gifts. In theory too the wife has no right to refuse the man offered in the place of her dead husband, or, if she feels an unconquerable repulsion, her group should supply a second woman to replace her. Similarly if the husband wishes to refuse the wife he has inherited he should supply another man in place of himself. In practice these regulations are not always carried out, and relatively seldom if the woman is childless; if the heritable spouse really dislikes her inheritor no compulsion is used to force her to marry him, nor are there any sanctions for this. (Gorer 1938:159)

REINDEER CHUKCHEE, SIBERIA

With group-marriage we find, among the Chukchee, the custom of levirate, according to which, after the death of one of several brothers, the next oldest becomes his successor. He takes care of the wife and children of the deceased, finds for them a dwelling in his camps, and acts as husband to the woman and as father to the children. The herd he unites with his own, but keeps it for the children of the deceased. When, however, the difference in age is very great, the brother does not exercise his levirate right, in order not to enter into marital relations with an old woman. In the absence of brothers, the levirate passes to cousins. It should be noted that levirate often has the character of a duty rather than that of a right. A woman left without a husband with her children and a herd to attend to, needs a protector; and the obligation to assist her falls on the nearest relative. . . . In case of need, even the nephew uses the right of levirate in regard to his widowed aunt; but the uncle is forbidden to do the same with the widow of his nephew. (Bogoras 1909:608)

MURNGIN, AUSTRALIA

The junior levirate is a prominent mechanism. When an older brother dies the brother next in age and consanguinity receives his wives and becomes father to the children. This is not only a privilege, but a duty. Frequently wives thus acquired, being past the age of bearing children or gathering food, are really an economic liability to the heir; yet he must take and look after them.

If *wawa* (Elder Brother) has four or five wives, he may say to a single *yukiyoyo* (Younger Brother), "You see that one—you take her and feed her." *Yukiyoyo* says, if *wawa* is an old man, "No, you are an old man. I'll wait until you die, then I'll have them all." *Wawa* replies, "No, you take her now, *yukiyoyo*. I have many wives and you have none." (Warner 1937:62)

So much for the levirate and sororate, and for the various reasons for arranged marriage. Before leaving the subject of arranged marriage, I must mention child betrothal and child marriage. With child betrothal, a child is promised or pledged to another group or individual as a potential spouse. An infant may be betrothed, or even an unborn child, (Reindeer Chukchee, Lesu, Murngin, Siwai, Toda, Trobriands). Sometimes these child-betrothals are not binding; when he grows up a child can "break his engagement" (Copper Eskimo, Fiji, Kwoma, Wogeo). In other cases, such as the English case we shall see presently, an actual marriage ceremony is performed over children. Nineteen societies in my ethnographic notes are said to have child betrothal or child marriage: Arapesh, China (Taitou), Reindeer Chukchee, Copper Eskimo, Fiji, Ifaluk, Kurtachi, Kwoma, Lepcha, Lesu, Murngin, Muria, Renaissance Europe, Siwai, Subanum, Tchambuli, Toda, Trobriands, and Wogeo. Here are three examples:

ARAPESH, NEW GUINEA

Before the little girl has become conscious of her sex, while she is still a slim, unformed child, the eyes of the fathers and uncles of other clans are upon her, judging her gently as a possible wife for one of their stripling lads. As it is upon the small girl that choice falls, it is about small girls that the Arapesh are most romantic; young men will comment with enthusiasm upon the feminine charm of a five-year-old, and sit about entranced by the coquettishness of some baby whose mother, for amusement, has decked her out in a grass skirt. There is no sexual emphasis in this choice; to regard children as sexual objects would be incredible to the Arapesh. It is merely that after girls are nine or ten years of age they are no longer possible objects of choice, either by one's self or for one's son, but are instead the betrothed wives of others. Not until a girl becomes a widow will she again be a person upon whose desirability one can speculate. And so mothers occasionally deck out their tiny daughters, and the conversation of a group of big boys is hushed for a moment as a small girl flips by, rustling her stiff little skirts. (Mead 1935)

REINDEER CHUKCHEE, SIBERIA

Most of the marriages between relatives are concluded at a tender age, sometimes when the bridegroom and bride are still infants. The marriage ritual is performed, and the children grow up, playing together. When a little older, they tend the herd together. Of course, the ties between them grow to be very strong, often stronger even than death: when one dies, the other also dies from grief, or commits suicide. . . .

I was told of a boy of two, who was still being nursed, and who had lost his mother. She had died of influenza. Since the family wanted a woman worker, the infant boy was almost immediately married to a full-grown girl. In due time the bride bore a child from a marriage-companion. When she was nursing her own child, she also nursed her infant husband. Chukchee boys are often nursed until five or six years old. (Bogoras 1909:577–578)

RENAISSANCE ENGLAND

Thus we find the case of one Elizabeth Hulse, married at four years of age to George Hulse, aged eleven, and seeking a divorce in the Bishop's court on the ground that "she could never fansie or cast favour to hym, nor never will do. . . ." The children were married in the chapel of Knotisford and on the girl being asked how she, a mere infant, knew of this fact, "she sais she knowis not, but bie the sayenge of her father and mother, forther, she sais, she was married to hym biecause he frendes thought she shuld have had a lyvinge bie hym." (Goodsell 1915: 258–259)

Frequency and Distribution of the Forms of Mate Choice, and Elopement

There are three main forms of mate choice: 1) arranged marriage; 2) free mate choice by one or both of the potential spouses, subject to the parents' consent; and 3) absolutely free mate choice, the parent's consent being unnecessary. In my ethnographic notes there are only five cases (in addition to our own society) in which absolutely free mate choice is customarily permitted. Six additional societies allow free mate choice subject to parents' or elders' approval. In twelve other societies, some marriages are arranged and others are the result of free mate choice (usually subject to parents' consent). Finally, for sixteen societies only arranged marriage (and occasional elopement) is mentioned. (See Table 1.)

All of these forms of mate choice have occurred in the history of Western society. There are records of arranged marriage for the Old Testament Hebrews, for the Anglo-Saxon tribes, and for Renaissance Europe (Goodsell 1915:186, 258; Reiss 1960:42). In the American Colonies, the parents' approval was frequently required even before courtship could begin (Goodsell 1915:357). And, of course, modern-day America follows the rather unusual custom of absolutely free mate choice.

What determines the forms of mate choice? Why should arranged marriage be so common, and free choice be relatively uncommon? My guess is that the form of mate choice is in part a function of extended kinship: when large kin groups are strong and important, then marriage tends to be a kin-group affair—it is taken out of the hands of the potential bride and groom. Table 1 shows some evidence that supports this view. In Table 1, I have correlated form of mate choice with two indices of the importance of kin groups: presence of unilineal kin groups; and presence of extended family households as the norm for a society. Table 1 shows a decided though imperfect tendency for marriage to be either arranged or by parents' consent when either unilineal kin groups or frequent extended-family households are present.

A good many societies with arranged marriage or marriage-by-parents'-approval do offer a "way out" for deviant individuals with strong personal preferences. For fourteen of the societies just cited, there is mention of institutionalized *elopement*—a more-or-less approved means by which determined individuals can disobey their elders and choose their own mates (Fiji, Gusii, Iban, Cheyenne, Kwoma, Mundugumor, Muria, Murngin, Ojibwa, Peyrane, Samoa, Siwai, Subanum and Tepoztlan). Elopement usually involves "running off," then waiting and hoping that the

TABLE 1
MATE CHOICE COMPARED WITH PRESENCE OF UNILINEAL KIN GROUPS AND EXTENDED FAMILY HOUSEHOLDS

Form of Mate Choice	Society	Unilineal Kin Groups Present	Extended family Households the Norm
Free mate choice, parents' approval not necessary:	Ifugao	no	no
	Jamaica	no	no
	Kaingang	no	no
	Barranquitas (Puerto Rico)	no	no
	San Pedro la Laguna (Guatemala)	no	?
	United States (Modern)	no	no
Free mate choice, parents' approval necessary:	Colonial America	no	?
	Hopi	yes	yes
	Iban	no	yes
	Peyrane (France)	no	no
	Samoa	no	yes
	Trobriands	yes	no
Both arranged marriage and free mate choice practiced:	Alor	yes	no
	Fiji	yes	yes
	Kaska	yes	no
	Kurtachi	yes	no
	Kwoma	yes	no
	Lepcha	yes	yes
	Murngin	yes	no
	Navaho	yes	no
	Ojibwa	yes	no
	Tikopia	yes	no
	Tepoztlan	no	?
	Wogeo	yes	no
Arranged marriage:	Anglo-Saxons	no	?
	Ashanti	yes	no
	Cheyenne	yes	no
	China (Taitou)	yes	yes
	Hindu India (Rajputs)	yes	yes
	Ireland (County Clare)	no	yes
	Hebrews (Old Testament)	yes	?
	Japan	no	yes
	Kipsigis	yes	no
	Muria	yes	?
	Mundugumor	yes	no
	Papago	yes	yes
	Pukapuka	yes	no
	Siwai	yes	no
	Subanum	no	no
	Tibet	yes	yes

marriage will finally be approved. To conclude this section, here is a description of elopement among the Iban:

IBAN, BORNEO

> When a young woman is in love with a man who is not acceptable to her parents, there is an old custom called *nunghop bui*, which permits him to carry her off to his own village. She will meet him by arrangement at the waterside, and step into his boat with a paddle in her hand, and both will pull away as fast as they can. If pursued he will stop every now and then to deposit some article of value on the bank, such as a gun, a jar, or a favor for the acceptance of her family, and when he has exhausted his resources he will leave his own sword. When the pursuers observe this they cease to follow, knowing he is cleared out. As soon as he reaches his own village he tidies up the house and spreads the mats, and when his pursuers arrive he gives them food to eat and toddy to drink, and sends them home satisfied. In the meanwhile he is left in possession of his wife. (Roth 1891:131)

Love

> "He loved every thread that sewed my frock. . . ." (Jamaica) (Clarke 1957:109)

> . . . there are very few societies in which young people are allowed a free hand in choosing their mates. Marriage brings the families on both sides into a series of new relationships, and it is natural that they should take an active interest in it. The commonest method[5] of solving the difficulty is to allow a limited choice among partners whom the family considers desirable. Actually, such an arrangement entails no great hardship. It does not agree with our own patterns of romantic love, yet it is interesting to speculate on how far these patterns are themselves a result of culture. The concept of romantic love did not appear in Europe until the time of the thirteenth century troubadours, and these experts ruled at first that it was impossible to married people. Even as late as the eighteenth century it played a very small part in European marriage. All societies recognize that there are occasional violent emotional attachments between persons of opposite sex, but our

[5] Doubtful.

present American culture is practically the only one which has attempted to capitalize these and make them the basis of marriage. Most groups regard them as unfortunate and point out the victims of such attachments as horrible examples. Their rarity in most societies suggests that they are psychological abnormalities to which our own culture has attached an extraordinary value just as other cultures have attached extreme values to other abnormalities. The hero of the modern American movie is always a lover just as the hero of the old Arab epic is always an epileptic. A cynic might suspect that in any ordinary population the percentage of individuals with a capacity for romantic love of the Hollywood type was about as large as that of persons able to throw genuine epileptic fits. However, given a little social encouragement, either one can be adequately imitated without the performer admitting even to himself that the performance is not genuine.

Most societies are less keen on romance than on congeniality. They train their young people to believe that any well-bred boy and girl, once married, will be able to live together contentedly and will in time develop a real fondness for each other. (Linton 1936:173–174)

Linton mentions two topics that I wish to say more about. The first is the historical development of the *notion* of romantic love in Western society. The second is the frequency of the *emotion* of romantic love (whatever that is) among our own and other populations. First, here is a synopsis of the history of romantic love, as traced by Ira Reiss:

One could not possibly understand sexual standards in America in the twentieth century unless he understood the roots of those notions of courtly love, or, as it is popularly called, romantic love, which the Normans brought to England, and which are still with us today. By the eleventh century, the notion of romantic love was becoming well known among the aristocrats. This notion basically consisted of the idea that one could become obsessed with the beauty and character of another person, and that this love would make one eternally happy as long as it were returned or eternally damned if one were spurned. . . .

To the knight and the troubadour, his lady was an angel, a

collection of perfection. The troubadour would come to serenade his lady; he would compose ballads of her beauty and his immortal love for her. Knights would engage in mortal combat in order to win honors for their chosen lover. Like our adolescents today, they would wear some object of their beloved person into battle—a handkerchief, a swatch of cloth around their necks in honor of their lady.

This account of romantic love may sound familiar, but lest one deceive himself, he should realize that this love affair was almost always between a bachelor knight or troubadour and a married aristocratic woman. Most of these love affairs were encouraged by their setting—a castle filled with bachelor knights and troubadours and but one or a few aristocratic ladies. There were many other reasons for bachelors and married women to be involved in love affairs; one basic reason was that people in those days generally believed that love and marriage would not mix, so they did not think of love in connection with their mates. At many points in the romantic love movement, it was also thought that to consummate love with sexual intercourse was to destroy it. Love, to last, must remain free of marriage and sex. In the year 1174, one of the many courts of love (which used to meet to discuss love questions just as many of our "advice to the lovelorn" columns do today) met at the house of the Countess of Champagne and stated officially that the "true" relation between love and marriage is as follows:

> "We declare and affirm, by the tenor of these presents, that love cannot extend its rights over two married persons. For indeed lovers grant one another all things, mutually and freely, without being impelled by any motive of necessity, whereas husband and wife are held by their duty to submit their wills to each other and to refuse each other nothing.
>
> "May this judgment, which we have delivered with extreme caution, and after consulting with a great number of other ladies, be for you a constant and unassailable truth. Delivered in this year 1174, on the third day before the Kalends of May, Proclamation VII."

In the early phases of courtly love, there was often little sexual element involved. It consisted mainly of admiration from a distance, with perhaps a kiss on the forehead as a reward for heroic duty or a newly-composed or well-sung ballad. The knights and troubadours, for a while at least, were content with the idealistic element of their love and even seemed to glory in their self-denial. Of course, in double-standard fashion, these bachelors had other lower-class women with whom they could release their sexual restraints. . . .

By the sixteenth century, the lovers' deeds began to be regularly rewarded by carnal favors rather than with a kiss on the forehead. The transition was slow from the beginning of romantic love in about the eleventh century. Even in the early days of romantic love, however, the knight or troubadour was often allowed to fully undress his beloved and put her to bed—providing, of course, that he did not take any sexual liberties. On other occasions, he was rewarded by spending the night with his lover if he swore continence. In the course of a few centuries the system broke down, and sexual intercourse became the reward which was *informally* taken; by the middle of the sixteenth century, extramarital coitus was *formally* given as the reward. (Reiss 1960:53–56)

Reiss goes on to describe how the concept of romantic love gradually filtered down to the lower social strata, and how romantic love finally became the proper motive for marriage.

In his book, *Sex and History*, G. Rattray Taylor describes how the Church imposed a repressive sexual code upon medieval Europe. Taylor points to various medieval social phenomena—monastic asceticism, the inquisitions and witch-hunts, the flagellate movements—which, he argues, were manifestations of psychopathology resulting from the harsh sexual code. Courtly love, I would guess, was another "psychopathology" of this sort—a symptom of and a solution to sexual fears and conflicts, resulting in a splitting of tender and sensual feelings. (See Beigel 1951.) Gradually, however, the conventions of courtly love became "corrupted," that is, the sexual component became less sublimated, and love and sex were joined, as were love and marriage.

In our present-day society, we are expected to marry "for love." But do we? Beigel says:

As with every institutionalized emotion, a certain amount of pretense is, of course, to be expected. Since love is considered the

> noblest motive for marriage, many people will profess love even though they have married for different reasons, family pressure, for instance, or material security or betterment of status. (Beigel 1951:332)

How many of us marry for love, or are even capable of the emotion of love? All of us? Most of us? Few of us? Nobody knows. A study has never been done. If such a study were tried, it would face grave difficulties. Aside from the difficulty of getting people to tell the truth about themselves (or knowing when they tell the truth and when they lie), there is the problem of defining and identifying the emotion. Just what *is* "love"? Is it one thing or many things? Is it merely a vague term, which different people attach to different emotions?

The term "love" or "romantic love" may, I think, refer to one, several, or all of the following things:

1. A strong attraction and attachment to a single person; this may or may not be accompanied by conscious sexual desire.
2. Possessiveness: expectation of sexual loyalty, and the potentiality for sexual jealousy.
3. Extremes of mood: elation and, at times, depression.
4. Idealization of the loved one.

Keeping in mind the difficulty of defining and identifying the emotion, let us see what the ethnographers have to say about romantic love in other societies. In my ethnographic notes, there are seven societies in which romantic love is said to occur "sometimes" (Alor, Reindeer Chukchee, Gusii, Jamaica, Muria, Siwai, and Trobriands); in five societies, it "seldom" occurs (China, Murngin, Navaho, Tepoztlan, and Ukrainians); and in seven other societies it may be completely absent (Arapesh, Ifugao, Kaingang, Lepcha, Manus, Samoa, and Siriono). Geoffrey Gorer says that "For the Lepchas of Zongu sexual activity is practically divorced from emotion; it is a pleasant and amusing experience, and as much a necessity as food and drink; and like food and drink it does not matter from whom you receive it, as long as you get it." (Gorer 1938:170) Among the Manus of the Admiralty Islands,

Mead says, there is no word for love in the language; there are no love songs, no romantic myths, and husbands and wives do not love each other (Mead 1931). According to Leighton and Kluckhohn: "Though the Navahos have been introduced to the white concept of romantic love in schools, it is still not widely held, and almost no emphasis is placed on psychological compatibility as a prerequisite for marriage. The Navaho theory is that one woman will do as well as another, so long as she is healthy, industrious, and competent." (Leighton and Kluckhohn 1948:79) As a final example, here is what Margaret Mead has to say about Samoa:

> In premarital relationships, a convention of love making is strictly adhered to. True, this is a convention of speech, rather than of action.[6] A boy declares that he will die if a girl refuses him her favours, but the Samoans laugh at stories of romantic love, scoff at fidelity to a long absent wife or mistress, believe explicitly that one love will quickly cure another. . . . having many mistresses is never out of harmony with a declaration of affection for each. The composition of ardent love songs, the fashioning of long and flowery love letters, the invocation of the moon, the stars and the sea in verbal courtship, all serve to give Samoan love-making a close superficial resemblance to our own, yet the attitude is far closer to that of Schnitzler's hero in *The Affairs of Anatol.* Romantic love as it occurs in our civilization, inextricably bound up with ideas of monogamy, exclusiveness, jealousy and undeviating fidelity does not occur in Samoa. Our attitude is a compound, the final result of many converging lines of development in Western civilization, of the institution of monogamy, of the ideas of the age of chivalry, of the ethics of Christianity. Even a passionate attachment to one person which lasts for a long period and persists in the face of discouragement but does not bar out other relationships, is rare among the Samoans. (Mead 1928)

Is the American a different sort of animal than the Lepcha or the Samoan, with basically different emotions? Or, is the supposedly widespread occurrence of romantic love among ourselves, and its rarity or apparent absence in other societies, due to more superficial cultural differences? These are questions that call for a

---

[6] Lewis says the same sort of thing about Tepoztlan.

speculative answer. My guess would be that both possibilities are partly true. There may be some fairly basic personality differences[7] between ourselves and such peoples as the Lepchas or Samoans, which make the emotion or emotions called "romantic love" actually more frequent in America. On the other hand, the apparent difference may be magnified by more superficial cultural factors. For one thing, in our country romantic love serves as a rationale for mate choice; it is the reason one gives, in our society, for his choice of a spouse. In societies with arranged marriage, such a rationale for mate choice is of course unnecessary, since the individual does not choose his own spouse. One possible reason, then, for the apparent frequency of romantic love among ourselves, is that the *notion* of romantic love—used as a *rationale* for marriage—has filled an ideological vacuum, caused by the disappearance of arranged marriage.

What is the origin of the *emotion*(s) of love? Why should the emotion be absent, or nearly so, in some societies? To answer this question, one would have to know the personality origins of love feelings—a subject about which there are several theories but little real knowledge. One such theory holds that the capacity to love develops from separation anxiety—the childhood fear of the withdrawal of mother's love (Reik 1944). Another theory holds that romantic love is a carry-over of Oedipal love—of the child's sexual love for the parent of the opposite sex (Fenichel 1945). As we shall see in Chapter 8, seen in world-wide perspective American child rearing is most deviant, unusual, and peculiar. No doubt it produces personalities which, in cross-cultural perspective, are also rather peculiar. It may be that some of the unusual aspects of our socialization practices—the early weaning, low diffusion of nurturance, generally rigorous child training, protracted period of adolescence, and so on—produce an unusually great capacity for romantic love.

Another possibility is that the feelings we term "romantic love" are a product of sex restrictions, as the old courtly love of the troubadours appeared to be. In Chapter 2 I noted that poly-

[7] That is, differences in the frequency of various personality traits or attributes.

androus societies tend to have very free and promiscuous sexual codes. From this I speculated that there is some sort of causal connection between sexual freedom and low potentiality for sexual jealousy (an apparent trait of polyandrous societies). Perhaps, where sex and sex partners are "cheap," where sexual experience begins in childhood and continues, with numerous partners, through adolescence, the capacity for jealousy is somehow lost or at least diminished. Maybe the same sort of thing can happen to the feelings subsumed under the term "romantic love": powerful attraction to a single person; possessiveness (with jealousy); great in-love elation; and idealization of the loved one. If sex partners are "cheap," if sexual experience is varied and starts early in life, capacity for these feelings may also be lost or diminished.

This could be a reason for variations between societies in the capacity for romantic love. What ethnographic data there are give some support to this interpretation, although there are some contradictory cases too. Of the seven societies I just cited in which romantic love may be completely absent, four are characterized by extreme sexual liberty: Ifugao, Kaingang, Lepcha, and Siriono. A fifth case, Samoa, also seems to have a fair degree of sexual freedom. But in the two other cases, Arapesh and Manus, the sexual code appears to be a bit more strict. Of the five cases in which romantic love "seldom" occurs, two have a good deal of sexual liberty: Murngin and Navaho; for the third case, the Ukrainians, there is no information on sex restrictions; but in the other two cases, China (Taitou) and Tepoztlan, sex restrictions are rather severe.

Marriage Finance

> "It's not man that marries maid, but field marries field,—vineyard marries vineyard,—cattle marry cattle." (*A German peasant*) (Goodsell 1915:189)

KURTACHI, SOLOMON ISLANDS

All the people with whom I discussed the matter in relation to marriage gave me the impression that no distinction existed in their minds between paying for a wife and paying for anything else of importance.

The rules governing the operation of the custom are entirely compatible with this view. If the woman refuses to perform the duties of a wife, her husband can, and does, divorce her and demand his currency back—he is not receiving what he paid for so he repudiates the purchase. But if she has cause to divorce him, he does not get his currency returned to him, since the breakdown of the transaction was not her fault. If she dies without giving him a child, he will expect to be repaid, unless he receives a sister in her place. (Blackwood 1935:98)

ALOR, EASTERN INDONESIA

"Boys are good. They give our death feasts. But girls are also good. We get their bride-price." (DuBois 1944:112)

ANCIENT BABYLON

Of their customs, whereof I shall now proceed to give an account, the following (which I understand belongs to them in common with the Illyrian tribe of the Eneti) is the wisest in my judgment: Once a year in each village the maidens of age to marry were collected all together in one place, while the men stood around them in a circle. Then a herald called up the damsels one by one, and offered them for sale. He began with the most beautiful. When she was sold for no small sum of money, he offered for sale the one who came next to her in beauty. All of them were sold to be wives. The richest of the Babylonians who wishes to wed bid against each other for the loveliest maidens, while the humbler wife-seekers, who were indifferent to beauty, took the more homely damsels with marriage-portions. . . . No one was allowed to give his daughter to the man of his choice, nor might any one carry away the damsel whom he had purchased without finding bail really and truly to make her his wife; if, however, it turned out that they did not agree, the money might be paid back. All who liked might come even from distant villages and bid for the women. This was the best of all their customs, but it has now fallen into disuse. (Herodotus)

MEDIEVAL AND RENAISSANCE EUROPE

Very generally girls were regarded as eligible mates in proportion to the size of the dowry they could bring their husbands.

Haggling by the parents over the essential matter of dowry was as open and unashamed as in any business transaction of the day. In Italy, at least, the wife's dowry was conveyed to the home of the husband immediately after the marriage ceremony had been performed, and a receipt was thereupon given for it. (Goodsell 1915:243)

Most societies look upon marriage as a legal contract either between the individuals involved or between their respective families. This leaves the way to divorce open, since the failure of either party to live up to the terms of the agreement renders the contract null and void. Such contracts become more binding when they involve property as well as mutual rights and duties. The commonest form of such ratification of contract by transfer of property is what which is, often rather erroneously, known as wife-purchase. In this the husband, or the husband's family, makes a payment to the wife's family. The converse condition, that is, a payment by the woman's family to the man's family or the man himself, is extremely rare. The old European system of providing a dowry for each daughter is one of the closest approaches to it. . . .

Wife-purchase is so foreign to the patterns of our own society, which leans rather toward husband-purchase, that we are prone to misunderstand its real significance. There are very few cases in which it degrades women to the level of chattels. A man may buy his wife, but there is hardly any society in which he can sell her again. The payment which he or his family makes to her family does not give him absolute rights over her. Although the purpose of the property transfer is interpreted somewhat differently in various societies, it usually has two main functions. It reimburses the woman's family for the loss of her services and, incidentally, makes it possible for them to replace her by another marriage. The bride-price which comes in is paid out again at a son's wedding. In this respect wife-purchase is really a substitute for daughter-exchange, a fairly common phenomenon among people of simple culture. Purchase has the same advantage over direct exchange that cash transactions have over barter. There is no need to wait for the other family to produce a daughter equal in age and value to your own. Moreover, it makes wives a highly desirable form of interest-bearing investment. With luck, the husband may get his money back several times over from the sale of his own daughters.

In some parts of Africa the husband regularly relies on the first installments paid on his daughter to meet the last installments due on the mother, while in some tribes of northern California a still more curious arrangement prevailed. Here the price paid for a woman set the rock-bottom price for her daughters, and the husband's family would give all they could afford for her, counting it a sound investment.

The other and in certain respects even more important function of the bride-price is to establish the rights of the families involved in the contract over the children which may result from the marriage. (Linton 1936:177–178)

Marriage finance is hard to summarize in any simple way, since it takes various forms and often tends to be complicated. I would, however, divide marriage payments into the following categories:

1. Bride price: payments to the bride's family and/or other kin, by the groom and/or the groom's family and kin. This is the most common form of marriage payment.
2. Bride service: the groom works for his bride's family, as a substitute for bride price.
3. Dowry: payments to the groom and/or his family and kin, by the bride's family and kin.
4. Gift exchange: both the boy's kin and the girl's kin make payments or exchange gifts with each other, the boy's kin making bride-price payments, and the girl's kin making dowry payments.
5. Woman exchange: two groups or individuals may merely trade women, no other payment being involved. For example, A gives his sister to B, who takes her as his wife; in return, B gives his sister to A, who takes B's sister as *his* wife.

In addition to these five types of marriage payments, marriage finance may take at least two other forms.[8] The first is the trousseau: payments to the bride by her kin, the groom's kin, or both.

---

[8] Bride auctions, as described above by Herodotus, do not to my knowledge appear elsewhere in the ethnographic literature. Perhaps we should take Herodotus' account of the Babylonian bride auction with a grain of salt.

This seems to be fairly rare; it occurs in my notes in three cases: China (Taitou), Siwai, and Wogeo. Finally, there are the marriage ceremonials and wedding feasts, which may be very expensive, and which must be financed by someone—by the groom and his kin, or by the bride's kin, or by both sets of kin.

In Murdock's *World Ethnographic Sample,* the frequency of these various forms of marriage payment are as follows:

Substantial bride price: 247 societies
Token bride price: 13 societies
Bride service (may be accompanied by bride price): 75 societies
Dowry: 24 societies
Gift exchange (relatives of bride and groom give approximately equal amounts): 15 societies
Woman exchange: 16 societies

No marriage payment: 152 societies (or about 30 percent of the entire sample)

Here are comparable figures from my own smaller sample:

Only bride price mentioned: twenty-four societies. Ancient Anglo-Saxons, Arapesh, Ashanti, Cheyenne, Baiga, China, Copper Eskimo, Gusii, Ifugao, Kipsigis, Kurtachi, Kwakiutl, Manus, Navaho, Nyakusa, Silwa (Egypt), Siwai, Somali, Subanum, Tchambuli, Teutons, Toda, Plateau Tonga, and Wogeo. In three of these societies, the bride price appears to be fairly small (Arapesh, China, Navaho).

Bride service: ten societies. Reindeer Chukchee, Homeric Greece, Old Testament Hebrews, Kaska, Lepcha, Muria, Ojibwa, Siriono, Subanum, and Tepoztlan. In two societies, a man has the option of paying bride price or doing bride service (Reindeer Chukchee, Muria). In four societies, he must do both; he must do bride service as well as pay bride price (Kaska, Lepcha, Subanum, Tepoztlan). Bride service often lasts fairly long: two months to two years for the Kaska; a few weeks to a few years for the Lepcha; three to five years among the Subanum; one or two years in Tepoztlan. In some cases, bride service involves living with the girl's parents as a sort of family servant (Lepcha, Reindeer Chukchee, Muria). In other cases it involves only certain limited tasks, such as hunting for in-laws (Siriono), or carrying wood and water (Tepoztlan). Finally, it is my impression that bride service commences *after* the marriage—or, at least, after the groom starts to cohabit with the bride.

Only dowry mentioned: two cases. Europe (Middle Ages and Renaissance), and Hindu India (Rajputs of Khalapur). Apparently the Romans introduced the dowry to Europe. The dowry—without bride-price payments from the groom's family—is a rare form of marriage payment.

Gift exchange: thirteen societies. Alor, Fiji, Guatemala (San Pedro la Laguna), Hopi, Ifaluk, Kwoma, Muria, Murngin, Pukapuka, Samoa, Siane, Tikopia, Trobriands. In one society, the Trobriands, the bride's people are reported to give more than the groom's people. In six societies the groom's people are said to give more: Alor, Fiji, Kwoma, Muria, Murngin, Siane. In one society, Samoa, gifts from both sides are supposed to be equal.

Woman exchange: one society, the Tiv. Among the Tiv a man may take his sister as a marriage ward and trade her to another man in return for a wife. Some Tiv wives are not traded for, but are instead paid for by bride price.

No marriage payment or bride service: one case, Kaingang. In addition, there is one borderline case, the Copper Eskimo. Jenness says that they usually do not pay bride price; they pay it only when the bride is being taken from her home territory.

Here are some of the forms of currency in marriage finance: Alor—gongs, pots, pigs, food; Arapesh—shell money, rings, food; Cheyenne—horses; Chukchee—reindeer; Fiji—mats, tapa, whale's tooth, food; Gusii—cows and goats; Hopi—food; Ifaluk—food; Ifugao—pigs; Kaska—blankets, skins; Kipsigis—cows and goats; Kurtachi—shell money; Kwakiutl—blankets; Manus—food, pots, shell money, dogs' teeth; Navaho—horses and sheep; Nyakusa—cows; Pukapuka—fish hooks, food; Rajput—money; Samoa—money, mats, food; Siane—shell money, pigs, axes, cloth, bird-of-paradise plumes; Siwai—shell money; Somali—spears, shields, horses, slaves, food; Tepoztlan—money; Tikopia—bark-cloth mats and sheets, bowls, food; Tiv—cows, cloth, brass rods; Toda—loincloths; Plateau Tonga—cows.

Marriage payments are often very expensive. Charley Nowell's wife cost 1200 blankets (Ford 1941:149, 152–Kwakiutl, Vancouver Island). Among the Subanum of the Philippines, a bride costs three to five years of bride service *plus* a bride price equal to several times the groom's family's annual income (Frake 1955). Among the Manus, the bride price is paid by the groom's economic backer—an elder brother, cousin, or uncle. This places the newly married man in a position of debt peonage; it will be years before he has paid off this debt (Mead 1931).

The foregoing are examples of bride price expense. Gift exchange, on the other hand, may also require a large-scale marshaling of wealth, but, if the exchange is fairly equal, it is not necessarily expensive to anyone concerned (since wealth is merely traded back and forth). In a marriage of Samoan aristocrats, for example, the girl's kin will give hundreds of bark-cloth mats to the boy's kin; the boy's kin will reciprocate with money payments, amounting to perhaps 1000 pounds sterling (Grattan 1948:153).

In some societies marriage payments are concluded at the time of the marriage; in other cases they may go on for years, perhaps a lifetime. In my sample, there are twenty-one societies in which the payments seem to end at marriage: Arapesh, Cheyenne, China, Copper Eskimo, Fiji, Gusii, Hopi, Ifugao, Kipsigis, Kwakiutl, Kwoma, Lepcha, Manus, Navaho, Rajput, Siwai, Somali, Tepoztlan, Toda, Plateau Tonga, San Pedro la Laguna. In a good many of these cases, however, there is a long betrothal period in which there is a series of payments: Arapesh, Fiji, Hopi, Ifugao, Kipsigis, Kwakiutl, Kwoma, Somali, San Pedro la Laguna, Toda, Plateau Tonga. For nine additional cases, payments go on after marriage: Alor, Kaska, Kurtachi, Murngin, Samoa, Siane, Subanum, Tikopia, Trobriands. In five of these cases, Alor, Kaska, Murngin, Samoa, and Trobriands, they last as long as the marriage.

What groups or individuals make and receive the marriage payments? For three societies, the groom pays bride price directly to the bride's father or parents: Copper Eskimo, Murngin, Pukapuka. In five societies, the groom's father pays bride price to the bride's parents: Gusii, Kipsigis, Kurtachi, Silwa, Siwai, and Tepoztlan. For two cases, marriage payments are exchanged between extended families: Taitou (China), and San Pedro la Laguna (Guatemala–Mayan). Finally, for ten societies marriage payments are exchanged between large groups of kin: Alor, Cheyenne, Fiji, Ifaluk, Navaho, Samoa, Subanum, Tikopia, Plateau Tonga, and Trobriands. In only three of these ten cases, however, does the *unilineal* kin group appear to be the marriage-payment unit: Ifaluk, Trobriands, and Plateau Tonga.

What are the consequences of marriage payments? One obvious consequence is the linking of scattered families and kin groups in commercial relationships. Being commercial, these relationships are not necessarily friendly. They are "business" relationships: buyer and seller, or–in the case of continuing marriage payments–debtor and creditor. Marriage payments may also serve to stabilize marriage by making divorce difficult, because divorce may mean that someone loses an investment.

For four societies, the ethnographer says that bride price offers protection to the bride: if her husband mistreats her, she will leave him and the bride price will not be returned (Kurtachi, Navaho, Subanum, Plateau Tonga). But in two other societies bride price has the opposite effect: it can trap a woman in an unhappy marriage. Among the Kipsigis, says Peristiany:

> The main effect of divorce is that the (bride-wealth cattle) must be returned. . . . This is the reason that makes divorce of very rare occurrence, as the wife's father or brothers will rather make a formal apology than give back what they have received. Very often the women are miserable because of this and they run away time after time, hoping that their husband will divorce them; but if their parents are mean, they will force them to go back to their husbands every time. (Peristiany 1939:92)

DuBois states that a similar situation prevails in Alor (DuBois 1944:88).

What is the origin of marriage payments? What causes them? We don't know. Perhaps, in some remote and indirect way, they are partly "caused" by large groupings of kin. In a previous section, we saw that arranged marriage tends to occur in societies with unilineal kin groups. Marriage payments show the same tendency: they are correlated with the presence of unilineal kin groups.[9] The correlation is not terribly strong, however, and there are numerous and striking exceptions. The Subanum of the Philippines, for instance, have the most expensive-looking bride price in my sample; yet they have a kinship system much like our own, with no unilineal kin groups and little in the way of kindred groupings or extended families.

Marriage Ceremonial

KWAKIUTL, VANCOUVER ISLAND

"Anyway, my older brother made arrangements for my marriage. He gave Lagius, the head chief of the Nimkis, two hundred blankets to keep Lagius from letting others have his daughter. . . .

"About a year later, my older brother gave this chief one thousand trade-in blankets. We got all the people of many tribes together to come and attend this marriage. The day before the marriage my brother got the head chief of every tribe to go and tell Lagius, the father of the girl I was to marry, that I was to marry her the next day. My brother paid each one of these men a pair of blankets.

"They go to the house where Lagius was staying, and they get up one by one and make a speech according to the rules of the Indian customs, asking his permission to let us get married the following day. After they finished, Lagius stood up before these chiefs and gave his consent. The next day the marriage was held. They all came in their canoes singing war songs and other songs to seem lively and let everyone know they are coming. When they all come in front of the house in canoes, the head chief of the Mamaleleqala was asked by my brother to stand up and make a speech—the marriage speech. He stands up and says: 'Lagius, the Owadi (this is the name of our chief) clan has come to you to take your daughter to be their wife. We have all come together as we should when anybody wants to marry your daughter, and we have all come to witness it. We have come in our canoes, which could go around the whole world looking for a wife.'

[9] G. P. Murdock, *World Ethnographic Sample.* See also in this connection Murdock 1960:6–7.

"He sits down, and then the Tlowitsis chief also stands up and gives a speech. He mentions his first ancestor, called Numas. This Numas came to this world already an old man, and used to go all around to all the different tribes looking for a wife. The chief says that they are using his canoe—the one Numas used to go around on. He says that this Owadi clan has come to get your daughter for a wife, and the Owadi clan has found her to be equal with them. Then the Tenaktak chief gets up in his canoe. He uses a blanket over his arms outspread like a bird. He says that he is the Thunderbird and that he became a man. He says, 'I have come to you in my Thunderbird dress to get your daughter to be married to the Owadi clan.' Then the chief of the Matilspe gets up and makes a speech: 'I am a bird that came down from the skies and became a man. I also have come to get your daughter to be married to the Owadi clan.' That is the last of the tribes; the others were not invited to this marriage.

"After they all finished, it goes back to the Mamaleleqala tribe. The chief of each of their clans gets up to finish all the speeches of these chiefs who has spoken. They correct and repeat everything that is said, so that there can be no mistake and everyone will hear them. Then they take up the blankets and begin to count them. Every time they count one blanket they say, 'Walk in with this.' This means that I am walking into his house to take his daughter with these blankets. They keep on like this until they finish all the blankets. When this is all finished, Lagius and the rest of the Nimkis chiefs stand up in front of their house and tell the people that they have got their wife. He says, 'Send all your young men to come and get her, and I will return some of the blankets for you to buy food for all the people you have asked to come and attend the marriage.'

"All this time I am sitting in the canoe with my older brother. Some of the young men brought her, and I took her in the canoe from her house to the one I was staying in at Village Island. Then everybody goes back to the places they are staying, and we are all invited to a potlatch. My older brother sends two men around to invite everybody to a feast—my wedding feast.

"The next day the blankets I get from my wife's father were all given away to all the men. That represented the belongings of my wife which she takes away with her from her father to my home, and I give a potlatch with these at Village Island to the Mamaleleqalas after my marriage.

"After this potlatch, my brother's wife called all the women together to give a feast to them. They send two women to go to the bedroom where my wife is and call her to come out to the feast, for this is the first time she is going to eat in her husband's house. When they all come in, they give my wife the highest seat. They call the feast, 'sitting together with a newly married girl that is going to have her first meal after her marriage.'

"They select a woman who has been good to her husband to take a piece of the food they are going to eat. She holds it in her fingers and tries to put it into my wife's mouth. They have to wait until my wife opens her mouth to eat. When she eats it, they sit down. Food is passed around to all the women, and they begin to eat. The wives of the chiefs, in order of rank, make speeches, telling the girl how she should be—that she is not to be proud, that she is not to go around with other men, that she must be good to her husband and not to go away from him but keep together with him as long as they are man and wife. The women that speak are the ones that are good to their husbands; they wouldn't let any woman that is not good to her husband make a speech. Every time she finishes, the woman says: 'You will be like me. I have stayed with my husband all these years. I have never grumbled and never tried to go away from him, and now you will do the same.' All these women that was asked to talk was paid by the parents of the man—sometimes blankets, sometimes money." (Ford 1941: 149–155)

IBAN, BORNEO

When a young man has been successful in his wooing, and has made an alliance with a maiden, he leaves her a ring as a pledge of his betrothal to her. After visiting her for some little time and finding her faithful to him, he asks for his parents' consent to marry. If his parents have no objection to his choice they go to see the girl's parents and take a cup with them to ask for their daughter. If the girl's parents approve of the contract they accept the cup. The cup is the final pledge of a marriage contract between the two parties. They then fix the day when the bride is to be fetched.

When the day appointed for the bride to be fetched has arrived, the parents of the bridegroom request their friends and relations, who are chiefly women and maidens, to accompany them to fetch the bride. They march to the bride's house in a long procession with flags and banners and also to the accompaniment of their musical instruments. If any village is passed they are greeted with mud, sand, and so forth, which is besmeared on their persons and in fact a little fun goes on. Sometimes, a fight takes place, when the women get the worst of it. Cases have been known when the fun went too far, assaults were being committed, and the offenders punished with a fine.

The marriage ceremony is very simple and is celebrated in the bride's house. It consists of splitting a pinang or areca nut into seven pieces and these are put on a brass tray with seven sireh leaves, seven pieces of gambier and seven small lumps of lime. All the friends and relations gather round the tray and eat its contents, at the same time talking over the binding nature of the marriage contract. It is to this effect. If a man leaves or puts away his wife unless she commits adultery or on account of an unlucky dream, or a bad omen, or inhospitality to a stranger, or bad temper, he will be fined according to the law laid down by their forefathers. Similar things are also said about the woman. The binding nature of a Dyak marriage in itself is good, if it be carried out. There are other rules connected with marriage among Dyaks, such as, if the wife in the natural course of things becomes blind, or diseased, and the husband puts her away, he must incur a heavy fine. Similar rules are binding on the wife.

If both parties agree to the compact they take the bride away in the procession. She is richly dressed and wears ornaments of various descriptions. The procession is generally picturesque and is accompanied with much excitement and laughter. The march is slow and stately owing to the heavy ornaments which the bride wears. Deafening sounds are produced by the beating of instruments in order that the cries of bad omens cannot be heard.

When the bridegroom's house is reached the bride is first conducted into another person's room where she relieves herself of her heavy ornaments. This being done, she takes some food. When the meal is finished she is conducted into the bridegroom's room and is requested to sit beside him. An elderly man who is considered to carry luck with him is asked to wave a live fowl over their heads, simultaneously pronouncing a benediction. It runs to this effect, "May you be settled down and properly unite! May you be fruitful as the caladium is surrounded by young plants! May you be well and comfortable! May you be blessed with wealth and paddy!" Many other words of welcome are also said.

The bride and bridegroom retire early for fear of hearing bad omens. The following morning anxious enquiries are made if either of them heard a bad omen or had a bad dream. For three days and three nights bad omens and bad dreams must be avoided. Should there be a bad omen or a bad dream the marriage would be dissolved.

The newly-married couple after having been three days and three nights in the bridegroom's house or room, go to visit the house of the bride and stay there for three days and three nights. Bad omens and bad dreams must still be avoided. Every visit they make they carry with them *pulut,* rice cooked in bamboos, or cakes. Upon their arrival in the houses of both the bridegroom and the bride, friends are invited to eat with them. It is called the ceremony of *ugundang pulut* or to return visits. The ceremony should be done three times over according to ancient custom, but, of late, it is only performed once. (Howell 1910:12–13)

MEDIEVAL ENGLAND

. . . let me . . . (describe) . . . the marriage ceremony as it may actually have occurred towards the end of the Middle Ages, and in the early days of the Reformation.

The bridal procession would set out from the house of the bride's father: first, the bride, accompanied perhaps by two pages, bearing a branch of rosemary, "gilded very fair" in a vase and hung about with silken ribbons. Next would come the musicians, fiddling and blowing, then a group of maidens. These would all be dressed in the same way as the bride, in order to confuse any demons, who might have been attracted by the odour of contamination, as to who was actually the bride; and if the bride happened to be called Mary they would all be in blue—the deep blue in which the Virgin is usually shown as being clad in medieval paintings. In Reformation times some of the bridesmaids would be carrying great bride cakes, others garlands of wheat finely gilded, or wheat sheaves on their heads—symbols of fertility and memories of Ceres—and they would throw gilded wheat grains over the couple. Thus it is in honour of a pagan deity that today trees are felled in Sweden or Canada, and converted into coloured paper discs that we may throw them at weddings and miscall them by the Italian name for a sweet-meat, confetto.

Last would come the bride's father. In Saxon times, the father would sell his daughter. . . . now he only comes to "give her away." The priest, appearing, asks if the man will take the bride to be his wedded wife—the *wed* being the bride-price—and he promises. The bride, promising in almost the same words as are used in England today, takes a similar oath, but adds the promise to be "bonere and buxum in Bed and at Boorde, if Holy Chyrch will it ordeyne." The bride and groom drink the wine and eat the sops—the Hereford missal attached special importance to this act, which was still practiced in Shakespeare's time, as we know from the reference in the *Taming of the Shrew.* After the Bride Mass has been said, the priest kisses the groom, who transfers the benediction to the bride by kissing her. The married couple, followed by their friends, might then play follow-my-leader all around the church. . . .

At nightfall there would be a banquet and dancing at the house of the bride's father, and bride and groom might remain there a week or more before going to their own home.

But the ecclesiastical precautions are not yet finished. The married couple retire with their friends, who help them undress and help them into bed, where they sit wearing their dressing-gowns. Next comes the ceremony of throwing the stocking. Two of the groom's friends sit on one edge of the bed, two of the bride's maids on the other; each man then throws one of the groom's stockings over his shoulder, hoping to hit the bride; then each girl throws one of the bride's stockings, in an attempt to hit the groom. If the stocking hits, the thrower is likely to marry before the year is out. Now appears the priest, and the benediction passed. . . . The priest blesses the bed, sprinkling holy water on the couple and censing the room, to dispel the demons who will undoubtedly be attracted by the performance of the sexual act which is presumably to follow—though not, if the couple are devout, until the three Tobias-nights have passed. Finally, the curtains of the bed are drawn and the guests withdraw, leaving the newly married couple to their own devices. (Taylor 1954:31–33)

Whatever a given society's system of age-sex categories may be, the individual's transfer from certain of these categories to those next in the age series is usually marked by ceremonial observances. . . . The one transition which is well nigh universally ritualized is that of entry into the adult group. In most societies full

> membership in this category comes with marriage, not, as is frequently assumed, with puberty. The marriage ceremony, like most rituals, has multiple functions. It not only marks the founding of a new conjugal family unit and the establishment of new relationships between the relatives of the parties immediately involved, but it is also a *rite de passage* relative to the age-sex system. A first marriage transfers the participants from the child or adolescent to the adult category. (Linton 1942:597)

As you may remember from Chapter 1, one of the defining attributes of marriage is that it begins with a public announcement. Usually this public announcement, which marks the beginning of a marriage, is elaborated into a ceremonial—with ritual observances, feasting and drinking, singing and dancing, pageantry and fancy dress, and so forth.

In my ethnographic notes, only four societies are without marriage ceremonial (Kaingang, Murngin, Papago and Siriono).[10] There are also six borderline or intermediate cases. Among the Kaska, Navaho, and Copper Eskimo, sometimes a marriage ceremony is held and sometimes marriage is begun without ceremony. For Ifaluk, Kwoma, and Trobriands, there is only a very minor ceremony associated with marriage; I am not sure that it should be termed a marriage ceremony. Here is what Whiting has to say about the Kwoma:

KWOMA, NEW GUINEA

> A Kwoma weds soon after he becomes adult. Adolescent courtship, culminating in the trial marriage in which the girl comes to live with the boy's parents, is finally terminated, if all goes well, by a special ceremony which makes the couple man and wife. The boy's mother determines when this ceremony shall take place. If she is satisfied with the girl and knows that her son is also, she tells her to cook the food for the afternoon meal. Hitherto the betrothed has cooked food only for herself, and the boy's food has been pre-

[10] In each of these cases, however, marriage does seem to begin with a public announcement. In addition to these, there are some of the "marginal cases" reviewed in Chapter 1, which are also without marriage ceremonial: Nayar (after the ritual marriage at puberty there are no further marriage ceremonials); Jamaica (common-law marriage); Kibbutz.

pared by his mother or sisters. The mother chooses an occasion when the boy is away from the house, so that, when he returns, he begins eating his soup unsuspectingly. When he has nearly finished his first bowl, his mother informs him that it was his betrothed who cooked the meal and that he is now married. At this announcement, it is expected that the boy will rush from the house and exclaim as he spits out the soup: "Faugh! It tastes bad! It is cooked terribly!"

After the wedding ceremony, the couple live together as man and wife. (Whiting 1941:125)

Finally, thirty-one additional societies have full-blown marriage ceremonials. Usually, these ceremonials are *very* elaborate.[11] In fact, they are often so elaborate that when an ethnographer attempts a fairly detailed description of one it covers many pages. Frequently, marriage entails not just one marriage ceremony but a series of several ceremonials.[12] Needless to say, they are often very expensive.[13] Nearly always, the wedding ceremonials include one or several wedding feasts. For twenty-five societies in my notes, marriage ceremonial includes feasting;[14] for six cases there is no mention of a wedding feast (Baiga, Gusii, Ifugao, Manus, Reindeer Chukchee, Tibet).

Marriage ceremonies may also have magico-religious overtones, although these are not as frequently mentioned as one might expect. The Christian cases in my sample have, naturally, "church weddings" (Dragaletvsy, Jamaica, Peyrane, Tepoztlan). The Hindu case (Rajputs) and Moslem case (Silwa) also have religious observances. Aside from these, religious references are few. Among the Hopi, bride and groom pray at the edge of the

---

[11] Baiga, China, Dragaletvsy (Bulgaria), Fiji, Gusii, Hopi, Iban, Ifugao, Kipsigis, Kurtachi, Kwakiutl, Lepcha, Muria, Manus, Pukapuka, Rajput (India), Samoa, Silwa, Somali, Tepoztlan, Tikopia.

[12] Fiji, Hopi, Iban, Ifugao, Kipsigis, Kurtachi, Kwakiutl, Lepcha, Muria, Rajput, Silwa, Tikopia.

[13] Baiga, China, Dragaletvsy, Fiji, Ifugao, Kurtachi, Kwakiutl, Lepcha, Muria, Manus, Samoa, Tepoztlan, Tikopia.

[14] Chenchu, China, Copper Eskimo, Dragaletvsy (Bulgaria), Fiji, Hopi, Iban (small ritual meals), Jamaica (noncommon-law marriages), Kipsigis, Kurtachi, Kwakiutl, Lepcha, Muria, Pukapuka, Rajput, Samoa, Silwa, Siwai, Somali, Subanum, Suye Mura (Japan), Tepoztlan, Tikopia, Tiv, Toda.

mesa. The Chukchee anoint bride and groom with reindeer blood; the Subanum anoint with chicken blood. The Iban, as we have seen, use noise-makers to drown out bad omens. The Muria employ demon-scarers. And that is all.

Marriage observances may also include ceremonialized expressions of hostility. In Pukapuka, the kin groups of the bride and groom engage in an insult contest, insulting not only each other but also the bride and groom (Beaglehole and Beaglehole 1938:296). In Silwa, there are mock fights between the two kin groups (Ammar 1954:94). The Gusii also have insult contests, as well as contests of other sorts—wrestling matches and dancing competitions (LeVine). As we saw in the beginning of this chapter when Don Taleyesva described his wedding, the Hopi have mud-smearing and insult contests between the women of the two kin groups. Among the Muria, bride and groom ceremonially beat each other (Elwin 1947). At times, there is a sexual initiation of the bride which has aggressive overtones. Among the Somali, the groom—apparently to demonstrate his manly superiority—beats the bride with a horsewhip before he deflowers her (Lewis 1955:136). The Gusii, from the appearance of their marriage ceremonial, seem to view sex as a form of combat:

GUSII, KENYA

A month after the transfer of cattle, the bride must be taken from her father's homestead to the home of the groom. Among the adjacent Luo and other East African tribes, it is customary for kinsmen of the bride to fight with kinsmen of the groom and attempt to prevent her departure. With the Gusii, however, it is the bride herself who resists, or who hides herself underneath the roof of a nearby house, . . . and her father, having received the bridewealth cattle by this time, may even help persuade her to go if her reluctance appears to be sincere. Five young clansmen of the groom come to take the bride and two immediately find the girl and post themselves at her side to prevent her escape, while the others receive the final permission of her parents. When it has been granted the bride holds onto the house posts and must be dragged outside by the young men. Finally she goes along with them, crying and with her hands on her head. This traditional resistance is usually token and not really intended to break off the marriage.

When the reluctant bride arrives at the groom's house, the matter of first importance is the wedding night sexual performance. This is a trial for both parties, in that the impotence of the groom may cause the bride to break off the marriage and the discovery of scars or deformities on the bride's body (including vaginal obstruction) may induce the groom to send her home and request a return of the bridewealth. The bride is determined to put her new husband's sexual competence to the most severe test possible. She may take magical measures which are believed to result in his failure in intercourse. These include chewing a piece of charcoal or a phallic pod commonly found in pastures, putting either of these or a knotted piece of grass under the marriage bed, and twisting the phallic flower of the banana tree. The groom for his part is determined to be successful in the face of her expected resistance; he fortifies himself by being well fed, which is believed to favor potency, by eating bitter herbs, and nowadays by eating large quantities of coffee beans, valued as an aphrodisiac. His brothers and paternal male cousins give him encouragement and take a great interest in his prospects for success in the impending sexual contest. Numerous young clansmen of the groom gather at the homestead in a festive mood; chickens are killed for them to eat and they entertain themselves by singing and dancing while waiting for the major events of the wedding night.

The bride usually refuses to get onto the bed; if she did not resist the groom's advances she would be thought sexually promiscuous. At this point some of the young men may forcibly disrobe her and put her on the bed. The groom examines the bride's mouth for pods or other magical devices designed to render him impotent. As he proceeds toward sexual intercourse she continues to resist and he must force her into position. Ordinarily she performs the practice known as *ogotega*, allowing him between her thighs but keeping the vaginal muscles so tense that penetration is impossible. If the groom is young . . . the young men intervene, reprimand the bride, and hold her in position so that penetration can be achieved on the first night. An older groom, however, is considered strong enough to take care of himself, and the young men wait outside the door of the house, looking in occasionally to check on his progress. It is said that in such cases a "fierce" girl in the old days could prevent the groom from achieving full penetration as long as a week. Brides are said to take pride in the length of time they can hold off their mates. . . .

Once penetration has been achieved, the young men sing in jubilation and retire from the house to allow the groom to complete the nuptial sexual relations. They are keenly interested in how many times he will be able to perform coitus on the first night, as this is a matter of prestige and invidious comparison. Six is considered a minimally respectable number of times and twelve is the maximum of which informants had heard. They claimed it was traditional to achieve orgasm twelve times but that performances in recent years were lower.

The explicit object of such prodigious feats is to hurt the bride. When a bride is unable to walk on the day following the wedding night, the young men consider the groom "a real man" and he is able to boast of his exploits, particularly the fact that he made her cry. (LeVine)

Akin to sexual initiation is the defloration ceremony, or ritualized virginity test, which is mentioned for Samoa (aristocrats), Tikopia, and various Moslem countries. Here is what Patai has to say about virginity tests among the Moslems of North Africa and the Middle East:

The public ascertaining of the bride's virginity has continued to be practiced in the Middle East in tradition-bound social strata down to the present day. Several variants of the custom have been reported both from Palestine and the neighboring countries. In Mecca it has been the custom on the morning following the wedding night, when the newlyweds leave their chamber, for the bride's mother to hurry to the bridal bed, gather up the bloodstained *sharshef*, and show it to all her women friends who used to spend the night with her. In the older form of the custom, as reported by Leo Africanus in the sixteenth century from Fez in Morocco, a woman used to be stationed in front of the wedding chamber, and as soon as the bridegroom had deflowered his bride he handed to her the bloodstained napkin, which she thereupon showed to all the assembled guests, proclaiming in a loud voice that the bride was found to have been a virgin. The public exhibition of the bloodstained garment is practiced to this day in Morocco.

In Egypt, down to the nineteenth century, the bloody garment was carried by the female relatives of the bride in triumph to the houses of neighbors, or hung over the door of the peasants' house.

In the Kuwait area it is the custom to this day that the young girl puts up a struggle on her wedding night in an attempt to save her virginity. Female relations on both sides listen to the sounds of the struggle and the screams of the bride from outside the tent or the door of the room. After cohabitation, the bridegroom takes out the bloodstained bed sheet to the bride's female and male relatives, displays it to them, and calls out in pride and pleasure: "God whiten your faces, you have indeed kept your daughter pure!"

Among the Jews of Kurdistan, an old man, or an old man and an old woman, both from the bride's family, used to be stationed in front of the nuptial chamber. As soon as he consummated the marriage, the bridegroom opened the door of the room so that all should be able to see the bloodstained sheet. It was especially important that women from the bride's family should be present, so that they should be able to bear witness in case the bridegroom, at a later time in a moment of anger, should calumniate his bride. When the women satisfied themselves that the bride was a virgin, they started their joyous "kilili" triller, and this sound, as well as the music of the band which was also started, made it public knowledge in the middle of the night that the bride was found to be a virgin. Thereupon a relative of the bride carried the bloodstained sheet to the house of her father. (Patai 1959: 67–68)

The marriage ceremonials may also include:

Instructions and harangues, delivered by the elders to the bride and groom (Hopi, Kwakiutl, Muria, Navaho, Tepoztlan)

Negotiation and legal "enactment" of the marriage contract (Iban, Silwa, Subanum)

Bride-price payments or gift exchange, as an integral part of the marriage ceremonies (Dragaletvsy, Gusii, Hopi, Ifugao, Kaska, Kipsigis, Kwakiutl, Muria, Manus, Navaho, Pukapuka, Samoa, Subanum, Tibet, Tikopia, Tiv, Toda)

Processions (Dragaletvsy, Iban, Kurtachi, Muria, Manus, Silwa)

Marriage ceremonies, like other kinds of ceremonials, usually contain a certain amount of ritual—that is, traditional, stereotyped acts of symbolic value. Sometimes, the symbolism in marriage ritual is fairly obvious. In the Hopi marriage described at the beginning of the chapter, Don's and Irene's hair is washed in yucca suds and twined together, symbolizing their union. The Gusii groom puts iron rings on his bride's ankles, indicating that she is henceforth his property. Sometimes marriage ritual persists as an anachronism, its original symbolic value being largely lost. Taylor gives two examples of anachronistic marriage ritual in Western society, when he describes symbolism in medieval weddings: the wedding cake (fertility symbol); and throwing confetti (also symbolizing fertility). According to Truxal and Merrill, our custom of giving a wedding ring is a symbolic remnant of giving bride price. The bride wears the ring on the fourth finger of her left hand because this finger was thought to be the "sinew or string from her heart." The ring, on this finger, symbolized the union of the wife's heart with her husband (Truxal and Merrill 1953:283).

To conclude this section, here is Verrier Elwin's description of Muria marriage ceremonial, along with his interpretation of its symbolism and functions:

MURIA, INDIA

The fundamental things [in the marriage ceremonials] seem to me to be these—the preparation of the bride in the *ghotul*, the ceremonial fetching of the bride by the bridegroom and his party, the building of a marriage-booth with its associated magical materials and patterns, the exchange of gifts and payment of a bride-price, the liberal use of oil and *haldi* to consecrate the bride and bridegroom, the procession round a marriage pole or booth seven times . . . , the tying together of the bridal pair, the pouring water over them . . . , minor rituals designed to emphasize the unity of the couple and to ensure the potency of the bridegroom, the last visit to the *ghotul* and the official bedding of the couple by the *chelik*.

The length, complexity and extravagance of the marriage ritual is necessary to impress on boys and girls who are so used to love and sex the importance of the steps they are now taking. Marriage here does not, as in so many other cultures, mark an initiation into the mysteries of sex.[15] It is not, usually, the binding together of two people who have fallen in love with each other. It represents instead the end of a life of sexual and domestic freedom and the companionship of young people. It marks the beginning of economic responsibility, a change of residence, a transformation of the whole way of life. The ritual is adapted to emphasize this. There is the long week of preparation in the *ghotul*[16] and the vigil of song and weeping that ends it; there is the parental fuss; the obvious trouble and expense for everyone; the solemn regard for omens; the new clothes and ornaments. I have often been reminded of the preliminaries to an operation—the bathing and shaving of the body, the tests and examinations, the rendering of the person aseptic, the creation of a sense that the patient is a being already separate and apart who will never be quite the same again. So now *chelik* and *motiari*[17] are prepared for an operation that will sever them forever from the carefree joys of youth.

The importance of this operation is further emphasized by the treatment of bridegroom and bride as the Raja and Rani of their brief matrimonial court. They are crowned; the leaders of their community defer to them and treat them with respect; their "army" and "police" accompany them everywhere, even when they go to perform their natural functions; they must never walk but always be carried about; at the time of *tika* everyone salutes them; they are "Raja and Rani for two days and a half."

This is a time of peculiar supernatural danger and the measures taken to avoid it find their parallels in many parts of the world. The crowns are not only symbols of royalty but correspond to the wedding-veil. Bride and bridegroom are also covered with a cloth both at the crisis of the Lagir and other important moments of the ceremony. This, and the refusal of bride and groom to look at each other, is connected partly with sexual modesty, partly with the belief that it is dangerous even to see dangerous persons. Bride and bridegroom remain silent for most of the ceremony; certainly they never speak to one another. . . .

---

[15] The Muria allow sexual freedom to children and adolescents.

[16] Adolescents' dormitory.

[17] Boy and girl.

The ceremonial beating of the bride by the bridegroom and of the bridegroom by the bride, which occurs several times during the ceremony, is regarded by Westermarck as intended to drive away evil influences and may also be connected "with the idea of gaining power." Protection from evil spirits is probably also the aim, or one of the aims . . . when a group of *motiari* including the bride dress up as boys and the bridegroom has to try to recognize his future wife.

Among the demon-scarers employed during the ceremony may be mentioned the brooms tied to the booth, the oil so freely used, the tying of the hair in plaits, the carrying of bride and groom over the threshold and the ceremonial bath. Brooms are important as sweeping away ghosts and spirits; sticks or grass from a broom are often used in magic or divination. . . .

The red ants scattered over the marriage party are perhaps intended merely as a joke; they may, however, represent a survival of some former custom or ordeal. . . .

Yet to the participants in the marriage it is probable that its financial and social aspect is of even greater importance than the supernatural atmosphere into which they have projected themselves. The allegiance of the two families is emphasized by the little rite of *samdhi-bhet* at the very beginning and by the farewell of the new relations-in-law at the end. Their prayer—"Let there be no quarrels. Let there be many children. As the root is below and branches above, so may we be united"—and again—"See, from of old was our relationship ordained. May the Departed guard and continue it"—indicates the importance of the ceremony for the family, the clan and the ancestors. This is still further shown by the presents made to various relatives and, above all, by the gifts offered to the Departed—to the Pot in the old home to compensate the ancestors for the loss of a girl, to the Pot in the new family to indicate that the bride has left her old clan and joined that of her husband. . . .

So far we have dealt mainly with rites of parting and separation; other ceremonies stress the social and sexual union of bride and groom and attempt to ensure its natural fertility. The giving of the bridal ring is a world-wide symbol of union, so is the ceremony of eating together. At the end of the Lagir circumambulation (itself a rite of aggregation with a subsidiary cathartic or prophylactic purpose), bride and groom are tied together and water is poured over them. On two occasions, the bridegroom or his friends carry off the bride; this may be a survival of an older tradition of marriage by capture or may merely be intended to stress the emphatic break with the old life and entry into the new.

The sexual interest is both manifest and latent. There is little concealment or symbolism about the ceremonial bedding of the married pair, the vagina carved on the main pillar of the booth, the obscene horseplay between relatives, the constant cries of "Penis" and "Vagina," the songs, the jokes, the abuse. . . .

Other incidents and objects in the ritual are of a symbolic character. Some are directly sexual: thus the *motiari* bang the *mahua* branch up and down on the site of the booth just as Bison-horn Maria girls use their dancing-sticks, professedly in imitation of sexual intercourse. The pouring of water over bride and groom is a symbol of world-wide distribution, and the breaking of wooden poles links up with many examples given by Westermarck, where things are broken to ensure or facilitate the consummation of the marriage. The Berber blow a cane to pieces. The Zulu bride breaks a spear. Among the Yakut dry rods are broken and burnt.

Haldi, with its yellow colour, is both a ghost scarer and a sex-symbol. It is significant that one of its forty-six ancient synonyms is *kamala*, "lustful" and others refer to it as "night." The oil with which it is mixed is, to the Muria mind at least, another sex-symbol, recalling the oil used in massage and that traditionally put on a lover's mat "to make it slippery."

Other objects are concerned more with the fruit of intercourse, for the fertility so carefully avoided in the ghotul is now passionately desired. The *kalsa*-pitcher is an obvious symbol of the womb; it is filled with fertile grain and a lamp (which stands for the act of love in folk-poetry as in Pahari paintings) covers its mouth. The arrow is another obvious sex-symbol; the very interesting song on p. 119 connects the marriage arrow with the arrow used to cut the umbilical cord of the first child. . . . The decorations of the booth, the strings of mango leaves so green and fertile, the coconut, the grain, the burning lamps, all hint at love and love's fruit. Even the curious rite where the bride and groom throw away their toilet-twigs and spit at each other may aim at ensuring union and productiveness. Most obvious of all the symbols are those connected with earth, for woman is everywhere the earth whom man must plough and sow.

The incidents and furniture of a Muria marriage, therefore, have not come together by chance. They are purposeful and charged with meaning. They express in vivid and dramatic form the working of the Muria mind. There could hardly be a more emphatic means of bringing home to a young couple their social, sexual and domestic union. (Elwin 1947:137–140)

Divorce

"This is to notify the public that my husband has left me from September 1953. I know nothing of his whereabouts. He is therefore not responsible for me any more."[18]

When a man has taken a wife and married her, and it comes to pass that she finds no favour in his eyes, because he hath found some uncleanness in her; then let him write her a bill of divorcement, and give it in her hand, and send her out of his house. (Deuteronomy 24:1)

Apparently, no culture has ever found the formula for perfect marital harmony. For some societies, marital *dis*harmony is so obvious and widespread that the ethnographer comments on it. But I know of no case where marriage is so blissful, so free from strife, as to receive special comment from the ethnographer.

Divorce, therefore, exists as a "way out," an avenue of escape from marriages in which the stress and strain has become intolerable. All societies, to my knowledge, permit divorce. The only possible exceptions are certain historic periods in Christian countries during which formal divorce was not permitted; but even then there were means of escape, in the form of annulments and informal separations (Goodsell 1915:174; Leyburn 1935:28).

Grounds for divorce are seldom mere incompatibility of husband and wife. Apparently, divorce is usually seen as a punishment inflicted on a spouse who has "done wrong," that is, violated the marriage contract in some way. For thirteen societies in my notes, adultery is given as a justification for divorce.[19] For the

---

[18] Newspaper notice, Jamaica. Clarke 1957:77.

[19] Hopi, Iban, Ifaluk, Kaska, Kipsigis, Kurtachi, Navaho, Ojibwa, Pukapuka, Samoa (aristocrats), Somali, Rajput, Wogeo.

Hopi, grounds for divorce also include stinginess, laziness, or violent temper. For the Iban, a bad omen or ominous dream can be a reason for divorce. For the Kaska, Trobriands, or Wogeo, physical violence may lead to divorce. Among the Ukrainians, a man may justifiably separate from his wife if she is a bad housewife, or a scold, or if she does him physical violence. Among the patrilocal Chukchee, the groom's parents may initiate divorce; if they do not like the new bride, they simply send her back.

Mere incompatibility is mentioned as grounds for divorce for the Muria, Pukapuka, Trobrianders, and Wogeo. Elwin, in his field work among the Muria, collected this list of reasons for divorce:

MURIA, INDIA

Reasons for divorce	Number of cases
"She ran away" (no reason given)	25
"We quarreled over work"	3
"She did not like me"	1
"She eloped from her parents' house before coming to me"	2
"She was a bitch"	2
"I was ill and she didn't like to stay with me"	1
"We did not like each other"	2
Impotence	2
"I could not satisfy her" (probably *ejaculatio praecox*)	9
"My older wife could not stand it when I married a second"	5
"My elder wife drove out the second"	4
"She was a thief"	1
"She was of bad character"	1

(Elwin 1947:635)

In some societies, such as the Ojibwa, Samoans, Kaska, Hopi, or Ifaluk, divorce is accomplished without legality or ceremony; it amounts to nothing more than an informal separation. In other societies divorce is a legal proceeding, a court case. Frake describes the legalistic divorce proceedings of the Subanum:

SUBANUM, PHILIPPINES

If a marital dispute leads to a divorce, the legal authorities settling the case must decide the disposition of the bride-price, of family property, and of the children, by determining which of the two parties is primarily responsible for the trouble and then making decisions in favour of the other party. In cases of equal responsibility, bride-price, property, and children are divided in half. . . . In cases in which the man is at fault, his family of procreation forfeits all right to the bride-price, must pay all amounts due on the price, loses the bulk of the property of the dissolved family, and gives up the children. When the woman is at fault, up to double the bride-price may be returned and the bulk of the family property and the children turned over to the man. . . . Usually a compromise is reached. (Frake 1955:183)

Grounds for divorce, particularly in court cases, may at times be more in the nature of excuses and justifications than they are the real reasons for breaking a marriage. Among the Kurtachi, for example, adultery is grounds for divorce. But, according to Blackwood, people are committing adultery all the time. Adultery is used as an excuse, when a person wants a divorce for some other reason (Blackwood 1935:117). A similar situation prevails in Pukapuka. There, too, people commit adultery frequently, even with their spouse's full knowledge; but deliberately flagrant adultery can still be grounds for divorce:

PUKAPUKA, POLYNESIA

If a married woman went from her house to sleep with another man and remained with him until daylight, she had committed adultery and belonged henceforth to her lover, for her act . . . was tantamount to divorce. If the woman returned to her husband's house before dawn, her behavior might be considered adultery, but it was not generally condemned, even though her husband was at liberty to whip her. A woman might obtain her husband's permission to sleep with another man, and no punishment befell her as long as she returned home before daylight. Similarly, if before going off with another woman a man told his wife where he proposed to go, and if he returned before dawn, there was no cause for divorce on grounds of adultery. (Beaglehole and Beaglehole 1938:297)

In some societies divorce is frequent; in other societies divorce is rare. In my ethnographic notes there are twelve societies in which divorce is said to be rather frequent. For eight societies, divorce is reported to be rare or uncommon. And for ten more societies divorce is uncommon after the birth of children.

Among the "frequent" cases, three ethnographers give approximate figures. Among the Alorese, about half of the men and one third of the women get divorced (DuBois 1944:97). For the Reindeer Chukchee, one third of the women are divorced (Bogaras 1909:598). In a sample of Hopi marital histories, 34 percent showed divorces (Titiev 1944:38). For nine other societies, divorce is said to be "frequent," "very frequent," "not uncommon," and so forth: Aymara, Kaska, Kurtachi, Lesu, Ojibwa, Papago, Somali, Toda and Trobriands.

For the "rare" or "infrequent" cases, again there are three ethnographers who give figures. In the Chinese village of Taitou, there had been one divorce in thirty years (Yang 1945:116). Among the Muria, divorce is less than 3 percent (Elwin 1947: 633). On Ifaluk, divorce is about 17 percent (Spiro 1949:135). For Dragetvsy, Kipsigis, and Lepcha, divorce is said to be rare. It is also reported to be of rather low occurrence in Barranquitas (Puerto Rico) and among the Siriono.

Finally, there are the ten cases in which divorce is frequent before children arrive, and much less common after there are children. Among the Siwai, about 40 percent of all marriages are dissolved before children are born; 10 percent are broken when the first child is an infant; 6 percent during the childhood of the first-born; and only 2 percent are dissolved after that (Oliver 1955:198). Among the Plateau Tonga, about 30 percent of the men and 25 percent of the women get divorced; but most of these divorces are in the early trial-marriage period, before there are children (Colson 1954:54). In the Egyptian village of Silwa, 50 percent of all divorces occur in the first two years of marriage; 77 percent occur in the first five years; and 91 percent in the first ten years (Ammar 1954:200). Among the Navaho, say Leighton and Kluckhohn:

> Only about one woman out of three and one man out of four reaches old age with the same spouse, and men who have had six or seven different wives in succession are frequently encountered. Some of these changes are the result of deaths, but the majority

are consequent upon desertion. "Divorce" is simple, consisting ordinarily in the return of one partner or the other to his or her own people. . . .

Marriages which last a few years have a good chance of continuing indefinitely. Out of 500 broken marriages in the Ramah area about half the breaks occurred during the first year and another third before the end of the second year. In short, less than one separation in five took place after the couple had lived together three years. This seems to be partly because children are a strong integrating force and become some guarantee of the stability of the marriage. (Leighton and Kluckhohn 1948:83)

Among the Copper Eskimo, says Jenness, a woman may be married and divorced two or three times in a single year; but after children come, divorce is rare (Jenness 1922:160). Among the Kaingang, according to Henry, early divorces are legion; but he knows of only one divorce which came after three children were born (Henry 1941:24). For the Iban, Murngin, Subanum, and Wogeo, divorce is also less likely after there are children.

For ten of these thirty societies, therefore, most divorces are said to come in the early years of marriage, before there are children.[20] This figure—ten out of thirty societies—is almost certainly too low; no doubt the early-divorce pattern occurs in some of the other twenty cases, but was simply not mentioned by the ethnographers.

Next I want to discuss the various impediments to divorce. In some societies, apparently, there *are* no effective impediments; divorce is easy (Aymara, Chukchee, Hopi, Ifaluk, Jamaica common-law marriages, Ojibwa, Pukapuka, Samoa). However, in other societies a person bent on divorce runs into various obstacles.

One such obstacle is the disposition of the children. In some cases the children are divided between the separating parents—the husband taking some, the wife taking others (Lepcha, Papago, Samoa, Siwai, Somali, Subanum). Occasionally, the husband keeps them all (Murngin, Ukrainians, Wogeo). In other

[20] This pattern also obtains in our own society. (Barnes and Ruedi 1951: 652–653)

cases, the wife keeps all the children with her (Jamaica, Kurtachi, Lesu, Navaho, Siriono, Trobriands). Love of one's children may keep a person from leaving his or her spouse. In Wogeo, for example, a mother will rarely initiate a divorce, since her husband has a right to keep the children (Hogbin 1935:323). The same is true among the Murngin (Warner 1937:77, 89). Among the Kurtachi, on the other hand; the mother keeps the children; she can use the threat of divorce as a weapon against her heavy-handed husband:

KURTACHI, SOLOMON ISLANDS

> If a woman is angry with her husband, her method of retaliation is to go off to her own people, if her village is within reach, taking the youngest child with her. This usually brings the husband over within a day or two, with entreaties to return, because he cannot bear to be parted from his baby. (Blackwood 1935:111)

There are other deterrents to divorce of a financial-legal nature. However, in view of the early-divorce pattern I have just described, it is my guess that the parent's love for his children is the most widespread effective obstacle to divorce.[21]

Another possible impediment to divorce results from the marriage payments. In Alor and Kipsigis, as we saw earlier, bride price must be returned at divorce; but the wife's family and kin are loath to give up the bride price they have received for her. This makes it very difficult for a woman to initiate a divorce. In cases of divorce among the Kurtachi, Navaho, and Subanum, disposition of the bride price depends on which spouse was "in the wrong." If the divorce is judged to be the wife's "fault," bride price is returned; but if it is the husband's "fault," he does not

---

[21] Actually, this should be stated more cautiously. What we know is that, in a number of societies, most divorces occur in the first few years of marriage. From this, I infer that something about the arrival of children curtails divorce. This inference is backed by the statements of some ethnographers that children really do impede divorce: Leighton and Kluckhohn for the Navaho; Henry for the Kaingang; Jenness for the Copper Eskimo; Hogbin for Wogeo; Blackwood for the Kurtachi; Warner for the Murngin. But as to *why* children hold marriages together, there may be many reasons.

get his money back. This seems to impede divorce among the Subanum; but for the Kurtachi and Navaho, it is apparently not an effective impediment (Blackwood 1935:98, 109; Leighton and Kluckhohn 1948:80; Frake 1955:183). Among the Copper Eskimo, Gusii, Lesu, Somali, Todas, and Plateau Tonga, divorce may also involve the return of bride price; but there is no indication for these cases whether or not this acts to lower the frequency of divorces.

In addition to disposition of children and marriage payments, there are other possible punishments or restrictions which may or may not act effectively to limit divorce. For the Iban, Ifugao, Subanum, and Todas, the "guilty" party in a divorce proceeding must pay fines. Among the Papago, the spouse who was "in the wrong" was publicly whipped. In the Bulgarian village of Dragaletvsy, both divorced spouses are subjected to social ostracism and disgrace.

In the Chinese village of Taitou, a divorced wife may not remarry, although her husband may. Among the Somali, a wife is simply not permitted to initiate divorce proceedings; but, again, her husband may. In Catholic Europe of the Middle Ages, and in Puritan New England, divorce was outlawed; although this still permitted informal separations and common-law remarriages, it no doubt was an effective impediment to divorce.

In his interpretation of Muria marriage ceremonies, Elwin expressed the belief that marriage ceremonial acted to inhibit separations and divorce. Benjamin Paul says the same sort of thing of marriage ceremonial in the Mayan village of San Pedro la Laguna. In San Pedro, marriage ceremony consists of a series of visits and gift exchanges between the extended families of bride and groom:

> In short, the elaborate negotiations and interchange between the two contracting bodies of kinsmen and the involvement of an outside arbiter not only serve to impress the couple with the seriousness of their new responsibilities, but also set up moral machinery to help stabilize the union. This machinery does not always hold the marriage together, but it helps. The system relies more on force of parental authority and fear of shame than on independence judgment and the dictates of conscience. (Paul 1950:489)

Among the Navaho, a divorce may disrupt a continuous marriage arrangement between two families or kin groups. The threat of such disruption can mobilize family pressure against a divorce:

> Relatives on both sides see in a marriage that fails a threat not only to original investment but to future good feeling and cooperation of all types between the two families. Hence the husband and wife are usually made to feel that a breakup is a defeat and implies some deficiency on the part of one or both of them. When a dissolution of one marriage is not only an economic inconvenience but also imperils other marriages between two family groups, the elders and all the brothers and sisters involved do their best to reconcile the estranged pair, and each side admonishes its representative to mend his or her ways. If the whole security, economic and otherwise, of the individual depends upon the full affection and support of his immediate and clan relatives, such sanctions are exceedingly powerful. (Leighton and Kluckhohn 1948:84)

Or, in the words of Left Handed's mother and Smooth Man's son:

> . . . I asked my mother, 'Who's that man who came here on horseback?' She said, 'That was my older brother.' She meant Smooth Man's Son. His clan was Walk Around You. His father and my mother's father had been brothers. Their clan was Salt. She said, 'He came and scolded me about your father. He said he met your father and asked him where he was going. He said your father said, "I'm going home. I've left the old woman." So that's why he came, and he gave me a good scolding. He asked me, "Are you having a good time by yourself? Do you think from here on you'll have a good life? And do you think from here on you'll have everything you didn't have before? I know you're acting now as if you're suffering from a very bad pain. Maybe you have a little, but that's nothing, because everything is all your own fault. It's not the old man's fault, and I'm not blaming the old man. I'm sorry for him. I'm sorry for him for your sake. You may not be sorry for him, but I am, because soon you won't be like you were before." This is the way my brother spoke to me, and a lot of other things besides.' " (Dyk 1938:144–145)

Although Leighton and Kluckhohn say this family pressure is

an "exceedingly powerful" sanction, it does not—according to their own divorce statistics—seem to have nearly the effectiveness in checking divorce as does the presence of children.

A final impediment to divorce is alimony: a separated or divorced husband must contribute to the support of his former wife's children. Alimony, of course, is a custom practiced in our own society. Its cross-cultural distribution is interesting. It is mentioned for just three cases in my ethnographic notes: the Copper Eskimo, the Iban of Borneo, and Jamaica. These three cases have something in common: absence of unilineal kin groups, frequent neolocal residence, and general weakness of extended kin groupings. Apparently, where large kin groupings are well developed, the support of the children is no problem in cases of divorce. A divorced woman and her children can always be provided for by other relatives. Alimony rules seem to occur only in a few cases where the nuclear family is relatively isolated from larger kin groupings: the Copper Eskimo, the Jamaicans, the Iban (to a lesser extent), and our own society.

Conclusion

The marriage customs of the United States, seen in worldwide perspective, are characterized by simplicity, informality, and cultural poverty. The elaborate marriage ceremonials and marriage finance, so common among other societies, are absent here, or nearly so. Along with this cultural poverty goes great freedom of mate choice—practically unparalleled in other parts of the world. However, while some of our marriage-related customs allow much freedom, others do not. Divorce, in the United States, is relatively difficult, and carries financial-legal penalties (not to mention the social penalty to the divorced mother who, with no sororate-levirate customs, may have trouble getting remarried). Marriage in the United States is a rather unusual combination of freedom and restriction: it is easy to begin, but hard to end.

5

Sex Restrictions

It is good for man not to touch woman. Yet for fear of fornication, let each man have his own wife, and let each woman have her own husband. But this I say by way of concession, not by way of commandment. But I say to the unmarried and to widows, it is good for them if they so remain, even as I. But if they do not have self-control, let them marry, for it is better to marry than to burn. (Paul, I Cor., 7)

"Ich am not cast away,
That can my husband say:
When we kisse and play,
In lust and liking,
He calls me his whiting,
His mulling and his mittine,
His nobes and his conny,
His sweeting and honny,
Thou are worth good and mony;
This make I my falyre Fanny,
Till he be dreame and dronny:
For, after all our sport,
Then he will rout and snort;
Then sweetly together we lye
As two pigges in a stye . . ."[1]

---

[1] The song of an ale-wife whose "visage would asswage a man's courage." Renaissance England. Quoted in Taylor 1954:141–142.

It is also an undoubted truth that, however much moralists may enforce the obligation of extra-matrimonial chastity, this obligation has never been even approximately regarded; and in all nations, ages, and religions a vast mass of irregular indulgence has appeared, which has probably contributed more than any other single cause to the misery and degradation of man.

The essentially exclusive nature of marital affection, and the natural desire of every man to be certain of the paternity of the child he supports, renders the incursions of irregular passions within the domestic circle a cause of extreme suffering. Yet it would appear as if the excessive force of these passions would render such incursions both frequent and inevitable. (Lecky 1869:298–299)

HOPI, ARIZONA

"Next to the dance days with singing, feasting, and clown work, love-making with private wives was the greatest pleasure of my life. And for us who toil in the desert, these light affairs make life more interesting. Even married men prefer a private wife now and then. At any rate there are times when a wife is not interested, and then a man must find someone else or live a worried and uncomfortable life. People cannot think that a man is doing wrong if he finds a single woman or a widow so long as he uses her right and rewards her. . . .

"If I caught her (my wife) in adultery, I would not fight her lover, but I would be terribly hurt and would speak to his relatives about it. . . . I probably would not have left her for that, but I would have given her a good scolding, and I might even beat her. A husband can't often catch his wife in another man's arms and stay happy." (Simmons 1942:281, 276)

NAVAHO, ARIZONA-NEW MEXICO

"I know all there is to know about such things. I know more about it than all of you people. I know just how it starts and how it happens, because I've been all through it. Lots of times the same thing has happened to me, but I tried never to think about it. I always put it out of my mind, because, when I think of it, it's nothing to me, there's nothing to it. We're all doing just the same to one another. All of you people who are here now are all wishing for another man's wife, even though you have a wife of your own. I know every one of you has been around with another man's wife.

Nothing can be done about it. It's always that way, with no end to it. And so I think there's no use talking about it. So we'll drop it and put it away."

"One day, when I was driving the horses to the water, I saw a woman riding along on horseback. She was the one we called Woman Who Flips Her Cards. She used to snap her cards down when she played, so that's what they named her. She was going after water. As soon as I met her I reached out for the bridle and held it. She said, 'What do you mean by that?' I said, 'I want you to ride away with me.' 'I'm after some water,' she said, 'because there's no water at my home.' I said, 'It won't take us long. We'll be over there in the wash. Nobody'll see us there.' So we went down in the wash, and I got off my horse, and she got down off hers. As soon as she got off she sat down, and as soon as she sat down I went up to her. We both liked it very much. This woman had a husband, and she said, 'You're better than my husband.' I said, 'You mustn't tell on me, because if you do your husband might get after me and kill me.' She said, 'I won't tell on you, because I know, sure enough, my husband would get after you.' I reached down in my pocket and got out two dollars and gave them to her. She liked it and was thankful." (Dyk 1938:247, 267)

KWAKIUTL, VANCOUVER ISLAND

"One thing you don't know is how we get a girl. What I do is tell some friend—maybe a man or maybe a woman. He goes and tells her I want to see her. He sees her husband or father is out of sight when he does this. Then he says that I want to meet her in a certain place in the woods. If it is a woman who is telling her, maybe she tells the girl to come to her house, and I go and sneak into that house to see her. Sometimes when the husband is away from the village, we would make arrangements that I'll go and stay with her at night, and during the night I sneak in very carefully so no one sees me, and I get up before daylight to get out of the house, looking around on both ways from the house to see there is no one seeing me come out of the house. Sometimes someone sees me, and they go and tell somebody, because they think it is a good joke, and then it comes around to the woman's husband. Then there is liable to be trouble between the woman and her husband, and maybe she gets a licking from him.

"I give those girls and women presents—sometimes blankets and sometimes money, maybe ten or maybe as much as fifty dollars at the beginning to start with them, and after that if she wants anything she asks for it. How much she wants at the beginning, that is all arranged by my friend. A lot of them wouldn't come with me for less than fifty dollars.

"I haven't any idea how many girls and women I spent money on like this. About two hundred, I guess. I think now there wouldn't have been so many after I was married, if I could have married the woman I wanted. Some of the girls I went with when I was young were married. A few weren't, and these were harder to get at, because they were so well watched, unless their parents wasn't alive. Some would be easy and wouldn't ask for anything. Others would be hard, and it seems those are the ones I want most usually. But the only reason I paid fifty dollars for one and not for the other was her busines; it doesn't matter to me.

"Sometimes there would be two at a time, and sometimes three. I stop when she or I gets tired of each other, and sometimes there is trouble between us. I sometimes gets jealous of her going with someone else, or she gets jealous if she knows I am seeing another girl at the same time. Sometimes, too, she has trouble with her husband, and she won't see me any more. And sometimes if the husband is too good to me, I don't like to hurt his feelings if he finds out I am laying his wife. There were some girls from my own tribe I goes with, but not so many as from other tribes. There was none from my own clan. These is all relatives and friends, and I never had anything to do with them like this. I didn't want to, because they all call me brother or nephew or uncle or cousin. It's all right to marry close, but none of us would go with one of our cousins or aunt or niece unless they are from other tribes. And if I have a very good friend, I wouldn't go and interfere with his wife or the wife of his near relatives either.

"My best friend goes between me and the girls and comes back with the answer. They used to be strict in the olden days, though, and the parents wouldn't let the girl out of their sight. The only girls that isn't married that I can get is the ones that doesn't have any parents, and their brothers and uncles is away working. And another thing, the girls that I go to, I don't go to when her folks is awake. I go and hide myself in the corners of the community house till I know that everybody is asleep, and I walk from my hiding place then, very careful that I don't step on a stick that will break. When I get near to where she is lying, I could hardly breathe in case that would wake the people near her. When I get to her, I just touch her by the foot and shake her a little. She tries to stay awake, for she knows every time that I was coming, and I go and lay down with her, and I have to be very careful all the time I am lying with her. Oh, it is a hard time to go with a girl when she is watched! We couldn't talk; we would just whisper as low as we can.

"I got caught once, at Fort Rupert. . . .

"Girls couldn't go around with men until they were married, and it was a great disgrace, especially to a chief's daughter, if anyone touches them. It doesn't make any difference in the money, but the husband might not like the girl and might not stay with her. The man usually doesn't want her, and when he is asked why he tells them she is not a virgin, and they go and spread it all over the place. They says they know when a girl has been touched, because the private of the girl is already too wide. My wife was all right." (Ford 1941:123–125, 155)

NAVAHO, ARIZONA-NEW MEXICO

"That was the last time we did anything, and that was the last time I saw her. Five days later they moved away towards the north, and I never saw her again. I sure did miss her. Every day and night I thought of her and wished she were with me always. But we were far away, and there was no way for me to go and see her.

"Two years later I heard she was married. After they held the wedding the boy who married her found out she wasn't a virgin, so he went back to his home and told his father and mother. His father went to where the girl lived and took back all the horses she'd got in marriage. They began asking her who the one was she'd been with, but she wouldn't tell. They tried and tried, asking her for a long time, but she never told anything at all." (Dyk 1938: 149–150)

. . . (if) the tokens of virginity be not found for the damsel: Then they shall bring out the damsel to the door of her father's house, and the men of her city shall stone her with stones that she die. (Deuteronomy 22:20)

Sex appears to be one of the more bothersome of human drives—a source of social problems. Everywhere it is hedged about by various taboos and restrictions. Sometimes these restrictions are effective and sometimes, as we shall see, they are not. Violation of the sex restrictions, particularly the rule against adultery, may bring punishments and suffering. The sex restrictions themselves pose further difficulties and privations.

I would divide sex restrictions into four categories: 1) occasional sex taboos, which restrict sex on certain occasions—such as pregnancy, menstruation, a ritual event, and so on; 2) incest taboos and their extensions (exogamous rules); 3) the prohibition against sexual intercourse before marriage; and 4) the prohibition against adultery (that is, after marriage sex must only be with one's spouse).

In most of the world's societies, apparently, premarital sexual intercourse is permitted. But this does not mean that sex restrictions do not apply to unmarried persons; they still must observe occasional sex taboos and incest taboos and, in some cases, may only have sexual intercourse with a particular category of person—a cross-cousin, perhaps, or an elder brother's wife.

The same applies to the rule against adultery. In those societies in which adultery is permitted, occasional sex taboos and incest taboos must be observed and, in some cases, adultery is limited to only particular occasions (ceremonial license) or to particular categories of persons (permissive sex relationships, as with a cross-cousin or a brother's wife).

The traditional sex restrictions of Western society limit sex to marriage. Western society (the United States included) is a bit on the strict side. Although some societies are probably stricter than we are, a good many more societies are less restrictive. However, in all known societies sexual intercourse is restricted to some extent. In the first place, incest taboos and their extensions seem to be found everywhere. Certain of the occasional sex taboos, particularly the menstrual sex taboo, seem to occur in almost all societies (Stephens 1962). A rather large minority of the world's societies prohibit premarital sex; and most societies try to curb adultery.

Premarital Sex Restrictions

As I said, a good many societies do permit sexual intercourse before marriage. In *Social Structure,* Murdock reports:

> . . . nonincestuous premarital relations are fully permitted in 65 instances, and are conditionally approved in 43 and only mildly disapproved in 6, whereas they are forbidden in only 44. In other words, premarital license prevails in 70 percent of our cases. In the rest, the taboo falls primarily upon females and appears to be largely a precaution against childbearing out of wedlock rather than a moral requirement. (Murdock 1949:265)

In my smaller sample, premarital sex is permitted in twenty societies.[2] In eight other societies, there is a rule against premarital intercourse, but the rule is apparently ineffective.[3] Six societies have a strict and apparently effective rule against premarital sex (Cheyenne, China-Taitou, Bulgaria-Dragaletvsy, Kurtachi, Manus, Egypt-Silwa). In four societies, girls are severely restricted but boys are not (Barranquitas, Kwakiutl, Papago, Tepoztlan). And for one case, girls are restricted and there is no information for boys (San Pedro la Laguna). In other words, almost half the societies in my sample have a rule against premarital sexual intercourse; in about one fourth of the sample, premarital intercourse appears to be effectively restricted.

Like Murdock, I found that premarital sex restrictions tend to rest more heavily on girls than on boys. However, the reason seldom seemed to be "a precaution against childbearing out of wedlock." More frequently mentioned was a premium on virgin brides, which often seemed extraordinary and rather quaint in view of the sexual freedom in some of the societies concerned (such as Navaho, Kwakiutl, Samoa, and Tikopia). The Navaho, for example, value a virgin bride, as illustrated by the quotation

---

[2] Baiga, Fiji, Hopi, Ifaluk, Ifugao, Kaingang, Kibbutz, Kipsigis, Lepcha, Marquesas, Muria, Murngin, Nayar, Pukapuka, Samoa (commoners) Siriono, Toda, Plateau Tonga, Trobriands, Wogeo.

[3] Alor, Gusii, Jamaica, Kwoma, Navaho, Ojibwa, Siwai, Subanom.

in the beginning of the chapter. Yet Kluckhohn found, in a sample of Navahos, that 99 percent of the men and about 50 percent of the women admitted having sexual intercourse before marriage (Kluckhohn 1948:101). Customs like the squaw dance make the preservation of virginity rather difficult:

NAVAHO, ARIZONA-NEW MEXICO

> ". . . I stood in the middle of the crowd, and after a while I went around and sat behind a woodpile. I was leaning over the wood, watching the dance, when, all at once, a girl held me. I don't know where she came from. I hadn't seen any of the girls walk out from the dance. There I was, lying and taking it easy, and she got hold of me. I said, 'I don't want to dance. I haven't anything to give you.' But she held on to me and began dragging me out, so I went with her and started dancing. After a while she stopped and wanted me to pay her. I gave her some of my buttons and told her to let me go. She let me go right away. I walked back to the woodpile, and just as I was going around behind it I got caught again. That was the same girl with whom I'd danced the night before. She was a big, strong girl. I tried to hold on to a log, but she pulled me right out. I paid her twice and told her to let me go. But she said, 'No, I want to dance with you until they stop.' Suddenly I got away, but just as I was going behind the group of singers she caught me again. But this time I was hanging onto a bush. Then I began to touch her legs, but she didn't move. Pretty soon I said to her, 'Let's go out of the crowd for a walk.' Right away she said, 'All right.' " (Dyk 1938:211)

In an earlier quote, Charley Nowell's lament was "Oh, it is a hard time to go with a girl when she is watched!" (Kwakiutl). In some societies girls are "watched"—chaperoned or isolated from men—in order to guard their virginity.[4] Girls were semisecluded in Europe, within certain groups and during certain historical periods. A female diarist writes that "the association with the op-

---

[4] Hindu India (Brahmins, Rajputs), a good many Moslem groups, ancient Greece, some communities in Latin America (Tepoztlan, Mexico; Barranquitas, Puerto Rico; San Pedro la Laguna, Guatemala), China (Taitou), Kwakiutl, Papago, and—apparently with less efficiency—in the Melanesian tribes Kwoma and Siwai.

posite sex was not yet invented then (about 1760) . . . and we were shielded from them as from chicken pox" (Beigel 1951:329; eighteenth-century Europe, urban middle class). A Jesuit missionary, traveling in China about 1650, has this to say about the seclusion of Chinese women, married and unmarried:

> Now to return to the metropolis of Hang Cheu, I must observe that having gone through a great part of it with my two companions, the throng of people was so great, that we could scarce make way through the streets. We saw not one woman tho' we looked about very carefully, only to be satisfied of the great retirement of those women. . . . During the forty days I traveled, I never saw more than three women, either in towns, upon the road, or at the inns. . . . Among us it will seem incredible, among them it will seem too much that I saw three. (D. F. Navarette, quoted in Thomas 1937: 241)

As a final example of guarding girls' virginity, here is what Oscar Lewis has to say about Tepoztlan:

TEPOZTLAN, MEXICO

> After menstruation occurs, the mother becomes more strict in her surveillance of her daughter. The most emphatic restriction and discipline are applied to the adolescent girl in her relations with boys. She is warned over and over that the worst thing she could do is speak to a boy or pay attention to anything he might say to her. She is told that boys are dangerous and often the cause of disgrace, and that only crazy or "bad" girls have anything to do with them before marriage. Girls are warned not to bring shame to the parents and they are threatened with severe punishment. Girls are so guarded that a delay in returning from an errand may be cause for a sharp scolding or slap. Ideally, the girl is not supposed to leave the house unaccompanied, though expediency frequently demands that she does.
>
> The responsibility of guarding the chastity and reputation of one or more daughters of marriageable age is often felt to be a burden by the mother. One mother said she wished her fifteen-year-old daughter would marry soon because it was inconvenient to "spy" on her all the time. (Lewis 1951:396–397)

In a society with a rule against premarital sexual intercourse, it is hard to know how faithfully this rule is followed. For example, in Kinsey's sample of Americans, about half the women and most of the men had intercourse before marriage—a figure that must have seemed shockingly high to some people (Kinsey, Pomeroy and Martin 1948:330; Kinsey 1953:550). In some societies, there may be so little privacy and so much "watching" that the rule is pretty effective; but again, it is hard to be sure. As Charley Nowell demonstrates, the truly dedicated philanderer can surmount many obstacles.

In a good many socicties, premarital sexual intercourse is formally permitted. Contrast, with the biblical quotations at the beginning of the chapter, this admonition from an Ifugao father:

IFUGAO, PHILIPPINES

> "My father never gave me any advice about sexual relations with my wife because, when I married, I already knew as much as he about that phase of life. But if a boy is big enough to begin his sex life and doesn't, his father will shame him. He will say, 'Do not be bashful. If she runs away from you and goes where your "sisters" are sleeping they will know that you are following her and will leave the *agamang* so that you may come up.' And if a boy should be discouraged by a girl's rebuffs or running away, his father advises him: 'Chase her down. Don't be fooled, otherwise she'll give it to somebody else. Follow her—it's well worth your while. Just look at So-and-So (another boy of the same age). His wife is pregnant already. Do as he did. It is well to learn even while you are a boy. Have children while you are young. Let them slope evenly downward from you, through the first, second, third, and so on down to the baby. My knees are hungry for grandchildren (including great-grandchildren). Whom can you be taking after, that you are like this—afraid of the *tadil* of a girl?' " (Barton 1938:55)

Sometimes premarital love affairs, although apparently permitted, are still carried out with a certain amount of discretion and secrecy, suggesting that there may be some subtle sanction against them (Hopi, Fiji). In other places, a premarital mateship may be as open and free of secrecy as a marriage (Ifugao, Kaingang, Kipsigis, Muria).

In some societies, premarital intercourse is allowed within a permissive sex relationship—between a boy and his cross-cousin or brother's wife, for example (Fiji, Lepcha, Murngin, Marquesas, Siriono, Toda). As Murdock has shown, permissive sex relationships seem to develop as a result of preferential marriage, either cross-cousin marriage, or the sororate-levirate. Permissive sex relationships between cross-cousins tend to occur in societies with cross-cousin marriage; permissive sex relationships between a boy and his brother's wife tend to occur in societies with the levirate; and permissive sex relationships between a girl and her sister's husband tend to occur in societies with the sororate. As Murdock says, "Future marriages may be said to cast their shadows before them." (Murdock 1949:270–273)

To conclude this section, here is Warner's description of the permissive sex relationship between cross-cousins among the Murngin:

MURNGIN, AUSTRALIA

A man always tries to obtain his actual mother's brother's daughter; if he cannot get her, he tries to marry someone as near to her in consanguinity as possible. [cross-cousin marriage]

Usually an older male *due* and male *galle* have an understanding that their sons and daughters shall marry. Such a betrothal could occur before the birth of either child. Sometimes a *gawel* will promise his wife's next daughter to his *waku*. Thus, even before birth there is a recognized relationship between *due* and *galle*. [infant betrothal of cross-cousins]

There are several degrees of marriage. As soon as a boy is circumcised and old enough to understand and remember what is told him, his *galle* is pointed out. At a similar age a *galle mielk* has her *due diramo* shown to her. This is done by the male parents of both children. [the children are shown, by adults, the cross-cousin(s) with whom the permissive sex relationship applies]

The young men and women older than the two usually tease the young couple with somewhat obscene jokes about their relationship and its meaning in their physical behavior. The youngsters are usually shy and ashamed when confronted with such humor; however, as small children, when away from the elders, they play house together. They are fully aware of the sexual act and of sex differences.

About the time facial hair appears upon a boy and the breasts of a girl swell, that is, when sexual intercourse is in their power and of interest to both, they start making love trysts in the bush. They may not copulate at first, but they simulate the act in close contact.

When a girl has her first menses the mother and older women put her inside a house (no special one) and leave her. She is supposed to remain in one place and move with digging sticks as crutches. This represents the myth of the two old women who made the present world, walking with the aid of digging sticks; the older of the two was menstruating. It is believed that menstruation is due to the sexual act, and that the blood is not dangerous to a woman since it comes from the abdomen and not from the heart.

When a girl's first menses are over, her father . . . says to her mother . . . , "You go make a house for them and fix a camp for them. She is big enough now."

After this, a young couple start living together and are recognized as husband and wife. They have been copulating before, frequently with the knowledge of the father and mother, but the latter pretend ignorance. (Warner 1937:75)

Restrictions on Adultery

Adultery is sexual intercourse—after marriage—with someone other than one's spouse. Most societies do have a rule against adultery although, as Murdock says, the rule is "sometimes more honored in the breach than in the observance." In *Social Structure*, Murdock reports that 120 of a sample of 148 societies have a rule against adultery (Murdock 1949:265). In *Patterns of Sexual Behavior*, Ford and Beach report that eighty-five societies—61 percent of their cross-cultural sample—have a rule against adultery, although in fourteen of these societies the rule applies only to women (Ford and Beach 1951:115).

In my sample of thirty-nine societies, twelve permit adultery.[5] Fourteen societies have an apparently ineffective rule against

[5] Baiga, Copper Eskimo, Fiji, Kwoma, Lepcha, Lesu, Marquesas, Murngin, Pukapuka, Siriono, Siwai, and Toda.

adultery.[6] Six societies have harsh penalties for adultery, which apparently effectively restrict it.[7] In six societies, men are allowed to commit adultery but women are not (Ancient Greeks, Ancient Romans, Gusii, Kipsigis, Papago, Tikopia). For one case, a wife's adultery is severely punished, and there is no information about restrictions on men (Brahmins, Hindu India). And two societies have a rule against adultery, with no comment from the ethnographer as to whether or not the rule is effective (Alor and Tiv). In other words, adultery is freely permitted in about 30 percent of the cases in my sample; adultery seems to be *effectively* restricted in 20 percent of the sample for men and in about 30 percent of the sample for women.

Where adultery is permitted, it is usually limited to some special situation, occasion, or kin relationship. The Kwoma, Marquesans, Murngin, Pukapuka, and Siwai have periods of ceremonial sexual license. The Copper Eskimo practice wife-lending. The Fijians, Lepcha, Marquesans and Siriono allow adulterous permissive sex relationships (with a cross-cousin, or with a potential spouse via the sororate-levirate).

In a few cases, Baiga, Lesu, Marquesas and Toda, there seems to be little if any bar to any sort of nonincestuous adultery. In Lesu, a woman's lover gives her gifts—*tsera*—which are to be handed over to her husband; adultery is open, fully permitted, and properly paid for (Powdermaker 1933:244–248; Lesu, New Ireland).

It is interesting that in some of these societies which allow adultery, the jealousy problem still exists; some people are still hurt when their spouses engage in perfectly proper and virtuous adultery. In Lesu, says Powdermaker, "Some men are jealous, and some are not. Some men gladly accept the *tsera* from their wives, who have received it from their lovers, and there is no rift in the family. However others, who are the exceptions rather than the rule, instead of taking the *tsera* fight the wife's lover. There is

---

[6] Aymara, Hopi, Ifaluk, Jamaica, Kaingang, Kurtachi, Kwakiutl, Navaho, Ojibwa, Subanum, Tepoztlan (Mexico), Plateau Tonga, Trobriands, and Wogeo.

[7] Cheyenne, Dragaletvsy (Bulgaria), Ifugao, Ireland (County Clare), Muria, Taitou (China).

the same difference in the woman's attitude toward her husband's mistresses." (Powdermaker 1933:248) Among the Fijians, Lepcha, and Siriono, permissive sex relationships are carried on with a certain amount of discretion and secrecy, suggesting some danger of jealousy and hurt feelings. And the Murngin, in their ceremonial license, are also discrete; they copulate secretly, in the bush, and tend not to choose the wives of band members or of close associates (Warner 1937:64).

In fourteen societies, as I said, there is a rule against adultery which is ineffective and "honored in the breach." In Kluckhohn's study of the sex lives of a group of Navaho:

> Married men under 30 attain 72 percent of outlet in marriage, 27 percent in other heterosexual contacts. . . . In men between 30 and 40 the extra-marital experience drops to 19 percent, between 40 and 50 to 12, over 50 to 4. . . .
>
> A group of thirteen men listed the number of individual women with whom they had had intercourse during approximately the first ten years of their active heterosexual lives. No list included less than eleven women, one man listed fifty-four different women. (Kluckhohn 1948:101, 102)

Among the Subanum, adultery may be punished by a rather stiff fine; yet all but two men questioned by the ethnographer admitted having adulterous affairs (Frake 1955:209).

In Tepoztlan, says Lewis, "Promiscuous sexual activity is considered a male prerogative, and men feel under pressure to have 'affairs.' Although male adultery is considered undesirable, it is also viewed as natural behavior and is widespread on the part of married men." A Tepoztlan husband tries to demonstrate his virility by seducing other men's wives; at the same time, he seems obsessively fearful—naturally enough—that other men will seduce *his* wife (Lewis 1951:326–328).

Among the Kaingang, according to Henry, people are sexually promiscuous; yet they still wish—rather pathetically—for marital fidelity:

KAINGANG, BRAZIL

> Once a couple are married they do not drop the liaisons formed before marriage. Their long training in philandering and the ab-

> sence of an ideal of faithfulness have not suited them to the stability that marriage implies. Furthermore the absence of binding legal forms or big property stakes, as well as the knowledge that a meal can always be found at one's father's or brother's fire, that one's mother or sister-in-law is ready to cook the food and spread the bed, makes marriage brittle and its rupture not sharply felt. Yet, in an utterly contradictory manner, the Kaingang believe that a man and woman, once they are "sitting together," belong to each other. . . . This theoretical possessiveness comes into constant conflict with the actual sharing in which the young people have taken part all their lives. The young man who for years before his marriage has dallied with the wife of anyone from his father to his second cousin, who has day in and day out enjoyed adultery with an equally delighted adulteress, decides suddenly, once he is married, that his possession should be exclusive. "I left my wife," Yuven told me, "because she took Kanyahe and Kundagn as lovers. She sleeps with everyone. All the women are that way. When their husbands go away they sleep with others. That is why I want to marry a Brazilian woman." (Henry 1941:25–26)

Sex, as I said, is a source of social problems. The urge to philander seems—in many societies, at least—to be very strong. And the urge to philander collides with feelings of possessiveness and sexual jealousy. When one spouse "cheats," the other spouse —if he or she knows about it—often suffers. In ten of the fourteen cases in my sample in which the rule against adultery is apparently ineffective, adultery does cause jealousy and is no doubt a considerable source of marital strain (Aymara, Hopi, Jamaica, Kaingang, Kwakiutl, Navaho, Ojibwa, Tepoztlan, Plateau Tonga, Wogeo). In three other cases there seems to be fairly high tolerance of infidelity (Ifaluk, Kurtachi, Trobriands); for Subanum there is no information.

Among the Navaho, say Kluckhohn and Leighton, "one of the principal sources of friction . . . is sexual jealousy." (Kluckhohn and Leighton 1946:179, 246) Among the Plateau Tonga, says Colson, "Husbands, despite their own affairs—or perhaps, because of them—seem considerably exercised about the possibility that their wives have lovers." (Colson 1958:165)

To conclude this section I will give two examples of sexual jealousy. The first is from Tikopia:

TIKOPIA, WESTERN POLYNESIA

Adultery by a married woman is stated in reply to casual enquiry never to occur, and in actual fact does seem to be very rare; only one case became public during my stay in Tikopia, though I have notes of a few others. . . . A married man, however, has not to suffer this restriction to the same degree. Convention allows him to go among the unmarried girls without suffering any real stigma. He may be chaffed or sneered at by other men for his lecherous conduct, but the only check that is liable to be put on his amorous exploits is that applied by the jealousy of his wife. Fear of a nagging tongue and sharp female nails are probably the most potent deterrent in keeping many husbands faithful. . . .

In such a case, if the husband goes out alone at night the wife does not sleep but watches for him anxiously. When the time draws on and it is near morning, then she knows "he has gone to the women" (the conventional Tikopia expression for lechery). When he returns, he thinks she is asleep, but no, she is waiting for him. She has a stick, with which she bangs him on the back and legs—the head is taboo—and she pinches his flesh until the skin is broken. This he must suffer as quietly as he can, in order not to arouse the whole household. (Firth 1936:132–133)

The second example is the Murngin who—outside the periods of ceremonial license—demand marital fidelity. Nevertheless, adultery appears to be common, and seems to cause a lot of trouble:

MURNGIN, AUSTRALIA

A beating is the usual punishment for a wife's adultery. Garawerpa, an old man of the Daiuror clan, put fire on his wives' vaginas, as did Binindaio when their *galles* copulated with Willidjungo, the medicine man. With the beating goes a severe tongue lashing. An outraged wife who has caught her husband in a sexual relation with another woman resorts to public abuse of her mate for his infidelities. Her obscenity and abuse are usually more proficiently and much more adequately expressed than a husband's.

At noon one day Bruk Bruk, the young and attractive wife of

Lika, who had inherited her from an older brother, accused Djolli. a man from a more distant clan, of trying to seduce her in the bush. A tremendous noise was made in the camp. All the relatives of the parties concerned talked at once, and the two men armed themselves with spears, spear-throwers, and clubs and charged at each other, exchanging curses.

Djolli was angry because he claimed to be falsely accused; and so was Lika because he knew something was wrong, for either his wife had defended her virtue against Djolli, or she had succumbed and then accused him. In either case his self-esteem had been injured. Djolli's wife, an older woman, no longer attractive, stood by, and instead of helping her husband, the usual thing for a wife, screamed at him: "You belong to me. I am your sexual partner. You are like a dog. You are incentuous and sleep with your own mothers and sisters. Why don't you keep your penis where it belongs—in me, not other women." (Warner 1937:81)

Sex and Civilization

Primitive tribes tend to have greater sexual freedom than do "civilized" communities.[8] There are exceptions, to be sure. Also, this trend does not seem to hold for incest taboos and occasional sex taboos. But civilized communities more often try to restrict sexual intercourse to marriage, and they more often seem to be effective at it. In my ethnographic notes, there are four cases in which sex seems to be effectively limited to marriage; three of these cases are civilized communities, Dragaletvsy (Bulgaria), Silwa (Egypt), and Taitou (China), and the other case is the Cheyenne. There are eight more cases in which a rather unsuccessful attempt is made to limit sex to marriage; two of these are civilized (Jamaica and Tepoztlan), and the other six are primitive tribes (Alor, Kurtachi, Kwakiutl, Navaho, Ojibwa, and Subanum). Finally, there are twenty-six cases in which some form of extramarital intercourse—either premarital or adulterous—is allowed. Two of these cases are civilized communities (Kibbutz and Nayar); the other twenty-four are primitive tribes (Baiga,

[8] "Civilization" defined: the culture of cities. Thus, a "civilized community" is a community which is part of a society that embraces cities.

Copper Eskimo, Fiji, Hopi, Ifaluk, Ifugao, Kaingang, Kipsigis, Kwoma, Lepcha, Lesu, Marquesas, Muria, Murngin, Papago, Pukapuka, Samoa-commoners, Siriono, Siwai, Tikopia, Toda, Plateau Tonga, Trobriands, and Wogeo).

In addition to the ethnographic notes, I have eleven more cases of civilized communities, gathered by means of ethnographer-interviews.[9] In none of these eleven cases is extramarital sex permitted to women; but in four of them a double standard prevails, and men are allowed extramarital intercourse (Chiaromonte, Italy; Naples, lower class, Italy; Yokohama, middle class, Japan; Nishapur, Persia). In four of these cases, sexual intercourse seems to be effectively restricted to marriage (Lasko, Yugoslavia; Villafranqueza, Spain; Madrid aristocracy, Spain; Hutterites, South Dakota). For one community, the rule against extramarital sex is present but apparently ineffective (The Bog, Nova Scotia). In the two final cases extramarital sex is not permitted, and the informant felt he could not guess about the effectiveness of sex restrictions (Chanzeaux and Peyrane, France).

So, an obligation to premarital chastity and marital fidelity seems to be one part of what Freud called "civilization and its discontents." Since we are not happy primitives, we must be faithful or risk the consequences. Of course, as we have seen, sexual freedom brings its own discontents; "primitives" are not necessarily "happy," even if their sex lives are usually more diversified. Also, although civilizations such as our own may prohibit extramarital sex and enforce the prohibition by means of various punishments, some people still break the rules. Kinsey found that most of the men in his sample and about half the women had premarital intercourse, and that by the age of forty about one fourth of the women and half the men had committed adultery (Kinsey, Pomeroy, and Martin 1948; Kinsey 1953). In fact, modern American and European sexual mores might be said to be in a state of "liberalization" or "decadence"—depending on one's point of view—following earlier historical periods in which sexual regulations were much stricter.

Why are civilized communities relatively strict about the

---

[9] See Appendix.

regulation of sex and primitive societies rather liberal? Although, of course, I do not know the exact cause-effect sequence, I think the answer ultimately lies in the development of the state. Until about 200 years ago, almost all civilized communities were parts of kingdoms, that is, autocratic agrarian states. Some primitive societies were also subject to kingdoms, but many were stateless, that is, they had no political organization beyond the community and kin-group level. The development of the kingdom seems to bring with it certain basic changes in the family. Among these are an elaboration of deference customs between family members and a tightening of sex restrictions. When the kingdom, the autocratic agrarian state, evolves into a democratic state, these family customs seem to gradually liberalize: family relationships become less deferential and more "democratic," and sex restrictions loosen. (I will have more to say about this toward the end of Chapter 7.)

As to the development of Western sexual mores, then, you might say that sexual strictness was "in the cards" as soon as states emerged. For the "original cause," you might point to the Roman legions, or to Charlemagne. However, an important secondary cause was the fact that Christianity became the state religion of the post-Roman feudal regimes. The Christian movement had, from its earliest days, been remarkable for its devotion to asceticism and sexual purity. Sex—even within marriage—was considered a poor second-best to complete celibacy, as is illustrated by the quotation from St. Paul, "But if they do not have self-control, let them marry, for it is better to marry than to burn." A crucial point, then, in the history of Western sex restrictions, was the ascendency of Christianity—rather than some other, less ascetic religious movement—as the state religion of Medieval Europe[10] (Lecky 1869:334–348).

A second turning point was, apparently, the adoption of celibacy by the Roman Catholic clergy. This was not easy; it was achieved after several centuries of struggle between intrachurch factions (Lecky 1869:347–353; Goodsell 1915:159). But when this was accomplished the ascetic Christian doctrine was reinforced, it

---

[10] For this reconstruction of European sex history, I am drawing on four sources: Goodsell 1915, Lecky 1869, Reiss 1960, and Taylor 1954.

seems, by the sexual frustration of the clergy; and the church gradually imposed a quite severe sex code upon Europe. Polygyny was outlawed, as were divorce and remarriage. Exogamous rules were extended. Many occasional sex taboos of religious significance were invented. And sanctions against premarital intercourse and adultery became very stiff indeed (Goodsell 1915:167; Lecky 1869:362–372; Taylor 1954).

After this, European sex history seems to follow an uneven course. In some periods and places, restrictions were relaxed and there was a good deal of sexual freedom. This seems to have been true of castle life in the early Middle Ages and, later, of the salon society in renaissance Italy and France (Goodsell 1915:230, 237). There were also countermovements—in particular, the Protestant Reformation—leading to greater sexual strictness (Taylor 1954: 122).

In seventeenth-century Massachusetts, adultery was punishable by death; "morals," no doubt, were pretty "good" (Goodsell 1915:354). Today, in twentieth-century America, formal sex restrictions are—in their general outlines—much the same as they were in the times of Tertullian, St. Augustine, Martin Luther, or John Wesley. Sexual intercourse is only permitted within marriage. Yet, as Kinsey and his colleagues have shown, the rules are "sometimes more honored in the breach than in the observance." We seem to be in a "decadent" phase of a long tradition, which began with an ascetic religion in some small agrarian states.

Incest Taboos

Incest taboos are prohibitions against sexual intercourse and marriage between kin. Within the nuclear family, sexual intercourse is, of course, permitted between husband and wife during nontaboo periods, but incest taboos apply to all other nuclear family relationships: mother-son, father-daughter, and brother-sister. Furthermore, incest taboos always extend beyond the nuclear family. These extended incest taboos, applied to more distant kin, are sometimes termed "exogamous rules" or simply "exogamy."

Incest taboos come close to being a true cultural universal. In a few ancient kingdoms, incest was permitted to kings and princes; within the royal families of ancient Egypt, Sumeria, Hawaii, Dahomey of West Africa, and the Inca empire of Peru, brother-sister marriage did sometimes occur (Ford and Beach 1951:112; Thomas 1937:179; Herskovits 1938:153). In Egypt, during at least one historic period (the period of Roman rule), open brother-sister marriage seems to have been practiced by the general population[11] (Middleton 1962:606). Excluding these few exceptions, all known societies prohibit sexual intercourse and marriage between brother and sister, father and daughter, and mother and son. Furthermore, all known societies extend incest taboos beyond the nuclear family, to include various more distantly related kin.

Incest taboos, being almost universal, constitute the omnipresent bare minimum of sex restrictions. Some societies permit adultery; some societies permit premarital sex; but no known society—aside from the above exceptions—permits incest. For example, the Nayars, as we have seen, allowed considerable sexual freedom; yet incest taboos were still observed. (In addition, the Nayars observed caste endogamy.) (Gough 1954:81) Ford and Beach cite seven other societies in which incest taboos—along with extended exogamous rules—appear to have been the only sex restriction;[12] Dieri, Gilyak, Hidatsa, Lesu, Masai, Toda, and Yaps (Ford and Beach 1951:113).

All known societies extend incest taboos beyond the nuclear family; yet the patterning of these extensions—which relatives are taboo and which are not—is subject to a good deal of intercultural variation. Murdock found that although incest taboos always (excluding the above exceptions) cover nuclear-family members, there is no single relative outside the nuclear family—cousin, aunt, grandmother—to whom incest taboos always apply in all societies (Murdock 1949:285). Cross-cousins, for instance, may frequently

---

[11] Frequency of occurrence is, of course, unknown. Also, we do not know whether there was actually no sanction against brother-sister marriage, or whether there was a weak sanction, which was violated.

[12] Excluding such occasional sex taboos as the menstrual sex taboc and the *post partum* sex taboo.

marry, as we saw in Chapter 3.[13] On the other hand, exogamy may embrace "kin" who are so distantly related to each other that they cannot even trace their genealogical ties.

> . . . incest taboos, in their application to persons outside of the nuclear family, fail strikingly to coincide with nearness of actual biological relationship. Regulations vary widely in different cultures; relatives with whom intercourse and marriage are strictly forbidden in one society are often privileged or preferred mates in another. Even within the same society, taboos frequently apply to certain distant relatives but not to other kinsmen who are genealogically closer. In approximately one fourth of our tribes, for example, certain second cousins are subject to rigid marital prohibitions while first cousins of particular types are allowed or even encouraged to marry. Very commonly, in fact, incest taboos exempt certain close consanguineal kinsmen but apply to adoptive, affinal, or ceremonial relatives with whom no biological kinship can be traced. (Murdock 1949:286-287)

What determines the intercultural variations in these extensions of incest taboos? Murdock found that, for one thing, they tend to pattern according to classificatory kin terms. For example, a male Ego's classificatory "mothers" (that is, female kin whom Ego calls by the same kin term as he calls his mother) will usually be sexually taboo. The same is true for classificatory "sisters" and "daughters" (Murdock 1949:287–288).

One key to the patterning of incest taboos is, no doubt, unilineal kin groups. As we saw in Chapter 3, unilineal kin groups are usually exogamous; since their members are "kin" to each other, they are not supposed to intermarry or have sexual relations. This means that in unilineal societies incest taboos are often enormously extended. In tribes like the Lesu and Murngin, divided into exogamous moieties, exogamous rules may—from the viewpoint of a given individual—extend to over half the entire society.

Murdock has a great deal more to say on this subject. However, rather than further repeat his findings, I shall refer you to

---

[13] It is rare, however, that parallel cousins are allowed to marry (Murdock 1949:287).

the original source: G. P. Murdock, *Social Structure,* Chapter 10. Before we go on to consider the strictness of exogamous rules, here is an example of their possible involvements and complications:

> . . . Warner has pointed out that a great deal of effort is expended among the Australians in preserving distance between incest groups. In the Murngin tribe it is as if a genealogical bureau were established to trace and record the lineage of every individual for generations back. The old men and women act, in fact, as such a bureau and as a court of decision in doubtful cases. A mother's mother's mother's mother's brother's son's son's son's daughter, for example, stands in a certain relation to a father's father's father's father's sister's daughter's daughter's daughter's son, and the two may or may not marry, according to the traditional definition of the situation. As in our law courts, there are doubtful cases and conflicting opinions. The ramifications of the prohibitions are so complicated that there have been cases where individuals were left with no one suitable to marry, and a special ruling was necessary. (Thomas 1937:103)

Exogamous rules apply to extramarital intercourse as well as to marriage; if this is not universally true, it must at least be extremely common. In a society with large exogamous kin groups, this means that many of the strangers a man meets are "relatives," and hence sexually taboo:

NAVAHO

> "While we were eating our lunch they started the dance, and the girl with the decorated-stick went out, and the rest of the girls went after her. I just lay over and went to sleep. All at once a girl grabbed me. I didn't notice anything until she was dragging me by the fire. When we got out of the shade I asked for her clan. She was Red Clay, and so I went ahead and danced with her. When she let me go I went back to sleep again. But then another girl grabbed me. This time I noticed her as soon as she took hold of me, and I asked about her clan and her father's clan. She said, 'My father's clan is Bitter Water, and my clan is Salt.' While she was holding me a fellow said, 'She's your granddaughter, because her mother's father belongs to your clan.' So she let me go, and I went back inside the shade and lay down again." (Dyk 1938:359)

It is easier to bar incestuous marriages than it is to effectively prohibit secret sexual liaisons. Marriage is open, and requires some sort of public ratification; extramarital sex may be obtained on the sly. Therefore, extended exogamous rules may effectively limit marriages, but they are more often violated in extramarital affairs. In Ifaluk, says Spiro, clan exogamy is followed for marriage; but for extramarital liaisons it is "violated with impunity." (Spiro 1949:26) The same is true for Kwoma, Trobriands, Tikopia (all clan exogamy), and Wogeo (moiety exogamy). Although they did not permit intraclan marriage, the Todas did not even have a rule against intraclan liaisons. However, other societies are stricter about violations of exogamy (outside of marriage). In Siwai, there are occasional love affairs in violation of sib exogamy; but these are severely condemned. In Ashanti, Ganda, and Lesu, violations of extended exogamous rules are punishable by death.

Finally, in some cases, even marriage may occur in violation of exogamous rules. The Kurtachi and Kwoma allow some people to marry within their clans. Among the Kaingang, Henry found incestuous marriages of all types—barring only brother-sister, mother-son, and father-daughter marriage.

Incest rules tend to be stricter for the "closer" kin relationships (Murdock 1949:286). In the Trobriands, clan incest is informally tolerated; but *sub*clan incest is much more serious. A Kwoma may philander with and even marry a classificatory "sister"; he would not think of doing such a thing with his real sister.

Finally, for the Baiga, Elwin presents a more complicated picture. Clan incest is punished by a rather light fine. Incest within the nuclear family is punishable by a heavier fine. In addition to these fines, there are supernatural penalties:

> . . . the Baiga will say that incest, in its more serious forms, never occurs; they will then declare that it could not occur because of severe social and supernatural sanctions which forbid it. For, in the first place, incest is the cause of earthquakes. . . . It brings leprosy, broken eyes, and worms in the feet. It is punished by social ostracism, it breaks up the family, it leads to barrenness and sterility.

However, Elwin continues, "the general day-to-day attitude is comparatively lax. 'It is not a very great sin,' said a 'civilized'

Bhaina Baiga of Bilaspur, 'to go to your mother or sister. The real crime is to kill a cow.'" (Elwin 1939:189–200; Baiga, India)

What is the origin of incest taboos and their extensions? Why are they almost universal? This has been a popular topic of speculation since the early days of anthropology. Some of the proposed "reasons" for the universality of incest taboos are:

1. Incest taboos arose as a result of the recognition, by primitive tribes, of the adverse biological effects of close in-breeding.
2. Humans, by innate "instinct," avoid incest (Lowie).
3. Incest taboos result from the fact that persons who are thrown into close contact in childhood (such as brother and sister, or a child with his parent) have no sexual interest in each other when they reach adulthood (Westermarck).
4. Incest taboos are a reaction to incestuous wishes; they are a rejection of the frightening childhood sexual attraction toward the opposite-sex parent (Freud).
5. Murdock's synthetic theory. Murdock rejects explanations (1), (2), and (3), accepts the Freudian interpretation as a partial explanation, employs learning theory principles and his own cross-cultural data, and constructs his own theory to explain the nature and universality of incest taboos (Murdock 1949:289–302).
6. Incest taboos are necessary to prevent disruptive sexual rivalry within the nuclear family (Kluckhohn 1960:46).
7. Incest taboos are necessary to prevent role confusion within the nuclear family (Davis 1949:399–405).
8. Incest taboos, with their extensions, serve to enlarge an intermarrying group, thus providing a survival advantage (Tylor 1889). To conclude the chapter, I would like to enlarge a bit on this one explanation for the occurrence of incest taboos.

In the first chapter I cited, as one of my "logical alternatives," a hypothetical society without incest taboos. In this imaginary case, people live in small, migratory hunting bands. Since there are no incest taboos, and since the bands are widely scattered, marriage is within the band: brother marries sister, cousin marries cousin. In some ways, life is simple. Each band is sexually self-sufficient. No one has to leave home to find a spouse. Marriage payments and bride service are unnecessary. And so forth. In fact, each band is so self-sufficient that, over time, it tends to develop a little culture all its own. It has its own distinctive customs, its own language, and so on.

Such an arrangement might be perfectly satisfactory from the point of view of individuals in the band. However, in the long run, the band culture has scant chance of survival. If the tiny band ever disappears because of the vicissitudes of famine, draught, disease, war, or simply irregularities in fertility, its culture also disappears.

As opposed to this hypothetical case, consider a hunting tribe that *does* have incest taboos. Because of the incest taboos, the small bands must exchange spouses with each other. Since there is a constant population mixing, there is also—presumably—a process of culture diffusion. Language and other customs tend to be fairly uniform within this collection of intermarrying bands. In this case, individual bands might disappear, but the culture (including the incest taboos) would persist; surviving bands would still be able to pass on the old customs to the next generation.

In other words, this is an analogy to a principle of ecology: a large gene pool (large intermarrying group) has a great survival advantage over a small gene pool (small intermarrying group).

This explanation for the "natural selection" of incest taboos "makes sense"; it has a nice Darwinian logic. However, I do not mean to say that I "believe" it. As a matter of fact, we do not know the reasons for the origin and prevalence of incest taboos.

6

Roles of Husband and Wife

". . . to make a good husband is but one branch of a man's duty; but it is the chief duty of a woman to make a good wife. . . . Woman, destined to be obedient, ought to be disciplined early to bear wrongs, without murmuring. This is a hard lesson; and yet it is necessary for their own sake."[1]

"I've thought about men and women, and I always thought a man was bigger and stronger. 'A man is sensible, and knows more, and he's smarter than a woman. The man is way ahead, and the woman is way behind, because a man can do anything. A man can do all the hard work. He'll haul big wood, he can carry anything that's big, and work on the farm. Even though it's a big field he'll do all the work on the farm by himself. He'll build a fence around it, and in the fall he'll gather up everything and have it ready for winter. He tends to the horses. He'll pick up a rope and

[1] From the tract "Loose Hints upon Education." Quoted in Goodsell 1915:310. (Eighteenth-century England)

rope a wild horse and break it. The horse may buck, but he tames it. He goes around and travels for long distances. Many things, even though hard to do, he does; he'll work on anything. A woman can do certain work, but all she does is cook and work on blankets and herd sheep and carry water for a short distance and carry just an armful of wood. And she'll do just a little work around the hogan.'

"I was that way for a long time, until I got gray hair; then I found out that a man is way behind and a woman is way ahead, because a woman can do all kinds of hard work too. I found out they're in many sufferings, and I found out that they can stand them. Like when they have their monthlies, they'll bleed a lot, but they'll stand it, and when they begin having babies; when they have babies they suffer so much. Even at that they'll stand it and start raising children. Soon they'll have a lot of children, and soon their children will have grown up and be married and start raising children of their own, and soon they'll have a lot of grandchildren. Then they'll all have hogans for themselves and sheep and horses and other things. That's all a woman's sufferings. She suffers a great deal through her generations.

"When I found this out I thought, 'A woman is stronger than a man. A man will beget children, he makes children all right, but he doesn't suffer, he only makes a woman suffer.' So that's why now, today, I think a woman is stronger than a man." (Dyk 1938: 48–49) (Navaho)

"Thus you see, young sparks, how the stile and method of wooing is quite changed . . . since the days of our forefathers (of unhappy memory, simple and plain men as they were), who courted and chose their wives for their modesty, frugality, keeping at home, good housewifery, and other aeconomical virtues then in reputation. . . . The virgins and young ladies of that golden age . . . put their hands to the spindle, nor disdain'd they the needle; were obsequious and helpful to their parents, instructed in the managery of the family, and gave presages of making excellent wives. Nor then did they read so many romances, see so many plays, and smutty farces; set up for visits, and have their days of audience, and idle pass-time. . . . Their retirements were devout and religious books, and their recreations in the distillatory, and knowledge of plants and their virtues, for the comfort of their poor neighbors and use of the family, which wholesome plain dyet and kitchen physick preserved in perfect health."[2]

"My son, when you get married, do not make an idol of the woman you marry; do not worship her. If you worship a woman she will insist upon greater and greater worship as time goes on. This is what the old people used to say. They always preached against those men who hearken too strongly to the words of woman; who are the slaves of women . . . After a while he will not be allowed to go to any feast; his wife will not let him. He will listen to the voice of his wife. His relatives will scold him, his sisters will think nothing of him. They will tell people never to go to visit him. Finally when he has become a real slave of his wife he will even hit his relatives if she asks him to. It is for these reasons that I warn you not to listen to women. You will be considered different from others. It is not good." (Radin 1926:72–73) (Winnebago, Wisconsin)

When I asked, could a wife be a friend, I was reminded politely of the facts of life in a Hindu joint family. A man's wife was chosen by his elders and the wedding usually takes place before, or soon after, she reaches puberty. Marriage is patrilocal, but for some years the young wife will come and go between her home village and that of her husband, spending a few weeks or months at each in turn, and while at the latter she must efface herself as much as possible in the presence of her in-laws. Out of respect for his parents, the bridegroom must act toward her with formal indifference. If she even wishes to hand him something while her mother-in-law is in the room, she must give it to her mother-in-law, who gives it to her son. Only years later, when she has had several children, and when they have established a separate hearth, can this constraint be fully relaxed; and even then, the best that my informants expected from their wives was that they should carry out their domestic responsibilities without complaining. To talk of "true friendship" with one's wife seemed irrelevant. (Carstairs 1958:45) (Deoli, India)

---

[2] Sir John Evelyn. Quoted in Goodsell 1915:307. (Seventeenth-century England)

In his treatment of his spouse, the peasant holds fast to the theory that "if you wish to have a good wife, you must strike into her as into a piece of wood." Other guiding principles are: "An unbeaten wife is like a dull scythe"; "A wife is like still water; unbeaten she stagnates"; "Love your wife with your heart, but flay her with your hands." The women, curiously enough, do not seem to object to this treatment. On the contrary, a wife whose husband never beats her feels that she is being neglected and that he no longer loves her. This attitude is expressed in the sayings: "A man does not love his wife unless he beats her"; "A woman does not care for a man who does not beat her." . . .

According to the prevailing division of labor by sex, household tasks such as cooking, washing, spinning, and sewing are considered strictly as woman's work. Milking and water carrying, too, are sometimes assigned exclusively to women. A man, as a rule, scorns to perform a task that has come to be regarded as feminine. A highlander, for example, will rarely degrade himself by fetching water from the well, "because it is woman's work." (Koenig 1937: 308–309) (Ukraine)

"We hold these truths to be self-evident: that all men *and women* are created equal." (From the Declaration of Sentiments of the first Women's Rights Convention, 1848. Quoted in Ditzion 1953:257)

In this chapter I will treat three aspects of husband-wife roles: togetherness versus separateness; men's work and women's work; and power and privilege. Each of these "aspects" or general topics has been further subdivided. Under "togetherness versus separateness," I will consider (a) property sharing versus separate ownership of property; (b) spatial segregation of husband and wife; and (c) public avoidance customs practiced by husband and wife. Under "men's work and women's work," I will (a) mention some cross-cultural regularities in the sex-typing of tasks; (b) discuss task segregation of husband and wife; and (c) make a general assessment of women's subsistence work. Finally, I will discuss a number of topics having to do with power and privilege: (a) women's participation in honorific and "important" undertakings and events; (b) the sexual double standard; (c) deference customs; and (d) power relationships between husband and wife.

Togetherness and Separateness

Then Almitra spoke again and said, And what of Marriage, master?
And he answered saying:
You were born together, and together you shall be forevermore.
You shall be together when the white wings of death scatter your days.
Ay, you shall be together even in the silent memory of God.
But let there be spaces in your togetherness,
And let the winds of the heavens dance between you.
Love one another, but make not a bond of love:
Let it rather be a moving sea between the shores of your souls.
Fill each other's cup but drink not from one cup.
Give one another of your bread but eat not from the same loaf.
Sing and dance together and be joyous, but let each one of you be alone,
Even as the strings of a lute are alone though they quiver with the same music.

Give your hearts, but not into each other's keeping.
For only the hand of Life can contain your hearts.
And stand together yet not too near together:
For the pillars of the temple stand apart,
And the oak tree and the cypress grow not in each other's shadow.

(Kahlil Gibran, *The Prophet*)

Marriage, in our society, ordinarily involves a certain amount of intimacy and sharing between husband and wife: living and sleeping together; eating together; going together to parties, on visits, and to various recreations; jointly owning house, car, and other possessions; and so forth. This degree of togetherness is usually *not* found in other societies.

In many societies, husband and wife do not even "live" together in our sense of the word. As I mentioned in Chapter 1, about one fourth of the societies in the *World Ethnographic Sample* are characterized by mother-child households. In these societies, the most common living arrangement is for each wife to have her own house (or hut); the husband either has another house of his own, or divides his time between the houses of his various wives.

In a great many societies, husband and wife do not sleep together during a large part of their married life. With the mother-child household arrangement, or with polygyny, husband and wife often sleep apart. In addition, there are the occasional sex taboos—in particular, the menstrual sex taboo and the *post partum* sex taboo—which must frequently, I imagine, necessitate separate sleeping arrangements. The menstrual sex taboo appears to be well-nigh universal (Stephens 1962). The *post partum* sex taboo is also quite common, and usually lasts a long time; in a sample of 100 primitive societies, fifty-one have a *post partum* sex taboo which lasts a year or longer (Stephens 1962).

In some societies, husband and wife do not eat together. This seems to be true for a sizable minority of the world's peoples (including a disproportionate number of cases from Africa). In my ethnographic notes, there are seven societies in which husband and wife do not eat together: Bemba, Dahomey, Ireland (County Clare), Jukun, Nyakusa, Silwa (Egypt), and Tepoztlan (Mexico). Also among the Nayars, who do not have "husbands" and "wives," men and women eat separately. In addition, for fifty-two ethnographer-interview cases:[3] in thirty-eight societies, husband and wife do eat together; in fourteen societies, husband and wife do not eat together (for some cases, "usually don't eat together"; for other cases, "never eat together").

Women are often excluded from public gatherings and public places; I will discuss this when I deal with power and privilege. However, even when women are not excluded, husband and wife are sometimes segregated. Among the Chiricahua Apache, says Opler, husband and wife do not share their recreations; for example, both may go to the same movie—but the husband will go with a group of men, the wife will go with a group of women, and they sit in different parts of the movie theatre (Opler:223; Chiricahua Apache, Southern Arizona). Titiev says the same sort of thing for the Hopi: husband and wife may both attend a ceremonial dance, but they will sit in different parts of the audience; also, they

---

[3] See Appendix.

rarely make visits together (Titiev 1944:16). Among the Bemba and Siwai, each spouse has his (her) own separate recreations (Richards 1956:50; Oliver 1955:142). In the Japanese village of Suye Mura, husband and wife do not even walk down the street together. They will rarely go to the same community activity. They may go together to visit another family, but even then men and women are seated on opposite sides of the room (Embree 1939:95; Suye Mura, Japan).

In our own society, husband and wife usually—for all practical purposes—jointly own all family property; this is my impression, anyway (Parsons 1943:27). In my ethnographic notes there is only one other case of this sort: the Chenchu, a hunting and gathering tribe of southern India. In twelve other societies, husband and wife are said *not* to own property jointly (or, to be more specific, the ethnographer mentions separate property ownership and does not mention joint property ownership). Among the Nama Hottentots, husband and wife each own their own cows (Schapera 1930:251). In the Trobriands, husband and wife own property separately. For example, the husband owns the house, and his wife owns the cooking utensils. But they do, from time to time, give each other presents (Fathauer 1954:32; Malinowski 1922:177; Silas 1926:149). Among the Ojibwa of Ontario, "Husband and wife have their own individual possessions, which they do not pool, though they lend one another things." (Landes 1937:106) In Alor, the wife owns all the crops (DuBois 1944:22). The Hopi wife owns the farm land, and other things besides:

> "I learned to respect Irene's rights, too. She owned the house and all the property that her relatives gave her, including orchards, stock, water holes, land, and personal possessions. She also owned any property she made with her hands, such as pots, baskets, milling stones, and clothes, or anything she earned for work or purchased with our money. She owned the fuel and foodstuffs that I brought into her house, as well as all household equipment and utensils. Whenever she received mutton, melons, fruit, corn, or any other produce from my hands and thanked me, it became hers." (Simmons 1942:13, 272)

Among the Plateau Tonga, husband and wife divide the crops:

> In working their fields, husband and wife with the children attached to their household form a single work team. . . . The husband with the assistance of the boys clears the land. . . . The wife with the assistance of the girls plants the seed, does most of the hoeing, and is largely responsible for the harvesting. The crop is then divided into two portions, depending upon the field in which it grew. The wife uses the crop from her field to feed her household, for brewing beer, and for gifts. Once stored in her granary, it comes under her strict supervision. No man has the right to go to his wife's granary or the privilege of arrogating to himself the right of doling out the daily provisions. (Colson 1954:60)

Among the Chagga, the situation sounds similar:

> Two containers symbolize the independence of the spouses: the milk calabash of the wife and the husband's storage basket for eleusine, standing under a special roof in the yard. The husband does not dare to drink milk of a calabash if his wife is absent or has not been informed beforehand. If the husband disregards this custom a serious marital discord may easily ensue. (Guttman 1926: 155)

Separate property ownership for husband and wife is also mentioned for the Ashanti, Ifugao, Haida, Kiwai, and the Moslems of the Middle East.

Public Prudery

RAJPUTS OF KHALAPUR, HINDU INDIA

Ideally a man and his wife are not allowed to talk to each other in front of the older members of the family. Since the mother-in-law is virtually always present in the courtyard and the young wife cannot leave the courtyard, this means in effect that the young couple may converse only surreptitiously at night.

A husband is not supposed to show any open concern for his wife's welfare; this is the responsibility of his parents. If the wife is sick, the mother-in-law and father-in-law see that she goes to a doctor; if they do not, neither she nor her husband should complain. (Triandis and Hitchcock)

SAMOA, POLYNESIA

. . . all expressions of affection are rigorously barred in public. A couple whose wedding night may have been spent in a room with ten other people will nevertheless shrink in shame from even touching hands in public. Individuals between whom there have been sex relations are said to be 'shy of each other' . . . Husbands and wives never walk side by side through the village, for the husband, particularly, would be 'ashamed.' So no Samoan child is accustomed to seeing father and mother exchange casual caresses. (Mead 1928)

IFALUK, MICRONESIA

This puritanism goes to great lengths. A man would never dream of kissing his wife goodbye, not because kissing does not constitute a form of displaying affection, but because of the absolute shame of being seen engaging in sexual activity. No man would even hold the hand of his wife for the same reason. Our adolescent pattern of handholding would shock any Ifalukian. Any overt form of sexual activity or display of fondness between the sexes is inhibited. The candid references to the sexual anatomy and physiology in the love songs stands in glaring contrast to their public attitude of shame. This means that one never sees overt affection displayed between spouses. One might interpret this as lack of affection, but this would be an untenable interpretation. In the intimacy of their homes, affection is shown, and patently felt. A wife will serve her husband, with no expressed feeling of gratitude on his part in public. But in private this pattern is different. (Spiro 1949:129)

TROBRIAND ISLANDS, MELANESIA

There is an interesting and, indeed, startling contrast between the free and easy manner which normally obtains between husband and wife, and their rigid propriety in matters of sex, their restraint of any gesture which might suggest the tender relation between them. When they walk, they never take hands or put their arms about each other in the way, called *kaypapa,* which is permitted to lovers and to friends of the same sex. Walking with a married couple one day, I suggested to the man that he might support his wife, who had a sore foot and was limping badly. Both smiled and looked on the ground in great embarrassment, evidently abashed by my improper suggestion. Ordinarily a married couple walk one behind the other in single file. On public and festival occasions they usually separate. . . . You will never surprise an exchange of tender looks, loving smiles, or amorous banter between a husband and wife in the Trobriands. (Malinowski 1929:109)

Most societies demand a certain amount of public avoidance between husband and wife. In my ethnographic notes, there are two societies in which husband and wife may show affection to each other in public (Kiwai and Maritime Chukchee); for eight other cases, the ethnographer says that husband and wife may *not* show any sign of affection toward each other while others are watching (Bemba, Chiricahua Apache, Jivaro, Ifaluk, Kurtachi, Samoa, Tikopia, Wogeo). Among the Mende of West Africa, spouses may hold hands, but other shows of affections are "against etiquette." (Little 1951:131) In the Egyptian village of Silwa, husband and wife may not engage in joking or physical intimacies in front of others (Ammar 1954:51). Among the Baiga of India, when a man returns to his wife after an absence, "he gives her no greeting and takes no notice of her whatsoever if other persons are about." (Elwin 1939:185) In the Chinese village of Taitou, a young couple may not sit together, walk together in public, mention each other too often, or praise each other (Yang 1945:54,56). In Dobu, it would be "scandalous" for husband and wife to touch in public (Fortune 1932:54, 244).

In my ethnographer-interview sample, in eleven societies husband and wife may show affection in public; in thirty-seven societies, they may *not* show affection in public.[4] Also, in over half the reported cases in the ethnographer-interview sample, husband and wife may not even touch each other in public.[5]

In many of these cases, this public prudery does not seem to

---

[4] See Appendix.

[5] May touch in public: Amman (Jordan), Anaguta, The Bog (Nova Scotia), Brno (Czechoslovakia), Chanzeaux (France), Konso, Lacandon-Maya, Lasko (Yugoslavia), Madrid aristocrats, Naples lower class, Peyrane

be part of a generally puritanical attitude toward sex. The Ifaluk, for example, sing graphically sexual songs; the Navaho have numerous joking relationships (that is, sexual joking); these two societies, as well as the Kipsigis, Baiga, Samoans, Tikopians, Trobrianders, and Wogeo, have rather loose sex restrictions. Yet all these societies demand rather extreme (from our point of view) public avoidance customs between spouses.

American couples—seen in world-wide perspective—are permitted a great deal of intimacy and informality. If they wish, they may show their mutual affection while others are present; they may touch, they may hold hands. They may even use terms of endearment. In a sample of American families, Schneider and Homans found:

> "Terms of endearment" fall into a series of classes; saccharine terms (honey, sugar, sweet, cookie, and so forth), affection terms (love, beloved, lover, and so forth), animal and vegetable terms (kitten, bear-cat, pumpkin, and so forth), and a large and varied collection of miscellaneous and idiosyncratic terms, some of them nonsense syllables (baby, pookum, and so forth) . . . (Schneider and Homans 1955:1202)

Terms of endearment—whether animal-and-vegetable, saccharine, or of the "pookum" variety—seem to be a rather special peculiarity of American married life. If other people use them, it must usually be only in the privacy of their bedrooms. In fact, a good many societies do not even permit husband and wife to call each other by name.

In nine societies in my ethnographic notes, a husband may not address his wife by her personal name (and vice versa); he must instead use the kinship term ("here, wife") or some circumlocution ("mother-of-my-children," for example) (Baiga,

---

(France), Subanum, Valley Tonga, Zinacantan (Mexico), Chiaromonte (Italy), Pecs (Hungary).

May not touch in public: Ashanti, Cook Islanders, Cuchumatan Mam (Mayan), Dragaletvsy (Bulgaria), Druz, Hutterites, Vaish (India), Yokohama middle class, Kipsigis, Kurds, Madiun (Java), Minangkabau, Navaho, Sherpa, Somali, Tenino, Toba Batak, Turkana, Valle Cana (Puerto Rico).

Chenchu, Dobu, Hopi, Manus, Ojibwa, Suye Mura, Eastern Timbira, and Tikopia). For two additional cases, the wife, reportedly, may not address her husband by his personal name, and there is no information on the form of husband-to-wife address (Dahomey and Silwa). For four societies in my ethnographic notes, it is reported that spouses may address each other by their personal names (Malaita, Ontong Java, Tallensi, and Ulithi).

In thirty-two cases of the ethnographer-interview sample, spouses may address one another by name (see Appendix). In three cases, they may not (Alor, Navaho, Tenino). In fourteen additional cases, the wife may not address her husband by his personal name, and there is no information on the husband-to-wife form of address.[6]

Firth has this to say about the personal-name taboo in Tikopia:

> Wife and husband do not use each other's personal names at all. . . . This is part of the native theory of domestic relations: husband and wife should show respect for each other, and avoidance of the personal name is one feature of this attitude. (Firth 1936: 135)

In Suye Mura, Japan, the personal-name taboo extends to many relationships:

> In ordinary family life a person is addressed according to his relation to the children. A man will be called "father" or "grandfather," a woman, "mother" or "grandmother"; children call nonrelative friends of the family "uncle" or "aunt" and all old people are called "grandfather" or "grandmother." Married couples address each other in the same manner. . . .
>
> People often avoid a name altogether and use some term such as "the over there grandmother," that is, the old woman who lives across the road; "the ne-ne grandfather," the old man who always says "Ne." People are very bashful about giving their own names. If a person is asked what his name is, he will smile and perhaps ask someone else to tell it. (Embree 1939:86)

---

[6] This lack of information is not the informants' fault; it is due to the wording of the interview-question.

To summarize: Traditional barriers frequently stand between husband and wife, curtailing their intimacy, sharing, and togetherness. They usually observe avoidance customs while in public; they may sleep in separate beds, live in separate houses, own separate property, eat separately, go separately to community gatherings, and—as we shall see in a moment—usually work at separate tasks. In most societies, spouses appear to follow the advice of Kahlil Gibran, to: "Fill each other's cup but drink not from the same cup. Give one another of your bread but eat not from the same loaf. . . . And stand together yet not too near together . . ." In our present-day American society, for some reason, these traditional barriers have largely disappeared. One of the ways in which American married life appears to be truly distinctive and unusual is in respect to this dimension of "togetherness."

Men's Work and Women's Work

NAVAHO

The husband takes the primary responsibility for building dwellings, corrals, and fences, although his wife and other women folk assist in plastering and chinking the hogan. The wife airs the bedding and keeps the dwelling and cooking utensils clean and orderly. She cooks, butchers mutton, gathers those crops from the field which are to be used for immediate consumption, and looks after the children, although the man will assist in all these tasks if the woman is ill, or under other special circumstances. The man is expected to cut most of the firewood, unless there are boys old enough to do this. All assist in bringing wood to the fire, although this is a special chore of children.

Men do most of the work in the fields, look after horses, wagons, saddles and cattle, and haul wood and water. At times of heightened activity in the care of the sheep, as when the lambs are being born, every able-bodied family member assists. At other seasons responsibilities are distributed according to availability of personnel and to arrangements within the extended family, but herding tends to be the duty of youngsters and of the old. Women spend their spare time in weaving, and occasionally in making baskets or pots. Dressing skins and making moccasins are male occupations. Some men are silversmiths, and women are also beginning to participate in this craft.

Many activities are sex-typed to such a degree that many adults would find it embarrassing to perform a task associated with the other sex. A young married man, for example, refused to be photographed milking a goat, protesting that "it wouldn't look right." Nevertheless the distinctions are less rigidly drawn in some respects than in white society. Many Navaho men find it no disgrace to cook, even when their wives are present. They will publicly assume responsibilities for babies and children which white men commonly evade. There is also highly specialized cooperation in many activities such as house-building, farming, and various work connected with the flocks and herds. At the sheep dip, for example, the men conduct the full-grown animals through the vats, but the women usually superintend the lambs and kids. And so, in many ways, the line between the sphere of men and the sphere of women is less obvious than in white society. . . . (Kluckhohn and Leighton 1951: 50)

TEPOZTLAN, MEXICO

The division of labor according to sexes is clearly delineated. Men are expected to support their families by doing all the work in the fields. . . .

Women's work centers about the care of the family and the house. . . .

In general, women's work is less rigidly defined than men's. Many women, especially widows, will do men's work without social censure. In contrast, men almost never do women's work and the few who do are objects of ridicule and are viewed as queer. Men carefully avoid housework of any kind or taking care of small children. Men build a fire and warm their food without compunction only in the fields where there are no women to do it for them. When a wife is ill or otherwise incapacitated, the husband will seek out the assistance of a female relative or, even though poor, may hire a servant. Occasionally, one hears of a widower or bachelor who cooks and sweeps the house, but never of a man who washes or irons or grinds corn to make tortillas. (Lewis 1951:98–99)

REINDEER CHUKCHEE, SIBERIA

Among the Reindeer Chukchee, women work much harder than men, especially the younger ones. The man's part of the work

> is the herding, catching, and slaughtering of the animals, the hunt, carrying of heavy logs and of the stones necessary to hold the tent firmly in place; also work on wood with axe, hatchet, and knife, and so forth. The harnessing of the reindeer is done by both sexes, also carrying fuel from the bush, and chopping wood and ice. The loading and unloading of sledges is performed for the most part by women. The care of the house, which in the nomadic life of an arctic climate requires almost uninterrupted toil, falls wholly to the share of the women, also skinning and butchering, gathering roots, preparing food, dressing skins, making garments, and much more, not to speak of the duties of the mother. Moreover, man almost never shares in the woman's part of the work; he does not even know how it is performed. Often, when wandering with a Chukchee camp, I had occasion to go to the newly chosen spot with the male members of the family. We drove on light sledges, and therefore arrived long before the women, who crept along slowly behind with the pack-sledges. Sometimes the difference of time was about two hours and a half; but the men would only unharness their reindeer; then they would loiter idly about waiting for the women, or begin some kind of men's work. Once in my presence a man took a snow-scraper and began to scrape the place for the tent, but after a couple of minutes he threw away the scraper. "Ugh!" he said, "this is woman's work." When I was trying to learn the Chukchee language, and took care to collect new words from everyone, I found, to my great amazement, that young men did not know the names of some parts of the house-frame, house utensils, preparations for dressing skins, and so forth. "Ugh!" they would say, "I don't know. That is the women's business."
>
> In the everyday life, the man, when at home, is idle, or occupies his time with the inspection of sledges, repairing their broken parts, and so forth. The women take care of everything in the tent and in the sleeping-room. (Bogoras 1909:547)

ARAPESH, NEW GUINEA

> . . . if one comments upon a middle-aged man as good-looking, the people answer: "Good-looking? Y-e-s? But you should have seen him before he bore all those children." (Mead 1935)

One thing marriage involves is a division of labor: wife does some tasks, husband does other tasks, and still other tasks may be performed by either husband or wife, interchangeably. Usually, or always, these tasks are "set," to some extent, by custom. For example, it is regarded "proper" for the wife to do the cooking, the husband to do the plowing, and so forth. The sex segregation of a given task may be more or less rigid or strict, as depicted by the following scale:

1. Wife does the task; husband would be ashamed to do it.
2. Wife usually does the task; husband may do it without shame.
3. Either husband or wife may do it.
4. Husband usually does the task; wife may do it.
5. Husband does it; wife is not allowed to do it (or would be ashamed to do it).

In the Navaho example just given, milking goats seems to exemplify scale-point 1; cooking probably falls at scale-point 2; farm work and livestock care seem to fall at scale-point 4.

The division of labor between husband and wife, as well as the more general division of labor between men and women, seems to have little to do with the biological capabilities and limitations of the two sexes. With the exception of bearing and nursing children, a man is biologically capable of doing anything a woman can do. Conversely, a woman should be able to do anything a man can do, including heavy physical labor. Since sex division of labor rests on little in the way of biological "givens," one might expect great intercultural variation in "men's work" and "women's work." That is, there should be some societies in which the husband keeps house and cooks the meals while the wife hunts buffalo and fights the enemy; where the wife does the plowing and the husband knits and embroiders; and so forth. As a matter of fact, there is much less intercultural variation than one might expect. Work around the house—cooking, cleaning, child care, bringing in fuel and water—is nearly always the province of the wife; the husband may or may not help her. Other tasks, such as hunting, herding large animals, handicraft with metals or stone, and boat building, are nearly always done by men. Murdock has made a large cross-cultural survey of the division of labor by sex. His data is given in Table 2.

TABLE 2

COMPARATIVE DATA ON THE DIVISION OF LABOR BY SEX*

ACTIVITY	Number of Societies in Which: Men always do it	Men usually do it	Either sex may do it	Women usually do it	Women always do it
metal working	78	0	0	0	0
weapon making	121	1	0	0	0
pursuit of sea mammals	34	1	0	0	0
hunting	166	13	0	0	0
manufacture of musical instruments	45	2	0	0	1
boat building	91	4	4	0	1
mining and quarrying	35	1	1	0	1
work in wood and bark	113	9	5	1	1
work in stone	68	3	2	0	2
trapping or catching of small animals	128	13	4	1	2
lumbering	104	4	3	1	6
work in bone, horn, and shell	67	4	3	0	3
fishing	98	34	19	3	4
manufacture of ceremonial objects	37	1	13	0	1
herding	38	8	4	0	5
house building	86	32	25	3	14
clearing of land for agriculture	73	22	17	5	13
net making	44	6	4	2	11
trade	51	28	20	8	7
dairy operations	17	4	3	1	13
manufacture of ornaments	24	3	40	6	18
agriculture: soil preparation and planting	31	23	33	20	37
manufacture of leather products	29	3	9	3	32
body mutilations, for example, tattooing	16	14	44	22	20
erection and dismantling of shelter	14	2	5	6	22
hide preparation	31	2	4	4	49

* Adapted from Murdock 1937.

TABLE 2 (*Continued*)

ACTIVITY	Number of Societies in Which: Men always do it	Men usually do it	Either sex may do it	Women usually do it	Women always do it
tending of fowls and small animals	21	4	8	1	39
agriculture: crop tending and harvesting	10	15	35	39	44
gathering of shellfish	9	4	8	7	25
manufacture of nontextile fabrics	14	0	9	2	32
fire making and tending	18	6	25	22	62
burden bearing	12	6	35	20	57
preparation of drinks and narcotics	20	1	13	8	57
manufacture of thread and cordage	23	2	11	10	73
basket making	25	3	10	6	82
mat making	16	2	6	4	61
weaving	19	2	2	6	67
gathering of fruits, berries, and nuts	12	3	15	13	63
fuel gathering	22	1	10	19	89
pottery making	13	2	6	8	77
preservation of meat and fish	8	2	10	14	74
manufacture and repair of clothing	12	3	8	9	95
gathering of herbs, roots, and seeds	8	1	11	7	74
cooking	5	1	9	28	158
water carrying	7	0	5	7	119
grain grinding	2	4	5	13	114

Table 2 shows that while there may be no cultural universals in the sex-typing of tasks, there are a number of near-universals. At the top of Table 2 are the tasks that are nearly always performed by men: weapon making, making musical instruments, hunting, mining, and so forth. At the bottom of the table are the tasks nearly always done by women: cooking, water carrying, and grain grinding, for example. There are two other tasks mentioned in my ethnographic notes, but not included in Table 2, which also always seem to be "women's work" (with the man sometimes helping): housekeeping and care of young children.

In most societies, woman's work is *not* confined to the home; in addition to minding the children and keeping house, she also helps in the subsistence work, that is, in the getting, growing, or processing of food. In a hunting and gathering society the men customarily hunt while the women gather plant food. In many agricultural societies, women do a large share of the farm work. For the agricultural societies in Murdock's *World Ethnographic Sample*: in 83 cases, women do most of the farm work; in 125 societies, men do most of the farm work; in 133 societies, men and women make approximately equal contributions to the agricultural work. In short, in most societies wives do a lot of work. In a good many societies, they work harder than their husbands:

ALOR, EASTERN INDONESIA

> . . . the wealthier and more important a man is, the more he considers physical labor beneath his dignity. Visiting, sitting, talking, and chewing areca are the only physical exertions worthy of a man aware of his importance. The very fact that one goes in for muscular labor makes one's status suspect. Muscular labor is the role of women and the young. (DuBois 1944:132)

IFALUK, MICRONESIA

> Women almost always have work to perform, whereas the men spend hours just sitting about in the canoe houses. (Spiro 1949: 135–136)

KIWAI, MELANESIA

> To an onlooker the distribution of labour between husband and wife often appears very unequal, particularly when the family are returning from work in their gardens, carrying their loads. The woman is frequently seen almost staggering under her burden . . .

Only on longer wanderings does he share part of his wife's load, but even then he looks almost ashamed of having to do so. (Landtman 1927:172)

ANCIENT TEUTONS

"All the bravest of the warriors, committing the care of the house, the family affairs, and the lands, to the women, old men, and weaker part of the domestics, stupefy themselves in inaction." (Tacitus, quoted in Goodsell 1915:208)

The *strictness* of task segregation between husband and wife involves two things:

1. The proportion of tasks allocated to either husband or wife, as opposed to work that both may do—in the terms of my scale, this is the proportion of tasks at scale-points 1, 2, 4, and 5, compared with the number of tasks at scale-point 3.
2. The latitude for exception within the sex-typed tasks: how many tasks would be shameful, degrading, or taboo for the husband (or wife) to perform? In terms of the scale: how many tasks are there at scale-points 1 and 5?

I have data only on this second point: latitude for exceptions in sex-typed tasks. In fact, my data bear only on the husband's helping with the wife's tasks, not on the wife's doing work ordinarily allocated to the husband. The data come from two samples: my ethnographic notes (that is, written accounts in ethnographies), and ethnographer-interviews (cross-cultural data gathered as a result of directly interviewing the ethnographer about his field work; see Appendix).

In all societies with which I am acquainted, the wife ordinarily does the "work around the house": preparing and cooking food, house cleaning, fetching fuel and water (where this is required), and child care. She may get help in large or small amounts—from her husband, her older children, or other persons —but in all the cases in my samples, these tasks are "wife's work," to some extent, at least.[7] For some societies, the ethnographer reports that the husband does, at times, help his wife with these household tasks. For other societies, the ethnographer says that he never does, or that he would be ashamed to do so.

In twenty-three sample societies, the husband does some of the cooking; in twelve other societies, the husband would be ashamed to cook.[8]

In five societies, the husband may help his wife with the house cleaning; in eleven other cases, he never does.[9]

In four cases, the husband may help his wife clean up after meals (dishwashing, or its local equivalent); in ten other cases, he never helps with this.[10]

---

[7] Murdock found that this is not universally true in all societies. He discovered a few cases in which men, unaided by women, do the cooking and water carrying (Table 2). But none of these cases are in my cross-cultural sample (Murdock 1937).

[8] *Ethnographic notes.* Husband helps with cooking: Arepesh, Baiga, Fiji, Haida, Hopi, Lesu, Maria Gond, Muria, Murngin, Navaho, Samoa, Siwai, Tchambuli, Tikopia, Toda, Wogeo. Husband never cooks, or would be ashamed to cook: Lepcha, Tepoztlan, Ukraine.

Ethnographer-interview sample. Husband helps with cooking: Alor, Chanzeaux (France), Chiaromonte (Italy), Kwoma, Naples lower class, Peyrane (France), Yokohama middle class. Husband never cooks: Berbers, The Bog (Nova Scotia), Hutterites, Konso, Lacandon-Maya, Lasko (Yugoslavia), Nishapur (Iran), San Juan Pueblo, Villafranqueza (Spain).

For a few of the cases in which the husband cooks, he does only special types of cooking, associated with special dishes or special occasions. In other words, cooking may be subdivided into sex-segregated tasks for these cases: Arapesh, Fiji, Lesu, Murngin, Peyrane, Yokohama.

[9] *Ethnographic notes.* Husband helps with house cleaning: Hopi. Husband never helps with house cleaning: Tepoztlan.

Ethnographer-interview sample. Husband helps with house cleaning: Alor, Chanzeaux, Chiaromonte, Peyrane. Husband never helps with house cleaning: Berbers, The Bog, Hutterites, Konso, Lacandon-Maya, Lasko, Nishapur, San Juan Pueblo, Villafranqueza, Yokohama middle class.

[10] *Ethnographic notes.* No cases.

Ethnographer-interview sample. Husband helps clean up after meals: Alor, Chanzeaux, Chiaromonte, Peyrane. Husband never helps clean up after meals: Berbers, The Bog, Hutterites, Konso, Lacandon-Maya, Lasko, Nishapur, San Juan Pueblo, Villafranqueza, Yokohama middle class.

In ten societies, a man helps his wife carry water for household use; in five cases, he never does.[11]

In fourteen societies, husband may help his wife fetch fuel (usually wood); in two societies, he never does this.[12]

In twelve societies in my ethnographic notes, the husband helps take care of infants and young children; in four other societies, he never does this.[13]

In the ethnographer-interview, there were two items concerned with child care: whether the father may carry an infant or young child; and whether the father may feed an infant or young child. In ten of these ethnographer-interview cases, the father may carry his young child; in five cases, he never does this.[14] In two cases, the father may feed his young child; in ten cases, he never does.[15]

In most primitive tribes, the sex division of labor does not seem to be too strict. At least this appears to be the case for the

---

[11] *Ethnographic notes.* Husband helps with water carrying: Baiga, Hopi, Tchambuli, Tibet. Husband never helps with water carrying: Ukraine.

Ethnographer-interview sample. Husband helps with water carrying: Alor, Chiaromonte, Hutterites, Nishapur, San Juan Pueblo, Villanfranqueza. Husband never helps with water carrying: Berbers, Konso, Kwoma, Lacandon-Maya.

[12] *Ethnographic notes.* Husband may fetch fuel: Chukchee, Hopi, Tchambuli. Husband never fetches fuel: no cases.

Ethnographer-interview sample. Husband may fetch fuel: Alor, Berbers, Chanzeaux, Chiaromonte, Hutterites, Lacandon-Maya, Lasko, Nishapur, Peyrane, San Juan Pueblo, Villafranqueza. Husband never fetches fuel: Konso, Kwoma.

[13] *Ethnographic notes.* Husband helps take care of infants and young children: Arapesh, Baiga, Copper Eskimo, Kaingang, Kaska, Kurtachi, Lesu, Manus, Muria, Navaho, Tikopia, Trobriands. Husband never helps take care of infants and young children: China, Gusii, Tepoztlan, Wogeo.

[14] *Ethnographer-interview sample.* Husband may carry his infant or young child: Alor, Chiaromonte, Chanzeaux, Hutterites, Lasko, Naples lower class, Nishapur, Peyrane, San Juan Pueblo, Villafranqueza. Husband never carries his infant or young child: Berbers, Konso, Kwoma, Lacandon-Maya, Yokohama middle class.

[15] *Ethnographer-interview sample.* Husband may feed his infant or young child: Alor, Naples lower class. Husband never feeds his infant or young child: Berbers, The Bog, Chanzeaux, Hutterites, Lacandon-Maya, Lasko, San Juan Pueblo, Villafranqueza, Yokohama, Kwoma.

items on which I have data; a man may usually help his wife with such household work as cooking, child care, and water carrying. This also seems to be true of industrialized Western democracies: France, Italy, England (see Bott 1957), Australia (see Herbst 1952), and the United States. On the other hand, in the "peasant" cases—communities that are, or have been until recently, part of autocratic agrarian states—the division of labor tends to be stricter. In these cases, the husband is more likely to be "ashamed" to cook, clean house, fetch water, mind the baby, and so forth.

To summarize this section on men's work and women's work:

1. There are strong cross-cultural regularities in the sex-typing of tasks. Some activities—those given near the top of Table 2—are always, or almost always, allocated to men. Other jobs—the ones listed near the bottom of Table 2—are usually given to women. The wife nearly always "keeps house" (cooks, cleans, fetches fuel and water, among similar tasks), and—in all known cases—has child-care duties (if she has children).

2. In most societies, wives do more than "keep house" and "mind the children"; they also contribute to the subsistence economy. In quite a few societies, the wife's subsistence work is more important than the husband's.

3. With regard to the *strictness* of task segregation: in some societies men help their wives with household work; in other societies they never do this or would be "ashamed" to do it. There is some tendency for task segregation to be stricter in peasant communities, compared with primitive tribes and industrialized Western democracies.

Privilege

"Being women, eat crumbs." (Bogoras 1909:548) (Saying, Reindeer Chukchee)

In most societies, apparently, the more "important," honorific jobs and offices are the province of men; women are excluded from them. In the Trobriands, for example, women can't hold office, own land, or participate in tribal councils (Malinowski

1929:36). Among the Tallensi, women have "the status of minors" in religious, jural, and political matters (Fortes 1949:99). Also among the Azande, Kiwai, Nuer (usually), Nyakusa, Rajputs, and in Tepoztlan, women may not hold positions of community leadership or play any part in public life. Such was also the case in Puritan New England. In contrast, there is one case in my ethnographic notes—the Haida of the Northwest Coast—in which women, reportedly, are allowed a voice in "politics" and may attend clan councils (Murdock 1934:371).

In a few cases, however, women may attain some *religious* prominence and leadership. Among the Nuer, women occasionally become prophets and magicians (Evans-Pritchard 1940:178). The Ojibwa, Copper Eskimo, and Haida have female shamans. And the Manus, in their seances with Sir Ghost, rely on female mediums (Mead 1931).

At times, women are not only excluded from public life; they are also barred from public gatherings. Among the Baganda of Africa, "Women were never allowed into public places such as courts or wrestling games." (Kalibala 1946:221) In the Egyptian village of Silwa, women—being unclean—may not enter the mosque (Ammar 1954:49). The Rajputs of Khalapur keep their women in purdah. The Rajput wife is confined to her household's courtyard; except for a few special occasions, she may not go anywhere (Triandis and Hitchcock).

Returning to my ethnographer-interview: one item asked the anthropologists whether or not the wife is excluded from a good many social gatherings (gatherings that her husband may attend). For thirty-three societies, it was reported that the wife *was* excluded from a good many social gatherings; for thirteen societies, she was not (see Appendix).

We have now reviewed several aspects of the widespread social inequality between men and women. Before, we saw that men (in this unfortunately small sample of cases) preempt the "important" jobs (including formal leadership) for themselves. Women are also excluded from social gatherings and public places of various sorts. In Chapter 2, we saw that polygyny is extremely common and that polyandry is quite rare; this, I think, is another facet of the social inequality between the sexes. And, as Whiting and D'Andrade discovered (Chap. 3), distant patrilocal residence is not uncommon, but distant matrilocal residence is rare. That is, it is a frequent occurrence—characteristic of a fair number of societies—for a newly married bride to move far from home in order to join her husband and his kin. The reverse —the groom's moving far from home in order to join his bride and her kin—seldom occurs.

I will now review some other aspects of this widespread, transcultural "discrimination" against women, starting with inequalities in sexual regulations.

The Double Standard

In a good many societies, sex restrictions are more severe for women than they are for men. For thirteen sample societies, premarital sex restrictions bear more heavily on girls than on boys: Chiaromonte (Italy),[16] China (Taitou), Ifugao, Jamaica, Kwakiutl, Ancient Hebrews, Moslems of the Middle East, Naples lower class,[16] Navaho, Nishapur (Iran),[16] Ojibwa, Tepoztlan, and Yokohama middle class.[16] For no society is it reported that premarital sex regulations are stricter for men than for women. Likewise, I know of no society in which restrictions on adultery are more severe for men than for women. On the other hand, in eight cases, husbands are free to practice adultery, but wives are supposed to remain faithful: Gusii, Kipsigis, Ancient Greeks, Ancient Romans, Moslems of the Middle East, Papago, Tikopia, and Yokohama.[16] For two other cases, adultery rules seem to be stricter for wives than for husbands (Ancient Hebrews and Tepoztlan).

Ira Reiss has traced the persistence of the double standard throughout the history of Western society (Reiss 1960). During medieval times, not only were women more severely restricted; sex was supposed to be women's "fault":

> The sexual obsessions of the Church bore with especial hardness on woman. By the Saxons she had been treated as property; now she was treated as the source of all sexual evil as well. Chrys-

---

[16] From the ethnographer-interview sample.

ostom, less vindictive than some, spoke of woman as a "necessary evil, a natural temptation, a desirable calamity, a domestic peril, a deadly fascination, and a painted ill." But by the Middle Ages even these qualifications were no longer acceptable. "A Good Woman (as an old Philosopher observeth) is but like one Ele put in a bagge amongst 500 Snakes, and if a man should have the luck to grope out that one Ele from all the snakes, yet he hath at best but a wet Ele by the Taile." It was argued that sexual guilt really pertained to women, since they tempted men, who would otherwise have remained pure. (Taylor 1954:64)

Deference

Another aspect of social inequality between the sexes has to do with deference customs. In Chapter 3 I described deference as follows: "Deference involves the general posture of respect, submissiveness, and obedience. It characterizes unequal relationships. The inferior, submissive person shows deference to the dominant, superior, privileged person." Some examples of deference customs are bowing, kneeling, hand kissing; speech etiquette, such as speaking to the deferred-to person in a low voice, or using special respectful language; mealtime etiquette, such as giving the deferred-to person a seat of honor, letting him be the first to start eating, giving him the choice food; body-elevation rules, such as not being higher than the deferred-to person, standing up when greeting him, and so forth. ". . . . deference is a sort of ritual expression of social inequality; the deference customs seem to say, 'you are strong, I am weak; you are noble, I am base; you are privileged, I am unprivileged.' "

In other words, deference customs imply two things: 1) *privilege*—the deferred-to person is more privileged than the deferential person; he has such privileges as the best seat, and the choicest food; 2) *power*—the deferential person is restrained and meek, obeys the deferred-to person's commands, and so on. Of course, the implication of power is an assumption. Deference does not necessarily *have* to mean power inequality. There are, no doubt, some wives, in some societies, who follow the prescribed deference customs—perhaps bowing to their husbands. and giving their husbands the seat of honor at the dinner table—and yet manage, by more or less subtle means. to hold their own in the family power struggle. However, perhaps we can more safely assume that a deference custom implies a *cultural expectation* of submissiveness on the part of the deferential party and of real power in the hands of the deferred-to party.

As you might expect, wife-to-husband deference customs are practiced in many societies. Husband-to-wife deference customs, on the other hand, are quite rare. Many societies expect wives to be deferential to their husbands. Practically no society expects husbands to be deferential to wives. Here are some examples of wife-to-husband deference customs:

GANDA, AFRICA

Women were required by custom to kneel down while greeting men. They did not kneel on their knees, but folded their legs behind them, with their feet turned inside out, forming a flat seat and settled down. They then extended both hands up, the man bent over to meet their hands and with the right hand exchanged the greeting. Even though the man had no rank, the woman greeted him with a sir or *sebo*. (Kalibala 1946:308)

The duties to which the husband attaches most importance are that his wife should wash his feet every night. (Mair 1934:96)

UKRAINE

. . . When they walk together, the wife usually keeps at least half a pace behind her mate, and when they enter the house he always precedes her. When there is only one animal at their disposal, it is the husband who rides upon the horse, while his wife trails behind on foot. If there is a burden to be carried, it is usually the woman who bears it. (Koenig 1937:307)

SUYE MURA, JAPAN

. . . He (husband-father) is first to take a bath, first to be served with food or *shochu*, and he has a special place to sit by the fire pit. (Embree 1939:80)

DRAGALETVSY, BULGARIA

A Dragaletvsy peasant saw nothing strange in the sight of a man riding a donkey while his wife trudged along behind carrying their purchases home from market.

The well-trained wife always deferred to her husband. If ever

I asked a question in the presence of both, the woman turned her eyes to see what response her husband made. If he made a gesture as though to say, "You go ahead and answer," then she began to talk, becoming silent whenever her husband wished to interject any comments. (Sanders 1949:95)

REINDEER CHUKCHEE, SIBERIA

After the reindeer is slaughtered, the woman has to skin it and butcher it; then she must carry everything to its proper place. She prepares the food, and presents it to her husband. She cuts off the best, and takes what is left, gnaws the bones, gathers all crumbs and scraps. Such delicacies as brains, marrow, and so forth, are eaten almost exclusively by men. Women are satisfied with licking their fingers when cutting the dainties into small pieces for the use of the men. "Being women, eat crumbs," is a saying of the Chukchee.

Women eat only after the men have finished. (Bogoras 1909: 548)

MODJOKUTO, JAVA

The father in the family traditionally receives better food, dresses better than the rest of the family. It is he for whom the one piece of meat is saved. In some families no one can eat the main meal till after father has had his pick. (Geertz 1956:126)

RAJPUTS OF KHALAPUR, HINDU INDIA

The subordinate status of women is further emphasized by the custom that women must crouch on the floor and pull their saris over their faces when in the presence of their husband or any man older than their husband. . . . When a man has entered the house for his meal, he will quickly retire to a room or behind the wall of his hearth. The women are then free to move about their business quietly. . . .

Because of this custom the men always announce their presence with a warning cough before entering the household and when possible send a boy, or the youngest male present on errands to the courtyard, since the younger the man the fewer are the women who must keep purdah from him. When the eldest male enters, the entire courtyard is immobilized until he has been safely attended. In nuclear families the wife usually does not cover her face before her husband, but only because the man usually requests her not to continue this custom. (Triandis and Hitchcock)

In six societies in my ethnographic notes, a wife must kneel or crouch before her husband: Rajputs; Tallensi (when offering him food); and Bemba, Ganda, Mende, and Nyakusa (when greeting him). In six societies, the woman is reported to walk behind her husband: Chiricahua Apache, Ifaluk, Mende, Nama Hottentots, Tallensi, and Ukraine. For five cases, the husband is said to get the choice food: Bemba, Reindeer Chukchee, Modjokuto (Java), Silwa (Egypt), and Taitou (China). For no society in my ethnographic notes is there any mention of husband-to-wife deference customs.

Additional data is supplied by the ethnographer-interview sample. In twenty-seven societies in the ethnographer-interview sample, the wife customarily walks behind her husband; in twenty-three societies, she does not (see Appendix). In two cases, the wife bows when greeting her husband (Yokohama and Nishapur); in forty-nine cases, she does not. For eleven cases, the husband sits on a chair, stool, or bench, while his wife sits or kneels on the floor (Alor, Ashanti,[17] Cuchumatan Mam, Greece,[17] Guaymi, Marian, Nishapur,[18] San Pedro la Laguna, Sherpa, Somali,[17] Zinacantan). In twelve other cases, the husband has a special sitting place, a "seat of honor," such as the seat at the head of the dinner table (Amman, Dragaletvsy, Hutterites, Konso, Lasko, Madiun, Magazawa, Minangkabau, Toba Batak, Vaish, Villafranqueza, Yokohama). In Barranquitas (Puerto Rico), a woman washes her husband's feet at night. In Dragaletvsy, a wife kisses her husband's hand when he returns from a trip. If others are present, a Kurdish woman stands when her husband enters the room. A Somali woman, if not especially busy, also rises when her husband approaches. In Madiun (Java), a woman must *not* be standing while her husband kneels or

---

[17] In these cases, if there is one seat the husband gets it; his wife sits on the ground.

[18] Here the husband sits in a chair while his wife remains standing.

stoops. For ten cases, when husband and wife are with other people, the wife stays in the background, lets her husband do the talking, and is elaborately respectful, submissive, and quiet (her manner sometimes changes, however, when she gets her husband alone) (Cook Islanders, Barranquitas, Dragaletvsy, Druz, Greece, Guaymi, Hutterites, Vaish, Kurds, and Toba Batak).

In three cases in the ethnographer-interview sample, the wife does receive some deference from her husband. In one case, a Berber group, the Dragaletvsy situation is reversed: the *wife* rides the donkey, and her husband walks behind, in her dust. The other two cases are European: Brno (Czechoslovakia) and Madrid (aristocrats). In Brno, the wife is seated first at the dinner table, and starts eating first. Among the Madrid aristocracy, the woman walks on her husband's right (the honorific side), has the most honorific seat at the dinner table, and is served first; a husband holds the chair for his wife, and stands when his wife enters the room (on formal occasions). These elegant "good manners" toward females are remnants of the old chivalric code, which—Beigel believes—began in the Middle Ages as a result of attitudes engendered by the conventions of courtly love or "romantic love," as first practiced, sung and popularized by the troubadours (Beigel 1951:328). Such chivalric customs still have some currency in modern-day America, partly because of their enthusiastic espousal by female arbiters of etiquette such as Emily Post. We (a few of us, anyway) hold the door for a woman, and let her enter first; give her the last unoccupied seat on the bus; stay on the streetside when walking down the sidewalk; and so forth. In this respect, Western society is very peculiar. Throughout the rest of the world (with the Berbers as the one exception known to me) such things simply are not done. Men are not chivalrous toward women. Women, instead, are chivalrous toward men.

Power

"Since you are a woman, be silent." (Bogoras 1909:547) (Saying, Reindeer Chukchee)

The *power* relationship between husband and wife has to do with who dominates and who submits; who makes the family decisions—husband, wife, or both jointly; who gets his (or her) way in case of disagreements; who is catered to; who commands; who obeys; and so forth. A deference custom, as I stated previously, is a ritual expression or cultural expectation of an unequal power relationship. Power, in a sense, is more fundamental than deference; it is "the real thing." It is also harder to find out about on a cultural or societal level.

In three respects, a cross-cultural assessment of husband-wife power relationships is difficult. In the first place, power relationships are harder for the ethnographer to observe than are deference customs. Traditional deference customs tend to be clear cut, standardized, and public. Customs such as the wife's kneeling to her husband, walking behind him, giving him the chair while she sits on the ground, are relatively easy for the ethnographer to observe and record. The customs—the cultural rules—are there. Informants can tell him about them, and he can see them in practice; the ethnographer need merely record them. Power relationships, on the other hand, tend to be less clear cut, less neatly summarized in cultural rules, and less "public," that is, less open to the ethnographer's scrutiny. Perhaps, in a given society, the husband is supposed to be "boss," and his wife gives him respect and obedience when they are in public; but what happens when they are alone, behind the walls of their home?

Secondly, I suspect that power relationships tend to vary a good deal within the same society. For example, in a society where the wife supposedly "obeys" her husband, there are, no doubt, some families in which the husband "obeys" his wife. Of course, deference customs may also admit exceptions; for example, in a society where women are supposed to walk behind their husbands, there may be a few wives who don't do this, or sometimes do it and sometimes don't. A deference *rule* may be violated by individuals. A power relationship, on the other hand, does not rest on a single "cultural rule"; it depends on many "rules" or customs, some of them fairly explicit and some of them not. It also depends on the personalities of the spouses. A power relationship is not a single "custom," in other words. It is the result of the complicated interaction of many things. My guess would be that in many societies there is great variation between families vis-à-vis husband-wife power relations. However, this intraculture variation is impossible to assess except in the crudest way: by noting that there are some families which are "exceptions" to the "normal" husband-wife power relationship.

The third difficulty with power relationships is that they are usually poorly reported in ethnographies. A few vague descriptive terms—such as "respect," "obeys," "fairly independent," "dominant"—and a few illustrative anecdotes, with perhaps some general allusion to jural rights (such as property-ownership)—is all the typical ethnographer gives us on the husband-wife power relationship. This is largely due to the other two difficulties just mentioned. Since power-relationships are hard to find out about, they tend to be ill-reported, that is, reported in a vague and fragmentary fashion. Deference customs, in contrast, being relatively clear cut and easy to find out about, are relatively well reported.

In this discussion of husband-wife power, I will be drawing again on two samples: the ethnographic notes (notes from written ethnographies) and the ethnographer-interviews (described in the Appendix). The ethnographic notes have all the difficulties and limitations just alluded to. The ethnographer-interview material is a bit better, in that it is somewhat more specific and clear; however, it, too, has the first two difficulties, the problem of intracultural variation, and the difficulty of knowing what *really* happens behind closed doors. I will begin with the ethnographic notes.

Twenty-one societies in my ethnographic notes are truly "patriarchal" (if we may believe the ethnographers).[19] In these cases the husband (in the "normal" or "most typical" family) is

---

[19] Araucanians, Arunta, Aymara, Azande, Reindeer Chukchee, Fiji, Ganda, Gusii, Ireland (County Clare), Kikuya, Mende, Moslems of the Middle East, Nuer, Orasac (Serbia), Rajputs of Khalapur (India), Samoa, Silwa (Egypt), Suye Mura (Japan), Tepoztlan (Mexico), Tonga, and Ukraine.

strongly and clearly dominant over his wife. Here is an example of a case of this sort:

GANDA, AFRICA

> The wife is expected to take a subordinate position; she should obey her husband and he is entitled to beat her if she does not do so. The household is organized for his convenience; meals should be ready at the times when he likes to eat, and the wife should not cook for herself in his absence. She should ask his permission to go visiting, and if she goes away from home to sleep he fixes the number of days that she may be away. (Mair 1940:13)

In six additional societies, the husband is reported to be only very mildly dominant over his wife (Baiga, Haida, Kiwai, Siwai, Tallensi, and Tarong). In five societies, husband and wife are said to normally have fairly equal power (Bemba, Chenchu, Ifugao, Murngin, and Trobriands). In six other cases, it is reported that husband and wife each has his or her own clear-cut sphere of authority; within her sphere, the wife is supreme (Chagga, Copper Eskimo, Hopi, Lakher, Nama Hottentot, and Nyakusa). Here is an example of separate spheres of authority:

NAMA HOTTENTOT, SOUTH AFRICA

> The status of the wife in Hottentot society is far from being that of an inferior. Although as a rule she plays a subordinate role in matters pertaining to tribal life, and in public always walks several paces behind her husband, yet her position in the household is supreme, and the education of the children is wholly in her hands. She is regarded as the mistress of the hut, which she brings with her at marriage, and of all its contents. She even has the right in certain circumstances to forbid her husband to enter it. She has her own property in cattle, some given to her by her parents while she was still a child, others when she was married, and her husband will not venture to sell or slaughter an animal belonging to her without her consent or in her absence. Even if he intends to barter his own stock he usually first consults her, and during his absence she also controls the pasturing of the herds. She supervises or herself does the milking which provides the household with most of its food, and controls all the provisions, allotting to each his food according to status and age, and brooking no contradiction.

> Her husband may not even take a mouthful of milk without first obtaining her permission, and should he do so, says Hahn, his nearest female relatives will put a fine on him. (Schapera 1930: 251)

Finally, in three cases in my ethnographic notes, the balance of power seems to rest with the wife. (Perhaps the Nama Hottentots should be added here, as a fourth case.) Among the Tchambuli of New Guinea, the men seem to have the greater jural rights. (The situation is unclear.) But, says Mead, the women "really run things"; since they do almost all the work, they also do most of the managing and decision making (Mead 1935).

In Modjokuto (Java), the husband seems to have a rather lofty, "honored" position; he receives formalized deference behavior from the rest of the family. However:

> . . . most men give all or the greater part of their earnings to their wives and are forced to ask for every cent of spending money as they need it. . . .
>
> The range of variation on the dimension of responsibility for major decisions of household management goes from dominance by the wife to a point of rather complete equality between husband and wife, with discussion over every major issue. . . .
>
> Anger is to be avoided if possible, and above all the neighbours must not know, must not hear the sounds of quarreling. . . . Many husbands—perhaps most—give in to their wives most of the time in order to avoid unpleasantness. (Geertz 1956:120–137)

The third case is the Jivaro, fierce head-hunters (and headshrinkers) of the Amazon basin. Here there is a conflict between ethnographers. Vigna says: "The husband is absolute master of his wife. If he finds that she is unfaithful, he will punish her harshly and severely, inflicting wounds with the machete in her head or body." (Later he adds, ". . . the rage, cunning and malevolence of the Jivaro women is beyond belief.") (Vigna 1945:44) However, if we are to believe Karsten, the Jivaro are ruled by their wives:

Some words may be added as to the position of the women. Those few writers who have touched upon the social position of the Jivaro woman have described it in that biased and erroneous way which has been the rule especially among missionaries when they have dealt with the position of women in savage societies: she is nothing but an oppressed slave, without rights, and hardly regarded as a personality at all. The truth is that the married Jivaro woman is not only completely independent within her own sphere of activity, but exercises a remarkable social influence and authority even in matters which mainly concern the husband. It is interesting to state in this respect that a family-father never sells fruit or other articles of food without the consent of his wife. There are, I think, few civilized societies where the man so unfailingly asks his wife's advice, even in unimportant matters, as among these savages. It occurred very frequently during my travels in the forest that I paid visits to the Jivaro houses to buy manioc or bananas, and received from the "autocrat" of the house the answer: "I must first ask my wife." Frequently the wife happened to be absent for the moment and then the answer was: "Wait a while until my wife arrives." I saw that there was a store of manioc and bananas in the house, and it would have been an easy thing for the man to give me immediately what I wanted to buy; yet he compelled me to wait for a long while, perhaps for hours, only to be able to ask his wife's permission to make the insignificant bargain. Still one can understand this consideration of the housewife when articles of food are in question. Since the wife is the keeper of the food and is responsible for the existence of a store sufficient for the needs of the family, it is natural that she should also be allowed to decide how much of it can be given to strangers. But her influence seems to be about the same in other matters. Both among the Jivaros and the Canelos Indians, when I tried to find an Indian to go with me on a certain journey, I frequently received the same answer: "I must first ask the advice of my wife." . . . When a thing, however insignificant, was to be bartered, the women always wished to have a voice—and their decision was generally final. It might seem natural that the men alone should have the right to decide, for instance, respecting feather ornaments and other ornaments which they themselves make and only they use, things which in fact are always regarded as strictly personal property. Still even when trying to barter for such ornaments I frequently received the usual answer: "I must first ask the advice of my wife." . . .

> . . . the women are natural arbitrators in the family, and when at the feasts the men get drunk and show fight, the women part them and deprive them of their weapons. (Karsten 1935:253–256)

In short, for three cases in the ethnographic notes—Tchambuli, Modjokuto, and Jivaro—wives seem to have a power advantage over their husbands. The Nama Hottentots might be included here as a fourth case. A final case comes from the ethnographer-interview sample: the Berbers, among whom the wife not only rides the donkey (while her husband walks behind, in her dust), but also customarily orders her husband about.

"Matriarchies"—societies in which women customarily rule (within the home)—are rare. The ethnographer-interview sample contains fifty-three cases, with just one possible "matriarchy," the Berbers (see Appendix). Forty-three additional cases are represented in the ethnographic notes; in these, there are three or four possible "matriarchies": Tchambuli, Modjokuto, Jivaro, and perhaps Nama.

Dominance-by-wife is mentioned as a variant pattern for a few other societies. Among the Tibetan peasantry, in instances of matrilocal residence (not the most usual living arrangement), the wife is said to rank her husband (Bell 1928:156). In Taitou, says Yang, a young wife is extremely submissive; however, if she lives long enough to have married children and grandchildren, she may eventually be the informal ruler of the household, although still according her husband formal deference (Yang 1945:56). And for six societies, there is mention of a few henpecked husbands (Andaman Islanders, Chenchu, Reindeer Chukchee, Kurtachi, Samoa and Siwai).

> The wife is often harshly treated by her husband. I have mentioned the case of a husband killing his wife with a blow of a firebrand. Blows, though less severe, are not infrequently dealt out to women; but it also happens that a wife ill-treats her husband. I recall one man of small stature, with but little physical strength, but very irascible. Quarrels between him and his wife were not rare. When it would come to blows, his wife would throw him, and keep him down, asking, "Have you enough? Will you cease?"

until he would say, "Enough, I will cease." His neighbors told me this story with much laughter. (Borgoras 1909:551) (Reindeer Chukchee, Siberia)[20]

In the language of politics, husbands and wives may be viewed as two separate and opposing interest groups. If a husband gains in power, his wife must lose power; if he gains in privilege, his wife loses privileges, and vice versa. Marriage—seen in these terms—is a power struggle. The husband may "win" (and become a dominating patriarch) or "lose" (and be a hen-pecked husband); or they may "tie" (and have an equalitarian marital relationship). One gets the impression that men usually have an initial advantage in this struggle. It looks as if men often make the rules to suit themselves; the deference customs, the jural rights, generally point in the direction of a power advantage for the husband. In the face of this initial handicap, a wife—if she wishes to fight back—must employ characteristically female weapons. Sometimes she does fairly well:

> "Whenever I failed in my duties to Irene, she found ways to torment me. She scolded, cried, even before relatives and neighbors, wasted our property, gossiped about me, teased me in public, and called me 'lazybones who sits in the shade.' That was one of the sharpest taunts to bear. She drenched me for sleeping after sunrise, denied me sexual pleasure by coldness, or by acting like a dead sheep, and sometimes threatened to drive me out of her house. She had the power and the means to make me so unhappy that my health might be endangered. A wife may even wish for her husband's death, fill his mind and system with bad thoughts, and then do nothing to save him. On the other hand, she may wish for her own death in order to punish her husband and thus cause

[20] For eleven societies, it is reported that wife beating is a frequent and socially accepted practice: Arunta, Azande, Reindeer Chukchee, Ganda, Gusii, Kiwai, Kurtachi, Kwoma, Lakher, Murngin, and Ukraine. Speaking of the Lakher of Burma, Parry observes: "Though a Lakher will beat his wife if he thinks she deserves it, he does not as a rule do so without good cause." (Parry 1932:276)

neighbors and even the poor man himself to believe that he is killing her.

"It was better for Irene to persuade than to compel me, and she learned to do this very well. She trained herself in nice quiet manners." (Simmons 1942:273) (Hopi)

To conclude this section on a Thurberian note, here is an episode in the age-old, transcultural War Between the Men and the Women:

> Perhaps the most curious tradition in the relation of the sexes is the old story of the Stiria Raj. Dhan Singh remembers it vividly when he was a young man in Kapripani fifty years ago. A great company of Baiga women were filled with one of those "inspirations" that descend from time to time on primitive tribes. They dressed up as men, adorned themselves with men's ornaments and tied turbans on their heads. Carrying spears and bows and arrows, they went out as an army. When they came to a village, they beat all the men, and drove them to take shelter in their houses. Then they caught a pig, cut off its ears and tail and gave them to the headman. They took the pig and marched home. Then the women of the village they had visited took the ears and tail from the headman and themselves formed an army and marched to the next village. There they repeated the process with another pig. Meanwhile the women of the original village captured a man and made him their servant. They made him kill the pig and roast it. Then they had a great feast and ended all with the Karma.
>
> "We men were very frightened," says Dhan Singh. "For the women had spears and they were mad. Who knew what they would do?" (Elwin 1939:238–239) (Baiga, India)

Conclusion

Morris Zelditch, in a previous cross-cultural survey, came to the conclusion that there are universal features to the patterning of husband-wife roles. Everywhere, says Zelditch, the husband-role has certain distinctive attributes, and the wife-role other, different, attributes. In all societies, he says, the husband is the *instrumental leader*, and the wife is the *expressive leader*. Expressive leadership—the wife's universal role—has to do with nurturance (feeding everyone, caring for the children, keeping house, plus the emotional concomitants of these nurturant tasks). Instrumental leadership—the husband's universal role—has to do with making the big decisions, being the ultimate disciplinarian, and taking responsibility for the family's economic security (Zelditch 1955).

Zelditch's generalization regarding the universal attributes of husband-wife roles needs some qualification. It is probably too much to claim that there is a certain type of role differentiation that is universal to *all* families. I feel sure Zelditch would agree to this. It would be safer to claim universality on a society level (thus allowing for exceptional families within societies), and even this is probably a bit rash. Further, I would not choose the labels "instrumental leader" and "expressive leader" to describe the attributes of husband-role and wife-role.

Still, making allowance for these qualifications, I think there is some validity to Zelditch's statement. There are extraordinary cross-cultural regularities in husband-wife roles. Zelditch, as far as I know, was the first to point this out. Murdock's and my data support him (that is, support the general drift of his argument). Perhaps there are no universal marital-role attributes. But there do seem to be some near-universals.

First, there are near-universals in the division of labor. As Murdock found, some tasks seem to be "inherently masculine": metal working, weapon making, hunting, boat building, mining, lumbering, and other tasks at the top of Table 2. Women do these tasks rarely; men nearly always do them. Other tasks seem to be inherently feminine: child care, housekeeping, grain grinding, water carrying, cooking, gathering of wild vegetable foods, sewing, and so forth (bottom of Table 2). Men seldom do these tasks; women nearly always do them. For some tasks, this near-universality in the division of labor "makes sense" (example: infant care in the hands of women). For other tasks, it does not make obvious sense. Why can't women do metal working, weapon making, or handicraft work in wood or stone? Why can't men fetch water and grind grain?

Second, it is probably true that every society does have a standard division of labor between spouses. That is, in every society, it is thought "proper" for wife to do some jobs (such as child care, cooking, housekeeping, water hauling), and for husband to do other jobs (such as hunting and fishing). This is, in truth, an unfounded generalization. I did not gather data specifically on this point. It is merely my impression that everywhere there is a traditional, culturally standardized division of labor between husband and wife. If there are any exceptional societies (in which each family may freely choose—or fight it out—to determine who does what), our own society probably comes as close as any.

Third, power and privilege tend to be in the hands of men. If there are social inequities between the sexes, women tend to be the "underprivileged minority group" in matters of marriage form (polygyny), sex restrictions, marital residence (moving far from home), and access to public gatherings and public office. Traditional cultural rules having to do with power relationships within the family appear to have been "made" by men. Deference customs are nearly always wife-to-husband, rarely husband-to-wife. Real power within the family also seems, in the majority of cases, to be in the hands of the husband. When it is not, it often appears to be a case of an overturning of the "proper" power relationship as a result of female subversion.

To summarize, these are the apparent near-universals of husband-wife roles:

1. A standard division of labor by sex.
2. The "essential femininity" of some tasks, such as child care, and the "essential masculinity" of other tasks, such as fishing.
3. Power and privilege: the husband's status is either equal to or higher than the wife's; matriarchies are rare.

In regard to this last point, the American housewife does extremely well. She does not have to observe deference customs toward her husband; if anything, he accords her deference. In general, her power position is a relatively strong one (Blood and Hamblin 1958; Blood and Wolfe 1960). Her position is also good vis-à-vis marriage form (absence of polygyny), sex restrictions, marital residence, and access to social gatherings and to "important," "honorable" jobs and offices. She has become "emancipated," partly as a result of political agitation (the feminist movement), and partly, no doubt, because of the peculiarities of the American family situation (the isolated nuclear family, the detraditionalized life style) (Parsons 1943; Reiss 1960:59–65).

In the allocation of power and privilege, our society—compared with other societies—treats its wives most generously.

7

Power and Deference

In the last chapter I began discussing power and deference. Now I will expand that discussion. First, we shall look at power and deference as they occur within other family relationships: child to father and child to mother. Then I will describe some patterning regularities that characterize deference behavior between kin. Finally, I shall talk about the autocratic family, and its occurrence within autocratic states. As in Chapter 6, we will be moving back and forth between two sets of cross-cultural data: 1) my ethnographic notes (notes taken from the written ethnographies); and 2) the ethnographer-interview (ethnographic data supplied by anthropologists in response to interview questions). The ethnographer-interview is described in the Appendix. Once more, we will be dealing with two related orders of phenomena—deference, and real power. To begin, I had better make a few review-comments on deference and power.

Formalized deference customs seem to represent a ritual expression or cultural expectation of an unequal power relationship. Deference does not *have* to signalize power, but most of the time, no doubt, it does. If, for example, the husband gets the best food, the best chair, special respectful language, in most cases he probably has real power over his wife. But there are instances where this is not the case—Modjokuto, for example, where the husband receives much formalized deference, but his wife usually seems to wield the informal control.

Real power has to do with who actually commands, leads, decides, manipulates, and so forth. Power is harder to observe and report than deference; in Chapter 6 I outlined some possible reasons for this. Power is less public, less easily observable than deference. Unlike deference, power is not neatly summarized in formal cultural rules. No doubt there is considerable intracultural variation (variation between families within the same society) vis-à-vis power relationships; this intracultural variation is not and probably cannot be adequately assessed by the ethnographers. Finally, the *language* for describing power relations used in most ethnographies is rather inadequate. Often, we are given little more than vague descriptive terms, such as "respects," "honors," "obeys."

There is another data problem here, which is serious—especially when we begin to examine power relations between child and parent. Power relations probably change over time. For example, a father may have differing degrees of power over his son, depending on whether the son is three years old, seven, twelve, eighteen, twenty-five, or fifty. (Usually, I imagine, the power tends to diminish with age.) No doubt there are points of role transition that mark a change in the power of father over son—particularly, when the son marries, when the son leaves home (if he ever does), and when the father "retires" from active work (if he ever does). Some ethnographers try to describe these life-cycle changes, but many don't. When one attempts a cross-cultural summary of father-son power relations, this time-dimension is an extra source of error and ambiquity. As a hypothetical example, let us take three societies in which the son is said to "obey" his father (with son's age unspecified). In one case, the ethnographer is really referring to an immature son, a little boy (although he doesn't say so). In the second case, the ethnographer refers to a son up to the time of his marriage. In the third case, the son "obeys" his father as long as the father lives.

In view of all this potential error, it may seem that any cross-cultural assessment of power in the family is necessarily doomed, that it is building on sand. I don't think this is the case. For one thing, I limit myself to the sort of generalizations which, I think, can be legitimately documented—even with relatively "bad" data. Secondly, the ethnographer-interview does, in some ways, offer "better" data than the ethnographic notes. In one respect, particularly, the ethnographer-interview is superior: it specifies the life-cycle stage. All ethnographer-interview data pertain to a male ego who is in his twenties, married, with at least one child. The father-son data, therefore, refer to the relationship between this male ego and his old father. The husband-wife material describes the relationship between a young married couple with at least one child.

Father and Child

> "If my father or my elder brother tells me to stand in one place, I'll stand there, dammit, all day if need be, until they tell me I can move." (Carstairs 1958:69) (Deoli, Hindu India)

> "One of the greatest benefits that God ever gave me is that he sent me so sharpe and severe Parents. . . . For when I am in presence of either father or mother, whether I speake, kepe silence, sit, stand, or go, eate, drinke, be merie or sad, be sewying, plaiyng, dauncing, or doing anie thing els, I must do it, as it were in soch weight, mesure, and number, even as perfitlie as God made the world, or els I am so sharply taunted, so cruellie threatened, yea presentlie sometyms, with pinches, nippes, and bobbes, and other waies which I will not name for the honor I beare them, so without measure misordered that I think myself in hell." (Goodsell 1915:285–286) (Seventeenth-century England)

The first fact to be noted here is that father is rarely submissive to child. In some societies the father is a stern, controlling autocrat; in other societies his power is relatively weak, and he gives his children a large measure of freedom. However, he rarely "obeys" his children or is submissive to them; they rarely "command" him or dominate him. The father frequently gets deference from his children; in only one case, to my knowledge, does he *give* his children deference.

The Father-daughter Relationship

For twenty-one societies in my ethnographic notes, the daughter is described as being submissive to her father.[1] In twelve of these cases, she also accords her father formal deference: she either bows to him, uses special respectful language to him, or cedes him various sorts of privileges and priorities, for example, the best food, and the most honorific seating place.[2] For six additional societies, daughter-to-father deference customs are mentioned, but there is no statement about the real power relationship between father and daughter.[3] In my ethnographic notes, there are only two cases in which a female may have a dominant position vis-à-vis her father: Marquesas and Truk. I shall have more to say about these cases in a moment.

In short, the father-daughter power relationship seems to be heavily weighted in favor of the father. It looks as if equality—or a "democratic" relationship—represents the highest possible power position for the daughter, and the lowest for her father. This generalization, like most such global generalizations, does require some qualification. In the first place, there are doubtless some exceptions. We have the cases of the Marquesans and Trukese. Also, in some societies there may be a few "henpecked fathers." Then, as we shall see in the next chapter, some peoples "spoil" their young children outrageously, by our standards. A child, if sufficiently spoiled and catered to, might be said to have a power advantage over his parents. Finally, there is scant mention in the ethnographic literature of "equalitarian" father-daugh-

---

[1] Araucanians, Aymara, Azande, Bemba, seventeenth-century England, Ganda, Ireland, Kikuyu, Moslems of the Middle East, Nuer, Nyakusa, Orasac (Serbia), Papago, Silwa (Egypt), Suye Mura (Japan), Taitou (China), Tallensi, Tepoztlan (Mexico), Thonga, Ukraine, and Valle Cana (Puerto Rico).

[2] Araucanians, Bemba, Ganda, seventeenth-century England, Kikuyu, Nuer, Nyakusa, Silwa, Suya Mura, Tallensi, Tepoztlan, Thonga.

[3] Jukun, Lamba, Modjokuto (Java), Rajputs of Khalapur (India), Toda, and Tonga.

ter relationships. Either the ethnographer comments on the power of father over daughter, or he has nothing to say about father-daughter power relations.

The Father-son Relationship

For this relationship, I have data from two samples: the ethnographic notes and the ethnographer-interview. Within the ethnographer-interview sample, there is no society in which the son customarily is dominant over his father. In twenty-nine of these fifty cases, the father is somewhat of an autocrat over his son. For twenty-one cases, the father also receives rather extreme-sounding deference from his son.

Turning to the data from my ethnographic notes, we see a similar trend, but with a few exceptions. For twenty-seven societies, the father is said to be customarily dominant over his son.[4] In twelve of these cases, the son also observes formalized deference customs toward his father.[5] In seven additional cases, son-to-father deference customs are mentioned, but there is no assessment of the real power relationship.[6] Opposed to these twenty-seven (or thirty-four) cases in which father is customarily dominant over son, there are eight more cases in which, apparently, he is *not* dominant. For two societies (Manus and Siwai), the ethnographer comments on the freedom, equalitarianism, and lack of "respect" in the father-son relationship. In two Australian tribes, Murngin and Yir-Yiront, the father is said not to discipline his son; disciplining is left to other kin. Among the Ifugao, a father is said to relinquish all authority over his son

[4] Aymara, Azande, Bemba, Reindeer Chukchee, Dahomey, Deoli (India), seventeenth-century England, Fiji, Gusii, Ireland (countrymen of County Clare), Kikuyu, Mende, Moslems of the Middle East, Nuer, Ontong Java, Orasac (Serbia), Papago, Rajputs of Khalapur (India), Silwa (Egypt), Suye Mura (Japan), Taitou (China), Tallensi, Tepoztlan (Mexico), Thonga, Tikopia, Ukraine, and Valle Cana (Puerto Rico).

[5] Reindeer Chukchee, Bemba, seventeenth-century England, Fiji, Gusii, Ireland, Orasac, Papago, Silwa, Suye Mura, Taitou, and Tepoztlan.

[6] Baiga, Ganda, Modjokuto, Jukun, Lamba, Nyakusa, and Tonga.

when the son marries. In the Philippine village of Tarong, an elderly, retired father slips to the lowly position of pensioner; he becomes a low-status dependent in the house of his son.

Finally, there are two extraordinary cases in which little boys are dominant over their fathers. One is Truk (Micronesia), where a father observes the following deference rules in relation to his son: "must not refuse a request," "must not speak harshly to," and "must not use fight talk." (Goodenough 1951) According to Anne Fischer, "The Trukese child has an enviable role in many respects, until, if a girl she reaches the age of about seven, or, if a boy, the age of ten or eleven. Until that time the word of the child is supposed to be obeyed by adults." (Fischer m.s.)

The second case of child dominance is the Marquesans (Polynesia), whose polyandrous marriage customs were described in Chapter 2:

> The eldest child of either sex, or the child who was adopted to take the position of the eldest, became the official head of the household from the moment of birth or arrival. . . . Of course, in practice, the father administered the household group until the child reached maturity, but socially the child outranked his father from the moment of birth. . . .
>
> Very little authority was exercised over children, and practically none over the eldest who, as has been explained, outranked the parents. These infant family heads could do practically anything they pleased. In the valley of Puamau, I once visited the local chief, who had a boy of eight or nine. When I arrived, the chief and his family were camping in the front yard, and the boy was sitting in the house looking both glum and triumphant. He had had a quarrel with his father a day or two before, and had tabooed the house by naming it after his head. Until he lifted the taboo, no one in the family could enter the house. The family were thus uncomfortably camping in the open until the child could be persuaded to lift the taboo and allow them to enter the house again. (Linton 1939:154–159)

To summarize both sets of data (ethnographic notes and ethnographer-interview):

In three cases, son is dominant over father: Tarong (when

father is retired), Truk (when son is a little boy) and Marquesas (eldest child only).

In five cases, the father-son relationship appears to be equalitarian; neither father nor son seems to have effective power over the other: Ifugao (after son's marriage), Manus, Murngin, Siwai, and Yir-Yiront.

In twenty-one cases (all in the ethnographer-interview sample), the father's authority over his *married* son seems to be either rather mild or completely absent.

In fifty-six other cases, father is dominant over son.

I would apply the same "rule" to the father-son relationship as I did to the father-daughter relationship: equality represents the highest possible power position for son, and the lowest possible status for father. Again, there are a few exceptions to this rule.

At this point, let us look at a few examples of the power of father over child.

REINDEER CHUKCHEE, SIBERIA

> . . . the bearing of the children before their father is very respectful. When the young herdsmen come home, they give their father a detailed account of the more important animals in the herd, about the pasture, the drinking-place, mosquitoes and reindeer flies. The father puts one question after another, and the son has to give short and clear answers without talking too much. He repeats often words like "Yes! yes! surely!" and other interjections, showing his respect for the words of his parents. He even feels it improper to sit down in the presence of his father, especially while other people are present. These relations continue while the son is not yet full grown. As soon as the young man has reached the age of about twenty-five, and his moustache begins to grow, or when he has a wife and a couple of children, he feels greater self-assurance and independence, though he may continue to watch his father's herd. He begins to bear himself towards his father, though with deference, without such extreme submission as in former years. (Bogoras 1909:554)

IRELAND

> The father and husband is normally owner and director of the enterprise. The farm and its income are vested in him. The farm

bears his name in the community and sons are spoken of as his "boys." In the draining of a field or the sale of cattle at a fair, the sons, even though fully adult, work under their father's eye, and refer necessary decisions to him. . . .

The behavior that reflects this state of affairs can be readily observed. Sons go to market and fair from the time they are ten or twelve, but they buy or sell little if anything. Father and sons can be seen together at the local markets, but it is the father who does the bargaining. . . .

Even at forty-five and fifty, if the old couple have not yet made over the farm, the countryman remains a "boy," both in farm work and in the rural vocabulary. . . . A countryman complained to me in words which tell the whole story. "You can be a boy forever," he said, "as long as the old fellow is alive." . . .

The relation extends to very small matters indeed. The better cup of tea, the bigger piece of bread, the two eggs instead of one, the pipeful of tobacco, go to the older men. (Arensberg 1950:54–123)

GUSII, KENYA

The homestead head is traditionally a patriarch with much control of family resources. He takes charge of all transactions from the negotiations for a daughter's bridewealth to the purchase of coffee seedlings. All the land and cattle of the homestead legally belong to him. . . .

In the relationship between a Gusii father and his adult son formality, respect and obedience are key qualities. The son is expected to act deferentially to his father, never contradict or embarrass him, and certainly never shout at him regardless of provocation. The father, however, may shout at the son and scold him abusively for misdeeds. Father and son may never bathe together, see each other naked, or discuss sexual topics in the presence of each other. . . . A good son is not only deferential but also obedient, and the father's commands may involve a son's marriages, economic affairs, and the welfare of his children. (LeVine)

TEPOZTLAN, MEXICO

The husband avoids intimacy with members of his family to be respected by them. He expects them to demonstrate their respect by maintaining a proper social distance. His contacts with his children are brief and reserved. The Tepoztlan husband expects his wife to see that the children are quiet when he is at home, and it is her obligation to teach them to fear him. Men are generally not talkative at home and contribute little to family conversation, nor do they seek or expect their children to confide in them. When the husband is at home during the day, he sits apart from the rest of the family; at night he eats alone or with his grown sons and goes out or retires soon after. The loftiness of the husband's position in the home makes him remote from the family. . . .

The relations between parents and children in Tepoztlan are also conditioned by emphasis on respect and authority. Children are reared to respect and obey their elders and to submit to the will of their mother and father so long as they live under the parental roof. Not long ago, all children in Tepoztlan kissed the hands of their parents, grandparents, and godparents in greeting; now only a few families continue this custom. . . .

The relationship between father and child is one of respect and avoidance of intimacy. The unvarying role of the father results in consistent behavior on the part of the children. They are always obedient, subdued, controlled, and inhibited in his presence and remain so well into adulthood. . . .

Boys generally do not speak much in the presence of their fathers. Talk about intimate subjects, telling jokes, or discussing women is strictly taboo. . . .

Regardless of age or marital state, a son is under his father's authority as long as he lives and works with his father. The son receives no recompense other than his support and care and what spending money he can get from his mother or father. (Lewis 1951:322–338)

As these examples illustrate—particularly the Gusii and Tepoztlan examples—deference involves more than power inequality. It also leads to a certain restraint in behavior, a lack of spontaneity, even a measure of avoidance. The deferent person is necessarily restrained, inhibited, and careful in his relations with the deferred-to person. But even the deferred-to person may act in a rather inhibited manner. The Tepoztlan father "avoids intimacy with members of his family to be respected by them." The Gusii father observes certain sex-connected avoidances in relation to his son. One gets the impression, from the ethnographic literature, that there is some sort of strong functional connection between power inequality and behavorial restraint or "formality." *Extreme* power inequality seems to beget inhibited "formal" behavior. Curiously, it is not merely the submissive person who is restrained. The *dominant* person is also "formal," withdrawn, and rather inhibited in his dealings with the submissive person. In societies where the father seems most "patriarchal," most all-powerful over his children, he also frequently is rather restrained in his intercourse with his children. He may order them about, but he tends not to play with them, to laugh with them, to let them sit on his lap, and so forth. In truth, I cannot document this in any clear-cut way (as with a cross-cultural correlation); all I can do is cite examples. But this is a phenomenon (or an apparent phenomenon) that strikes one's eye when one scans the ethnographic literature.

If it *is* generally true that great power inequality necessarily leads to restrained, semiavoidant behavior, this is most curious. It is particularly curious that the *dominant* person should be restrained. What is there about extreme dominance that demands a "formal" demeanor? It is possible to imagine a domineering father who is all-powerful (in relation to his children), yet also expressive and informal when he is with them—who orders them about, but also laughs with them, jokes with them, plays with them, lets them sit on his lap. There may, in fact, be a few individual fathers like this. But this is not the sort of picture that emerges on a societal level (that is, in ethnographic accounts). In "patriarchal societies" where fathers seem customarily to be extremely dominating, they also receive deference from their children. When deference customs are observed, they seem to set up a "respect" relationship that restrains the father's behavior as well as the child's.[7] At least, this is my impression.

To conclude this section, here are a few examples of "respect"

[7] Needless to say, this effect also obtains within other family relationships—Child to Uncle, Child to Grandparent, Younger Brother to Elder Brother, even Wife to Husband.

relationships that involve inhibited behavior on the part of both the deferent and the deferred-to person.

NAYAR

The *karanavan*[8] was traditionally unequivocal head of the group. . . . He could command all other members, male and female, and children were trained to obey him with reverence. . . .

Under the *karanavan*, men of the group are ranked by seniority. All those older than ego are sometimes collectively called *karanavar* and are accorded respect and obedience . . . all younger, whether they be mother's brothers, younger brothers, maternal nephews or great nephews, may be commanded and disciplined. The social distance between men of a property-group is great. . . . Indeed, though learning and skills are passed on between them, the relationships between men are, when possible, formalized to the point of avoidance. By traditional etiquette, a man may not touch his *karanavan* or any maternal uncle; before approaching him he must remove his upper cloth. To speak to the *karanavan* he stands respectfully half hidden from sight behind a pillar, holding his hand before his mouth lest his breath should reach the hearer. With younger mother's brothers more intimately responsible for his education, a youth's etiquette is necessarily relaxed, but he observes the greatest possible formal respect before them. A similar etiquette is preserved before older brothers and classificatory brothers: after puberty these never joke, sit or chew betal and areca nuts together. (Gough 1954:64–69)

TAITOU, CHINA

The father's attitude is dignified, even remote; his authority is unquestioned and he expects submissiveness from his sons. . . . by the time the boy reaches the age of fifteen, the father assumes a more dignified attitude toward him and is frequently severe. . . . When father and son do work together, they have nothing to say, and even at home they speak only when there is business to discuss. At street gatherings or in places of amusement, they mutually avoid each other.

In the winter, when the men are not busy in the fields and

[8] Mother's brother, who is head of the household.

supper is usually finished earlier, sons, wives, and grandchildren will gather in the old mother's room and the grandmother will play with her youngest grandchildren, while the wives and older grandchildren and the sons talk about what they have seen and heard outside. The father may take part in this gathering if he likes, but he usually keeps himself aloof in order to maintain his patriarchal status. If he attempts to disrupt the free atmosphere, he will be chased out by his old wife. (Yang 1945:57–59)

MOKJOKUTO, JAVA[9]

Beginning in the juvenile period the boy is expected to be especially respectful to the father, to avoid speaking to him unless necessary, never to eat with him at the same table. Once I was sitting with a father on his front porch when his twenty-year-old son came in unexpectedly on the train from a nearby city, after an absence of six months. . . . He (the son) stayed a whole weekend, and my notes are full of statements like "father in front room, son out back talking to mother," "father out back, son on front porch." I do not believe they had a face-to-face conversation the whole time he was there. (Geertz 1956: 117–118)

Mother and Child

The father-child relationship tends to be characterized by formalized deference customs, "respect," and inequality of real power. The father tends to dominate, and "command," and the child to submit, and "obey." The father tends to get such traditional marks of deference as a bow, a kiss on the hand, the best food, the best or only chair, special deferential language; father and child tend to be rather "formal" and restrained in their intercourse. This is not to say that all fathers are patriarchs, demanding obedience, deference and formality. Societies, as well as indi-

---

[9] Geertz says, "Respect is shown in several ways: by posture, gestures and tone of voice, term of address, and above all by the language-level spoken." The grandfather is the most respected; father and uncles receive a somewhat lesser degree of respect; elder brothers receive still less. "The father in the family traditionally receives better food, dresses better than the rest of the family. It is he for whom the one piece of meat is saved. In some families no one can eat the main meal till after father has had his pick." (Geertz 1956:36, 37, 126)

vidual families, vary along this dimension of "patriarchality." Some fathers are relatively autocratic or "strong"; other fathers are relatively equalitarian or "weak." But marked power inequality, deference, and formality do frequently characterize the father-child relationship.

The mother-child relationship stands in marked contrast. In only three societies in my ethnographic notes is the mother said to receive formalized deference from her children: Papago, Tepoztlan, and seventeenth-century England (Goodsell 1915:284–285). Likewise, there is little mention of "respect" or "formality" between mother and child; the nearest approach to this is a mild degree of sex avoidance, such as refraining from sexual jokes. The mother-child relationship is usually described in such terms as "warm," "affectionate," "relaxed," "informal," "loving." The mother generally seems to exert less power over the children than the father. For twelve societies in my ethnographic notes, the father is described as stricter and demanding of more obedience than the mother: Dragaletvsy (Bulgaria), Dahomey, Fiji, Gusii, Ifaluk, Rajput (India), Silwa (Egypt), Taitou (China), Tepoztlan (Mexico), Tikopia, Tonga, and Valle Cana (Puerto Rico). No ethnographer says that the mother is customarily stricter than the father.[10]

In short, in contrast to the father, the mother tends not to receive deference, demands less in the way of "formality" and "respect," and is less strict. The contrast between mother-role and father-role seems most marked in those "patriarchal" societies where the father has a rather exalted position and is domineering and "formal" with his children. (Of the twelve cases I just gave, all but Ifaluk and Tikopia seem markedly "patriarchal.") On the

---

[10] Since the mother, not the father, is usually the main caretaker of young children, she may do more actual disciplining. That is, since she is around them more, she may discipline the children *more* than the father does—punish them more often, restrain them more frequently. In this sense—frequency of disciplinary action—she might be said to often be "more powerful" than the father. However, in the sense of *strictness* of discipline, severity of restraints, and intolerance of disobedience, she is never the more powerful parent; no ethnographer, in my notes, describes the mother as "stricter" than the father.

other hand, in the more equalitarian cases, where the father is not domineering and demands less respect, the contrast is less pronounced and may possibly, at times, disappear. This particular generalization is, unfortunately, based on a small sample of only twelve reported cases; however, reference to child-to-mother deference customs is conspicuous by its absence, compared to the frequent references in the ethnographic literature to child-to-father deference.

No doubt there are exceptions to this rule, in the form of individual families in which the mother is stricter than the father and the father-child relationship is characterized by greater informality, intimacy, and expressiveness. But I know of no *society* in which such a situation is said to be the cultural norm.

As mentioned in the conclusion to Chapter 6, Morris Zelditch posits certain universal attributes to husband-wife roles. Everywhere, he says, the husband is the instrumental leader, and the wife is the expressive leader. One thing Zelditch apparently meant by this universal role differentiation was this very dimension of power/deference/formality: the husband-father (the instrumental leader) is the more powerful, more deferred-to person; the wife-mother (the expressive leader) has a "warm," "informal" relationship with her children. The husband-father, by contrast, gets more obedience and respect and is less "warm" (Zelditch 1955). Once more, I agree with the general drift of Zelditch's argument, making allowance for occasional deviant cases. This does seem to describe—approximately and roughly—a pronounced cross-cultural regularity in family relationships.[11]

To up-date my conclusion to Chapter 6, there appear to be four near-universal aspects of husband-wife roles:

1. A standard division of labor by sex.
2. The "essential femininity" of some tasks, such as child care, and the "essential masculinity" of other tasks, such as hunting and fishing.
3. Power and privilege, in relation to each other: the husband's status is equal to or greater than the wife's.

---

[11] For speculation about possible reasons for this phenomenon, I refer you to Parsons and Bales, *Family, Socialization, and Interaction Process.*

4. Power over the children, and deference received from the children: the husband-father is as strict or stricter than the wife-mother (rarely if ever less strict); the husband-father frequently receives deference from the children, but the wife-mother rarely does.

To conclude this section, here are two examples of the "respected" father and the relatively "warm" mother:

SILWA, EGYPT[12]

Having more contacts with children's problems of upbringing, the mother tends to be the target of their ambivalence; they wrangle and quarrel with her, are rude to her, run outside the house and throw stones at the door or climb the wall and swear at her. On the other hand, children feel that the mother is their most reliable source of care and affection, and that she is more accessible and amenable than the father. In this capacity she is the one usually approached for expressing their wishes or asked to mediate between them and the father. Mothers themselves recognize their treatment of children is different from that of the father. This is epitomized in the mothers' popular saying to their children in persuading them to obey them: "On the death of my father I eat dates; on the death of my mother I eat hot coal." In this way the mother tries to win from her offspring assistance and service as she is not invested with the same power or authority as the father. On the other hand, withdrawal from the father, keeping away from his bed while he is asleep, and keeping quiet while he is about the house, is told and retold to children by the mother or older siblings for fear of punishment. The father's authority cannot be flouted; and a change in the tone of his voice must be seriously considered. Although his punishment might be less frequent than that of the mother, yet it is certainly more severely administered. While the former pinches the ear, or the thigh, and seldom slaps, the latter normally slaps and thrashes with a rope or a cane. (Ammar 1954: 138)

VALLE CANA, PUERTO RICO

The difference between the father-child and mother-child strictness situations is that between the enforcement of immutable

---

[12] Son-to-father deference customs, in Silwa, were described in Chapter 3.

laws by a god who only descends his throne to execute measures in "serious offenses" and disciplinary measures by his aide for run-of-the-mill offenses. The wife, being removed from the seat of ultimate power and therefore closer to the subjects, may be more amenable to childish pleas for mercy or forgiveness. The father, in his own eyes, appears to be quite indulgent at times, like a benevolent despot, since

> His sceptre shows the force of temporal power,
> The attribute to awe and majesty,
> Wherein doth sit the dread and fear of kings;
> But mercy is above this sceptred sway . . .

The paternal sceptre is the strap on the wall, his subject the child, his prime minister (who must assuage him as well as administer his kingdom) the wife-mother. The ruler is superhuman and above the populace, farther away and therefore more awe-inspiring. But his prime minister always has an ear turned to the crowd. (Landy 1959:148–149)

Deference within Other Kin Relationships

The father-child relationship appears to be merely one part of a larger patterning effect, which can be described as follows:

Deference is received by older men. It is rarely given to women, and almost never given to younger kinsmen. In other words, deference between kinsmen depends on two factors, age and sex. With rare exceptions, Ego only gives deference to men, and only gives deference to men who are older than he (or she) is.[13]

Some kin relationships may or may not be characterized by deference, depending on the society: Ego to father, elder brother, uncles, and grandfathers—in fact, Ego to any older male relative. In all these relationships, deference (when it does occur) is given to the older man by his younger relative. Ego always *gives* defer-

[13] The only relationship that seems not to fit this pattern is the husband-wife relationship. As we have seen, wife frequently gives deference to husband, whether or not he is older than she is.

ence to uncle, grandfather, elder brother, and so forth; he (or she) never *receives* deference from them.

Some other kin relationships are very rarely characterized by marked deference customs. These are the ones between a male or female Ego and *older female relatives*: Ego to mother, elder sister, aunts, and grandmothers.

Here are the cross-cultural data:

For twenty-seven societies in my ethnographic notes, there is mention of marked deference being given to some older male relative(s) (other than Father).[14] For eighteen additional societies in the ethnographer-interview sample, marked deference is reported to some older male relative(s) (other than the father).[15]

In contrast to these, I know of only one case (excluding Truk and Marquesas) in which Ego gives deference to a *junior* relative. This is Tonga (Polynesia), where Ego defers to his sister (whether older or younger), his sister's children, and his father's sister's children (whether older or younger).

There are five more exceptional cases, in which Ego gives deference to *elder female relatives*. In seventeenth-century England, the mother apparently received formalized deference. Among the Papago and in Tepoztlan, deference is given to all elder male and female kin. Among the Chagga, the elder sister gets deference. Among the Lakher of Burma, the grandfather and grandmother are "given the highest respect." And, of course, the Tonga can be included here too, since they give deference to sister, father's sister, and father's sister's children.

---

[14] Araucanians, Aymara, Azande, Bemba, Chagga, Fiji, Ganda, Gusii, Ireland, Jukun, Kikuyu, Lakher, Lamba, Modjokuto (Java), Nayar, Orasac (Serbia), Papago, Rajput (India), Samoa, Silwa (Egypt), Suye Mura (Japan), Taitou (China), Tepoztlan (Mexico), Thonga, Tikopia, Toda, and Truk.

[15] Alor, Ashanti, Atrisco, Dragaletvsy (Bulgaria), Cuchumatan Mam (Mayan. Guatemala), Greece, Kipsigis, Kurds, Madiun (Java), Madrid (aristocracy), Magazawa, Menangkabau, Nishapur (Iran), San Pedro la Laguna (Mayan. Guatemala), Vaish (India), Villafranqueza (Spain), Yokohama (middle class), Zinacantan (Mexico).

To summarize: only elder men may receive deference (barring the few exceptional cases just cited). Women and juniors rarely receive deference, in any society. In those societies which do observe deference customs between kin, it is the elder men who are the recipients of deference.

There is a related pattern here, a sort of all-or-none effect. In societies where Ego gives marked deference to father, Ego also gives about the same degree of deference to some other older male relatives. In societies where Ego is not deferrent to father, he does *not* defer to other elder male kin. In other words, the world seems to be divided into deference societies, which have *several* deference relationships, and nondeference societies, which have *no* deference relationships. The child-to-father relationship appears to be the "hub" or focus of this pattern: if you defer to your father you will also defer to some other elder kinsmen; if you don't defer to your father you will not defer to other elder kin.

I have fair cross-cultural evidence to support this last generalization, although it could be better. In the ethnographic notes, there are the usual cases of "no information," that is, cases in which a deference relationship between child and father is described, but where there is no information on other kin relationships, such as Ego to father's brother, to elder brother, mother's brother, father's father. However, there is no case in the ethnographic notes in which only one relative receives marked deference—be he father, father's father, mother's brother, or some other older male—and all other relatives clearly do not. And there are twenty-seven societies in the ethnographic notes for which several deference relationships (deference to father, plus deference to some other elder male relative or relatives) are described.

Turning to the ethnographer-interview sample, there are two cases that probably are exceptions to this pattern: Subanum and San Juan Juquilla. Among the Subanum, the father receives marked deference, but uncle, grandfather, and elder brother do not. For San Juan Juquilla, father receives deference, father's brother does not, and other kin relationships are unreported. There are two other marginal cases, Nishapur and Madrid (aristocrats). In both these cases, father receives extreme deference and other kin receive slightly less. In sixteen additional cases in the ethnographer-interview sample, father receives marked deference,[16] as do various other elder male kin.[17] Finally, there is *no* case in the ethnographer-interview sample in which the father *does not* receive marked deference[18] while some other older kinsman *does.*

To summarize this all-or-none effect: if father does not get deference, no other elder kinsman does; if father does get deference, other elder male kin will get a similar degree of deference. These "extensions" of deference customs to father may be more or less inclusive. In some societies, they may include all elder male kin. In other societies, they may only include all male kin of father's generation, plus elder brother (thus excluding grandfather); or, they may include only elder male kin on the father's side of the family (thus excluding mother's brother and mother's father).[19]

Finally, there is one more patterning regularity—which I will call the *patriarchal pattern.* When father receives marked deference from son, he also tends to receive marked deference from mother. In other words, son-to-father deference and wife-to-husband deference are positively correlated.[20] This last so-called pattern is merely a trend; there are a good many exceptional cases.

The correlation between son-to-father and wife-to-husband

---

[16] Cases with scale-scores of 3, 4 or 5. See Appendix.

[17] Alor, Ashanti, Atrisco, Cuchumatan Mam, Dragalėtvsy, Greece, Kipsigis, Kurds, Madiun, Magazawa, Menangkabau, San Pedro la Laguna, Vaish, Villafranqueza, Yokohama, and Zinacantan.

[18] Cases with scale-scores of 2, 1 or 0. See Appendix.

[19] Dorian Apple, in her cross-cultural study of grandparenthood, reports data that fit this pattern I have just described (Apple 1956). She finds that when an old man retains authority over his married son, he receives deference from his grandchildren. When he does not retain authority over his married son, he does not receive deference from his grandchildren; in this case, the grandparent-grandchild relationship is characterized by "friendly equality." In Apple's cross-cultural sample, forty-seven societies conformed to this trend; there were seven exceptional cases.

[20] The same is probably true for daughter-to-father deference, but I do not have adequate data on this point.

deference is shown in Table 3. This table is based on the ethnographer-interview data. For descriptions of the son-to-father and wife-to-husband deference scales, I refer you to the Appendix.

Here is a shorthand summary of all these deference patterns:

1. Husband over wife.
2. Father over child.
3. Father is stricter than mother.
4. Elder men get deference; women and juniors don't.
5. If Ego defers to father, he also defers to uncle and/or grandfather and/or elder brother. If he does not defer to father, he does not defer to uncle or grandfather or elder brother (the all-or-none effect).
6. If father is dominant over some family member, he is dominant over all family members (the patriarchal pattern).

None of these are universal laws of nature. The first five are strong trends, with few apparent exceptions. The last is a relatively weak trend, with numerous exceptions.

Finally, deference and marked power inequalities (between kin) do not occur in all societies. The above "rules" merely specify the directions and combinations deference will assume when it *does* occur. Some societies, like our own, are fairly equalitarian in their kin relationships. In these, husband tends not to dominate wife, father does not get marked deference from child, nor—by virtue of pattern number 5—do grandfather, uncle, or elder brother. In other societies the father is a domineering, deferred-to patriarch; in nearly all of these cases—by virtue of patterns 5 and 6—some other kin relationships are similarly autocratic.

What, then, determines whether or not a society will have autocratic kin relationships? What "causes" them? My guess is that the most powerful original cause or antecedent condition is political organization. The autocratic state begets the autocratic family.

Autocratic Family and Autocratic State

Here I must leave the subject of the family for a moment, and talk about politics. To begin, I will divide societies into types,

TABLE 3

THE PATRIARCHAL PATTERN: CORRELATION BETWEEN SON-TO-FATHER AND WIFE-TO-HUSBAND DEFERENCE

Son-to-father	Wife-to-husband Deference					
Deference	5	4	3	2	1	0
5	Nishapur	Madrid Vaish		Magazawa Menangkebau		
4		Cuchumatan Mam San Pedro la Laguna Valle Cana	Greece Konso Villafranqueza	Ashanti Dragaletvsy Lasko Zinacantan Madiun		Brno Lacandon Maya Navaho San Juan Juquilla
3	Yokohama	Atrisco	Amman Kipsigis	Alor	Druz	Subanum
2			!Kung	Sherpa	Berbers Valley Tonga	Anaguta Kaktavik Tenino
1			Barranquitas Guaymi Ojibwa	Chanzeaux Peyrane	Chiaromonte Kwoma Naples Turkana	San Juan Pueblo
0				Somali	The Bog	

according to their mode of political organization. The first type of society I shall call the *kingdom*; the second type is the *tribe*.

A kingdom has the following characteristics:

1. The people in the society are subject to a *state*. A state is a centralized organ of political control, with coercive power over the populace. The state makes its power felt by means of an army, a police force (which may coincide with the army), and control over law and law courts. The state levies taxes. In kingdoms, the power of the state is either centered in or at least symbolized by a single supreme office, held by a single person—a "king," "lord," "raja," or "sultan," for example. Succession to this supreme office is hereditary. (By this definition, a small feudal regime is considered a separate "kingdom," even if it controls a small geographic area, and even if it owes a loose allegiance to some larger political unit.)

2. The kingdom is socially stratified; it is divided into two or more hereditary social classes or castes. The upper class—the "nobles"—mans the state apparatus, thereby exercising control over the lower class—the "commoners."

3. The kingdom's economic base is agrarian. Wealth is produced by the commoners, in the form of agricultural products. Incidental wealth accrues as a result of handicraft manufacturing and public works; the labor for this is also supplied by the commoners.

4. The kingdom is characterized by economic exploitation of the commoners, by the nobles. The nobles extract wealth from the commoners either indirectly, through their access to tax funds, or directly, in the form of rentals, protection payments, or obligatory gifts.

5. The regime is legitimatized by means of a state religion. That is, the state fosters a body of supernatural belief that rationalizes the king's rule as "god-ordained," as it does the laws and procedures of the state, the control of commoners by nobles, and the resulting economic exploitation. Occasionally, a kingdom will evolve its own, individual state religion, as did ancient Egypt. More frequently, the state religion is "borrowed" from another kingdom. Hence, the world's four major religions—Christianity, Buddhism, Hinduism, and Islam—have each, in their various

forms, served as state religions for many kingdoms. This is not to say that these four religions were "tailor-made" to legitimatize autocratic regimes (although this may have been the case for Hinduism). Rather, they have been "borrowed" by kingdoms, set up as the official state religion, and adapted for the purpose of legitimatizing the state and the social hierarchy.

These are the defining attributes of the kingdom: a state, nobles and commoners, an agrarian economic base, exploitation of commoners by nobles, and a state religion.

The other type of society—the *tribe*—is a society without a state. It is not subject to "a centralized organ of political control, with coercive power over the populace," with an army and tax collectors. Although the tribe may evince some rudimentary form of social stratification, it does not have "nobles" who have the power to economically exploit "commoners." Neither, needless to say, does the tribe have a state religion. The tribe's subsistence may come from one or several of three sources: agriculture, animal husbandry, hunting (and/or fishing), and gathering.

A tribe never embraces cities. A kingdom may; some kingdoms have cities, and some do not. Some kingdoms are also characterized by a group of culture traits that are commonly termed "civilization"—large public works, and esoteric arts and sciences (written language, mathematics, astronomy, and so forth). Tribes never have "civilization," thus defined.

The tribe was the first political form to appear. During the earliest periods of human history, people managed to get along without any sort of state government whatsoever. Kingdoms represent a cultural emergence, a later-appearing sociopolitical form. The kingdom, I would guess, was a cultural invention that materialized as the result of war and conquest; it was a formula by which a conquering group could hang onto conquered territory, maintain continuous control over conquered peoples, and exploit them. That is, tribal groups fight each other, and may achieve conquests of sorts. But these conquests are limited to raiding and, perhaps, driving the enemy from his territory. To conquer a *people*, and keep them subjugated, the kingdom formula was necessary. When a tribe did consolidate its conquests by applying the kingdom formula, it ceased to be a tribe and became a kingdom (became the "nobility" in the newly created kingdom).[21]

Kingdoms, over time, multiplied and spread. By means of conquest, they engulfed peoples who had previously lived in tribes; also, of course, they occasionally engulfed each other. Whereas once all of mankind had lived in tribes, now some peoples lived in tribes and others lived in kingdoms.

This represents the state of affairs until about 200 years ago, when new sociopolitical types—the democratic state, and, later, the industrialized totalitarian state—began to emerge in Europe and among overseas Europeans, and then to diffuse to other parts of the world. Prior to this time, I think the world could have been neatly divided into these two types of societies, tribes and kingdoms. Nearly all societies would have fit into either one or the other of these two types. There would have been very few societies that would have constituted exceptions, that could not have been termed either "tribe" or "kingdom."

What I am saying is that the kingdom represents another culture-patterning regularity—this time on a grand scale. It constitutes what Julian Steward would call a *cross-cultural type* (Steward 1955). Its defining attributes—state, state religion, nobles and commoners, and so on—were functionally interrelated, so that they always went together, in a "package," so to speak. Prior to the recent emergence of new forms of the state, the world was divided into societies without states (tribes) and societies with states (kingdoms). Whenever a state emerged, the other attributes of the kingdom accompanied it: a single, hereditary, supreme office (the kingship), exploiting nobles and exploited commoners, and a state religion. All states (with rare exceptions) were necessarily autocratic and exploitive.

Today, these old sociopolitical types seem to be on their way to extinction. The remaining autonomous tribes are fast being "put on reservation" and then assimilated by expanding and newly-emerging states. Some of the old kingdoms, in turn, have

---

[21] This historical reconstruction is impressionistic; I will not try to document it. However, some of the points I am raising are, I think, amenable to cross-cultural-historical research.

been engulfed by democratic states and industrialized totalitarian states. Others are evolving (or have already evolved) in the direction of these newer sociopolitical forms.

So much for historical reconstruction and political types. Let us return to the question: what "causes" autocratic family and kin relations? One important cause, I think, is the kingdom.

In Table 4, degree of son-to-father and wife-to-husband deference is correlated with type of political organization—kingdom versus tribe. The cases—all of which come from the ethnographer-interview sample—are ordered according to degree of son-to-father deference. At the top of the page are the cases that got the highest score on son-to-father deference—"5." Below them are the cases scored "4," then the 3's, and so on.

These deference scores are based on a cumulative scale, which has the following items (or code categories): a) the son may not address the father by his personal name (may not call him "Joe," for example); b) the son rarely expresses verbal aggression toward his father; c) the son rarely disputes with his father; d) the son must speak to his father in a soft voice; and e) the son either kneels or bows when greeting his father.

Cases scored "5" have all of these deference customs, that is, the cross-cultural coders scored them "yes" for all of these code categories. For cases scored "4," either "speaks softly" or "kneels or bows" was scored "no"; all the other items were scored "yes." Cases scored "3" observe the first three deference customs ("does not address father by his personal name," "rarely expresses verbal aggression toward father," and "rarely disputes with father"), but do not have the last two ("speaks softly" and "kneels or bows"). Cases scored "2" have the first two deference customs but not the last three. In the "1" cases, the son does not address his father by the father's personal name, but the other deference customs are absent. Finally, in the "0" cases, none of the deference customs were coded present; the son may even address his father by his personal name.

While I term this a "deference scale," the scale also—to some degree—is a gauge of real power (in the sense of strictness). This is particularly true of scale-item 3—the son "rarely disputes" with his father.

TABLE 4

FAMILY DEFERENCE CUSTOMS CORRELATED WITH PRESENCE OR ABSENCE OF KINGDOMS

	Degree of Son-to-father Deference	Degree of Wife-to-husband Deference	Part of a Kingdom, Now or in the Past		A Tribe
Madrid (aristocrats)	5	4	x		
Magazawa (bush Hausa)	5	2	x		
Menangkabau	5	2	x		
Nishapur (Iran)	5	5	x		
Vaish (India)	5	4	x		
Ashanti	4	2	x		
Brno (Czechoslovakia)	4	0	x		
Cuchumatan Mam (Mayan)	4	4	x		
Dragaletvsy (Bulgaria)	4	2	x		
Greece	4	4	x		
Kurds	4	•	x		
Konso	4	3			x
Lacandon Maya	4	0	x		
Lasko (Yugoslavia)	4	2	x		
Madiun (Java)	4	2	x		
Navaho	4	0			x
San Juan Juquilla (Zapotec)	4	0	x		
San Pedro la Laguna (Mayan)	4	4	x		
Valle Cana (Puerto Rico)	4	4	x		
Villafranqueza (Spain)	4	3	x		
Zinacantan (Mexico)	4	2	x		
Alor	3	2			x
Amman (Jordan)	3	3	x		
Atrisco (Spanish-Americans)	3	4	x		
Druz	3	1	x		
Kipsigis	3	3			x
Nkundo	3	•		???	
Subanum	3	0		???	
Yokohama (middle class)	3	5	x		

* Cases marked with an asterisk represent communities that are part of Western democratic states.

TABLE 4 (*Continued*)

	Degree of Son-to-father Deference	Degree of Wife-to-husband Deference	Part of a Kingdom, Now or in the Past		A Tribe
Anaguta	2	0			x
Berbers	2	1		???	
*Hutterites (South Dakota)	2	•	x		
Kaktavik Eskimos	2	0			x
!Kung	2	3			x
Pecs (Hungary)	2	•	x		
Sherpa	2	2		???	
Tenino	2	0			x
Valley Tonga	2	1			x
Paiute	•	0			x
Barranquitas (Puerto Rico)	1	3	x		
*Chanzeaux (France)	1	2	x		
*Chiaromonte (Italy)	1	1	x		
Guaymi	1	3		???	
Kwoma	1	1			x
*Naples (lower class)	1	1	x		
Ojibwa	1	3			x
*Peyrane (France)	1	2	x		
San Juan Pueblo	1	0		???	
Turkana	1	1			x
*The Bog (Nova Scotia)	0	1	x		
Somali	0	2			x

Scores on wife-to-husband deference are given in the second column of Table 4. These scores are also based on a cumulative scale; for its description, I refer you to the Appendix. The wife-to-husband scale is inferior to the son-to-father scale. The cumulative pattern is less pronounced; there are more scale errors. Also, it is less clearly an indicator of real power relationships.

Now, what does Table 4 "say"? It says that nearly all the cases with extreme son-to-father and wife-to-husband deference represent groups and communities which are, or were until recently, parts of kingdoms. Most of the tribes are fairly "low" on the deference scales, with a few exceptions—most notably, the Konso of Ethiopia and the Kipsigis of Kenya. Six cases are drawn from Western democratic states—the Hutterites (United States), The Bog (Canada), Chanzeaux and Peyrane (France), and Chiaromonte and Naples (Italy). These cases are also rather "low" on the deference scales.[22]

Sometimes tribes have marked family deference customs, and sometimes they do not. It looks as if most of the time they do not, but there are not enough data to really draw a conclusion about this. Kingdoms, on the other hand, seem to almost always have marked deference customs. Also, Table 4 suggests that when the kingdom evolves to a democratic state the family deference customs, after a time, diminish. After the state becomes democratic, the family also becomes relatively democratic. Again, this is merely a suggestion from the data, since there are so few cases of this sort.

How can I draw a cause-effect conclusion from this correlation? That is, how can I conclude—merely because kingdoms and family deference accompany each other—that the kingdom acts to "cause" extreme family deference customs? I base the conclusion on two grounds. First, in the light of my historical reconstruction—the picture of expanding, conquering kingdoms subduing and assimilating neighboring tribes—it seems reasonable to assume that the kingdom "came first" (was the antecedent) and that family deference "came afterward" (was a consequence, or result, of subjugation by a kingdom). Second, there is the suggestion in the data that when the kingdom disappears (in lieu of a democratic state) the extreme family deference customs also disappear. Neither of these arguments is unassailable, so I must offer the conclusion tentatively. I *think* that the kingdom "caused" extreme family deference, but I cannot "prove" it.

How—by what process—might the kingdom act to cause or intensify family deference? We do not know.

---

[22] Four other cases are marginal in respect to duration and intensity of contact with Western democratic states—Atrisco, Brno, Barranquitas, and Valle Cana. Three of these cases (all but Barranquitas) do evince marked family deference customs.

One thing we see here is another patterning regularity, of sorts, a parallel between family relationships and the larger social hierarchy. Autocratic societies, that is, autocratic agrarian societies—kingdoms—have autocratic families. As the king rules his subjects and the nobles subjugate and exploit the commoners, so does husband tend to lord it over wife, father rule over son, and—by virtue of pattern number 5, again—Ego defer to grandfather, uncle, and elder brother. The family, in such societies, looks like a sort of kingdom in microcosm. As Ego defers to father and grandfather, so do the commoners defer to the nobles; and the deference customs are quite similar. Sometimes, the *same* deference custom is given both to one's own father and to the local lord. Here are some examples of the parallel between family and social class relations:

RAJPUTS OF KHALAPUR

Dominance behavior is likewise patterned by the caste system and the authoritarian family structure. People are dominant toward their subordinates, and submissive or obedient toward their superiors. The adult Rajput man, obedient to his father or older brothers, is dominant with his wife, his children, men of less powerful families, and the lower-caste servants. (Triandis and Hitchcock)

TONGA

In the family itself the father held the highest rank, the daughters came next, and the sons in order of age. In accordance with the general principle that in the classificatory system behaviour to more distant relatives is modelled on behaviour to members of the family, the same grading was extended outside the family. Thus elder brothers and their children were of higher rank than younger brothers and their children. . . The man whose rank was highest, the descendant of a succession of eldest sons, acted as their chief. . . . At the head of the whole system were the *tui Tonga*, the sacred king, and the *tui kanokupolo*, the secular king. Of these the *tui Tonga* had the highest rank. . . . The formal marks of respect which every person had to show to his superiors in rank were to refrain from eating in their presence, from standing when they were seated, or in any other way raising his head above theirs, and to *moemoe* them, or place their feet on his head, whenever he met them. When a chief passed, all commoners had to bow their heads. . . .

The privileges reserved for chiefs as a class were such rights as that of bathing in special wells, of wearing a distinctive dress, eating certain foods and playing certain games . . . (Hogbin 1934: 237–238)

NAYARS OF MALABAR

By traditional etiquette, a man may not touch his *karanavan* or any maternal uncle; before approaching him he must remove his upper cloth. To speak to the *karanavan* he stands respectfully half hidden from sight behind a pillar, holding his hand before his mouth lest his breath should reach the hearer. . . .

Rules of ritual pollution decreed . . . that members of each lower caste, according to their ritual rank, must refrain from approaching members of the "good" castes within distances ranging from 15 to 40 feet. (Gough 1954:68, 26)

SIXTEENTH-CENTURY POKOM-MAYANS, GUATEMALA

The upper class, perhaps better called nobility, filled the offices of lords, priests of the upper brackets, ambassadors, permanent war captains . . . judges and upper level tax collectors. These offices all carried titles and prerogatives of dress, address and certain activities. . . .

Only lords and their immediate families wore *chachal*, strings of precious stones and gold, very long fingernails, like tigers' claws and the *lichik*, a mantle of thin delicate cloth. Ladies wore one over the face. At special public rituals lords were entitled to one or more canopies depending on their status. . . . Courteous and courtly manners . . . were essential behavior. . . . Wealth, knowledge and age or any two of these entitled a person to reverential terms of address . . .

(*Here Miles quotes from the journal of the Jesuit, Las Casas:*)

"Fathers taught and exhorted with great care that children honor and obey and serve their parents . . . and the same their lords and principales; and they hanged promptly men who became proud and haughty toward the lords, aspiring to lordship or obstructing the vassals, who do not obey them, or those who donned distance of manner to attend the tributes and service which they owed the lord." (Miles 1957:766–774)

VALLE CANA, PUERTO RICO

His sceptre shows the force of temporal power,
The attribute to awe and majesty,
Wherein doth sit the dread and fear of kings . . .

The paternal sceptre is the strap on the wall, his subject the child, his prime minister (who must assuage him as well as administer his kingdom) the wife-mother. The ruler is superhuman and above the populace, farther away and therefore more awe-inspiring. But his prime minister always has an ear tuned to the crowd.

There is one fly in this overliterary ointment: The father, it is true, is kingpin in his own household. He is not, however, kingpin in the outside world; being a caneworker he has a low social status. Thus a father powerful at home may be ordered around in a very imperious manner by a middle-class woman and sometimes even a child. And to middle- or upper-class men he is "*el jibaro,*" a hill-billy, a creature not ordinarily respected. . . .

Man, woman and child are expected always to be at the service of the upper class, and while there is usually some type of recompense, however little, for most work, it is not unusual for lower-class persons to perform services free for middle- and upper-class members, because this is their . . . [tr. "work of obligation"]

Lower-class men, especially the older ones, commonly use this phrase, but even some of the younger generation seem to have fallen heir to this feudal service ethic. A striking example: One Sunday most of the husbands could not be found for interviewing. Not one was at home and we went through Valle Cana searching for them. We finally found them on the canefields of Don Pedro, a middle-class landowner who often made his contempt of the lower-class men emphatic to us and to them. He felt they were "no-good, spendthrift, shiftless, not very bright" and "would allow themselves to be worked for anything." Several of the men explained to us that they were helping Don Pedro since he was a poor man (he has fairly large holdings and his son had just built one of the best houses in the barrio) and could not afford to pay for Sunday work. He was their neighbor, they said, and furthermore, since he was spending thousands of dollars on cortisone treatments for his arthritis, how could he pay them? Don Pedro's three strapping sons stood around and watched. Later we asked one husband we knew why he was not there. "In the past I have worked for him as my obligation many times. But for some reason he was angry with me last year and now I'm afraid to bother him—since otherwise I would have been working too." (Landy 1959:148, 149, 49, 50)

The kingdom emerges as a kind of pecking-order social system, in which similar deference behavior is repeated throughout many social relationships: wife to husband, child to father, child to father's brother, commoner to noble. Commoner women are at the bottom of this pecking order. They are ordinarily deferent to many persons, and deferred-to by no one. Commoner men are deferred to by their wives and by junior relatives, but deferent to elder male relatives; also, I assume, they must defer to the nobles, whether men or women, older or younger. Noble women are, apparently, deferred to by commoners; they, in turn, defer to their husbands and to elder male kin. Noble men defer only to their elder male kin; they receive deference from their wives, from younger kin and family members, and from commoners.[23]

As one informant said, "It really isn't so bad. In fact it's rather nice. You have to do it to some people. But then, other people have to do it to you."

What else characterizes the kingdom? For one thing, the data presented in Chapter 6 on the strictness of sex division of labor (women's work which men can't do) show a trend in the direction of more sharply segregated sex roles in kingdoms. Also, kingdoms tend to have tighter sex restrictions (Chap. 5). Finally, it is my impression—unsupported by data—that people in kingdoms tend to be generally inhibited in the expression of their impulses.

---

[23] The analogy to the pecking order is not completely accurate because some remaining social relationships are not characterized by deference; these include relationships between male or female Ego and older female kin.

Kingdoms, in contrast to tribes, seem to have less in the way of orgiastic ceremonials, drunkenness, and dancing and singing; their media of artistic expression, such as music, appear to take more restrained, controlled forms. Perhaps the most interesting problem in this area is the effect of socialization, in the autocratic family, on character formation. Do all kingdoms—all communities that are, or were until recently, parts of kingdoms—evince some common personality syndrome, which results from their family deference customs?[24] Time and future research, perhaps, will tell.

---

[24] See in this connection G. Rattray Taylor's description of the "patrist" personality syndrome, which includes, among other things: a restrictive attitude toward sex; a view that women are inferior; political authoritarianism; inhibition, fear of spontaneity; fear of homosexuality; maximum emphasis on sex differences; and asceticism, fear of pleasure (Taylor 1954:81).

8

Child Rearing

CHILDHOOD VIGNETTES: HOPI *

"When we were within our mother's womb, we happened to hurt her. She has told me how she went to a medicine man in her pain. He worked on her, felt her breasts and belly, and told her that we were twins. She was surprised and afraid. She said, 'But I want only one baby.' 'Then I will put them together,' replied the doctor. He took some corn meal outside the door and sprinkled it to the sun. Then he spun some black and white wool, twisted the threads into a string, and tied it around my mother's left wrist. It is a powerful way to unite babies. We twins began, likewise, to twist ourselves into one child. My mother also helped to bring us together by her strong wish for only one baby.

"My own mother was my best friend and my earliest memories are of her. She was always busy as a bee or an ant, cooking, grinding corn, bringing water, making baskets out of rabbitweed or pots out of clay. I well remember how my father frightened me over her when I was perhaps three. It happened after the snow had disappeared in the springtime. We had moved back up the ladder into our summer house. My parents and I were sleeping in the same room where I was born. I was lying on a sheepskin in the northwest corner. When I awoke I heard struggling and felt the floor shaking. The noise and movements made me wide awake. From the sounds that my mother was making I thought she was suffering and that my father must be killing her. I cried out and covered up my face and head with a blanket. Pretty soon they quieted down and my mother got up and came over to me with kind words. She lay down beside me, and I went back to sleep. The next morning at breakfast, I felt angry, first at my father but later at my mother also, because she was still so kind and polite to him. The next night I slept with my grandfather in another room.

"I later saw some giantlike Katchinas[1] stalking into the village with long, black bills and big sawlike teeth. One carried a rope to lasso disobedient children. He stopped at a certain house and called for a boy. 'You have been naughty,' he scolded. 'You fight with other children. You kill chickens. You pay no attention to the old people. We have come to get you and eat you.' The boy cried and promised to behave better. The giants became angrier and threatened to tie him up and take him away. But the boy's parents begged for his life and offered fresh meat in his place. The giant reached out his hand as if to grab the boy but took the meat instead. Placing it in his basket, he warned the boy that he would get one more chance to change his conduct. I was frightened and got out of sight. I heard that sometimes these giants captured boys and really ate them.

"When I was four or five I was captured by the Spider Woman and nearly lost my life. One morning in May as I played in the plaza in my shirt my father said that he was going to his field. I wanted to go. But as he filled his water jar he said, 'You had better stay here, my jar does not hold enough for us both.' I began to cry. As he started down the south side of the mesa I followed along the narrow path between two great stones and came to the bottom of the foothill near the Spider Woman's shrine. My father had disappeared among the rocks. I happened to look to my left at a rock by the shrine where some clay dishes had been placed as offerings to the Spider Woman. There sat the old woman herself, leaning forward and resting her chin in her hands. Beside her was a square hole in the ground. She said, 'You are here at the

[1] A masked dancer, who impersonates a supernatural.

right time. I have been waiting for you. Come into my house with me.' I had heard enough about the Spider Woman to know that no ordinary person ever sits by the shrine. I stood helpless, staring at her. 'Come into my house,' she repeated. 'You have been walking on my trail, and now I have a right to you as my grandson.'

"My father had heard me crying as I followed him, so he asked a man whom he met coming up the mesa to take me back to the village. As this man came around the corner of a rock the old woman disappeared. She had been sitting close by the pile of firewood that the people had placed on the shrine for her as they passed up and down the mesa.

"I thought I had not moved, but when the man saw me I was standing right under the rock and was being drawn into the hole. The old Spider Woman has the power to do strange things. I had been caught in her web and could not step backward. When the man saw me he shouted, 'Boy, get out of the shrine! The Spider Woman may take you into her house!' I laughed in a silly manner but could not move. The man rushed up quickly and pulled me out of the shrine. As he took me up the mesa I felt sick and was unable to play any more that day.

"During the night I had an awful dream. The Spider Woman came for me and said that now I belonged to her. I sat up and saw her heel as she disappeared through the door. Crying, I told my parents that the Spider Woman was after me. Every time I closed my eyes I could see the old woman coming again. My father, mother, and grandmother talked about what had happened at the shrine and took turns watching me. Once when I cried and said to my father, 'The Spider Woman will get me,' he put his hand on my head and replied, 'Well, my boy, you went too near her shrine. I fear you are hers now and that you will not live long.'

"Learning to work was like play. We children tagged around with our elders and copied what they did. We followed our fathers to the fields and helped plant and weed. The old men took us for walks and taught us the use of plants and how to collect them. We joined the women in gathering rabbitweed for baskets, and went with them to dig clay for pots. We would taste this clay as the women did to test it. We watched the fields to drive out the birds and rodents, helped pick peaches to dry in the sun, and gather melons to lug up the mesa. We rode burros to harvest corn, gather fuel, or herd sheep. In house-building we helped a little by bringing up dirt to cover the roofs. In this way we grew up doing things. All the old people said it was a disgrace to be idle and that a lazy boy should be whipped.

"My father and grandfather excused my mischief a little, explaining that it was due to the antelope power in me because I was a twin. But even a threat of the giants failed to make me behave. I got into some new mischief almost every day. One day Archie, a clan brother, and I pulled all the tail feathers out of my godmother's turkeys. Whenever I saw an ugly-faced or snotty-nosed child I wanted to whip him. When it rained, I walked through the street throwing mud into the windows at girls grinding corn. When women went down to the spring for water, I placed sharp sticks in the path for them to step upon with their bare feet, and watched gleefully from a hiding place. I persuaded other children to engage in mischief and sometimes licked them to make them join me.

"By the time I was six, therefore, I had learned to find my way about the mesa and to avoid graves, shrines, and harmful plants, to size up people, and to watch out for witches. I was above average in height and in good health. My hair was clipped just above my eyes, but left long in back and tied in a knot at the nape of my neck. I had almost lost one eye. I wore silver earrings, a missionary shirt or one made of a flour sack and was always bare-legged, except for a blanket in cold weather. When no Whites were present, I went naked. I slept out on the housetop in summer and sometimes in the kiva with the other boys in winter. I could help plant and weed, went out herding with my father, and was a kiva trader. I owned a dog and a cat, a small bow made by my father, and a few good arrows. Sometimes I carried stolen matches tucked in the hem of my shirt collar. I could ride a tame burro, kill a kangaroo rat, and catch small birds, but I could not make fire with a drill and I was not a good runner like the other fellows. At the races people teased me and said that my feet turned out so far I pinched my anus as I ran. But I had made a name for myself by healing people; and I had almost stopped running after my mother for her milk." (Simmons 1942:25–72)

DIARY OF A FOURTEEN-YEAR-OLD JAMAICAN GIRL

"*Wednesday.* I got up at six o'clock tidy up one room. I shine three pairs of shoes. Comb my hair my self. I went to the Bakery to buy Bread. I had my bath at seven o'clock under a shower in a zinc round bathroom but it had a top. My Aunt prepared breakfast for my Step Uncle and seven others. I had for breakfast bread an butter an a can of choclate tea and some corn meal porrige. I went to school a little later at half past nine. Two health nurses came to school. My heart beat heard for I was a little afraid. She came to give us injection. I got my own, at first a moneta for the school came and rub my left hand with a bit of cotton and some lotion on it. The nurse took the needle and fill it with medicine she sent it right up in my arm but I did not cry, then another moneta rub my arm a second time. I went home for dinner at 12 o'clock. I got one cassava flour dumplin a piece of yellow yam pumpkin sweet potatoes and a piece of beef and I came back to school but all this time my hand was paining me, but I continued my school work. About half past three I went to drawing class I draw a flower pot. At four o'clock I was back home. When I came home I went to cottage to a lady. I spend a long time up there playing with the children. When I went home my aunt quarrelled with me and she hit me over my back and said 'This will learn you that when I send you out again you must not stay long.' She gave me a sixpence to buy bread for supper I got for my supper Bread and butter and fry plaintain and a can of corn porrige. I wash up all the supper thing and caught up a fowl with eight chickens.

"*Thursday.* I got up a halfpast five, clean out the drawing room and dust down the chairs. I tidy out one bedroom. I sat down reading a piece of old paper an my aunt said to me, 'what the hell you doing with the piece of old paper an you have a lot of things to do before you go to school.' I clean three pairs of shoes, comb my hair, an catch up the fire at six o'clock. I went an buy penny half penny worth of chocolate for the tea. My aunt told me to leave the fireside an she will complet the breakfast. I bought a six pence worth of bread for the breakfast. I had my bath and dress myself for school. At half past eight she send me up to Red

Hazel for some grape fruits. I made my return very quick for I was feeling hungry I got for my breakfast a can of chocolate an bread an butter an a Johny cake. When I look on the clock it was five minutes to nine she said that I 'must go to the sea side and buy fish.' I told her I could not go because I was late. She said to me you bitch you you see what you eat 12 o'clock for your dinner. I said 'I don't care.' As she was going to knock me I ran out of the house and go to school. I went to school quarter past nine. Thursday morning it always scripture so I read my bible. We had grammar an arithmetic test. At 12 o'clock I went home for my dinner, my aunt did not say anything about what I told her this morning. I got for my dinner plain rice, yellow yam, potatoes and fish. I went back to school at 1 o'clock. When I was leaving the house I hear my aunt and her husband having a little quarrelled it was about. When the dinner ready he won't come home befor the dinner cold. Hear him what the hell you worrying me for my good woman. I went home from school ten to five. When I went home she was sleeping. I took my own time and undress my self an catch up the fire. I cooked the supper we had for supper fry fish, Johnny cake and bread and tea. I wash up my supper things an catch up my chickens when I went in side my aunt said to me 'you bitch you' and flogged me and send me to bed. I went to bed half past eight. I don't even tell anyone goodnight.

"*Friday*. I got up at 7 o'clock. I did not clean any shoe, I comb my hair and go to the bakery. I did not bath, because the pipe was, lock off. They were working on the pipe. All the same I use water. I got for my breakfast bread an butter and a can of mint tea. I went to school at half past eight. I began to do my hand work, because Friday morning is our hand-work day. I have completed on mat. I went home for my dinner at 12 o'clock I did not get plenty dinner so I was vexed I only got a pece of yellow some rice and cod fish an a piece of pear. My aunt saw that I was vexed so she said to me, 'you bitch you, you provided any thing Hear you just come out of the house an leave me in peace!' I took my mat an came to school. When I came back I took my composition Book and transcribe my work in a new book. I try to be neat as possible. I went home at half past four. When I came home from school I carried some milk up to a lady. When I came back I began to peel a roast breadfruit the breadfruit drop from me and a big piece break off. I ate it I said to myself that is to make up for my dinner. When I went inside with it my aunt said to me 'Eileen! is the whole of the breadfruit that,' I said 'Yes mam.' She said 'you bitch you. . . .' " (Henriques 1953:182–183)

CHILD REARING, ACCORDING TO JOHN WESLEY'S MOTHER

"Dear Son—According to your desire, I have collected the principal rules I observed in educating my family; which I now send you as they occurred to my mind. . . .

"The children were always put into a regular method of living, in such things as they were capable of, from their birth; as in dressing, undressing, changing their linen, and so forth. The first quarter commonly passes in sleep. After that, they were, if possible, laid into their cradles awake, and rocked to sleep; and so they were kept rocking, till it was time for them to awake. This was done to bring them to a regular course of sleeping; which at first was three hours in the morning, and then in the afternoon; afterward two hours, till they needed none at all. . . . (At six o'clock, as soon as family prayers were over, they had their supper, at seven the maid washed them) and got them all to bed by eight; at which time she left them in their several rooms awake; for there was no such thing allowed of in our house, as sitting by a child till it fell asleep.

"As soon as they were grown pretty strong, they were confined to three meals a day. At dinner their little tables and chairs were set by ours, where they could be overlooked, and they were suffered to eat and drink (small beer) as much as they would; but not to call for anything. If they wanted aught, they used to whisper to the maid which attended them. . . .

"Mornings they had always spoon-meat; sometimes at nights. But whatever they had, they were never permitted to eat, at those meals, of more than one thing, and of that sparingly enough. Drinking or eating between meals was never allowed, unless in case of sickness; which seldom happened. . . .

"When turned a year old (and some before), they were taught to fear the rod, and to cry softly; by which means they escaped abundance of correction they might otherwise have had; and that most odious noise of the crying of children was rarely heard in the house; but the family usually lived in as much quietness as if there had not been a child among them. . . .

"They were very early made to distinguish the Sabbath from other days, before they could well speak or go. They were as soon taught to be still at family prayers, and to ask a blessing immediately after, which they used to do by signs, before they could kneel or speak."

(*Rules about punishment*)

"That whoever was charged with a fault, of which they were guilty, if they would ingenuously confess it, and promise to amend, should not be beaten. . . .

"That no sinful action . . . should ever pass unpunished.

"That no child should ever be chid, or beat twice for the same fault; and that if they amended, they should never be upbraided with it afterwards.

"That every signal act of obedience, especially when it crossed upon their own inclinations, should be always commended, and frequently rewarded, according to the merits of the case.

"That if ever any child performed an act of obedience, or did anything with intention to please, though the performance was not well, yet the obedience and intention should be kindly accepted; and the child with sweetness directed how to do better for the future. . . .

"As self-will is the root of all sin and misery, so whatever cherishes this in children insures their after wretchedness and irreligion; whatever checks and mortifies it promotes their future happiness and piety. This is still more evident, if we further consider, that religion is nothing else than doing the will of God, and not our own: that the one grand impediment to our temporal and eternal happiness being this self-will, no indulgences of it can be trivial, no denial unprofitable. Heaven and hell depends on this alone. . . .

"In order to form the mind of children, the first thing to be done is to conquer their will, and bring them to an obedient temper. To inform the understanding is a work of time, and must with children proceed by slow degrees as they are able to bear it; but the subjecting the will is a thing which must be done at once; and the sooner the better." (quoted in Gesell 1930)

From time to time, throughout this book, I have referred to the peculiarities of American family customs: the fact that we sometimes give deference to our females, that we allow free courtship and mate choice, that we have practically nothing in the way of patterned kin behavior, that American husbands and wives do not observe public avoidance customs, that the American nuclear family tends to be isolated from larger kin groupings, and so forth. Child rearing is another one of those areas in which the United States is rather deviant. In regard to a number of child-rearing issues, it seems that practically the whole world "does it one way," whereas we "do it another way." In this chapter I will review a few of those child-rearing areas within which our customs are noticeably at odds with the practices current in most other societies.

Birth

American birth customs are unusual for the relative absence of supernaturalism. Not that we are completely without birth magic and birth-associated taboos. However, we have very little of this sort of thing. In the typical primitive society or peasant community, birth is surrounded by a luxuriance of supernaturalism—all manner of "superstitions" or supernatural beliefs, magical precautions of various types, and, especially, taboos. The Navaho, for example, have over forty birth-associated taboos (Bailey 1950:43).

Birth customs seem to conform to Malinowski's observation that supernaturalist practices (which he terms "magic") tend to occur at points and times of uncertainty, where the issue is in doubt, much is at stake, and hazards are involved (Malinowski 1948). Birth is certainly a time of uncertainty. Much is at stake. Particularly where modern medical technology is not available, the survival of mother and child is certainly in doubt. Perhaps this is one reason why there is a profusion of supernatural beliefs and practices associated with the event of birth.

The most nearly universal birth precaution appears to be the food taboo. In nearly all societies pregnant women are not allowed to eat certain foods. Barbara Ayres found that thirty-three societies in her cross-cultural sample insisted upon pregnancy food taboos; only two societies had no food taboos (Ayres 1954:49).

Sex taboos are also a common accompaniment of birth, although apparently less common than food taboos. In Ayres' sample, eighteen of twenty-nine societies had a pregnancy sex taboo. Usually this taboo begins in about the second month of pregnancy (Ayres 1954:21). After birth, most societies demand a *post partum* sex taboo; in many cases this taboo lasts several years (Whiting and Kluckhohn, m.s.; Stephens 1962).

Still less frequently cited but still, apparently, pretty common, are various activity taboos (examples: the expectant mother should not kill chickens; she should not look at a snake), and various positive magical acts (examples: she *should* kill white chickens; it is lucky if she sees a little green snake).

Here are some examples of these birth practices:

MEDIEVAL EUROPE

The nurses and midwives of these days were saturated with superstitions and practised all manner of strange traditional rites which were believed to help the little stranger on the strenuous path of life that lay ahead of it. Sometimes a fresh egg, the symbol of fruitfulness, was laid in the baby's bath; or a coin was placed there to insure to the little one ample means in its later life. Again, after its bath, the new-born child was laid close against the left side of its mother in the belief that she would draw from it all the sickness and protect it thus from child-pains, leprosy and the falling-sickness. Against these and many other superstitious practices, kept alive by ignorant midwives, municipal laws were occasionally directed. For example, an ordinance of Gotha, as late as the seventeenth century, after enjoining midwives to be God-fearing and lead Christly lives, continues: "On the contrary all superstition and misuse of God's name and word . . . such as use of written characters, drawings, gestures, and making the cross, amputation of the navel-string with certain questions and answers . . . sprinkling before or after the bath, and such-like are forbidden. . . ." (Goodsell 1915:212)

LESU, MELANESIA

During this period the pregnant woman has no sexual intercourse, either with her husband or anyone else. . . . Other pregnancy taboos affect the husband and not the wife. No man with a pregnant wife can fish or hunt wild pig. If he does, it is thought that he will have no success. . . .

It is interesting to note in this connection that a man and his wife observe the same sexual taboos, although for a much shorter time, when their pigs are giving birth. The owner of a pregnant pig and his mate are continent when the pig is expected to give birth, and also for the first month that the infant pig is being suckled. Should this taboo be broken it is thought that the young pig would sicken and die; and pigs are very valuable property. (Powdermaker 1933:62, 79)

LEPCHA, SIKKIM

It would be tedious to give a complete list of the pre-natal precautions to be observed, but the following are some typical examples. If either of the parents are engaged in making a fence he or she must do the whole work by himself; otherwise the baby cannot be born properly. The father must not take any fish out of a trap in the river or the child will be born with its nose stopped up. Neither parent must lock up anything except their own box or the child will not be able to be born until what is closed is opened; even the house door must not be fastened. Neither parent may eat animals which have met their death by accident or by being killed by a wild beast; the father must never look at a recently killed animal; he can kill animals but must run away at once. The father must not touch the iron or rope of a horse's bridle; should he do so the mother and child are liable to die, but this can be prevented if a bridle is kept in the house which can be *pek* over the woman during delivery. If either parent should be weaving a mat or cloth he or she must never quite finish it but must leave a little bit over. The mother must not eat any joined fruit such as double banana or the child's toes will be webbed. Neither parent must stick poles into the ground or tie knots or drive in nails or put small stones into the cracks between bigger stones when building a wall; all of these prevent proper delivery. Expectant parents must not look at a solar or lunar eclipse or the child will be born dead; in the case of a solar eclipse both parents must stay in the house all day. If a child has recently died the paths it used to walk in and its house must be avoided; and as a general precaution it is better to avoid the paths and houses of all recently dead people. Expectant parents must not watch a dog being born; if they do so the child will have one eye smaller than the other. If expectant parents move a sacred image the child will be born dumb. Should either parent look at or kill a field-mouse or should they eat rice which has stuck to the bottom of the cooking-pot the placenta will not descend. There are a very great number of prohibitions similar to those listed above; the second half of pregnancy is a period of constant watchfulness for both parents. . . .

For the first three days of life the baby is considered to be still in the womb and all the pre-natal precautions have to be observed. It is not even referred to as a human child; it is called a rat-child. During those three days the mother must on no account touch the ground; were she to do so the blood clot would not descend. The father may go out but must not do heavy work such as lifting stones or cutting trees; such actions would cause the woman pain in her belly. Also nobody except those who live in the house must enter the house or see the child; should they do so the mother will have terrible pains. (Gorer 1938: 284, 289)

KIPSIGIS, KENYA

The mother is confined to her hut for three days after the birth of a girl, and for four days after the birth of a boy. For six days after birth she cannot touch anything in the hut with her hands and must eat her food with a stick. On the seventh day her hair is shaved and she bathes in the river; but for a whole year she will not be able to touch anything with her hands without washing at . . . a calabash full of water, suspended from a tree. This ceremonial uncleanness is called *chepengobit,* and it is believed that, if the mother is not careful and touches anything with her hands, not only that object but all others of the same species belonging to her husband will suffer. Thus, if she touches meat or milk, the cows of her husband will become barren; if she touches her porridge, his fields will wither, and so on. . . . A month after the birth, the husband returns to his home. During this time no man can see the baby, as a man's face is said to frighten it so much that it will stop crying and will eventually become so feeble that it will die. (Peristiany 1939:76, 77)

ARAPESH, NEW GUINEA

When the mother's breasts show the characteristic swelling and discolouration of pregnancy, then the child is said to be finished—a perfect egg, it will now rest in the mother's womb. From this time on, all intercourse is forbidden, for the child must sleep undisturbed . . . she (the mother) must observe certain precautions: she must not eat the bandicoot or she will die in hard labour, for the bandicoot burrows too far into the ground, nor the frog, or the child will be born too suddenly, nor the eel, or the child will be born too soon. She must not eat sago that comes from a *marsalai* place, nor coconuts from a tree that has been tabooed by the *tamberan*, the supernatural patron of the men's cult. If the woman wants the child to be male, other women will tell her never to cut anything in half, for this cutting will produce a female. . . .

At the moment of birth the father cannot be present. . . . Nevertheless, the verb to "bear a child" is used indiscriminately of either a man or a woman, and childbearing is believed to be as heavy a drain upon the man as upon the woman. . . .

The father now comes to share his wife's task of caring for the new-born child. . . . He is now, in native phrasing, "in bed having a baby.". . .

The father lies quietly beside his new-born child, from time to time giving the mother little bits of advice. He and she fast together for the first day. They may not smoke or drink water. From time to time they perform small magical rites that will ensure the child's welfare and their ability to care for it. . . .

The father of a first child is in an especially delicate position, more delicate than is the mother. . . . After a five-day period during which he remains in strict seclusion with his wife, not touching tobacco with his hands, using a stick to scratch his person, and eating all food with a spoon, he is taken to the water-side (where he is ritually purified). . . .

Still the child's life depends upon the constant special attention of the father as well as the mother. The father must sleep each night with the mother and baby, and there is a strict taboo on intercourse. . . . If a child is puny and ailing or if its bones are weak and it fails to walk quickly, this is the fault of its parents, who have not observed the taboo. (Mead 1935)

KWAKIUTL, VANCOUVER ISLAND •

". . . the fourth day after my birth, my father and mother gathered all the rotten stuff they could find—rotten wood, moss, the green stuff that grows on the outside of canoes, . . . everything that was rotten. They brought these things into the house and set a fire on to that and put the cradle on top of the smoke four times, so that I will be mild and won't cry much. Then they went out and found water on the top of old stumps, and bathed me in that four times. This makes me meek, too. After that, once a day for four days, they do the same thing with the water, but they only smoke me once. . . .

"From the time I am first put in my cradle, they be watching for the string to come off from the button of my belly. If you want your baby to be a canoemaker, they give it to a man to put on his wrist while he is making a canoe. They gave mine to my father, and he put it on his right wrist while singing. They say they took me out of my cradle and wrapped me up and put me inside a wooden drum. He began to hit the drum with his fists and began to sing. He put me in the drum and sing like this four times to make me like he was—a maker of songs. I could have been like him, and I was when I was a young man. I made winter dance songs and love songs, but we don't make them any more.

"When I was in my cradle, I cried all the time. My parents wanted me to sleep. They got some boys with poles, in the evening, to catch a bat. They put it under my cradle. They say the bat sleeps all the time in the day, and that will make me sleep all the time during the day. Then they begin to wonder who was crying the way I was now crying. They think of a woman crying for a dead person, and asked this woman to come and pretend to cry. I was all covered up. They always do this when a baby cries too much, and they say it will stop him. But it didn't stop me.

"If a baby's skin get yellow, they say that the parents of the baby have seen a frog. His parents go and find a frog and come in with the frog alive. They take the baby out of the cradle and cover him with something, and take the frog by the legs and pass it down near the back of the baby saying, 'This is the cause of your sickness.' They do this four times. If the baby doesn't get well, they do it the next day and so on until the fourth day. If the parents see a dead man or a dead woman, they take a rag and go to the dead person and wipe it on the face with a rag. And they say when a child has no breath and is like a dead person, they use this the same way on a child. When they hear crows crowing or any bird making a noise when a woman is pregnant, then the baby may make a noise like that. Anything they see or hear or smell while she is carrying, if it frightens them, the child will be like that." (Ford 1941:43–46)

KURTACHI, SOLOMON ISLANDS

No men are permitted to enter the hut in which the woman is confined, from the time the pains begin. The husband may not enter it for three days after the birth of the child, and other men only after he has done so. . . .

Failing to observe the (sex) taboo is supposed to bring ill-health to the child. An obviously sick baby will be taken as an indication that its parents have been indulging in sexual intercourse during the prohibited period. . . .

During pregnancy a woman may not eat the megapoda *iowa* nor the fish called *turo*. Her husband should also observe this rule. . . . While labour is in progress the husband must abstain from food of any kind. . . . After the birth, for an indeterminate period, the parents may not eat pig, fish, opossum, shell-fish, or barringtonia fruit. . . . The effect of the other prohibitions is to confine the parents to a vegetarian diet; this is thought to be of advantage to the child. The mother is subjected to further restrictions. She must chew with her areca-nut only the leaf of the betel-pepper, not touching the catkin-like fruit, which is much preferred in the ordinary way. . . . The nursing mother must also abstain from bananas and canarium almonds. . . .

As soon as the expectant mother feels the pains beginning, her husband must stop working, and remain indoors, not in the hut where his wife is confined, but in that of another of his wives, or of a neighbor. He must spend his time in sitting idle or dozing, and must on no account carry, or even lift, anything heavy, or touch a knife, axe, or any sharp or pointed instrument. To do the former would injure the child, the latter would cause it to die. This continues for three days. On the fourth day he may go into the hut and see his child. After this he is allowed to walk about the village, but must not go outside it. He must still refrain from working. On the fifth day he goes, with his wife, and washes in the sea; these are his first ablutions since the child was born. Then he may take an axe or a knife and go into the hut and pretend to cut the child; this removes the taboo on his use of sharp instruments, and he may now resume his usual activities. (Blackwood 1935:155–159)

There are several other aspects to birth precautions that I have not mentioned yet. For one, the father, as well as the mother, often becomes involved in the birth magic and taboos (Alor, Arapesh, Reindeer Chukchee, Copper Eskimo, Kurtachi, Ifaluk, Lepcha, Lesu, Maria Gonds, Muria, Siriono). At times, father and mother collectively observe about the same food taboos. Or, the father may be bound by activity taboos that are, within his sphere of work, analogous to the mother's. Occasionally the father even "lies in," apparently simulating his wife's parturition trauma (Arapesh, Copper Eskimo).

Also, infant and mother are frequently isolated in a special birth shelter or at home, both during the birth and for a period afterward—shielded from the gaze of men and/or strangers. (See Ford 1945.)

Finally, there is the question of the reasons for these taboos and magical precautions. The *professed* reasons generally have to do with the safety, health, and well-being of the infant (Arapesh, Reindeer Chukchee, Gusii, Hehe, Kipsigis, Kurtachi, Kwakiutl, Kwoma, Lepcha, Rajputs, Silwa, Siriono). Also mentioned are magical measures for the health and safety of the mother (Azande, Lepcha, Tepoztlan). A few societies combine isolation of the mother with notions about some supernatural quality of power-danger or uncleanness attached to the mother (Ifaluk, Kipsigis, Maria, Rajput, Silwa, Ulithi). One gets the impression that the horror of menstrual blood at times generalizes to the act of birth, the afterbirth, and *post partum* bleeding, thus serving as one reason for birth seclusion and birth taboos.

A final topic I would like to discuss here is the somatic difficulties of the parturient mother. Such questions as—Is she sick during pregnancy? Is labor difficult? Is she markedly incapacitated by the act of giving birth? For fourteen societies in my ethnographic notes, the ethnographer has something to say on this subject. For most of these cases, pregnancy is apparently not noticeably debilitating, nor is birth such a major physical trauma.

An Alorese woman continues with her usual farm work throughout her pregnancy. Births seem to occur with little difficulty, and without extreme pain. "One gathers the impression that birth is considered an easy and casual procedure and that problems in beginning nursing never occur. . . . In the half-dozen births I witnessed, the mothers at no time showed signs of pain beyond acute discomfort. They groaned softly and perspired freely but seemed on the whole to give birth with little difficulty." (DuBois 1944) After giving birth the mother rests for about a week. Within two weeks she is back working in the fields.

There are six other cases in my notes in which the pregnant woman continues with her normal work up until the time of delivery: Reindeer Chukchee, Ifaluk, Lesu, Navaho, Papago, and Pukapuka. In Tepoztlan the pregnant woman's work is curtailed a bit; she stops lifting heavy loads. As far as *post partum* work is concerned: in Samoa, the mother resumes work after a few hours; among the Ojibwa, she gets one day's rest after giving birth; among the Navaho and Copper Eskimo, she rests for about two days. For four cases, a new mother does have a vacation from her normal economic chores. In Ifaluk she undergoes a three-month ritual seclusion, which exempts her from many of her normal duties. In Tepoztlan she rests for several months. A Rajput mother gets about three weeks' rest, and an Azande mother two or three weeks.

Nausea during pregnancy (or "morning sickness") is reported present for two cases (Pukapuka and Tepoztlan); among the Papago it is said to be present but infrequent; and it is, apparently, absent among the Arapesh and Ifalukians.

The mother performs the birth unassisted in three cases: Ifaluk, Maria, and Siriono. Here is Spiro's description of birth in Ifaluk:

> While in labor, the mother kneels on a mat, catching the baby in her arms when it emerges. . . . Though the mother is accompanied by her mother and her mother's sister, they do not serve as midwives, except in the event of a difficult delivery, in which case they will extract the baby from the womb. Ordinarily, however, the mother delivers her own baby. She is, moreover, not to indicate her pain by any overt manifestations. Should she cry out, she would shame both her mother and herself. (Spiro 1949:84)

Finally, here is Margaret Mead's account of birth in Samoa:

> There is no privacy about a birth. Convention dictates that the mother should neither writhe, nor cry out, nor inveigh against the presence of twenty or thirty people in the house who sit up all night if need be, laughing, joking, and playing games. The midwife cuts the cord with a fresh bamboo knife and then all wait eagerly for the cord to fall off, the signal for a feast. . . . Then the visitors

go home, the mother rises and goes about her daily tasks, and the new baby ceases to be of much interest to any one. (Mead 1928)

Nursing and Early Nurturance

When one reads an ethnographic account of child rearing in a primitive society, one will usually find some statement to the effect that the people "love their babies." Often this statement is couched in superlatives; the ethnographer seems amazed at the amount of affection, care, attention, indulgence, and general "fuss" lavished upon infants and young children. Here are a few examples of what I mean:

IFALUK, MICRONESIA

. . . the infant is exposed to the faces and arms of many people. For the westerner, the amount of handling the infant receives is almost fantastic. The infant, particularly after it can crawl, is never allowed to remain in the arms of one person. In the course of a half hour conversation, the baby might change hands ten times, being passed from one person to another. This transference of the infant is not due to the fatigue of the person who is holding it at the time, but is done at the request of the others. The adults, as well as the older children, love to fondle the babies and to play with them, with the result that the infant does not stay with one person very long. . . .

Infants are not only greatly desired, as we have already seen, but they are given the greatest care and indulgence possible. The infant is idealized to the point that its over-indulgence and pampering become phantasies from the standpoint of Western standards. We have seen that no infant is ever left alone, day or night, asleep or awake, until it can walk. To isolate a baby would be to commit a major atrocity, for if a baby is left alone, "by and by dies, no more people."

Should an infant cry, it is immediately picked up in an adult's arms, cuddled, consoled or fed. Thus the baby is in a state of almost complete dependence on the adults about it. This oversolicitude extends to the two- and three-year-olds as well, assuming that another baby has not entered the household. Should the baby fall, and begin to cry, he is immediately picked up. . . .

To claim that the infant is king in Ifaluk is not to exaggerate the situation at all. The infant is in control of a social situation, and easily dominates the adults, bending them to his will. (Spiro 1949: 89–94)

KWOMA, NEW GUINEA

Kwoma infants up to the time they are weaned are never far from their mothers. It is, in fact, very seldom that they are not actually in physical contact with her. Having turned over most of her household duties to her co-wife or some female relative, the mother may hold the child all day and give it her undivided attention. She sits either on the earth floor or on a bark slab under the porch of the family dwelling with the baby nestling on her outstretched legs. At night the infant sleeps cuddled by her side. Whenever she has to move, she carries the child with her cradled in her arm, sitting on her neck, or, less frequently, straddling her hip. . . . The mother keeps her breast constantly available. . . .

As regards prestige, the Kwoma infant enjoys in a sense the most dominant social position that he will ever attain. His every command is obeyed, and all his wants are attended to. (Whiting 1941:24, 30)

LESU, NEW IRELAND

The whole hamlet regards the youngest infant as its pet and plaything. Whenever there are a group of natives together, whether it is the women resting and chattering after their communal cooking, or the men idling on the sand, the child is tossed about from one to the other, fondled, patted, jumped up and down, and kissed. (Powdermaker 1933:70)

NAVAHO

Within a few hours after birth the baby is given to the mother or placed near her in its temporary cradle. This relationship of almost constant physical proximity between child and mother is unbroken until weaning. Night and day, wherever the mother goes, whatever she is doing, the baby is either being held by her or is within sight of her eye and almost always within reach of her hand. As soon as she is physically able, the mother herself responds immediately to every manifestation of want or discomfort on the part of her child. Her first response whenever the child cries is to place it to her breast. . . .

> The baby gets a good deal of affectionate attention. He is, of course, fed and held by the mother. He is also held, touched, and talked to by the father, older brothers and sisters, and indeed all relatives who come and go in the hogan. The relative joggles the cradle or makes affectionate noises. All Navahos make a fuss over babies. They receive, from the start, a very great amount of attention and a great deal of facial stimulation by touch. Their faces are patted and their ears are plucked. Their limbs are also stroked when they are out of the cradle, but this occurs far less often. . . .
>
> A well infant of a few months may nurse only six times during daylight and once or twice during the night. Older children nurse much more frequently. Children close to a year old have been observed to be put to the breast on the average about thirty times during a 24-hour period, and more than sixty such contacts during this interval are by no means unknown. Sometimes a child will be fed three times within fifteen minutes. . . .
>
> White observers often comment that The People "spoil" their younger children. They do *indulge* them, but they do not "spoil" them in the original sense of the word, that is, to deform or ruin the character. (Leighton and Kluckhohn 1948:18, 27, 28, 33)

Thirteen more societies in my ethnographic notes are reported to be similarly extravagant in respect to early nurturance: Arapesh, Arunta, Azande, Reindeer Chukchee, Copper Eskimo, Kaingang, Kurtachi, Lepcha, Muria, Murngin, Silwa, Siriono, and Tikopia. In contrast to these, there are four cases in which the ethnographer comments on the low degree of early nurturance: Gusii, Mundugumor, Rajputs, and Samoa.

How does our society rank, in comparison with other societies, with respect to parental warmth and nurturance given to babies and very young children? It is possible that we are a bit on the cold side. Whiting and Child rated American parents less nurturant[2] than about 75 percent of the other peoples in their cross-cultural sample (Whiting and Child 1953:93). I say this is merely "possible," since this Whiting and Child finding has two understandable drawbacks. To represent American child rearing, they

---

[2] The Whiting and Child variable I am referring to here is "initial indulgence of dependency."

chose a study of child rearing practices within a sample of Chicago families, which was done by Davis and Havighurst about twenty years ago. There is no telling, of course, how representative or nonrepresentative these Chicago families were of our country as a whole, or whether any such localized sample could be taken to represent "American child rearing." A second possible drawback has to do with their cross-cultural sample. It was heavily loaded with primitive societies, containing very few "peasant" or "kingdom" cases. I suspect that further differences between tribes and kingdoms exist in the area of child rearing. It may be, for instance, that primitive tribes are generally "high" in respect to early nurturance and infant indulgence, whereas kingdoms are relatively "low"; that we are relatively cold in our treatment of little children, when we are compared with a sample of primitive tribes; but that we are not nonnurturant as compared with the kingdom cases.[3]

At any rate, one is on shaky ground when one tries to compare American parents with other peoples in respect to emotional qualities, such as parental love, proneness to nurturance and indulgence, and the like. However, in the more simple and clear-cut area of mere body contact with the mother—being carried by her, lying next to her, feeling her skin, sucking at her breast—the American infant is undoubtedly "deprived" compared with infants in most other societies.

For one thing, in most societies the infant sleeps next to its mother for several years after birth. In forty-five of sixty-four societies in Whiting and D'Andrade's sample, the nursing infant customarily sleeps by its mother's side (Whiting and D'Andrade; Stephens 1962:9).

Second, there is the matter of waking body-contact. Descriptions of fairly constant holding, fondling, and carrying of the infant by the mother and other caretakers—cases such as the Kwoma and Ifaluk—are almost (but not quite) as common in ethnographies as are descriptions of great over-all infant indulgence.

---

[3] I think this is true, but I cannot document it.

Third, there is manner of nursing. For fifteen cases in my notes, the infant is "nursed whenever he cries."[4] Apparently, this means more than our conception of "demand feeding"; this means that the breast is used as a pacifier, with a consequent high frequency of feedings, as described above for the Navaho. In only three cases in my notes is the infant not "nursed whenever he cries"; in Alor, in Jamaica (Rocky Roads), and among the Rajputs of Khalapur, he sometimes has to wait a while.

Finally, we wean our infants from the breast at an extraordinarily early age. In Whiting and Child's cross-cultural sample, the median age of weaning was two and a half years. Only one society out of fifty-two weaned at approximately the same age as we do (at about six months)—the Marquesans. The usual procedure in primitive societies is to wean the child at about the time when the next baby is born. Particularly in societies with a long *post partum* sex taboo, this means a nursing interval of two years or more. When a mother has no more babies, she may nurse her last child more or less indefinitely—for four or five years, or even longer:

BAIGA, INDIA

"In Dadargaon I lived with my parents for one year. Then we all came to Kotalwahi. It was then that I stopped drinking my mother's milk. She suckled me till after my marriage, till I was twelve years old." (Elwin 1939:136)

KWAKIUTL, VANCOUVER ISLAND

I know a relation of mine, a girl. We used to go and play, maybe on the beach and maybe in the back of the houses. We must have been about four or five years old and the same age, only she was a little younger. She used to say, 'I'm getting hungry,' and we used to go home together with her in her house, and she goes right up to her mother and pulls out her mother's breast and begins

---

[4] Arapesh, Kurtachi, Kwoma, Lepcha, Manus, Navaho, Ojibwa, Papago, Pukapuka, Samoa, Silwa, Siriono, Tepoztlan, Thonga, and Wogeo.

to feed on it. I remember I wasn't nursing then, and I thought I ought to be if this girl was." (Ford 1941:47)

OJIBWA, ONTARIO

"My youngest brother used to be playing with a bow and arrow and, with them in his hands, come running up to mother to nurse." (Landes 1937:28)

KURTACHI, SOLOMON ISLANDS

Some women have very pendulous breasts, but I have not seen any long enough to be thrown over the shoulder to a child carried on the back. I have often seen a woman bend down with her hands on her knees so that a child standing beside her could suck. (Blackwood 1935:162)

LEPCHA, SIKKIM

A youngest child will continue sucking until the mother's milk dries up, or until the child "becomes ashamed"; this may continue up to puberty. Gongyop's only surviving son took the breast until he was ten; and Pursang, Chano's second "son," was suckled by a childless aunt until her death, which occurred when he was eleven. (Gorer 1938: 293–294)

The "typical" picture, then, of infancy and early childhood in a primitive society, is: many magical precautions at birth and birth-associated taboos; in contrast to all of this concern with the supernatural, a relative nonchalance about the mother's physical hardship during pregnancy and at parturition; a superlative amount of love, attention, and nurturance lavished upon the infant; high frequency of body contact with adult caretakers—especially with the mother, who sleeps with the infant; the ultimate in "demand feeding"—the breast is used as a pacifier; and a prolonged nursing period, lasting for two or more years. Typically, too, these "golden years" end at weaning. As Spiro says of Ifaluk—baby is king, but at weaning the king is dethroned. A new infant ascends the throne, and the weaned child is left out in the cold. Gone is the mother's breast; gone also is much of the nurturance, love, and attention to which the child had become accustomed. Usually, the weaned child stops sleeping with his mother; his place has been taken by his new baby sibling. Traumatic weaning is described for eleven cases in my notes: Hehe, Ifaluk, Lepcha, Kwoma, Lesu, Navaho, Ojibwa, Taitou (China), Tepoztlan, Thonga, and Valle Cana (Puerto Rico). Only in one case is weaning said to be not especially upsetting—the Rajputs, who are unusual for their low degree of nurturance given to babies.

To conclude this section, here are some descriptions of the dethronement of King Infant:

KWOMA

When a child is weaned he may no longer sit in his mother's lap by day nor lie by her side at night. This is apparently felt as the most severe frustration experienced at this period of life. No longer is it possible to attain the vantage point from which all drives have hitherto been satisfied. . . .

With weaning, then, many of the demands which the Kwoma child has learned to make during infancy become no longer successful. His mother no longer responds in the same helpful way to many of his requests. His demands to be taken into her lap, scratched, patted, or warmed, are now ignored. When she no longer heeds his demands, he becomes more vociferous. Unless he is in serious danger, she still does not cater to him. . . .

If a child is too vociferous and persistent in his demands, he is actually punished. . . .

Weaning greatly increases a child's experience of anxiety. His desire to sit in his mother's lap and his fear of being pushed away and scolded for it, the desire to suckle and the belief that there is a *marsalai*[5] in his mother's breast, the wish for his demands to be heeded and the punishments he receives for crying, all are anxiety-producing sources of conflict. . . .

In the realm of prestige, the Kwoma child during the period of weaning plunges from the very top to the very bottom of the social hierarchy. (Whiting 1941:33–36)

IFALUK

As we have emphasized repeatedly the baby is king in Ifaluk. Not only are babies desired, not only are their every wants fulfilled,

---

[5] Monster.

but they are the constant center of attention. They are always the focal point of the household. This orientation, moreover, remains constant. The adult eyes are always focused on the babies, so that once the baby grows older he is out of focus, so to speak, and a new baby is now in focus. There is little eye accommodation, which would enable both the infant and the growing baby to be in focus. In other words, the king is dethroned. His place of centrality is now usurped by a younger infant. From the position of extreme overt love and attention he now finds himself ignored. Adults are still concerned about him, but they leave him to shift for himself. He is free to come and go when he wants, to eat where he wants, as long as he is not too far from sight. But what is even more important, the constant overt affection displayed towards him when young, is now withdrawn. I have seldom seen a child four or five years old being held in an adult's arms, kissed, hugged, or in general receive overt physical affection. From a state of infancy—overabundant love—they pass directly to a state of adulthood, as far as the display of affection is concerned. The result of this differential treatment is a child starving for affection. (Spiro 1949:100–101)

THONGA, SOUTH AFRICA

The very day of his weaning, the child must leave the village of his parents and go to stay with his grandparents. A little mat and a few clothes have been prepared for him and the grandmother comes to take him. . . . Sometimes father and mother accompany their offspring themselves, during the night, to make the separation easier. It is a sad day for them as well as for the child! The following day the parents go again to see how the little one has stood their absence. They do not enter the village. They remain hidden in a little copse and look at their child through the branches! He must not see his mother, otherwise he would cry. . . . A touching scene indeed! (Junod 1927, Vol. I:60)

NAVAHO

Except for ill health, the Navaho child's troubles may be said to begin only at the weaning period. Weaning, however, is late, and it is gradual. In cases where the next baby does not come for some time or at all, the child may often be said to wean itself.

To the child, weaning means less and less of the mother's attention. Deprivation of the breast is merely one sign of a general loss.

For the weaned child is no longer allowed to sleep every night by the mother's side. His sleeping place is now under the blanket which also covers the two or three other children nearest him in age. The mother surrenders to these older children most of the care of the weaned baby. Crying is less immediately responded to and less fully tolerated. A weaned baby who gets in the mother's way may be rather roughly jerked aside. Moreover, the mother starts to make demands of him. . . .

Children who have recently been weaned seem to find the sight of the new baby at the mother's breast a disturbing experience. . . .

Children who happen to be the last in the family or whose following brother or sister dies very soon after birth leaving them the youngest again, undergo life experiences in this period which are different in important respects from those of the average child. Preliminary analysis of materials which the authors have collected indicate, in fact, that adult Navahos who were actually or psychologically "last-born" have a personality structure which differs consistently from that of other Navahos. They tend to be more stable, more secure, less suspicious, generally "happier." It must be realized that the number who are "psychologically" last-born is large, for the infant mortality rate is very high. (Leighton and Kluckhohn 1948:33–37)

TEPOZTLAN

Most mothers nurse their infants until they know that they are again pregnant. . . .

When the mother decides to wean the child she places a bitter substance (*savila*) on the nipple, often in the child's presence, and tells him that her breast is sore and that he may no longer nurse. . . . Crying, even if prolonged over eight days, is viewed as a normal part of weaning. . . .

Illness and death are frequent in children after weaning. . . .

Affection shown by the grandmother, the father, and older brothers and sisters also serves to comfort younger children. Demonstrative affection from the mother is almost entirely absent after the new baby is born. In general, it is rare for a child over five to be held, hugged, or kissed, and by the time the child reaches ten this never occurs. . . .

After the birth of a new sibling the next youngest child no longer sleeps with the mother. (Lewis 1951:376–379)

Caretakers

Here we come to an area in which our society is strikingly deviant. In all the societies in my ethnographic notes, with the lone exception of the Copper Eskimo, people ordinarily live within residential kin groups that are larger than the nuclear family. A married couple lives either with or near the husband's kin (patrilocal residence or avunculocal residence), or they live with or near the wife's kin (matrilocal residence). It is only in the infrequent, deviant cases, in these societies, that the nuclear family is "isolated"—geographically distant, and more or less cut off from other kinfolk.

Our society is unusual for the relatively high frequency of isolated nuclear households; because the nuclear family is usually isolated from other kin, the job of caring for young children is left largely in the hands of the mother. She is either the only caretaker, or she is by far the most important caretaker. Talcott Parsons points out that the isolated nuclear family, as opposed to larger kin-groupings, constitutes a small, "tight," social-interaction system. It is an all-your-eggs-in-one-basket situation. Mother —and how mother feels—is very important, because she is the only mother you have; there are no surrogate mothers in the form of aunts, grandmothers, or older cousins. When mother becomes angry or estranged, there is no place to go, no one else to turn to. (Mother, too, has a job which permits no rest, needless to say.) As Parsons says, since there are no mother-surrogates, there is a very high degree of "affective involvement" between mother and child.[6] Or, to use Bacon, Barry, and Child's term, there is very little "diffusion of nurturance"; mother is the only nurturer.

Let us now turn to the cross-cultural literature and see how unusual we are in respect to "diffusion of nurturance."

For four cases in the ethnographic notes, the mother is said

---

[6] Parsons thinks this arrangement aggravates emotional insecurity in the child and makes more likely cross-sex identification in boys (Parsons 1949: 256–258).

to be the only caretaker for the nursing infant: Azande, Hehe, Kwoma, and Taitou (China). However, in each of these cases, this situation lasts only until the child is weaned. After weaning, apparently, the child (in these four cases) usually has a number of caretakers. Even this situation seems to be rather unusual. In most societies the mother appears to get a great deal of help, even during the nursing period.[7]

In most of the reported cases in my notes, the father seems to be an important caretaker of young children, that is, of children too young to work, under five years of age (Alor, Arapesh, Baiga, Copper Eskimo, Ifaluk, Kurtachi, Lesu, Muria, Pukapuka, Tikopia, and Trobriands). Among the Manus and Wogeo, the father does not help during the first year; after that he is a major caretaker. In Taitou the father tends to avoid a nursing child; after weaning, he seems to be a fairly important caretaker. And in five societies men appear to have little to do with young children: Azande, Deoli (Hindu India), Gusii, Kwoma, and Tepoztlan.

In most societies, fairly young children are apparently pressed into service as caretakers for still younger children. Although girls may have more continuous duties of this sort, it seems that both boys and girls usually serve as surrogate parents before they are ten. In some societies—such as Samoa, to be cited below—the child-nurse actually relieves the mother of many of her caretaking and mothering duties. Only two societies in my notes are said not to rely on child-nurses: Kwoma and Manus. In two cases, Pukapuka and Valle Cana, child-nurses are used, but they seem to be rather unimportant. Fifteen other societies are said to place heavy reliance on child-nurses (Alor, Baiga, Gusii, Ifaluk, Kurtachi, Lepcha, Muria, Navaho, Ojibwa, Samoa, Silwa, Tepoztlan, Tikopia, Plateau Tonga, and Wogeo).

Finally, for fourteen societies, the mother is reported to receive help from numerous other surrogate mothers: grandmothers, aunts, co-wives, and nonkin neighbors (Arapesh, Fiji,

---

[7] Alor, Arapesh, Baiga, Copper Eskimo, Gusii, Iban, Ifaluk, Kurtachi, Lepcha, Lesu, Navaho, Ojibwa, Pukapuka, Samoa, Silwa, Tepoztlan, Tikopia, Wogeo.

Iban, Ifaluk, Kurtachi, Lepcha, Lesu, Muria, Navaho, Ojibwa, Samoa, Silwa, Tikopia, and Wogeo).

Here are some examples of the diffusion of nurturance:

IFALUK

Though the family is the most important institution in defining patterns of interaction, the family is not as crucial a group here as it is in other cultures for two reasons. In the first place, the family is seldom together at one time. The father is in the canoe house, the mother in the taro patch, the children are playing, the young people are about their activities. There are few meals at which the entire family is present, or required to be present, people eating when and where they choose. On the other hand, there is little distinction between one's own relatives and "strangers." Every one knows every one else in the village, so that the child moves in a world in which there are no strange faces or strange people towards whom one's behavior must be different. All individuals look alike and all treat him alike. If he is hungry any of them give him food; if he needs something anyone will try to satisfy his need. Every house is open to him and he never has to learn that some houses are different from others; he can walk into any house (without knocking) at any time of the day or night. (Spiro 1949:97)

NAVAHO

One of the most common sights in an extended Navaho family is that of a toddler (especially one who has been recently weaned and feels himself somewhat rejected by his mother) running from one woman in the group to another and receiving some sign of affection from each. . . .

In an extended family group the child may well have not merely three or four but fifteen or more persons whom he calls "my older brother." And the Navaho child calls not one but a number of women "my mother." Once the worst emotional shock of the weaning process is over, the mother's sisters often become almost completely adequate substitutes for the real mother. Indeed there are cases where it appears that a young man or woman actually feels closer to one of these secondary mothers. . . .

What does all this mean in terms of the dynamics of personal relations? It means that the Navaho child's emotional energy tends to be spread over a much wider surface than is the case with white children. He is not likely to have the same degree of intense emotional involvement in a very few persons. Naturally, the reverse is equally true. The mother is devoted to her own children, but her feeling toward them grades off almost imperceptibly into that for her sisters' children. . . . The child, after he has reached the toddling stage, finds ready and immediate succor and comfort in one of his secondary mothers whenever he feels that his own has been cross or has temporarily rejected him. (Leighton and Kluckhohn 1948:38, 48–49)

SAMOA

Babies sleep with their mothers as long as they are at the breast; after weaning they are usually handed over to the care of some younger girl in the household. . . .

The chief nurse-maid is usually a child of six or seven. . . .

The weight of punishment usually falls upon the next oldest child [that is, the child-nurse], who learns to shout, "Come out of the sun," before she has fully appreciated the necessity of doing so herself. By the time Samoan girls and boys have reached sixteen or seventeen years of age these perpetual admonitions to the younger ones have become an inseparable part of their conversation, a monotonous, irritated undercurrent to all their comments. I have known them to intersperse their remarks every two or three minutes with, "Keep still," "Sit still," "Keep your mouths shut," "Stop that noise," uttered quite mechanically although all of the little ones present may have been behaving as quietly as a row of intimidated mice. On the whole, this last requirement of silence is continually mentioned and never enforced. The little nurses are more interested in peace than in forming the characters of their small charges and when a child begins to howl, it is simply dragged out of earshot of its elders. No mother will ever exert herself to discipline a younger child if an older one can be made responsible.

If small families of parents and children prevailed in Samoa, this system would result in making half of the population solicitous and self-sacrificing and the other half tyrannous and self-indulgent. But just as a child is getting old enough so that its wilfulness is becoming unbearable, a younger one is saddled upon it, and the whole process is repeated again, each child being disciplined and socialized through responsibility for a still younger one. . . .

The close relationship between parent and child, which has such a decisive influence upon so many in our civilization, that submission to the parent or defiance of the parent may become the dominating pattern of a lifetime, is not found in Samoa. Children reared in households where there are a half dozen adult women to care for them and dry their tears, and a half dozen adult males, all of whom represent constituted authority, do not distinguish their parents as sharply as our children do. The image of the fostering, loving mother, or the admirable father, which may serve to determine affectional choices later in life, is a composite affair, composed of several aunts, cousins, older sisters, and grandmothers; of chief, father, uncles, brothers and cousins. Instead of learning as its first lesson that here is a kind mother whose special and principal care is for its welfare, and a father whose authority is to be deferred to, the Samoan baby learns that its world is composed of a hierarchy of male and female adults, all of whom can be depended upon and must be deferred to. (Mead 1928)

Severity of Socialization

Severity of socialization has to do with the strictness with which the child—the spontaneous, natural little barbarian—is made to conform to the rules of social living. Whiting and Child divided socialization into five spheres or drive-areas: the oral (which has to do with nursing and weaning), the anal (toilet training), dependency (or training in independence and self-reliance), sex, and aggression. Within each sphere, training may begin early or late (example: a child may be toilet-trained at nine months or at two years of age), punishment for infractions may be mild or severe (example: if a child is caught fighting with his younger sibling, his parents may merely restrain him, or they may whip him), and demands for drive control may be more or less strict (example of strictness: parents may tolerate absolutely no expression of sexuality or aggression).

How do we in the United States compare with the rest of the world, vis-à-vis severity of socialization? It looks as if we are rather harsh parents. For four of the five drive-areas, Whiting and Child rated American socialization as more severe than average (in comparison with the other societies in their cross-cultural sample). For oral training, America was rated somewhat more severe than average. For toilet training, America and the Tanala of Madagascar were rated the most severe. For sex training, we ranked more severe than about three fourths of the sample. For severity of independence training, we are about average. (America received the median score.) For socialization of aggression, we rated more severe than average. Finally, as far as over-all severity of socialization is concerned: the Dobuans were rated most severe, we and the Ashanti were rated next most severe, and forty-four other societies were rated less severe (Whiting and Child 1953).

Of course, these Whiting and Child findings are subject to the same limitations as the previous finding regarding early nurturance. "America" is represented by one little sample of Chicago families. And their sample contained many tribes and few kingdom cases.

There is some evidence that kingdoms are more severe than tribes in several areas of socialization. For one thing, kingdoms tend to have tighter sex restrictions (Chap. 5). This may mean that they also allow children less latitude for sexual expression; I suspect this is true, but I do not have enough cross-cultural data on sex training within kingdom or peasant cases to demonstrate it. Kingdoms do seem to be relatively strict in the area of obedience demands.[8] This trend is shown in Table 5. This is to be expected, since obedience is closely related to the issue of power and deference; and—as we have seen—in the kingdom-cases, fathers tend to be relatively powerful and to get marked deference from their children.

I want to spend the rest of this section on these last-mentioned two areas of socialization, obedience (of child to parent) and sex. The first thing to note here has to do with the history of child rearing within our own society. It may be that, even now, we are a bit on the strict side, when our child rearing is compared with that of a sample of primitive societies. However, historical documents indicate that we have recently become more liberal; formerly, we were much stricter with our children. The "blame"

---

[8] Obedience training is a sphere of socialization which falls outside Whiting and Child's classification (that is, outside their five drive-areas).

TABLE 5

SEVERITY OF OBEDIENCE DEMANDS COMPARED WITH TYPE OF POLITICAL ORGANIZATION

Severity of Obedience Demands (Obedience demanded of a 5-year-old son by his father)*	Tribe	Part of a Kingdom Now or in the Past
SEVERE:	Kipsigis Somali Tenino Turkana	Amman Ashanti Barranquitas Chanzeaux Druz Kurds Lacandon Maya Lasko Madiun Madrid Magazawa Peyrane San Pedro la Laguna Valle Cana Villafranqueza
MILD:	Alor Kaktavik Eskimos !Kung Kwoma Navaho Ojibwa Valley Tonga	Chiaromonte Cuchumatan Mam Hutterites Vaish

* For coding rules, see Appendix.

for our historic harshness toward our children is ordinarily laid at the door of ascetic Protestantism:

Religious doctrine played an important part in the moral training of the child, not only in the obvious form of religious training, but even more importantly as the ideological basis for child-raising theory and practice. Foremost among these doctrines during this

> period[9] was the Calvinist theory, which was adhered to not only by the New England Puritans but also by many of the other Protestant sects, such as the Presbyterians, Methodists, and Congregationalists. The keystone of Calvinist doctrine regarding child rearing was "infant depravity," which, leaving theological subleties aside, consisted in the belief that the infant was born "totally depraved" and doomed to depravity throughout life unless given careful and strict guidance by the parents and, ultimately, saved through Grace. "No child," wrote one New Englander, "has ever been known since the earliest periods of the world, destitute of an evil disposition—however sweet it appears."
>
> Complete obedience and submission were thus requisite if the child was to be kept from sin and evil. The parents were considered responsible and so had to exact such obedience in order to carry out their duty. As a corollary, the safety and health of the child depended upon complete submission. . . .
>
> Submission was obtained by "breaking the will" of the child—a concept not restricted, however, to those actually members of Calvinist religious groups. "Will" was seen as any defiance of the parents' wishes, at any age. "The very infant in your arms will sometimes redden and strike, and throw back its head, and stiffen its little rebellious will." The child was not to have what it wanted, for its desires were sinful, "depraved." (Sunley 1955:159)

Here is another statement of this same ideology, made by a Pilgrim pastor:

> "Surely . . . there is in all children (though not alike) a stubberness and stoutness of minde arising from naturall pride which must in the first place be broken and beaten down that so the foundation of their education being layd in humilitie and tractableness other virtues may in their turn be built thereon." (quoted in Goodsell 1915:397)

Sex training, too, appears to have been quite strict. Masturbation in particular was looked upon with a good deal of horror, since it supposedly led to disease, insanity, and even death (Sunley 1955:157).

---

[9] Early nineteenth-century America.

I will now conclude this section with some child-rearing examples. First, obedience demands. Then, some examples of sex training and childhood sexuality.

KWAKIUTL

"My brothers always stopped me when I was doing wrong. They had to. A boy can't learn good if he isn't. Especially my eldest brother, who loved me so much that he looked after me better than my parents. If I do anything wrong he takes down my pants, if I have any on, and puts me on his lap, backside up, and slaps my backside, which hurted me awful bad. He would do that for quite a while, and that pain will teach me to think of it, and I wouldn't do again for a long time what he didn't want me to do. He takes me in the house to do this. The most hurt to my feelings is he makes me stand up in front of him, when he finished slapping my butt, and uses kind words when he talks to me, and I see tears coming out of his eyes while he talks and tells me it hurted him most, and if he didn't love me so much he wouldn't care. But he does love me so much, he has to do this to show me the thing I done is not right. And the way he talked and the tears in his eyes hurted me, and I thought to myself I'll never do it again. That was worse punishment than the whipping. . . .

"Any time I think of the thrashing I am going to have, I feel it already and don't do it. He never used to punish me the first time. He used to warn me that if I do it again I always get my thrashing. The most that hurts me though is his kind words, and I always think of those kind words and I use them for my children and grandchildren after I thrash them." (Ford 1941:77, 83)

YIR-YIRONT, AUSTRALIA

The father indulges his son at every turn; nor does he interfere when the spoiled son throws spears at the mother or otherwise mistreats her. (Sharp 1937:102)

MURNGIN, AUSTRALIA

There is constant tribal pressure on a mother to be good to her children. No Murngin mother would dare correct her children in the manner of a European woman, for she would be considered cruel and inhuman. Camp gossip and opinion would uniformly condemn her and liken her to an animal. On the other hand, there is less restraint on a son and daughter concerning their mother than in our own society. They frequently curse her, and there is no taboo on the conversation used before her. . . .

To a European, the children are almost intolerable in their demands on their parents and those around them. (Warner 1937: 98, 91)

KURTACHI, SOLOMON ISLANDS

While they are very small, the children are subjected to little or nothing that we should describe as discipline. . . . Scenes like this are enacted in every village every day. Father is sitting on the verandah or on a log somewhere about the village, his pipe has gone out. He says to his small daughter, aged perhaps five, "*Di ma ta tsura.*" "Fetch me some fire." "*Tsuga.*" "I don't want to," says she, without moving. Father takes no notice at all, but goes on with what he happens to be doing without his pipe, and presently gets up and fetches his fire for himself. (Blackwood 1935:172)

WOGEO, MELANESIA

All Wogeo children who cannot as yet talk properly are thus to our way of thinking sadly spoiled. Never in any circumstances slapped or beaten no matter how naughty they may have been, they accept the granting of their most outrageous demands as a matter of course. Parents keep the household knives concealed in order to avoid having to refuse requests that these be handed over, but fragile ornaments like ear-rings are presented at once. Although such objects, never intended for rough treatment, are often broken within a few minutes, I never remember hearing a single expression of annoyance or irritation. . . .

Anxiety for the child's welfare ensures it an audience for its smallest woes, and, if at a slightly later stage it falls down, everyone in sight rushes to pick it up. (Hogbin 1946:296)

Temper tantrums at this age frighten the whole village, and everyone hurries with a gift of food to distract the child's attention . . . The whole of Dap became a hubbub on one occasion when Jauon discovered that her mother proposed to leave her behind with an elderly relative and go off alone on a day's gardening. Although still only a tiny tot, she threw herself on the ground screaming and, every time one of the women tried to pick her up, fought, kicked, and bit. Her father, Marigum, ran up and down wringing his hands, calling out, "Spirit, stop; Jauon, Jauon, Jauon; your mother will look after you. She will not go to the garden." After the passion had subsided the mother sat nursing the child for the whole day and when leaving the village on later occasions always took care to slip away unobserved. (Hogbin 1943:297)

Finally, here are some descriptions of peoples who permit—even encourage—the sexuality of children.

HOPI

"My crippled uncle Naquima, who lived with us, was a good friend of mine. . . . He often picked lice off my head and played with my privates to give me pleasure." (Simmons 1942:38)

ALOR

. . . the child is given genital satisfaction through deliberate masturbation. One of the favorite substitutes for offering the breast in an effort to pacify a child is to massage its genitals gently. (DuBois 1944)

NAVAHO

Tony (a boy of twenty-six months) kept fighting for her breast, and half stood up on his feet, bending across her knees to nurse and at the same time manipulating his genitals with one hand and wiggling in a decidedly passionate manner. Presently he fell asleep and she held him on her lap. He woke at intervals and nursed more quietly, lying on her lap while she stroked his hair. Just before we left, he was lying on his back in her lap, when he began wiggling and fighting for her breast again, and had a prolonged erection. His mother, noticing it, played with him and stroked his penis while he nursed. If she left off, he continued by himself. He seemed very pleased and even left off nursing once to smile at all about him. Finally he relaxed and crawled away, his sister playing with him for awhile, and then his brother tussled with him (Kluckhohn 1947:69)

KAINGANG, BRAZIL

The sexuality of little boys is stimulated by their mothers by manipulation of the genitals before they can walk. . . . Yet with all this I never saw or heard of intercourse among children. . . . The children receive so much satisfaction from adults it is hard to see why they should bother with one another. They are at the beck and call of anyone who wants a warm little body to caress. As Monya, age two, wobbles by on fat uncertain legs Kanyahe calls to him. He slowly overcomes the momentum of his walk, turns about, smiles and wobbles obediently over to Kanyahe. Children lie like cats absorbing the delicious stroking of adults. The little children receive an enormous amount of adult attention and one never sees them caress one another or lie down together. It is impossible to keep track of children around the campfire. By choice and from necessity they literally sleep all over the place. They like to cuddle next to an uncle, aunt or step-mother. In the winter when there may be only one blanket to shelter a family, the little ones are driven to crawling under the cover of someone else who welcomes the additional warmth of the little bundle. This wandering around often culminates in the sexual experience to which the grown-ups are eager to introduce the child, and he is generally enjoyed first by a person much older than he. Some married men have nicknames that bear a humorous reference to their experience in trying to deflower young girls. Yakwa was called, "You pierced your mother" because he had deflowered a young girl who had the same name as his mother. Kovi received a nickname because his first cousin clawed his penis when he tried to deflower her. The growing child's sexual experience is primarily humorous, often illicit, administered by adults, and apt to be violent in the case of girls. (Henry 1941:17–18)

BAIGA, INDIA

Their sexual consciousness is developed very early. Parents may insist on their children going to work and to work hard, but they rarely interfere with their pleasures. . . . Even when they see their children indulging in erotic play, they simply laugh tolerantly. "Sometimes we say, 'Why do it now? Wait a little.' But the children grow excited, so what should they do?" Lahakat might be expected to adopt this tolerant attitude; but Dhan Singh, a much stricter and chaster man, echoed it. "If a child of seven goes to a girl, what does it matter? It does no harm. But of course when they are grown up and go to the bazaars, then there is something in it." Sujji of Kawardha told me that "if I catch my young daughter with a boy I let her alone. I don't beat her or abuse her; otherwise the neighbors may say, 'Is she your wife or your daughter that you are so jealous? Why are you making trouble, you impotent old man? Let her do what she likes.' " . . .

The Baiga themselves believe that children are born with a complete equipment of phallic knowledge. Certainly the language of even the youngest children is amazingly well-informed. Soon after the child is born, directly it is able to talk, it says, "I'll copulate with your mother." I know a small boy of about four years old who drives the cattle to the accompaniment of a stream of sexual *gali* of which you would not expect his father to be competent.

When the children are out in the fields or forest, watching the *bewar*, or grazing cattle, they play a good many impromptu games. The official recreations of the tribe are described elsewhere, and do not have any special sexual meaning. But here in the privacy of the jungle, the children quickly improvise such entertainments as Cow and Bull, Horse and Mare, Cock and Hen, Pig and Sow, and play them with a wealth of realistic detail which reveals considerable physiological knowledge. . . .

Another favorite game is Houses, and a number of Baiga have told me that it was during this game that they had their first sexual encounters. This is played when boys and girls wander together into the jungle. They pair off and make little huts out of leaves and branches. . . .

Dhan Singh was only nine years old when he had his first sexual experience. "We were plucking *mahua*. I was laughing at her. I seized her and had her under the tree. There was no blood. I came to love her and married her in the end." (Elwin 1939: 230–232)

Learning the Supernatural

A child in a primitive society must learn to cope not only with the living and the real, but also with the nonliving and the unreal. Typically, his world teems with supernatural beings and entities, and his actions are hedged by supernatural injunctions and precautions. Taboos must be learned. Demons, ghosts, and witches must be recognized and avoided. Perhaps a spirit-helper must be wooed and won.

In this section I will merely give a few illustrations of the child's encounter with this unreal—yet real—world of the supernatural.

KWOMA—THE MARSALAI, AND SORCERY

Parents and older siblings extend their warnings to include supernatural dangers. They tell the child that huge, snakelike monsters which cause storms dwell in the swamp, and that it is dangerous to go near their dwelling places. This danger is brought within the sphere of experience of the child when his mother tells him that a *marsalai* occupies her breast and vivifies the story by putting a leech on it. A child is also warned, during the weaning period, not to venture out at night, for this is the time when ghosts are abroad; and not to go too far from the house unless accompanied by an older person, for if he does a sorcerer may kill him. . . .

A Kwoma child learns that, in addition to things naturally inedible, there are also foods which are made poisonous by sorcerers. Boys and girls are told never to eat food given them by a stranger or a nonrelative, for it may be poisoned by the insertion of a magical white powder.

A child is warned about another type of sorcery which also pertains to food but is concerned with how and where a person can safely eat rather than with what he can eat. A child is taught to be very careful with his crumbs and other food leavings. He is warned that, if someone steals such material and performs a certain magical rite upon it, he will sicken and die, and that, therefore, he should be particularly careful if he eats anywhere but in his own house. It is difficult for a thief of sorcery material to steal leavings from the floor or rubbish heap of your own dwelling because he would be killed on the spot if he were caught at it, but a sorcerer can pick up food leavings left in the forest with little danger of discovery. Since relatives may not sorcerize one another, one may eat in their houses if one is careful, but parents warn children never to eat in the house of a nonrelative, for a crumb may fall, no matter how careful they may be, and nonrelatives are not to be trusted. A child is warned that his blood is another material which must be kept from the hands of sorcerers; therefore, if he cuts himself, he should take care to catch or wipe up the blood in a leaf which he should burn or hide in a safe place. He is also warned that his blood "goes into" any animal that he kills, so that he must be careful not to spill the blood of such an animal.

A child does not have to be warned frequently about the dangers of sorcery because his parents show fear of it. Whenever anyone is sick in the hamlet, practically the only subject of conversation is sorcery. Adults speculate about the identity of the sorcerer and curse those whom they suspect. Everyone is worried and emotional. The almost hysterical reaction of his parents to sorcery impresses the seriousness of the danger upon the child so vividly that it is not difficult to teach him to be careful. (Whiting 1941:35, 39–40)

ARAPESH—LEARNING ABOUT SORCERY

Children hear the mutterings and cursing of their parents when the arrogant Plainsmen pass through; they hear death and misfortune laid to the sorcerers' doors. When they are only five or so they are cautioned: "Never leave any half-eaten food lying about in a place where there are strangers. If you break off a sugarcane stem, be careful that no stranger sees you do it, or he will return and pick up the butt and use it to sorcerize you. If you eat an areca-nut be careful not to throw part of the kernel away in the husk. If you eat the durable tough yam, eat it all; do not leave a piece that a stranger may seize and use against you. When you sleep in a house where there are strangers, lie with your face up, that none of your saliva may drip on the bark, later to be carried away and hidden by the enemy. If anyone gives you an opposum-bone to gnaw, keep the bone until you can hide it somewhere when no one is looking." And a little boy is given a palm-leaf basket, a little girl a tiny net bag in which to carry about these food leavings so that they may not fall into the hands of the stranger. This constant cautioning about "dirt" makes everyone in Arapesh culture obsessive on the subject. By eating, by chewing areca-nut, by smoking, by sex-intercourse, one is constantly having to relinquish some portion of one's person that may fall into the hands of strangers, and falling there cause one to fall ill, or die. (Mead 1935)

NAVAHO—MENSTRUAL TABOOS, AND PRAYER

"One morning I went out with the herd again in the canyon. . . . I saw what I thought was a sheep pelt. I went close and looked at this thing, and it was tied with a rope. I took it out of the brush and thought, 'What a nice soft kid's skin it is.' But in the middle there was something on it. Then I broke off a willow and put it between my legs for my horse with the skin for a saddle and started to run.

"When I got home with the sheep my mother was walking around outside. I ran up to her and said, 'I found a nice, soft kid's skin.' As soon as she saw it she was afraid of it. She said, 'Throw it on the ground! That's a dangerous thing to have. It'll kill you. It'll break you all in pieces. That thing will set on all your joints; it will get on every joint of yours. That's what's called menstrual.' It was what the women used at that time for their monthlies, and there was blood on it.

"She picked it up with a stick and took it away and told me not to leave. 'Stay there and stand there.' She ran up to a cliff, halfway to the top of the canyon, and from there she brought weeds and roots and leaves of various things and different brushes. She mashed it up with rocks and put it in a big pan of water and mixed it and told me to drink some. And she took off my clothes and washed me all over with it. Then she put my clothes in it and washed them. That was a medicine for this thing.

"Then she told me to go inside. I went in and put a robe around me, and after she'd washed my clothes and spread them out to dry she came into the hogan and talked to me again. 'Those things, they use them when they're passing blood. All women, every month, pass blood. That's a dangerous thing to handle.' I asked her again, 'What will it do to you?' She said, 'I told you before. If you handle those things it'll break your foot, or your legs. It'll get on any of your joints, around your fingers and your back, around your ribs. It'll get on every joint and twist your feet and fingers to all directions. It'll break you, break all your joints, and at last it'll kill you, if you don't get medicine for it.' She scared me again. From there on I used to be afraid to touch anything that lay in the brush. . . .

"My mother had many prayers. When she made corn-mush—she made it every other day—she had sticks to stir it with, and when she thought the mush was done she'd take the sticks out and raise them. While she was holding them up she'd say a little prayer. She used to say, 'We'll have something all the time. Our stocks and our hogan will be in good shape, and we'll live well all the time. We'll have lots of property and all kinds of beads and turquoise. And we'll have lots to eat all the time.' That's the way she used to say her prayers. After we ate we all said our prayers too. We always gave thanks for our food and always prayed for more things to eat. We used to pray for everything." (Dyk 1938: 13–14, 216)

OJIBWA—FASTING FOR A VISION

Small children—4, 5, or 6 years old—after having had their faces blackened were merely sent out into the woods to spend the day there. "In the early days both boys and girls were sent out alone to wander around in the woods. Each one was sent alone; never were two sent together. Here the spirits were to talk to them, and they to the spirits." Children were usually sent out in the spring or fall. While wandering around they would probably see someone in the woods, someone like manito, for example. They might see things, too, in the shape of trees, and so forth, these things being spirits would have pity on them and give them more power or longer life. This is done before the girl becomes a woman or the boy a man. The person must still be a child. . . .

"They waited, in those old days, for the sun to peep up—the sun had to be looking at us when we got our faces blackened. And just as the sun went down we had our faces washed—the sun was supposed to see us get washed. I fasted one day when I was about 5 years old: I got no bread nor water nor any food all day. Those who fasted more than one day were usually permitted to drink, but not to eat.

As the children grew older, greater significance was attached to fasting. The number of days was increased so that many children, especially boys, spent 4 or more days without food, consequently sleeping and dreaming. A child that did not return after 4 days of fasting was thought to be receiving extraordinary powers—that he was being given the "power" to be a medicine man or medicine woman. "Such a child was learning how to cure certain diseases and how to combine certain herbs for certain medicines, and so forth." "Some received such powerful medicine that they could pull someone's mouth to one side, cripple him, make him crazy, or even cause him to die." . . .

Parents obliged their children to fast because they were desirous of having them contact the spiritual world and obtain a medium in it in the form of a guardian spirit. (Hilger 1951:41, 43)

WINNEBAGO—FASTING FOR A VISION

"After a while we got fairly well started on our way back. I fasted all the time. We moved back to a place where all the leaders used to give their feasts. Near the place where we lived there were three lakes and a black hawk's nest. Right near the tree where the nest was located they built a lodge and the war-bundle that we possessed was placed in the lodge. We were to pass the night there, my older brother and myself. It was said that if anyone fasted at such a place for four nights he would always be blessed with victory and the power to cure the sick. All the spirits would bless him.

"The first night spent there one imagined oneself surrounded by spirits whose whisperings were heard outside the lodge, they said. The spirits would even whistle. I would be frightened and nervous, and if I remained there I would be molested by large monsters, fearful to look upon. Even (the bravest) might be frightened, I was told. Should I, however, get through that night, I would on the following morning be molested by ghosts whom I would hear speaking outside. They would say things that might cause me to run away. Towards morning they would even take my blanket away from me. They would grab hold of me and drive me out of the lodge, and they would not stop until the sun rose. If I was able to endure the third night, on the fourth night I would really be addressed by spirits, it was said, who would bless me, saying, 'I bless you. We had turned you over to the (monsters, and so forth) and that is why they approached you, but you overcame them and now they will not be able to take you away. Now you may go home, for with victory and long life we bless you and also with the power of healing the sick. Nor shall you lack wealth. So go home and eat, for a large war party is soon to fall upon you who, as soon as the sun rises in the morning, will give the war whoop and if you do not go home now, they will kill you.'

"Thus the spirits would speak to me. However if I did not do the bidding of this particular spirit, then another one would address me and say much the same sort of thing. So they would speak until the break of day, and just before sunrise a man in warrior's regalia would come and peep in. He would be a scout. Then I would surely think a war party had come upon me, I was told.

"Then another spirit would come and say, 'Well, grandson, I have taken pity upon you and I bless you with all the good things that the earth holds. Go home now for the war party is about to rush upon you.' And if I then went home, as soon as the sun rose the war whoop would be given. The members of the war party would give the war whoop all at the same time. They would rush upon me and capture me and after the fourth one had counted coup, then they would say, 'Now then, grandson, this we did to teach you. Thus you shall act. You have completed your fasting.' Thus they would talk to me, I was told. This war party was composed entirely of spirits, I was told, spirits from the heavens and from the earth; indeed all the spirits that exist would be there. These would all bless me. They also told me that it would be a very difficult thing to accomplish this particular fasting.

"So there I fasted, at the black hawk's nest where a lodge had been built for me. The first night I stayed there I wondered when things would happen; but nothing took place. The second night, rather late in the night, my father came and opened the war-bundle and taking a gourd out began to sing. I stood beside him without any clothing on me except the breach-clout, and holding tobacco in each hand I uttered my cry to the spirits as my father sang. He sang war-bundle songs and he wept as he sang. I also wept as I uttered my cry to the spirits. . . .

"When I found myself alone I began to think that something ought to happen to me soon, yet nothing occurred so I had to pass another day there. . . . On the third night I was still there. My father visited me again and we repeated what we had done the night before. In the morning, just before sunrise, I uttered my cry to the spirits. The fourth night found me still there. Again my father came and we did the same thing, but in spite of it all, I experienced nothing unusual. Soon another day dawned upon us. That morning I told my elder brother that I had been blessed by spirits and that I was going home to eat. However I was not telling the truth. I was hungry and also knew that on the following night we were going to have a feast and that I would have to utter my cry to the spirits again. I dreaded that. So I went home. When I got there I told my people the story I had told my brother; that I had been blessed and that the spirits had told me to return. I was not speaking the truth, yet they gave me the food that is carefully prepared for those who have been blessed. Just then my older brother came home and they objected to his return for he had not been blessed. However, he took some food and ate it. . . .

"The following spring we moved to the Mississippi in order to trap. I was still fasting and ate only at night. My brothers used to flatter me, telling me I was the cleverest of them all. In consequence I used to continue to fast although I was often very hungry. . . . all that I desired was to appear great in the sight of the people. To be praised by my fellow-men was all that I desired. And I certainly received all I sought. I stood high in their estimation. That the women might like me was another of the reasons why I wanted to fast. However, as to being blessed, I learned nothing about it, although I went around with the air of one who had received many blessings and talked as such a one would talk." (Radin 1920:388–391)

Steps to Adulthood

The road from childhood to adulthood is marked by many little signposts. For a boy in our society, these may include being allowed to cross the street alone, the first bicycle, the first long pants, the first date, the first part-time job, driver's license, school graduation, and—eventually—full-time job, marriage, and parenthood. These little steps, these points in the transition from child role to adult role, I would divide into three categories:

1. Those having to do with work and the adult occupational role.

2. Those having to do with marriage and parenthood: the transition in family roles, from a child in the family of orientation to spouse-parent in one's (newly founded) family of procreation.

3. Those having to do with the child's "emancipation" from his parents' authority: the transition from a situation in which the child must "mind" his parents and must account to them for his actions, while they are "responsible" for him, to one where the child is autonomous, is no longer his parents' responsibility, and is no longer subject to their authority.

In this matter of transition from child role to adult role our society is, again, quite deviant compared with other societies. In regard to category 3, our society is unusual for the sudden, radical nature of the child's emancipation from his parents' authority. As far as category 2 is concerned, age of marriage and parenthood is apparently rather late in America—although a generation ago our society was much more unusual in this respect. Regarding the first category, "going to work" and assumption of the adult occupational role, we are definitely odd.

In nearly all the societies in my ethnographic notes, children are put to work by the age of ten. Typically, work begins somewhere between the ages of three and six, the load of duties and responsibilities is gradually increased, and sometime between the ages of nine and fifteen the child becomes—occupationally speaking—a fully functioning adult. Some of these children's duties are strictly "children's work," and will have little carry-over to adulthood—errand-running, for example. However, in nearly all cases, the bulk of children's work is a clear-cut, specific apprenticeship to the adult occupational role. That is, typically a little girl works at being a little mother (a child-nurse), a little housekeeper, a cook, and a farmer (in societies where women do agricultural work); little boys work at being herdsmen (in herding societies), farm workers (in societies where men do farm work), and, in hunting and gathering societies, boys work (or play) at being hunters. Frequently (not always) the bulk of this work apprenticeship is done in the presence of the adult role model: little girls follow their mothers and other older females around, are taught by them, and work with and for them; little boys do their work apprenticeship in the company of their fathers, older brothers, and other older males. (A résumé of the ethnographic notes on work apprenticeship is given at the end of the chapter.)

What are the consequences of this early work apprenticeship, in terms of the child's emotional development? The child, for one thing, is an economic asset—helping with the crops, taking responsibility for livestock or for a young sibling. Being "valuable," responsible, and relied-upon would—one would think—boost his (her) self-esteem. The child is allowed to "grow up"—grow up quickly—within the occupational sphere, at least. This early work and adult-role practice may have subtler and more profound effects. To quote Parsons:

> Our kinship situation, it has been noted, throws children of both sexes overwhelmingly upon the mother as *the* emotionally significant adult. In such a situation "identification" in the sense that

> the adult becomes a "role model" is the normal result. For a girl this is normal and natural not only because she belongs to the same sex as the mother, but because the functions of housewife and mother are immediately before her eyes and are tangible and easily understood by a child. Almost as soon as she is physically able, the girl begins a direct apprenticeship in the adult feminine role. It is very notable that girls' play consists in cooking, sewing, playing with dolls, and so on, activities which are a direct mimicry of their mothers'. But the boy does not have his father immediately available; in addition—especially in the middle class, but increasingly perhaps in the lower—the things the father does are intangible and difficult for a child to understand, such as working in an office, or even running a complicated machine tool.
>
> Thus the girl has a more favorable opportunity for emotional maturing through positive identification with an adult model. (Parsons 1949:257)

In other words, the American mother's occupation role is easily perceived by the child, whereas the adult male occupational role is less so. Furthermore, a little girl may practice her future adult role through play and by helping mother. This is less possible for boys. Playing cowboys and Indians is a less real apprenticeship to adulthood than playing with dolls or helping mother dust the house. Therefore, Parsons thinks, boys—in our society—stand in greater danger of confused sex identity and retarded emotional maturity.

Contrast this situation in America with the societies in the ethnographic notes. For all but one society (Manus) in my notes, little girls do not merely play at being women; they *work* at it. It is "for real." By the age of about twelve they are actually functioning as adults in regard to work. The same is true of boys in all but five cases. (In two of these five exceptional cases, Alor and Ifaluk, adult men seldom do productive work either; in these two cases, one might say that the boys are practicing the adult male occupational role—loafing.)

In our society childhood work is largely replaced by going to school. Schooling is, to be sure, preparation for adult work, especially in the case of boys. However, it is not, in itself, adult work. Transition to the adult role in the occupational sphere is extraordinarily retarded in our society. Whether or not the results of this are as sinister as Parsons thinks, this is a most unusual condition of child rearing which, quite possibly, fosters personality characteristics distinctive to our culture.

Before going on to consider age of marriage, here are a few descriptions of work apprenticeship:

BAIGA

"When I was four or five I had to spend all day looking after my eldest brother's son. I had no time to play." . . .

"When I was born, in those days we cut *bewar.*[10] I had to work very hard in my youth. When I was about five, my father took a new wife. That year we left Kumnijhiria and went to Daldal. There too we cut *bewar.* When I was five or six I had to look after my little brothers and sisters. I used to feed them and bring them water in tiny earthen pots." (Elwin 1939:136, 147)

REINDEER CHUKCHEE

The reindeer-breeding Chukchee send boys of ten, and girls hardly much older than that, to help in tending the herd. I remember having met one summer-time two such young reindeer-breeders, a boy and a girl. They were from ten to twelve years old. They were walking through the bushes quite alone, staff in hand, and wallet on back. They had to walk some ten miles before they could reach their herd. It was strange to see these young children wandering in the bush without any protection and shelter. (Bogoras 1909:553)

MURIA

But directly a child is old enough to play, he is regarded as old enough to work. The early stage of "eating while playing and playing while eating" is soon over and the little girls and boys have to take their share of the work of the house. Tiny girls may often be seen staggering about with the youngest baby in their arms or helping their mothers to cow-dung the house. Sometimes you may see a line of boys and girls following their elders back from the jungle, each with a tiny basket of fruit or a minute bundle of leaves on their heads. During this period the children are very

---

10 Slash-and-burn agriculture.

dependent on their parents and go everywhere with them. A boy takes his little axe and follows his father to the jungle. A girl takes a pot and goes with her mother to the well. (Elwin 1947:76)

COPPER ESKIMO

A girl receives a little elementary education in cooking and sewing and in dressing meat. She is encouraged to make dolls and to mend her own clothing, her mother teaching her how to cut out the skins. Both boys and girls learn to stalk game by accompanying their elders on hunting excursions; their fathers make bows and arrows for them suited to their strength. One of their favourite pastimes is to carry out, in miniature, some of the duties they will have to perform when they grow up. Thus little girls often have tiny lamps in the corners of their huts over which they will cook some meat to share with their playmates. . . .

The children naturally have many pastimes that imitate the actions of their elders. Girls make dolls out of scraps of skin, and clothe them like real men and women. Their mothers encourage them, for it is in this way that they learn to sew and to cut out patterns. Both boys and girls play at building snow houses. In summer, with only pebbles to work with, they simply lay out the ground plans, but in winter they borrow their parents' snow-knives and make complete houses on a miniature scale. They trace too figures of men and animals in the snow, and carve them out of single blocks; for example, two small boys one day set up a snow-rabbit on top of a hill; one ran and stabbed it through the heart with his knife, while the other completed its demolition by slicing off its head. Sometimes they make toy sleds of ice, like the real ones that are used by their parents in emergencies. One of their games in which the adults sometimes join imitates the killing and cutting up of a bearded seal. A child lies flat on the ground while the others gather around him and pull him about as though they were hewing him to pieces. In Victoria island the children spent an idle summer's day partly in splashing about in a neighboring lake, partly in setting up rows of stones and turf, *inyukhuit*, as for a caribou drive, and digging shallow pits, *tallut*, from which they launched their shafts at imaginary deer. (Jenness 1922: Vol. XII, pp. 170, 219)

SAMOA

As soon as the girls are strong enough to carry heavy loads, it pays the family to shift the responsibility for the little children to the younger girls and the adolescent girls are released from baby-tending. It may be said with some justice that the worst period of their lives is over. Never again will they be so incessantly at the beck and call of their elders, never again so tyrannized over by two-year-old tyrants. All the irritating, detailed routine of housekeeping, which in our civilization is accused of warping the souls and souring the tempers of grown women, is here performed by children under fourteen years of age. A fire or a pipe to be kindled, a call for a drink, a lamp to be lit, the baby's cry, the errand of the capricious adult—these haunt them from morning until night. With the introduction of several months a year of government schools these children are being taken out of their homes for most of the day. This brings about a complete disorganization of the native households which have no precedents for a manner of life where mothers have to stay at home and take care of their children and adults have to perform small routine tasks and run errands. (Mead 1928)

PLATEAU TONGA, NORTHERN RHODESIA

Girls from the time they can toddle are gradually introduced to the tasks of the housewife, and very soon after this to the work in the fields as well as the gathering of relish and firewood. This happens as a small girl follows around after her mother or the older woman in whose care she is. At no one stage is she suddenly introduced to a new type of work. Instead the encouragement to experiment with all that is going on about her lapses into an insistence that she take more and more responsibility for the routine tasks of the household and that she meet the standards of her woman guardian in performing them. By the time she reaches puberty, she is expected to be competent both as a housewife and as a worker in the fields, though she may not be capable of planning ahead sufficiently to be in full charge of a household. Boys have a less uniform training and their competence, perhaps because of this or perhaps because some of the work assigned to men requires the strength of the mature male, does not come till a later date. Small boys may help with some of the work of the household, especially in planting season when it is their job to lead the oxen before the plough. About the age of six to seven they are introduced into the ranks of the herdboys, where they remain until roughly the age of fourteen to fifteen. Here they are under the supervision of older boys, and only secondarily directed and

> instructed by their male guardians. After this apprenticeship, they again begin to work in the fields and have the task of learning farming methods. . . .
>
> All children receive some training in the care of infants and toddlers. Most small girls and some small boys spend a period as nursemaids to smaller children, which gives them a notable skill in handling infants and an apparent pleasure in doing so which lasts into later life. . . . If a girl is not needed at home to care for a younger sibling, she is very likely to be borrowed by an older sister or some other relative with an infant. It is most unusual for a girl to reach puberty without having spent several years in such service. (Colson 1958:262, 264)

In regard to age of marriage, my cross-cultural data are rather scanty. There are eleven cases in my notes in which the age of marriage appears to be pretty early—by our standards, at least. Opposed to these, there are three cases of apparent late marriage. Among the Subanum, says Christie, a man's marriage may be deferred "for years" after puberty because he is unable to raise the bride price (Christie 1909:54). The Kipsigis, according to Peristiany, formerly had "very late marriage" for both men and women (Peristiany 1939:54). And in Ireland, average age of marriage is definitely later than it is here (Arensberg 1950:96).

In contrast, we have the cases of child betrothal discussed in Chapter 4, in which marriage becomes semiofficial in infancy or early childhood; however, in these cases, it does not appear that child spouses do become spouses in fact until much later. Among the Toda, for example, a girl is "married" in childhood; but she usually does not move in with her husband until she is fifteen or sixteen (Rivers 1906:502).

Among the Siriono, marriage often takes place before physical maturity (Holmberg 1950:83). In the Hindu town of Deoli, girls are usually wed before they reach puberty[11] (Carstairs 1958:45). Among the Murngin, says Warner, "Men obtain their wives at almost any age after they have reached maturity, the first usually

---

[11] "Eleven years old and not married! Shocking it truly was in India, and especially in such an orthodox and aristocratic family as mine!" (Ranade 1939:1)

when the beard begins. . . . The proper time for a girl to marry is when her breasts first start developing." (Warner 1937:129) Among the Lepcha, "girls are betrothed and occasionally married from the age of eight onwards, and boys from the age of twelve" (Gorer 1938:316). For the Kwoma, marriage occurs soon after the puberty initiation (Whiting 1941:88). In Tepoztlan, girls are "married at a very early age." (Lewis 1951:399) Among the Somali, "Most girls marry between the ages of 12 and 15 and few are without a husband at 20." (Lewis 1955:135) In the Egyptian village of Silwa, it is "not unusual for girls to get married by the age of twelve and thirteen. . . . Nowadays, boys usually marry after eighteen" (Ammar 1954:183). Among the Gusii, the average age of marriage for girls is fifteen; for boys, it is eighteen to twenty (LeVine). And, among the Plateau Tonga, women are usually married between sixteen and eighteen (Colson 1954: 49).

The data suggests (merely suggests, since the evidence is so fragmentary) that primitive societies and peasant societies tend to have quite early marriage, and that girls are frequently married at an earlier age than boys. Why should there be this age differential between the sexes? Two possibilities have already been suggested. The first possible reason, advanced by Murdock, is polygyny. One way to "correct" the sex ratio in a polygynous society is early marriage for girls and later marriage for boys. A second possible reason is marriage finance. Since bride-price payments are usually greater than dowry payments, this may pose added obstacles to a boy's marriage.

As to the reason for the generally early age of marriage—why not? As we have seen, work apprenticeship begins during early childhood in these societies. By puberty, most of these people are functioning as adults in the work and economic spheres. If they can do a man's work (or a woman's work) at puberty, why shouldn't they get married?

So it appears that in most of the known cases an individual is married some time between the ages of twelve and eighteen, and makes a basic family-role transition; he (she) moves from the status of child in the family of orientation, to spouse in his (her) new family of procreation. Actual "procreation"—parenthood—does, I imagine, follow soon afterward,[12] and by the age of twenty, perhaps, the full cycle of family roles has been completed: from child to spouse to parent.

Age of marriage evokes the third general area of role transition from childhood to adulthood—"emancipation," the transition from childhood subservience to parents' authority to the autonomy, the freedom from parents' authority, of adulthood. In this area our society also appears to be unusual, but in this case it is not because we are "late." Rather, it is because emancipation is so sudden, radical, and early in our society.

Everywhere, no doubt, emancipation is to some extent a gradual process. As the child "grows" and accumulates skills and knowledge, he is given greater and greater latitude for independent decision making, more responsibility, and greater freedom. Emancipation ordinarily occurs gradually; it is also a matter of degree. Many people, in most societies, do not become fully "emancipated" until their parents' (or at least father's) death. Perhaps even then they are not fully emancipated; that is, even then they may play a sort of child role (authority-wise) vis-à-vis some surviving older kinsmen—elder brothers, and uncles, for example. This delayed emancipation is due to two widespread social conditions: 1) deference customs, which in many societies are due elder male kin as long as they live; and 2) the extended family.

In regard to the extended family: about one fourth of the societies in Murdock's *World Ethnographic Sample* are characterized by extended-family households. Many additional societies—typically, African societies—have extended-family compounds. In such a situation, some married people (the in-married spouses) continue to live with their parents. It is my impression that in such cases a young person, even after his (or her) marriage, still is somewhat subordinate to parents and older kin. Status-wise, he is to some extent a married child. Out-married persons, in these cases, may be fairly free of their own parents'

---

[12] I have no data on age of parenthood.

authority, but they are subordinate to their spouses' elder kin. A person who out-marries into an extended-family household or compound becomes, in a manner of speaking, the spouse of a married child.[13]

Of course, in nearly all other societies the nuclear family is closely tied to larger kin groups—either unilineal kin groups, or less concentrated residential kin groups (that is, less concentrated than the extended-family household or compound), or both. In such cases young married people may frequently be somewhat subordinate to a variety of elder kinsmen. I assume this is often the case, but I am not sure, since usually the authority picture for these larger kin groups is pretty hazy.

In any event, because of the rarity of the isolated nuclear household throughout most of the world, "emancipation" is gradual and often, apparently, never complete. A person is not suddenly set free of parental authority as the result of marriage. Our society is unusual in this area since, as the result of our high frequency of neolocal residence and isolated nuclear families, marriage usually marks a sudden, radical, and fairly complete emancipation from parental authority. In other words, in our society two of the major "steps to adulthood"—marriage and emancipation from parental authority—are joined; marriage automatically brings emancipation. In most other societies this is not the case: marriage does not end the parents' authority; after marriage, one continues in a quasi childlike authority relationship either with one's own elder kin or in relation to one's spouse's kin (in the case of out-marrying). In the words of the Irish countryman, "You can be a boy forever, as long as the old fellow is alive." (Arensberg 1950:59)

---

[13] I do not have data to document this. It is merely my impression that the extended-family household or compound usually constitutes a single economic and property-owning unit, with ownership and jural rights in the hands of the old man, or old men.

In a good number of these cases, apparently, young married people are not subservient in the sense that they owe marked deference to the elders; it is merely that elders exercise authority and jural control, in the manner, perhaps, of an American parent vis-à-vis his high-school-aged child.

To summarize this discussion of the steps to adulthood, and the comparison of the United States with the rest of the world:

1. In the occupational sphere, maturity is extraordinarily retarded in our society. We have little or nothing in the way of an early work apprenticeship. Instead, we merely send our children to school.

2. In the area of family role transition, marriage and parenthood seem to occur relatively late in our society.

3. In regard to breaking the bonds of parental authority, our society is unusual in the joining of marriage with sudden, radical emancipation.

Summary of Ethnographic Notes on Work Apprenticeship

ALOR Girls start to work earlier, and work harder, than boys do. (However, even Alorese men do little work.) Both boys and girls serve as child-nurses; at times, they resent this. In addition, girls weave baskets, sew pandanus mats, make bark cloth, cook, and do farm work in the company of their mothers. By nine or ten years of age, a little girl can cook the family meals.

ARAPESH Girls serve as child-nurses; apparently boys do too, to a lesser degree. Girls carry burdens, gather plant food and firewood, and do garden work, such as weeding. At harvest time, little girls join together in work bees. Boys follow father and other older men into the forest to hunt; they also play at being hunters.

AZANDE Girls start serious work at five or six–grinding flour, preparing food, gathering firewood, getting water, and serving as child-nurses. A boy, taught by his father, starts working at about six–wood cutting, farm work, hunting and trapping.

REINDEER CHUCKHEE Both boys and girls are herding reindeer by the age of ten.

COPPER ESKIMO The work apprenticeship seems to be largely in the form of play.

DRAGALETVSY (Bulgaria) Children run errands and, apparently, do some farm work. At seven years of age they start school.

FIJI "Very early," a boy begins to help his father, and a girl begins to help her mother. This "helping" is at first rather playful, and gradually becomes more serious and arduous. By fifteen or sixteen children are functioning economically as full adults.

GUSII After weaning, a child starts to work: chasing chickens, running errands, carrying food, and so on. If the family has cows, a boy joins the herd boys at about the age of three; three-year-old girls are taught to carry water (in pans, placed on their heads). From the age of three, both boys and girls help their mothers in the field work. A girl starts serving as a child-nurse at five or six.

HEHE "Little boys" herd cattle and "perform other tasks" under the father's supervision.

HOPI (See quotation at beginning of chapter.)

IBAN "At an early age," girls help their mothers in household work. At about twelve, both boys and girls apparently start helping with the farm work. At an earlier age, they serve as child-nurses.

IFALUK Boys, like men, do little work. An eight-year-old girl helps her mother, cooks, does other household chores, serves as child-nurse.

JAMAICA (Rocky Roads) Girls start household work at five years of age. At seven, children start school. At ten, boys begin helping their fathers with the farm work. At about fourteen, a boy is a full-time farmer.

KWOMA Economic duties are assumed gradually; full adult work is not undertaken until adolescence. However, small children do help in the gardens and help tend the pigs. Little girls carry water; little boys hunt.

LEPCHA At about six years of age, children start serious work, in the company of their elders. This includes farm work. A six-year-old girl "should be an active help to her mother"; boys of this age are less useful. Children fetch wood and water. By twelve, children do full adult work.

LESU Little children run errands. Between the age of six and puberty, their work gradually increases. Girls work harder than boys. By ten, girls help their mothers in the gardens; they work about half as long as adult women do; they also serve as child-nurses. Boys are also child-nurses, and help a little with cooking and food preparation.

MANUS Apparently, children do absolutely no work—the only case of this sort in the sample. They do not even seem to "practice" adult work in their play. Near puberty, girls start going fishing with their mothers. Boys in early adolescence are still idle.

MARIA GONDS Little boys do field work in the company of older men. Little girls work around the house with their mothers.

MURIA (See quotation.)

MURNGIN At four years, a girl follows her mother and is taught the gathering of plant food. Little boys play at hunting.

NAVAHO Economic tasks are learned gradually, from the age of six onwards. Children begin to herd at six or seven, chop and gather firewood, haul water, help in food processing. Girls learn to cook and serve as child-nurses. Girls learn to card and spin at about ten, learn to weave a little later. A father teaches his son the care of livestock, farming, and house building.

OJIBWA Starting at about seven years of age, children are taught economic tasks by parents and grandparents. Boys go hunting. Little girls run errands, carry wood and water. At eight, children help their mothers set fish traps. Boys start trapping animals at about twelve.

PAPAGO Starting at about four years of age, economic tasks, including child nursing, are gradually assumed.

RAJPUTS Preschool children do not work. After starting school, children do chores. Girls wash dishes, do housekeeping, care for babies, serve food, wash clothes. Boys run errands, serve as herd boys, help men with farm work.

SAMOA (See quotations under "Caretakers" and "Steps to Adulthood.")

SIRIONO Little boys play at hunting. At eight years a boy starts going hunting with his father. By twelve, he is a full-fledged hunter. A little girl has an early work apprenticeship, following and helping her mother.

SILWA Both boys and girls serve as child-nurses, but girls do more of this. A girl becomes a child-nurse at about five years of age. By seven, she is running errands, fetching wood and water, doing housework and cooking. Boys start farming at about seven, do much farm work in a subordinate capacity, and acquire all the agricultural skills by seventeen. Recently, children have started to go to school.

SUBANUM "Children" do agricultural work.

TEPOZTLAN No work before five years of age. Children go to school. "Girls play in snatches between errands and chores, and as they grow older, less and less time for play is available.

The burden of household work usually falls on the eldest daughter . . . (in) most families all girls over ten are pressed into continual service. . . ." (Lewis 1951:389) Girls drop out of school early to give full time to household chores. They care for younger siblings. Formerly, boys were doing full-time farm work by ten; now they do not start working full-time until about fifteen.

THONGA Boys "stay with the goats" until they are ten or eleven; then they start herding cattle.

TIKOPIA Children run errands. Girls carry wood and water, and fish with their mothers. Boys also fish.

PLATEAU TONGA (See quotation.)

VALLE CANA Less than half the children under seven years of age have regular tasks, such as wood gathering, child nursing, house cleaning. After seven, tasks increase sharply, and "for some children tend to become a harassing burden." (Landy 195:141)

WOGEO Work starts at about eight years of age.

9 Cross-cultural Regularities

One of the first and most stunning messages of anthropology was the variability of human behavior. "Human nature," human character is very much the product of culture, and hence subject to cross-cultural variability. As a result of the writings of Ruth Benedict, Margaret Mead, Clyde Kluckhohn and other anthropologists, this message has, no doubt, by now been widely disseminated.

Being plastic, human nature may be molded by culture into a variety of psychic forms, shapes, and sizes. Cultures too, needless to say, may also take on various forms, shapes, and sizes. Does this mean that human nature is infinitely malleable, and that cultures are infinitely varied? Is nothing constant? Are there no cultural universals?

There are, to be sure, some cultural universals. All human societies have spoken languages. Every known society has a religion (if religion be broadly enough defined). All societies have the family (???). And so forth.

When one begins to do cross-cultural research and begins to compare many societies with respect to fairly discrete items and areas of culture, one makes another discovery. There are *many* cultural universals. They are innumerable. They are legion. Perhaps human nature is malleable. But human culture, in many of its details, is surprisingly constant. Some peculiar-looking, arbitrary-seeming little customs appear again and again, throughout a great range of societies. The manner in which customs pattern or combine often shows an even more remarkable sameness. Sometimes these cultural universals make a certain amount of "sense." (Example: a mother living with and caring for her young children.) But often they occur for no apparent good reason. (Example: why should a wedding always include a wedding feast?)

In this final chapter I want to go over some of the cultural universals having to do with the family. Before launching into this, I must retract something. "Cultural universal" is too strong a term. Perhaps the only universals we can be really sure of are language and the use of tools. There are, no doubt, a few more true universals. However, since the ethnographic coverage is somewhat less than complete, it is a bit risky to talk unqualifiedly about universals. Furthermore, my researches are always based on samples of societies; they take in only a small fraction of the known, reported cases. Also, most of the so-called "universals" I just alluded to are not true universals at all; for most of them, there are one or several known exceptions. Instead, they appear to be almost-universals, quasi-universals.

So, this revelation I am about to make about the sameness of cultures is not quite so remarkable as first advertised. But it is still, I think, pretty remarkable. These are merely trends, to be sure. But they are extremely strong trends, with very few apparent exceptions. Also, most of them were unexpected. Few of them could have been predicted by anyone. There must be, I'm sure, a "reason" for each of these regularities, but the "reasons" are rarely obvious. Perhaps none of them are really understood.

Here is a list of the apparent near-universals that have been alluded to throughout this book:

Chapter 1. A mother lives in the same house with her young children. Incest taboos. The menstrual sex taboo. Societies with a fairly high percentage of mother-child households require a change of residence for all adolescent or prepubertal boys (that is, the boy no longer sleeps under the same roof as his mother). Mothers are expected to be married (absence of the mother-child family, as the cultural norm). Marriage is not undertaken for a specified, short-term period (as with *mut'a* marriage). Recognition of kin ties beyond the nuclear family.

Chapter 2. None.

Chapter 3. The pattern of focal avoidance relationships with their extensions. The personal name may not be used when addressing father, uncle, or grandfather. Method of assignment to unilineal kin groups: recruitment is either patrilineal (all children belong to father's group) or matrilineal (all children belong to mother's group); alternative methods of recruitment, such as the Mundugumors' "ropes," are rare. In a unilineal society, at least some unilineal kin group segments are exogamous. Distant matrilocal residence is rare (although distant patrilocal residence is common).

Chapter 4. A marriage ceremonial includes feasting.

Chapter 5. None.

Chapter 6. Women are rarely more privileged and powerful than men. Some tasks, such as hunting, are nearly always done by men; other tasks, such as grain grinding or housekeeping, are nearly always done by women. Men rarely give deference to women (unless it is a commoner man and a noble woman).

Chapter 7. Deference is given to older male kin; it is rarely given to female kin or to juniors. Within the father-child relationship, equality represents the lowest possible status for the father and the highest possible power position for the child. Mother is rarely stricter than father. The all-or-none effect: if father gets deference from Ego, so do various other older male kin; if father does not get deference, neither do other older male kin. Kingdoms are characterized by marked family deference customs.

Chapter 8. Pregnant women observe food taboos.

One of these near-universals was unearthed by Barbara Ayres (1954): the last one. Two were discovered by Whiting and D'Andrade (m.s.): the association between mother-child households and change of residence for adolescent boys, and the fact that an out-marrying man rarely moves very far from his natal home. D'Andrade has discovered another one, a pattern that dictates the order in which family members will move away from home (unpublished). It is somewhat similar to the cumulative patterns I shall discuss in a moment; I will not try to describe it here. Finally, four of the above near-universals were discovered (or, if not discovered, first properly documented) by G. P. Murdock: incest taboos, method of assignment to unilineal kin groups, unilineal kin-group exogamy, and the near-universal regularities in the sex typing of some tasks.

In addition to single traits or clusters of traits that are near-universally found, there are also near-universal patterning regularities that dictate how certain customs—when they *do* occur—will combine. These patterning regularities are, to my mind, the most astonishing of all the cultural near-universals. At this point I want to describe two types of these patterning regularities. The first is the cumulative pattern, which can be represented by a Guttman-type scale. The second is the pattern of "extensions," which characterizes avoidance and deference relationships. First, the cumulative pattern.

So far, to my knowledge, six of these cumulative patterns have been discovered. Roy D'Andrade found one—mentioned above—having to do with household composition. Freeman and Winch (1957) have reported another, which has to do with level of societal complexity. I have found four: a cumulative pattern of menstrual taboos, a cumulative pattern of kin-avoidance customs, and two cumulative patterns having to do with deference customs (one for son-to-father deference, the other for wife-to-husband deference). These last two patterns are described in the Appendix. Of these four, the "best" one—that is, the most clear cut, unequivocal, and free from scale errors—is the menstrual taboo pattern. (The "worst" is the wife-to-husband deference pattern.) To illustrate this cumulative patterning phenomenon, I will describe the menstrual taboo scale.

Menstrual taboos are avoidance customs that obtain between menstruating women and men, plus associated superstitions about the hurtful properties of menstrual blood.[1] They are very common the world over. Some menstrual taboos are idiosyncratic to specific societies or culture areas. Others are widely distributed. That is, a few taboos, or very narrowly defined types of taboo customs,

---

[1] For a more extended treatment of menstrual taboos, see Stephens 1962, Chapter V.

tend to occur again and again, throughout aboriginal North America, South America, Oceania, Asia, and Africa. I picked out three of these (there are probably more). They are: the menstruating woman may not have sexual intercourse; the menstruating woman may not cook for her husband; and women, during their menstrual periods, must stay in menstrual huts, special dwellings that men may not enter. I was then able to make a Guttman-type scale, using these three taboos plus two looser, more all-embracing code categories. The scale is as follows:

4. The menstruating woman stays in a menstrual hut.

3. She may not cook for her husband.

2. Many other menstrual taboos (taboos not accounted for by the other scale-points) are present.

1. The menstruating woman may not have sexual intercourse. Also, there is a belief current that menstrual blood is dangerous to men.

The cumulative pattern is as follows: whenever a society can be coded "yes" for one of these scale-points, it can never be checked "no" for some "lower" scale-point; when a society is checked "no" for a particular scale-point, it is never checked "yes" for some "higher" scale-point. Examples:

For some societies that had menstrual huts, there was no information on the presence or absence of some of the other taboos—cooking taboo, sex taboo, and so forth. However, out of my sample of seventy-two societies, there was *no* case in which menstrual huts were reported to be present while one of these other taboos was reported to be absent.

Some societies had the menstrual cooking taboo but did not have menstrual huts. However, no society with the cooking taboo was reported to be without the menstrual sex taboo, the belief in danger to men, or "many" other menstrual taboos.

No society without the menstrual sex taboo (there were very few of these) had the menstrual hut, the cooking taboo or "many" other menstrual taboos.

Likewise, no society without the belief that menstrual blood is dangerous to men had menstrual huts or the menstrual cooking taboo. There was one "error" in the scale, represented by the Lakher of Burma. They were apparently without the belief in danger to men, yet they were judged to have "many" other menstrual taboos.

The remarkable thing about this scale is that it is only to a minimal extent an artifact of the coding rules. The scale represents an actual cross-cultural regularity in culture patterning. These menstrual customs just "behave" this way. For some reason, it simply does not happen that a society without the menstrual sex taboo has a menstrual cooking taboo, or that a society with menstrual huts does not have the menstrual cooking taboo. The pattern is doubly curious since it does not make any obvious "sense." Why shouldn't some peoples have a menstrual cooking taboo without the sex taboo, or have the menstrual hut without some of the other taboos? The pattern seems arbitrary and accidental. Yet, obviously, it is neither arbitrary nor accidental. There must be some sort of strong functional imperative which dictates that these customs may only combine according to one particular sequence—for, apparently, this is the way it always happens.

A second, different type of patterning regularity has to do with patterned kin behavior, namely, deference and kin avoidance. The over-all effect seems to be that patterned kin behavior within several "focal" kin relationships dictates the nature of patterned kin behavior within other kin relationships.

I described one of these patterning regularities in Chapter 7—the one having to do with family deference customs. In this case the focal kin relationship is Ego-to-father. The extensions to this focal relationship are kin relationships involving Ego with other older male kin, uncles, grandfathers, and elder brothers. The pattern is as follows: when marked deference occurs within the Ego-to-father relationship, it also occurs within some (not necessarily all) of these other relationships—Ego to elder brother, uncles, and grandfathers; when Ego does *not* give father deference, neither does he give deference to *any* of these other older male kin.

The second instance of this sort of patterning regularity involves avoidance, and was briefly mentioned in Chapter 3. In this case there are three focal kin relationships: male Ego to sister, male Ego to wife's mother, and male Ego to son's wife. Each of these focal relationships carries some extensions. Thus, if Ego avoids his sister, he also usually[2] avoids female cousins. If he avoids his mother-in-law, he also usually avoids others of his wife's consanguineal kin. If he avoids his daughter-in-law, he usually avoids others of his son's wife's consanguineal kin. Furthermore, if the focal person is not avoided, extensions are rarely avoided. If Ego does not avoid his sister, he rarely avoids female cousins. If he does not avoid his mother-in-law, neither does he avoid others of his wife's kin. And, if he does not avoid his daughter-in-law, he doesn't avoid other kin of his daughter-in-law.

Finally, *degree* of avoidance within the focal relationship appears to set limits on the degree to which extensions may be avoided. With rare exceptions, severity of brother-sister avoidance will be *equal to or greater than* severity of Ego-to-cousin avoidance. The same is true of the other avoidance relationships. In societies where Ego avoids his mother-in-law, he will observe an equal or diminished degree (never greater) of avoidance toward the extensions to the mother-in-law, which typically include wife's mother's sisters, wife's mother's mother, and wife's father. Likewise for the son's wife avoidance, with its extensions.[3]

So this is the second type of patterning regularity—focal relationships with extensions. As with the first type, the cumulative pattern, this appears to be an inevitable, standard form, which must be followed by any society that "wishes" to practice deference or avoidance.

These focal relationship/extensions patterns carry with them other regularities that dictate who *may not* be deferred to and who *may not* be avoided.

In the case of deference, as we have seen, junior relatives are almost never deferred to, and women are seldom deferred to.

---

[2] I suspect that instances in which a focal avoidance does not carry extensions—for example, when Ego avoids sister but does not avoid any female cousins—are rare. However, because of the usual cases of "no information," I cannot be sure about this.

[3] For a lengthier treatment of kin-avoidance, see Stephens 1962, Chapter VI.

Deference is limited to only particular kin relationships, and within these it may go only one way—to the elder male relative.[4] In the case of avoidance: persons of the same sex are rarely avoided (exception: extensions to the mother-in-law or son's wife avoidance); and consanguineal kin of different generations are rarely avoided (that is, a man rarely avoids his mother, aunts, nieces, grandmothers, or granddaughters).

This completes the list of cultural near-universals. Considering the paucity of cross-cultural studies, this is a fairly long list. Since the scant cross-cultural literature *has* yielded such a collection of near-universals, this must mean that they are extremely numerous, obvious, and easy to find—easy to find, that is, as soon as one sets about systematically gathering data on discrete, small topics and areas, for a reasonably large sample of societies. Consider the fact, too, that nearly all of these were stumbled across by accident. It has rarely happened that a cross-cultural researcher has actually gone looking for these near-universals. Further systematic comparisons of the ethnographic literature would, I am sure, yield more of these. However, I do think such an exploration would be gravely limited, now, by the shortcomings of most ethnographies in regard to completeness and specificity of reporting.[5]

Future studies will, no doubt, add to this strange little list, and widen our perspective on this mysteriously constant quality of culture (that is, constant in some areas, varied in others). With more and better studies, we may even begin to understand *why*.

---

[4] Exception: wife-to-husband deference.

[5] Cross-cultural research will never progress very far until ethnographers —a good many ethnographers, at least—agree to adopt some sort of standardized reporting format. This might be on the order of a standard check list of culture traits, which would be applied by many ethnographers, reporting on a fair-sized sample of societies (with good geographic distribution). Such a project would yield a body of vastly superior ethnographic data (from the viewpoint of the cross-cultural researcher, anyway)—clear, specific, and comparable from case to case. Many new areas could then be investigated. Old studies could be redone with improved data.

As far as I know, nothing of this sort is being undertaken at present. Perhaps it will be a long time in coming. Perhaps it will never come.

Appendix

The Ethnographer-interview Data

The ethnographer-interview was an attempt to get data on family deference customs and power relations that would be—it was hoped—more detailed, specific, and complete than those offered by the written ethnographies. Most of the people interviewed were anthropologists; there were also several sociologists, a historian, and a number of foreign students. Each respondent was asked to report on a fairly small, circumscribed group of people—a small tribe, a peasant village, or a subgroup within a large city. The interview-questions ranged from queries about discrete items of formalized deference (such as bowing to, or walking behind, the deferred-to person) to requests for rather difficult generalizations about behavior (such as whether the son "rarely disputes" with his father). I want to say, at this point, how impressed I was at the quality of cooperation I received. With rare exceptions, the informants were extremely gracious, seemed most conscientious, and—although conscious of the difficulties and dangers inherent in such generalizations as "rarely disputes"—appeared to do their utmost to give the best possible answer. (Even if the best answer, in some cases, was an informed and responsible guess.) Anthropologists are excellent informants.

Below are listed the ethnographer-interview cases, fifty-three in all, together with the informant for each case.

ALOR (Small island in eastern Indonesia.) Cora DuBois, Department of Anthropology, Harvard.

AMMAN (City in Jordan.) Ahmed Dakhgan, Department of City Planning, Massachusetts Institute of Technology.

ANAGUTA (Tribe in Nigeria.) Stanley Diamond, Laboratory for Socio-Environmental Studies, NIH, Bethesda, Md.

ASHANTI (Ashanti living in city of Koforidua.) Daniel F. McCall, African Studies Center, Boston University.

ATRISCO (Spanish-American village in New Mexico.) Florence Kluckhohn, Department of Social Relations, Harvard.

BARRANQUITAS (District in the east-central highlands of Puerto Rico.) Robert Manners, Department of Anthropology, Brandeis University.

BERBERS (A Berber group in the Riff Mountains of Spanish Morocco, near city of Tetuan.) Therese Kemp, Department of Anthropology, Harvard.

THE BOG (Rural slum district in Nova Scotia.) Robert Rapoport, Department of Social Relations, Harvard.

BRNO (City in Czechoslovakia.) Jaromir Matula, c/o Language Research, Harvard.

CHANZEAUX (Village in northern France.) Laurence Wylie, Department of History, Harvard.

CHIAROMONTE (Village in southern Italy.) Laura Banfield, Cambridge, Mass.

COOK ISLANDERS (Living in Auckland, New Zealand.) Anthony Hooper, Department of Anthropology, Harvard.

CUCHUMATAN MAM (Highland Mayans, Northeast Guatemala.) Suzanne W. Miles, Department of Anthropology, Brandeis University.

DRAGALETVSY (Village in Bulgaria.) Irwin T. Sanders, Department of Sociology and Anthropology, Boston University.

DRUZ (Village of Ammatour, Lebanon.) William R. Polk, Center for Middle Eastern Studies, Harvard.

GREECE Irwin T. Sanders, Department of Sociology and Anthropology, Boston University.

GUAYMI (Tribe in Panama.) Olga Linares, Department of Anthropology, Harvard.

HUTTERITES (Collective-farming religious sect community in South Dakota.) Herman Bleibtreu, Department of Anthropology, Harvard.

KIPSIGIS (Tribe in Kenya.) Robert Manners, Department of Anthropology, Brandeis University.

KAKTAVIK (Eskimo village on Barter Island.) Norman Chance, Department of Anthropology, University of Oklahoma.

KONSO (Tribe in Ethiopia.) Richard Kluckhohn, Department of Social Relations, Harvard.

KURDS (Kurdish community in Damascus, Syria.) Yusuf Ibish, c/o Center for Middle Eastern Studies, Harvard.

!KUNG (Bushmen of Kalahari Desert, South Africa.) Lorna Marshall, Peabody Museum, Harvard.

KWOMA (Tribe in New Guinea.) John Whiting, Laboratory of Human Development, Harvard.

LACANDON-MAYA (Jungle-dwelling Mayan group in Chiapas, Mexico.) Therese Kemp, Department of Anthropology, Harvard.

LASKO (Village in northwest Yugoslavia.) Otmar Sprah, Language Research, Harvard.

MADIUN (City in Central Java.) Ali Budiardjo, National Planning Board, Jakarta, Indonesia.

MADRID (Aristocracy.) Father Juan Cortes, c/o Department of Social Relations, Harvard.

MAGAZAWA (Bush Hausa, in northern Nigeria.) Stanley Diamond, Laboratory for Socio-Environmental Studies, NIH, Bethesda, Md.

MENANGKABAU (Central Sumatra.) Dr. and Mrs. Makaminan Makagiansar, c/o Graduate School of Education, Harvard.

NAPLES (Lower class.) Anne Parsons, McLean Hospital, Belmont, Mass.

NAVAHO (Tribe in Arizona-New Mexico.) Clyde Kluckhohn.

NKUNDO (Tribe in the Congo.) Donald Edwards, c/o African Studies Center, Boston University.

NISHAPUR (District in Iran.) Joseph Upton, Center for Middle Eastern Studies, Harvard.

OJIBWA (Luc de Flambeau reservation, Canada.) William Caudill, Laboratory for Socio-Environmental Studies, NIH, Bethesda, Md.

PAIUTE (Harney Valley, Oregon.) Beatrice Whiting, Laboratory of Human Development, Harvard.

PECS (City in southwest Hungary.) Jolan Banyay, c/o Language Research, Harvard.

PEYRANE (Village in southern France.) Laurence Wylie, Department of History, Harvard.

SAN JUAN JUQUILLA (Zapotec village in southern Mexico.) Laura Nader, Department of Anthropology, University of California.

SAN JUAN PUEBLO (Deculturated Pueblo Indians near Santa Fe, New Mexico.) Robert Lee Munroe, Laboratory of Human Development, Harvard.

SAN PEDRO LA LAGUNA (Highland Mayan village in Guatemala.) Lois Paul, Center for Community Studies, Boston.

SHERPA (Solu-Khumbu area in Nepal.) Allain Thiollier, c/o Department of Anthropology, Harvard.

SOMALI (Galjaal-Barsana tribe in Somalia.) David Marlowe, Department of Anthropology, Harvard.

SUBANUM (Tribe in the Philippines.) Charles O. Frake, Department of Anthropology, University of California.

TENINO (Warm Springs Reservation, Oregon.) Dr. and Mrs. Del Hymes, Department of Anthropology, University of California.

TOBA BATAK (Western Sumatra.) Osman R. I. Bako, National Planning Board, Jakarta, Indonesia.

TURKANA (Tribe in Kenya.) Philip H. Gulliver, African Studies Center, Boston University.

VAISH (Caste group in Ambala City, India.) Taj Gupta, Language Research, Harvard.

VALLE CANA (Village in Puerto Rico.) David Landy, Graduate School of Public Health, University of Pittsburgh.

VALLEY TONGA (Tribe in Northern Rhodesia.) Elizabeth Colson, Department of Anthropology, Brandeis University, and Thayer Scudder, Department of Anthropology, Harvard.

VILLAFRANQUEZA (Village in eastern Spain.) Father Juan Cortes, c/o Department of Social Relations, Harvard.

YOKOHAMA (Middle class.) Sadako Imamura, c/o Laboratory of Human Development, Harvard.

ZINACANTAN (Tsotsil village in Chiapas, Mexico.) Benjamin N. Colby, Department of Anthropology, Harvard.

The interview-questions pertained to a male Ego who is in his twenties, married, with at least one child. The first series of questions asked about the father-son relationship—that is, the relationship between this male Ego and his father. Then the informant was asked about the relationship between this male Ego and his wife. The informant was asked to make a generalization about his (or her) entire "case," which was either a tribe, a village, or a subgroup within a city. The answers, therefore, try to represent the "normal," "usual," "customary" father-son and husband-wife relationships within this social group. The interview questions follow.

Ethnographer-interview

Son-to-father

1. Does the son address his father by the father's personal name?
2. When talking to the father, does he follow any of these rules of verbal restraint: don't argue with father; speak softly to father; speak only a little when around father; don't tease father?
3. Does he kneel or bow when greeting his father?
4. Does he observe a touch-taboo in relation to his father?

5. May father and son eat together?

6. Does the father have a seating priority in relation to his son? Does the father have an honorific seating place, that is, a seat of honor?

7. May father and son laugh and joke together?

8. Are there any other taboos on personal intimacies between father and son?

9. May father and son talk about sex?

10. Characterize the son when he is five years old, as to how obedient he is to his father, how strict are the obedience rules placed on him, how shocked people would be if he were disobedient to his father, and how severe the punishment for disobedience (to his father). If there is a transition time—with regard to the severity of the father's obedience demands—how old is the child when this transition takes place?

11. (Married son once more.) How frequent is son-to-father verbal aggression—that is, angry disagreements and verbal fights?

12. Does the son, in his father's presence, have to observe some rule of body elevation? (Examples: stand until father sits, always sit lower than father, stand when father enters the room or gathering.)

(The informant was then asked to compare the father-son relationship with the relationship of Ego of elder brother, uncle, and grandfather vis-à-vis these deference customs.)

Wife-to-husband

1. May the wife address her husband by his personal name?

2. When talking to her husband, does the wife follow any of these rules of verbal restraint: don't argue with husband, speak softly to husband, speak only a little when around husband, don't tease husband?

3. Does she kneel or bow when greeting her husband?
4. When they are walking together in public does the wife walk behind her husband?
5. Is there a rule against husband and wife touching, when in public?
6. May husband and wife eat together?
7. May husband and wife be together in public?
8. Is the wife excluded from a good many gatherings which her husband may attend? What sort of gatherings is she excluded from? What sort of gatherings is she not excluded from?
9. Does the husband have a seating priority or seat of honor in relation to his wife?
10. How frequent is wife-to-husband verbal aggression (angry disagreements, verbal fights)?
11. Does the wife, in her husband's presence, have to observe some rule of body elevation? (Examples: stand until husband sits, sit lower than husband, stand when husband enters a room or gathering.)
12. Is there a good deal of joint decision making by husband and wife—talking over and deciding together on questions of household, children, jointly-held property, other family business? Or, does the husband alone tend to make the decisions, without consulting his wife?

(Subsequently, a few informants gave data on sex-restrictions and husband-wife division of labor. These data are given in Chapters 5 and 6.)

The interview-answers were recorded and then coded. (Most, but not all, of the material was coded. Some code categories coincide with questionnaire items; others cut across the questionnaire items, that is, embrace several questions, or only part of one question.) Here are the coding rules.

Coding Rules

General Instructions

An entry of "x" means "yes, the respect rule is present."

An entry of "–" means "no, the respect rule is absent."

Leave blank: if there is no response in regard to the respect rule (that is, code category), or if you feel the response is too ambiguous to be coded.

If the respondent says he is unsure, but then answers a particular question, code.

If the respondent says a particular respect rule was present "in the old days" but is disappearing now, code for "the old days."

Son-to-father

A. (Question 1) Son doesn't address the father by his personal name.

B. (Question 2) Son rarely disputes with his father. (Code "x" if respondent says son "doesn't argue"—and vice versa. Code "x" if respondent says disputing and arguing is "severely disapproved"—and vice versa.)

C. (Question 2) Son must speak softly to his father.

D. (Questions 3 and 12) When greeting his father, does the son kneel, bow, kiss father's hand, or stand (if previously sitting)? (Code "–" if respondent says he only does any of these under special—not usual, daily—circumstances. Code "–" if Question 3 is answered "no," and Question 12 lists some other rule of sitting etiquette, such as letting father have the only chair.)

E. (Question 11) Son rarely expresses verbal aggression (anger) toward his father (when interacting with father). (Code "x" if respondent says verbal aggression is "shocking" or "severely disapproved"—and vice versa.)

F. (Question 10) A father places strict obedience demands on his *five-year-old* son. (Code "x" for such statements as "strict obedience," "rare disobedience," "very obedient." Code "–" for such statements as "often disobedient," "not strict obedience demands." There will be a number of ambiguous, doubtful, borderline cases. Feel free to code such cases "•"—"no rating." There will be a few cases where the informant states both the ideal rule and the actual behavior, which departs from the ideal rule. In such cases, code the actual behavior.)

Wife-to-husband

A. (Question 1) The wife doesn't address her husband by his personal name.

B. (Questions 2 and 10) The wife rarely disputes with her husband. (Code "x" if respondent says wife "doesn't argue"—and vice versa. Code "x" if respondent says disputing and arguing are "severely disapproved"—and vice versa.)

C. (Question 3) The wife kneels or bows when greeting her husband.

D. (Question 4) The wife walks behind her husband when outside the house. (If there are several arrangements, code for the most frequent one.)

E. (Question 5) When nonnuclear-family members are present, spouses do not show affection to each other by embraces, caresses, patting or hand holding, or endearing terms.

F. (Question 6) Spouses do not eat together (at the same table or hearth at the same time). (If there are several arrangements, code for the most frequent one.)

G. (Question 8) The wife is excluded from a good many social gatherings, which her husband may attend.

H. (Questions 9 and 11) The wife gives her husband a seating priority. (Examples: at meals husband has most honorific seating place, such as at the head of the table; husband sits on a chair or bench and wife sits on the ground; husband has a special chair; if there is one chair, the husband takes it; wife stands until husband sits.)

I. (Question 12) The husband dominates family decision making. (Code "x" if (1) the husband makes the family decisions unilaterally, or (2) the husband has the last word on family decisions, although he may consult his wife before deciding. Code "–" if (1) each spouse has his/her own sphere of influence in family decision making, in which he/she is sovereign, or (2) family decisions are jointly made.

These coding rules were applied, independently, by three cross-cultural coders: Diane D'Andrade, Judith W. Stephens, and myself. Coder-agreement was as follows:

Son-to-father

A. Doesn't address by personal name: 98 percent agreement.

B. Rarely disputes: 92 percent agreement

C. Speaks softly to: 85 percent agreement.

D. Kneels or bows to (or stands when father enters room or gathering): 85 percent agreement.

E. Rarely expresses verbal aggression toward: 79 percent agreement.

F. The father places strict obedience demands on his five-year-old son: 84 percent agreement.

Wife-to-husband

A. Doesn't address by personal name: 99 percent agreement.

B. Rarely disputes: 83 percent agreement.

C. Kneels or bows to: 98 percent agreement.

D. Walks behind: 94 percent agreement.

E. No public affection-display: 96 percent agreement.

F. Can't eat with: 94 percent agreement.

G. Excluded from a good many social gatherings: 80 percent agreement.

H. Gives a seating priority: 91 percent agreement.

I. Husband dominates family decision making: 86 percent agreement.

Each code category, for each case, was then assigned a final score, by the following conventions:

If two or three coders scored it "x," it got a final score of "x."

If two or three coders scored it "–," it got a final score of "–."

If two or three coders did not score it (deciding there was insufficient information), it did not receive a final score. Such instances of "no information" are indicated by a dot—"•"—in Table 6.

Over-all scores on degree of son-to-father and wife-to-husband deference were then assigned, on the basis of the following cumulative scales:

Scale Measuring Degree of Son-to-father Deference

This scale is made up of the following scale-points (from high to low):

5. (highest possible scale-score) Both "son kneels or bows to father" and "son speaks softly to father" scored "present" (or "x").

4. One (but not both) of the above items scored "present": either "kneels or bows" or "speaks softly."

3. "Son rarely disputes with father" scored "present."

2. "Son rarely expresses verbal aggression toward father" scored "present."

1. "Son does not address father by his personal name" scored "present."

Scale Measuring Degree of Wife-to-husband Deference

This scale has the following scale-points (from high to low):

5. "Wife kneels or bows to husband" scored "present."

4. "Wife rarely disputes with husband" scored "present."

3. "Husband dominates family decision making" scored "present."

2. "Husband has a seating priority" scored "present."

1. "Wife is excluded from a good many social gatherings" scored "present."

Scale-scores were assigned according to the following conventions:

a. A society's score is equal to the highest scale-point that was scored present. Examples (from the son-to-father scale): The Vaish get a score of 5, since they were scored "present" for all scale-points; Yokohama is scored 3, since it is scored present only for points 1, 2, and 3; Barranquitas gets a score of 1, since it scored "present" only on point 1; the Somali get a score of 0, since they scored "absent" or "–" on scale-point 1.

b. If a society's rightful scale-score is in doubt because two or more consecutive scale-points are unscored (because of lack of information), that society does not receive a scale-score. Examples (from the son-to-father scale): Cook Islanders, Toba Batak, Paiute.

c. If a society's rightful scale-score is in doubt because of no score at only *one* scale point, that society is still given a scale-score, on the basis of rule (a). Examples (son-to-father): Sherpa, Nkundo, Atrisco.

Table 6 gives coded items and final scale-scores, and also illustrates the cumulative scale-pattern.

TABLE 6

CODED DATA FROM THE ETHNOGRAPHER-INTERVIEW*

			(Son-to-father)								(Wife-to-husband)					
	X	1	2	3	4	5	Y	6	7	8	9	10	11	12	13	14
Alor	3	x	x	x	•	–	2	–	x	–	–	–	x	x	x	–
Amman	3	x	x	x	•	–	3	x	x	x	–	–	x	–	x	–
Anaguta	2	x	x	–	–	–	0	–	–	–	–	–	–	x	–	x
Ashanti	4	x	x	x	x	–	2	x	x	–	–	–	x	x	x	x
Atrisco	3	x	x	x	•	–	4	x	–	x	x	–	–	–	•	–
Barranquitas	1	x	–	–	–	–	3	x	–	x	–	–	–	x	x	–
Berbers	2	x	x	–	–	–	1	x	–	–	–	–	–	–	x	–
The Bog	0	–	–	–	•	–	1	x	–	•	–	–	–	–	–	–
Brno	4	x	x	x	x	–	0	–	–	•	–	–	–	–	x	–
Chanzeaux	1	x	–	–	–	–	2	x	x	–	–	–	–	x	–	–
Chiaromonte	1	x	–	–	•	–	1	x	–	•	–	–	–	–	–	–
Cook Islanders	•	x	x	•	•	–	2	x	x	•	–	–	–	•	x	–
Cuchumatan Mam	4	x	x	x	x	•	4	x	x	•	x	–	x	–	x	–
Dragaletvsy	4	x	x	x	–	x	2	x	x	•	–	–	–	–	x	–
Druz	3	x	–	x	–	–	1	x	–	•	–	–	x	x	x	–
Greece	4	x	•	x	–	x	3	•	x	x	–	–	•	x	x	x
Guaymi	1	x	–	–	•	–	3	x	x	x	–	–	–	x	x	x
Hutterites	2	x	x	–	–	–	•	x	x	•	•	–	–	•	x	x
Kaktavik	2	•	x	–	–	–	0	–	–	–	–	–	•	x	•	–
Kipsigis	3	x	x	x	•	–	3	x	–	x	–	–	–	x	x	x
Konso	4	•	x	x	x	–	3	x	x	x	–	–	–	–	–	–
Kurds	4	x	•	•	•	x	•	x	•	•	•	–	–	x	x	–
!Kung	2	x	x	–	–	–	3	–	–	x	–	–	–	x	x	–
Kwoma	1	x	–	–	–	–	1	x	–	–	–	–	x	x	x	•
Lacandon Maya	4	•	x	x	x	–	0	–	•	•	–	–	•	•	•	–
Lasko	4	x	x	–	–	x	2	•	x	•	–	–	–	–	–	–
Madiun	4	x	x	x	x	–	2	–	x	–	–	–	x	–	x	–
Madrid	5	x	x	x	x	x	4	x	–	–	x	–	x	–	x	–
Magazawa	5	x	x	x	x	x	2	x	x	•	–	–	–	x	x	x
Menangkabau	5	x	x	x	x	x	2	x	x	•	–	–	–	–	x	–
Naples	1	x	–	–	–	–	1	x	–	–	–	–	–	–	–	–
Navaho	4	x	x	x	x	–	0	–	–	–	–	–	x	x	x	–
Nishapur	5	x	x	x	x	x	5	x	x	•	•	x	x	x	x	x
Nkundo	3	x	x	x	•	–	•	•	•	•	–	–	–	x	x	•
Ojibwa	1	x	–	–	–	–	3	•	•	x	–	–	–	–	x	–
Paiute	•	x	•	•	•	–	0	–	–	•	–	–	x	x	x	•

TABLE 6 (*Continued*)

	(Son-to-father)						(Wife-to-husband)									
	X	1	2	3	4	5	Y	6	7	8	9	10	11	12	13	14
Pecs	2	x	x	–	–	–	•	•	•	•	–	–	–	–	–	–
Peyrane	1	x	–	•	•	–	2	x	x	–	–	–	–	–	–	x
San Juan Juquilla	4	x	x	x	x	–	0	–	–	–	–	–	–	x	x	–
San Juan Pueblo	1	x	–	–	–	–	0	–	–	–	–	–	–	–	•	–
San Pedro la Languna	4	x	x	x	x	•	4	x	x	•	x	–	–	x	x	x
Sherpa	2	x	x	–	–	–	2	x	x	•	–	–	•	x	x	x
Somali	0	–	–	•	•	–	2	x	x	•	–	–	–	x	x	–
Subanum	3	x	x	•	•	–	0	–	–	–	–	–	–	–	–	–
Tenino	2	x	x	–	–	–	0	–	–	•	•	–	x	–	x	–
Toba Batak	•	x	x	•	•	–	2	•	x	•	–	–	x	x	x	–
Turkana	1	x	–	–	–	–	1	x	–	–	–	–	–	x	x	–
Vaish	5	x	x	x	x	x	4	•	x	x	x	•	x	–	x	x
Valle Cana	4	x	x	x	x	–	4	x	x	x	x	–	–	–	x	x
Valley Tonga	2	x	x	–	–	–	1	x	•	–	–	–	x	x	•	x
Villafranqueza	4	x	x	x	x	–	3	x	x	x	–	–	–	–	x	–
Yokohama	3	x	x	•	•	–	5	x	x	x	x	x	x	x	x	–
Zinacantan	4	x	x	–	–	x	2	x	x	•	–	–	x	x	–	x

* Column headings are as follows:

X. Son-to-father deference scale-score.
1. Son can't address father by personal name.
2. Son rarely expresses verbal aggression to father.
3. Son rarely disputes with father.
4. Son speaks softly to father.
5. Son kneels or bows to greet father, or stands when father enters room or gathering.

Y. Wife-to-husband deference scale-score.
6. Wife excluded from a good many social gatherings.
7. Husband has a seating priority.
8. Husband dominates family decision-making.
9. Wife rarely disputes with husband.
10. Wife kneels or bows on greeting husband.
11. Wife doesn't address husband by his personal name.
12. Wife walks behind husband.
13. Spouses don't show affection in public.
14. Spouses don't eat together.

Entries are as follows:

"x" is "yes"
"–" is "no"
"•" indicates "no final code"
Numerical entries in columns X and Y indicate the deference scale-scores.

Evaluation of the Deference Scales

These data do have shortcomings, namely, 1) probable reporting error, due to the nature of the interview-questions, and 2) defects in the cumulative scales.

Probable Reporting Error

We can only guess, of course, about how "accurate" the informants' reports were. However, there were a number of factors that must have made a certain amount of error inevitable. In the first place, the informant was asked to generalize about an entire group (a tribe, village, or subgroup within a city). This immediately introduces the problem of variations within each group (which has already been discussed in Chapters 6 and 7). My guess is that reports were most accurate when they dealt with discrete items of etiquette, summarized in clear cultural rules (such as "doesn't address by his personal name"), and that the informants' generalizations were most subject to error when they tried to describe the more power-relevant behavior (such as "rarely expresses verbal aggression toward," "rarely disputes with"). Real power is simply harder to find out about than formalized deference is.

Some of the interview-questions could have been more specific. This is particularly true of "does the husband dominate family decision making" and "is the wife excluded from a good many social gatherings." Perhaps more specifically worded questions would have reduced error on a few items.

Finally, reporting error is no doubt compounded by some coding error. I imagine this is most true of the code categories that yielded low average agreement between the coders, namely, "the son rarely disputes with his father," "the wife is excluded from a good many social gatherings," and "the wife rarely disputes with her husband."

Evaluation of the Scales

As cumulative scales go, these are rather poor. Both scales are weak in respect to marginals; there are only two cases at point 5 on the wife-to-husband scale, and only 2 cases at point 0 on the son-to-father scale. As far as scale-errors[1] go, the son-to-father scale is good enough (with two scale-errors), and the wife-to-husband scale is not so good (with nine scale-errors). Also, of course, numerous items were uncoded and left blank.

Why do I use these scales, then? Because they are the best I can do. On the plus side, a cumulative scale—even a rather poor cumulative scale—has two advantages. In the first place, it does indicate a continuum (which, in this case, I have termed "degree of deference"), and it gives some empirical basis for ordering cases along this continuum. By virtue of the cumulative pattern, the "high" cases have what the "low" cases have, plus something extra. As an example, the Vaish have a score of 5 on degree of son-to-father deference, and the Hutterites have a score of 2. The Vaish have what the Hutterites have ("doesn't address by personal name" and "rarely expresses verbal aggression toward") plus something extra—"rarely disputes," "speaks softly to," and "kneels or bows."

Also, I would guess that this 6-point scale—as opposed to a 2-point scale (in which cases are scored "present" or "absent," or "high" or "low")—acts to cut down measurement error. Assume, for example, that I had never undertaken the ethnographer-interview—that, instead, I had merely used the written ethnographies. In this case, I would have probably coded degree of deference on a 2-point scale. Some societies would have been coded "high" (on, for example, son-to-father deference). These would have been cases in which the ethnographer said the son "respects" his father, or "obeys" him, or cases where the father's strictness was described, or cases in which extreme-sounding

[1] Exceptions to the cumulative pattern, in which a "high" item is coded "x" while a "lower" item—for the same case—has been coded "–."

formalized deference customs were reported. Other societies would have been coded "low": where the father "does not demand much obedience," or where descriptions are given indicating that the father is not very strict (and where there is no mention of formalized deference). If I had done this, and separated societies into "highs" and "lows" on degree of son-to-father deference, there would have been, I'm sure, a certain amount of error. Some cases that "should have been" coded "high" would have been scored "low," and vice versa. Furthermore, error—when it occurred—would have been total. Error would act to transfer a case from the top of the scale ("high") to the bottom of the scale ("low"), or to transfer it from the bottom of the scale to the top.

Now, to return to thc cumulative scales based on the ethnographer-interview. Even if these scale-scores do contain some error—and I'm sure they do—the error is much less likely to be total. Say, for example, that the Vaish really don't bow to their fathers. The "real" score for the Vaish should be 4, and not 5. Still, error has only changed this from a moderately high score (4) to an extremely high score (5); it has not transferred a lowest possible score (0) to a highest possible score.

Therefore, I think (although I cannot prove it) that these cumulative scales, based on the ethnographer-interview data, are less tainted with error than an alternative measure—a 2-point scale[2]—would have been. True, I could have used a multipoint scale and ranked scale-points in some arbitrary manner instead of using a cumulative scale. However, I think even a rather poor cumulative scale—which nevertheless gives some empirical basis for ordering scale-points—is preferable to arbitrary ranking.

---

[2] The data from the ethnographies were not complete enough to permit other than a 2-point, high/low scale.

Bibliography of Cross-cultural Studies

Aberle, David F., "Matrilineal Descent in Cross-cultural Perspective" in David M. Schneider and Kathleen Gough (eds.), *Matrilineal Kinship*. Berkeley: University of California Press, 1961.

Apple, Dorrian, "The Social Structure of Grandparenthood," *American Anthropologist*, Vol. 58, No. 4, August 1956.

Ayres, Barbara C., "A Cross-cultural Study of Factors Relating to Pregnancy Taboos," Doctoral thesis, Radcliffe College, 1954.

Bacon, Margaret, Herbert Barry, and Irving L. Child, Unpublished Ratings of Socialization Practices. Yale University, Department of Psychology.

Barry, Herbert A., "The Relationship between Child Training and the Pictorial Arts," *Journal of Abnormal and Social Psychology*, Vol. 54, No. 3, May 1957.

Barry, Herbert A., Margaret K. Bacon, and Irving L. Child, "A Cross-cultural Survey of Some Sex Differences in Socialization," *Journal of Abnormal and Social Psychology*, Vol. 55, No. 3, November 1957.

Devereux, George, *A Study of Abortion in Primitive Societies*. New York: Julian Press, Inc., 1955.

Fischer, John L., Ratings of the Occurrence of Totemism with Food Taboos. Unpublished. Tulane University, Department of Sociology & Anthropology.

Ford, Clellan S., "A Comparative Study of Human Reproduction," *Yale University Publications in Anthropology*, No. 32, 1945.

Ford, Clellan S., and Frank A. Beach, *Patterns of Sexual Behavior.* New York: Harper & Row, Publishers, 1951.

Freeman, Linton C., and Robert F. Winch, "Societal Complexity: An Empirical Test of a Typology of Societies," *American Journal of Sociology*, Vol. 62, No. 5, March 1957.

Friendly, Joan P., "A Cross-cultural Study of Ascetic Mourning Behavior." Honors thesis, Radcliffe College, 1956.

Homans, George C., and David M. Schneider, *Marriage, Authority, and Final Causes.* New York: The Free Press of Glencoe, 1955.

Lambert, William W., Leigh Triandis, and Margery Wolf, "Some Correlates of Beliefs in the Malevolence and Benevolence of Supernatural Beings: a Cross-cultural Study," *Journal of Abnormal and Social Psychology*, Vol. 58, No. 2, March 1959.

Murdock, George Peter, "Comparative Data on Division of Labor by Sex," *Social Forces,* 1937, Vol. XV, pp. 551–553.

———, "Family Stability in Non-European Cultures," *Annals of the American Academy of Political and Social Science,* Vol. 270, 1950.

———, *Social Structure.* New York: The Macmillan Company, 1949.

———, "World Ethnographic Sample," *American Anthropologist,* Vol. 59, No. 4, 1957.

———, "Cognative Forms of Social Organization" in G. P. Murdock (ed.), *Social Structure in Southeast Asia.* Chicago: Quadrangle Books, 1960.

———, and John W. M. Whiting, "Cultural Determination of Parental Attitudes: The Relationship Between the Social Structure, Particularly Family Structure, and Parental Behavior" in Milton J. E. Senn (ed.), *Problems of Infancy and Childhood.* New York: Josiah Macy, Jr. Foundation, 1951.

Spiro, Melford E., and Roy G. D'Andrade, "A Cross-cultural Study of Some Supernatural Beliefs," *American Anthropologist*, Vol. 60, No. 3, June 1958.

Stephens, William N., *The Oedipus Complex: Cross-cultural Evidence.* New York: The Free Press of Glencoe, 1962.

Tylor, E. B., "On a Method of Investigating the Development of Institutions; Applied to Laws of Marriage and Descent," *Journal of the Royal Anthropological Institute*, Vol. 18, 1889, pp. 245–269.

Whiting, Beatrice B., "Paiute Sorcery," *Viking Fund Publications in Anthropology*, No. 15, 1950.

Whiting, John W. M., "Sorcery, Sin and the Superego: A Cross-cultural Study of Some Mechanisms of Social Control," Nebraska Symposium on Motivation, 1959.

———, and Irving L. Child, *Child Training and Personality*. New Haven: Yale University Press, 1953.

———, and Roy G. D'Andrade, Cross-cultural Ratings of Residence and Sleeping Arrangements. Unpublished. Harvard University, Laboratory of Human Development.

———, and Richard Kluckhohn, Unpublished Ratings of Duration of the *Post Partum* Sex Taboo. Harvard University, Laboratory of Human Development.

———, Richard Kluckhohn, and Albert Anthony, "The Function of Male Initiation Ceremonies at Puberty" in E. E. Maccoby, T. M. Newcomb, and E. L. Hartley (eds.) *Readings in Social Psychology*. New York: Holt, Rinehart and Winston, Inc., 1958.

Zelditch, Morris, "Role Differentiation in the Nuclear Family: a Comparative Study" in Talcott Parsons and Robert F. Bales, *Family, Socialization and Interaction Process.* New York: The Free Press of Glencoe, 1955.

General Bibliography

Abrams, Charles, and John P. Dean, "Housing and the Family" in R. N. Anshen (ed.), *The Family: Its Function and Destiny.* New York: Harper & Row, Publishers, 1949.

Aginsky, Bernard Willard, "An Indian's Soliloquy," *American Journal of Sociology,* 1940. Vol. 46, pp. 43–44.

———, "Kinship Systems and the Forms of Marriage," *Memoirs of the American Anthropological Association,* No. 45, 1935.

Barnes, H. E., and O. M. Ruedi, *The American Way of Life.* Englewood Cliffs, N. J.: Prentice-Hall, Inc., 1951.

Beigel, Hugo G., "Romantic Love," *American Sociological Review,* Vol. 16, No. 3, June 1951, pp. 326–334.

Blood, Robert O., and Robert L. Hamblin, "The Effects of the Wife's Employment on the Family Power Structure," *Social Forces,* Vol. XXVI, May 1958, pp. 347–352.

———, and Donald M. Wolfe, *Husbands and Wives.* New York: The Free Press of Glencoe, 1960.

Bott, Elizabeth, *Family and Social Network.* London: Tavistock Publications, 1957.

Cottrell, Leonard S., "The Adjustment of the Individual to His Age and Sex Roles," *American Sociological Review,* Vol. 7, No. 5, October 1942.

Davis, Allison, and Robert J. Havighurst, "Social Class and Color Differences in Child-rearing," *American Sociological Review*, Vol. 11, December 1946.

Ditzion, Sidney, *Marriage, Morals and Sex in America*. New York: Bookman Associates, 1953.

Durand, John D., "Married Women in the Labor Force," *The American Journal of Sociology*, Vol. 52, November 1946.

Fenichel, Otto, *The Psychoanalytic Theory of Neurosis*. New York: W. W. Norton & Company, Inc., 1945.

Fortune, Reo, "Incest," *Encyclopaedia of the Social Sciences*. New York: The Macmillan Company, 1932.

Frazier, E. Franklin, "The Negro Family" in R. N. Anshen (ed.), *The Family: Its Function and Destiny*. New York: Harper & Row, Publishers, 1949.

Freeman, Linton C., "Marriage without Love: Mate-selection in Non-Western Societies" in Robert F. Winch, *Mate-Selection*. New York: Harper & Row, Publishers, 1959.

Freud, Sigmund, *Totem and Taboo*. New York: W. W. Norton & Company, Inc., 1950.

Geertz, Clifford, "Cultural Ecology." Manuscript. University of California, Berkeley, Department of Anthropology.

Gesell, Arnold, *The Guidance of Mental Growth in Infant and Child*. New York: The Macmillan Company, 1930.

Gibran, Kahlil, *The Prophet*. New York: Alfred A. Knopf, Inc., 1960.

Glick, Paul C., "Family Trends in the United States, 1890 to 1940," *American Sociological Review*, Vol. 7, August 1942.

Goodsell, Willystone, *A History of the Family as a Social and Educational Institution*. New York: The Macmillan Company, 1915.

Herbst, P. G., "The Measurement of Family Relations," *Human Relations*, Vol. V, No. 1, 1952, pp. 3–35.

Herodotus (Selections). *University of California Syllabus Series*, Number 101. Berkeley: University of California Press, 1919.

Kinsey, A. C., *Sexual Behavior in the Human Female*. Philadelphia: W. B. Saunders Company, 1953.

Kinsey, A. C., W. B. Pomeroy, and C. E. Martin, *Sexual Behavior in the Human Male*. Philadelphia: W. B. Saunders Company, 1948.

Kluckhohn, Clyde, "Variations in the Human Family" in Norman Bell and Ezra Vogel (eds.), *A Modern Introduction to the Family*. New York: The Free Press of Glencoe, 1960.

Komarovsky, Mirra, "Cultural Contradictions and Sex Roles," *The American Journal of Sociology*, Vol. 12, November 1946.

Leach, E. R., "The Structural Implication of Matrilateral Cross-cousin Marriage," *The Journal of the Royal Anthropological Institute of Great Britain and Ireland*, Vol. 81, 1951.

Lecky, William Edward Hartpole, *History of European Morals from Augustus to Charlemagne*, Vol. II. London: Longmans, Green & Co., Ltd., 1869.

Leyburn, James G., *Frontier Folkways*. New Haven: Yale University Press, 1935.

Linton, Ralph, "Age and Sex Categories," *American Sociological Review*, Vol. 7, No. 5, October 1942, pp. 589–603.

———, *The Study of Man*. New York: Appleton-Century-Crofts, 1936.

Lowie, Robert H., "Exogamy and the Classificatory Systems of Relationship," *American Anthropologist*, Vol. 17, April–June 1915.

Lowrie, Samuel H., "Dating Theories and Student Responses," *American Sociological Review*, Vol. 16, No. 3, June 1951.

Malinowski, Bronislaw, *Magic, Science and Religion*. Boston: The Beacon Press, 1948.

Mead, Margaret, *Male and Female*. New York: William Morrow & Company, Inc., 1949.

Middleton, Russell, "Brother-sister and Father-daughter Marriage in Ancient Egypt," *American Sociological Review*, Vol. 27, No. 5, October 1962, pp. 603–611.

Miller, Daniel, and Guy E. Swanson, *The Changing American Parent*. New York: John Wiley & Sons, Inc., 1958.

Ogburn, William F., "The Changing Family," *The Family*, Vol. 19, 1938.

Olson, Ronald L., "Clan and Moiety in Native North America," *University of California Publications in American Archaeology and Ethnology*, Vol. 33, 1934. Berkeley: University of California Press, pp. 351–422.

Parsons, Talcott, *Essays in Sociological Theory Pure and Applied.* New York: The Free Press of Glencoe, 1949.

———, "The Kinship System of the Contemporary United States," *American Anthropologist*, Vol. 45, 1943, pp. 22–38.

———, and Robert F. Bales, *Family, Socialization and Interaction Process.* New York: The Free Press of Glencoe, 1955.

Phillpotts, Bertha Surtees, *Kindred and Clan in the Middle Ages and After.* London: Cambridge University Press, 1913.

Radcliffe-Brown, A. R., "The Social Organization of Australian Tribes." *Oceania*, Vol. I, 1930.

Redfield, Margaret Park, "The American Family: Consensus and Freedom," *The American Journal of Sociology.* Vol. 52, November 1946, pp. 175–183.

Reik, Theodore, *A Psychoanalyst Looks at Love.* New York: Holt, Rinehart and Winston, Inc., 1944.

Reiss, Ira L., *Premarital Sexual Standards in America.* New York: The Free Press of Glencoe, 1960.

Sapir, Edward, "Terms of Relationship and the Levirate," *American Anthropologist*, Vol. 18, 1916.

Schneider, David M., and George C. Homans, "Kinship Terminology and the American Kinship System," *American Anthropologist*, Vol. 57, 1955, pp. 1194–1208.

Smith, Raymond T., *The Negro Family in British Guiana.* New York: Humanities Press, Inc., 1956.

Steward, Julian, *Theory of Culture Change.* Urbana: University of Illinois Press, 1955.

Sunley, Robert, "Early Nineteenth-century American Literature on Child Rearing" in Margaret Mead and Martha Wolfenstein (eds.), *Childhood in Contemporary Cultures.* Chicago: University of Chicago Press, 1955.

Taylor, G. Rattray, *Sex in History.* New York: Ballentine Books, Inc., 1954.

Thomas, William I., *Primitive Behavior.* New York: McGraw-Hill Book Company, Inc., 1937.

Titiev, Mischa, "The Importance of Space in Primitive Kinship," *American Anthropologist*, Vol. 58, No. 5, October 1956.

———, "The Influence of Common Residence on the Unilateral Classification of Kindred," *American Anthropologist,* Vol. 45, 1943.

Truxal, Andrew G., and Francis E. Merrill, *Marriage and the Family in American Culture.* Englewood Cliffs, N. J.: Prentice-Hall, Inc., 1953.

Winch, Robert F., *Mate-Selection.* New York: Harper & Row, Publishers, 1958.

Wyndham, Richard, *The Gentle Savage.* New York: William Morrow & Company, Inc., 1936.

Ethnographic Bibliography

ALOR **Eastern Indonesia**

Cora Dubois, *The People of Alor.* Minneapolis: University of Minnesota Press, 1944.

ANDAMAN ISLANDERS (HRAF)[1]

E. H. Man, *On the Aboriginal Inhabitants of the Andaman Islanders.* London: Trubner, 1883.

ARAPESH **New Guinea**

Margaret Mead, *Sex and Temperament in Three Primitive Societies.* New York: William Morrow & Company, Inc., 1935.

ARAUCANIANS **South America (HRAF)**

Mischa Titiev, *Araucanian Culture in Transition.* Ann Arbor: University of Michigan Press, 1951.

ARUNTA **Australia (HRAF)**

Herbert Basedow, *The Australian Aboriginal.* Adelaide: F. W. Preece, 1925.

Geza Roheim, "Women and Their Life in Central Australia," *Journal of the Royal Anthropological Institute of Great Britain and Ireland,* Vol. 63, 1933, pp. 207–265.

ASHANTI **West Africa (HRAF)**

R. S. Rattray, *Ashanti.* New York: Oxford University Press, 1923.

---

[1] The entry "(HRAF)" indicates that this case was, at the time of writing, included in the ethnography collection of the *Human Relations Area Files.*

R. S. Rattray, *Ashanti Law and Constitution.* New York: Oxford University Press, 1929.

ATRISCO New Mexico

Florence R. Kluckhohn, "The Spanish-Americans of Atrisco," Manuscript, Harvard University, Department of Social Relations.

AYMARA Andes of South America (HRAF)

Harry Tschopik, "The Aymara of Chucuito, Peru: 1. Magic," *Anthropological Papers of the American Museum of Natural History,* Vol. 44, 1951, pp. 133–308.

AZANDE African Sudan (HRAF)

E. E. Evans-Pritchard, *Witchcraft, Oracles and Magic among the Azande.* New York: Oxford University Press, 1937.

P. M. Larken, "An Account of the Zande," *Sudan Notes and Records.* Vols. 9 and 10, 1926–1927.

C. G. and B. Z. Seligman, *Pagan Tribes of the Nilotic Sudan.* London: Routledge & Kegan Paul, Ltd., 1932.

BAIGA India

Verrier Elwin, *The Baiga.* London: John Murray, 1939.

BARRANQUITAS Puerto Rico

Robert A. Manners, "Tabara: Subcultures of a Tobacco and Mixed Crops Municipality" in Julian Steward (ed.), *The People of Puerto Rico.* Urbana, Ill.: University of Illinois Press, 1956.

BEMBA Northern Rhodesia (HRAF)

Audrey Richards, *Chisungu.* London: Faber & Faber, Ltd., 1956.

———, *Land, Labour and Diet in Northern Rhodesia: An Economic Study of the Bemba Tribe.* New York: Oxford University Press, 1939.

BERBERS North Africa

George Peter Murdock, Africa: Its Peoples and Their Culture History. New York: McGraw-Hill Book Company, Inc., 1959.

CHAGGA Kenya (HRAF)

B. Gutmann, *The Tribal Teachings oj the Chagga.* (tr. by W. Goodenough and D. Crawford) Munich: C. H. Beck'sche Verlagsbuchhandlung, 1932.

O. F. Raum, *Chaga Childhood.* New York: Oxford University Press, 1940.

CHENCHU India

C. Furer-Haimendorf, *The Chenchus.* New York: The Macmillan Company, 1943.

CHEYENNE Wyoming-Nebraska-Colorado-Kansas

K. N. Llewellyn and E. A. Hoebel, *The Cheyenne Way.* Norman, Okla.: University of Oklahoma Press, 1941.

CHIRICAHUA APACHE Arizona and Northern Mexico

M. E. Opler, *An Apache Life Way.* Chicago: University of Chicago Press, 1941.

———, "Chiricahua Apache Social Organization" in Fred Eggan (ed.), *Social Anthropology of North American Tribes.* Chicago: University of Chicago Press, 1937.

REINDEER CHUKCHEE Siberia (HRAF)

Waldemar Bogoras, "The Chukchee," Part 3, *Memoirs of the American Museum of Natural History,* Vol. 11, 1909.

COPPER ESKIMO (HRAF)

Diamond Jenness, "The Life of the Copper Eskimos," *Report of the Canadian Arctic Expedition, 1913–1918,* Vol. 12, 1922.

DAHOMEY West Africa

Melville J. Herskovits, *Dahomey: An Ancient West African Kingdom,* Vol. 1. Locust Valley, N. Y.: J. J. Augustin, Inc., 1938.

DAKOTA South Dakota-Wyoming-Nebraska

John G. Neihardt, *When the Tree Flowered.* New York: The Macmillan Company, 1951.

DEOLI Hindu India

Morris Carstairs, *The Twice-Born.* Bloomington: University of Indiana Press, 1958.

DOBU Melanesia (HRAF)

Reo Fortune, *Sorcerers of Dobu.* New York: E. P. Dutton & Co., Inc., 1932.

DRAGALETVSY Bulgaria (HRAF)

Irwin T. Sanders, *Balkan Village.* Lexington: University of Kentucky Press, 1949.

DRUZ Lebanon

Victor F. Ayoub, "Political Structure of a Middle East Community." Doctoral thesis, Harvard University, 1955.

FIJI Oceania (HRAF)

A. M. Hocart, "Lau Islands, Fiji," Bernice P. Bishop Museum, Bull. 62, 1929.

Laura Thompson, "Southern Lau, Fiji: an Ethnography," Bernice P. Bishop Museum, Bull. 162, 1940.

GANDA Uganda (HRAF)

Ernest B. Kalibala, "The Social Structure of the Baganda Tribe of East Africa." Doctoral thesis, Harvard University, 1946.

Lucy P. Mair, *An African People in the Twentieth Century*. London: Routledge & Kegan Paul, Ltd., 1934.

———, "Native Marriage in Buganda," The International Institute of African Languages and Cultures, Memorandum 19, 1940.

John Roscoe, *The Baganda*. New York: The Macmillan Company, 1911.

GUSII Kenya

Robert and Barbara LeVine, "Culture and Personality Development in a Gusii Community" in Beatrice B. Whiting (ed.), *Child Rearing in Six Societies*. New York: John Wiley & Sons, Inc., in press.

HAIDA North America: Northwest Coast

George Peter Murdock, "Kinship and Social Behavior among the Haida," *American Anthropologist*, Vol. 36, No. 3, 1934, pp. 355–385.

HEHE Tanganyika

Elizabeth F. Brown, "Hehe Grandmothers." *Journal of the Royal Anthropological Institute of Great Britain and Ireland*, Vol. 65, 1935, pp. 82–96.

HIDATSA North America: Plains

Robert H. Lowie, "Notes on the Social Organization and Customs of the Mandan, Hidatsa, and Crow Indians." *Anthropological Papers of the American Museum of Natural History*, Vol. 21, 1917.

HINDU INDIA (see also DEOLI, RAJPUTS, NAYARS)

David G. Mandelbaum, "The Family in India" in R. N. Anshen (ed.), *The Family: Its Function and Destiny.* New York: Harper & Row, Publishers, 1949.

D. N. Mitra, "A Hindu Wife," *The American Journal of Sociology,* Vol. 52, 1946.

Ramabai Ranade, *Himself: The Autobiography of a Hindu Lady.* New York: David McKay Company, Inc., 1939.

HOPI Arizona-New Mexico

Leo W. Simmons, *Sun Chief.* New Haven: Yale University Press, 1942.

Mischa Titiev, "Old Oraibi," *Papers of the Peabody Museum of American Archaeology and Ethnology, Harvard University,* Vol. 22, No. 1, 1944.

IBAN Borneo (HRAF)

J. D. Freeman, *The Iban.* Canberra: The Australian National University, 1958.

Edwin H. Gomes, *Seventeen Years among the Sea Dyaks of Borneo: A Record of Intimate Association with the Natives of the Bornean Jungles.* London: Sealey & Company, 1911.

William Howell, "The Sea Dyak," *The Sarawak Gazette,* Vol. 38–40, 1908–1910.

H. Ling Roth, "The Natives of Borneo," *Journal of the Royal Anthropological Institute of Great Britain and Ireland,* Vol. 21, 1892, pp. 110–137.

IFALUK Micronesia (HRAF)

E. S. Burrows, "The People of Ifalik," (1948)

and

Melford E. Spiro, "Ifaluk: a South Sea Culture," (1947) Unpublished manuscripts: Coordinated Investigation of Micronesian Anthropology, Pacific Science Board, National Research Council, Washington, D.C.

IFAGAO Philippines (HRAF)

R. F. Barton, "Ifugao Law," *University of California Publications in American Archaeology and Ethnology.* Vol. 15, 1919.

R. F. Barton, *The Half-way Sun.* New York: Brewer and Warren, 1930.

———, *Philippine Pagans: The Autobiographies of Three Ifugaos.* London: Routledge & Kegan Paul, Ltd., 1938.

IRELAND (rural)

C. M. Arensberg, *The Irish Countryman.* Gloucester, Mass.: Peter Smith, 1950.

C. M. Arensberg and S. T. Kimball, *Family and Community in Ireland.* Cambridge: Harvard University Press, 1940.

JAMAICA

Edith Clarke, *My Mother Who Fathered Me.* London: George Allen & Unwin, Ltd., 1957.

Yehudi A. Cohen, "Structure and Function: Family Organization and Socialization in a Jamaican Community." *American Anthropologist.* Vol. 58, No. 4, 1956.

Fernando Henriques, *Family and Colour in Jamaica.* London: Eyre and Spottiswoode, 1953.

JIVARO Brazil (HRAF)

R. Karsten, *The Head-hunters of Western Amazonas.* Helsinki: Centraltry-cheriet, 1935.

J. Vigna, "Bosquejo Sobre los Indios Shuaras o Jibaros" (tr. by Elinor Stewart) *America Indigena,* Vol. V, 1945.

JORDAN

George L. Harris, *Jordan.* New Haven: HRAF Press, 1958.

JUKUN African Sudan

C. K. Meek, *A Sudanese Kingdom.* London: Routledge & Kegan Paul, Ltd., 1931.

KAINGANG Brazil (HRAF)

Jules Henry, *Jungle People.* Richmond: William Byrd Press, 1941.

KARIERA Australia

A. R. Radcliffe-Brown, "Three Tribes of Western Australia," *Journal of the Royal Anthropological Institute of Great Britain and Ireland,* Vol. 43.

KASKA Western Canada (HRAF)

John J. Honigmann, "Culture and Ethos of Kaska Society." *Yale University Publications in Anthropology,* No. 40, 1949.

John J. Honigmann, "The Kaska Indians: an Ethnographic Reconstruction," *Yale University Publications in Anthropology,* No. 51, 1954.

James A. Teit, "Field Notes on the Tahltan and Kaska Indians: 1912–1915," *Anthropologica,* No. 3, pp. 39–171.

KIBBUTZ Israel

Melford E. Spiro, *Kibbutz: Venture in Utopia.* Cambridge: Harvard University Press, 1956.

———, *Children of the Kibbutz.* Cambridge: Harvard University Press, 1958.

———, "Is the Family Universal?—The Israeli Case" in Norman Bell and Ezra Vogel (eds.), *A Modern Introduction to the Family.* New York: The Free Press of Glencoe, 1960.

KIKUYU Kenya

Charles Dundas, "The Organization and Laws of Some Bantu Tribes in East Africa." *Journal of the Royal Anthropological Institute of Great Britain and Ireland,* Vol. 45, 1915.

Jomo Kenyatta, *Facing Mount Kenya: The Tribal Life of the Gikuyu.* London: Secker and Warburg, 1953.

KIPSIGIS Kenya

J. G. Peristiany, *The Social Institutions of the Kipsigis.* London: Routledge & Kegan Paul, Ltd., 1939.

KIWAI Melanesia

G. Landtman, *The Kiwai Papuans of British New Guinea.* New York: Macmillan Company, 1927.

KURTACHI Solomon Islands (HRAF)

Beatrice M. Blackwood, *Both Sides of Buka Passage.* New York: Oxford University Press, 1935.

KWAKIUTL Vancouver Island

Clellan S. Ford, *Smoke from Their Fires.* New Haven: Yale University Press, 1941.

KWOMA New Guinea

John W. M. Whiting, *Becoming a Kwoma.* New Haven: Yale University Press, 1941.

LAKHER Burma

N. E. Parry, *The Lakhers.* New York: The Macmillan Company, 1932.

LAMBA Northern Rhodesia

Clement M. Doke, *The Lambas of Northern Rhodesia.* London: George G. Harrap & Co., Ltd., 1931.

LEPCHA Sikkim (HRAF)

Geoffrey Gorer, *Himalayan Village.* London: Michael Joseph, 1938.

LESU New Ireland (Melanesia)

Hortense Powdermaker, *Life in Lesu.* New York: W. W. Norton & Company, Inc., 1933.

MALAITA Solomon Islands

H. Ian Hogbin, *Experiments in Civilization.* London: Routledge & Kegan Paul, Ltd., 1939.

MANUS Admiralty Islands (Melanesia)

Margaret Mead, *Growing up in New Guinea.* London: Routledge & Kegan Paul, Ltd., 1931.

———, "Kinship in the Admiralty Islands," *Anthropological Papers of the American Museum of Natural History,* Vol. 34, Part 2, 1934.

MARIA GONDS India

W. V. Grigson, *The Maria Gonds of Bastar.* Bombay: Oxford University Press, 1938.

MARQUESAS Polynesia (HRAF)

E. S. C. Handy, "The Native Culture of the Marquesas," Bernice P. Bishop Museum, Bull. 9, 1923.

Ralph Linton, "Marquesan Culture" in Abram Kardiner, *The Individual and His Society.* New York: Columbia University Press, 1939.

MAYANS Central America (see also Pokom-Mayans, San Pedro la Laguna)

George M. and Merle A. McBride, "Highland Guatemala and Its Maya Communities." *The Geographical Review,* Vol. 32, 1942.

Sylvanus G. Morley, *The Ancient Maya.* Stanford: Stanford University Press, 1946.

MENANGKABAU Sumatra

Fay-Cooper Cole, *The Peoples of Malaysia.* Princeton, N.J.: D. Van Nostrand Company, Inc., 1945.

MENDE Sierra Leone (HRAF)

K. L. Little, *The Mende of Sierra Leone.* London: Routledge & Kegan Paul, Ltd., 1951.

MODJOKUTO Java

Hildred S. Geertz, "Javanese Values and Family Relationships." Doctoral thesis, Radcliffe College, 1956.

———, *The Javanese Family.* New York: The Free Press of Glencoe, 1961.

MOSLEMS OF THE MIDDLE EAST (see also Silwa)

Arthur Jeffery, "The Family in Islam" in R. N. Anshen (ed.), *The Family: Its Function and Destiny.* New York: Harper & Row, Publishers, 1949.

Raphael Patai, *Sex and Family in the Bible and the Middle East.* New York: Doubleday & Company, Inc., 1959.

MUNDUGUMOR New Guinea

Margaret Mead, *Sex and Temperament in Three Primitive Societies.* New York: William Morrow & Company, Inc., 1935.

MURIA India

Verrier Elwin, *The Muria and Their Ghotul.* Bombay: Oxford University Press, 1947.

MURNGIN Australia

W. Lloyd Warner, *A Black Civilization.* New York: Harper & Row, Publishers, 1937.

NAMA HOTTENTOTS South Africa (HRAF)

I. Schapera, *The Khoisan Peoples of South Africa.* London: Routledge & Kegan Paul, Ltd., 1930.

NAVAHO Arizona-New Mexico (HRAF)

David Aberle, "Navaho," in David Schneider and Kathleen Gough (eds.), *Matrilineal Kinship.* Berkeley: University of California Press, 1961.

———, "Navaho Kinship: a Trial Run." Manuscript, Social Science Research Council Seminar on Kinship, Harvard University, 1954.

Flora L. Bailey, "Some Sex Beliefs and Practices in a Navaho Community," *Papers of the Peabody Museum of American Archaeology and Ethnology,* Vol. 40, No. 2, 1950. Harvard University.

Walter Dyk, *Son of Old Man Hat.* New York: Harcourt, Brace & World, Inc., 1938.

Clyde Kluckhohn, "As an Anthropologist Views It" in A. Deutsch (ed.), *Sex Habits of American Men.* Englewood Cliffs, N.J.: Prentice-Hall, Inc., 1948.

———, "Some Aspects of Navaho Infancy and Childhood" in G. Roheim (ed.), *Psychoanalysis and the Social Sciences,* Vol. 1, 1947.

———, and Dorothea Leighton, *The Navaho.* Cambridge: Harvard University Press, 1951.

Dorothea Leighton and Clyde Kluckhohn, *Children of the People.* Cambridge: Harvard University Press, 1948.

NAYAR **Hindu India**

E. Kathleen Gough, "The Nayars and the Definition of Marriage," *Journal of the Royal Anthropological Institute of Great Britain and Ireland,* Vol. 89, Part 1, 1959.

———, "The Traditional Kinship System of the Nayars of Malabar." Manuscript, Social Science Research Council Summer Seminar on Kinship, Harvard University, 1954.

David M. Schneider and Kathleen Gough, *Matrilineal Kinship.* Berkeley: University of California Press, 1961.

NUER **African Sudan (HRAF)**

E. E. Evans-Pritchard, *Kinship and Marriage among the Nuer.* New York: Oxford University Press, 1951.

NYAKUSA **Africa (HRAF)**

Monica Wilson, *Good Company.* New York: Oxford University Press, 1951.

OJIBWA **Ontario (HRAF)**

Victor Barnouw, "Acculturation and Personality Among the Wisconsin Chippewa," American Anthropological Association, Memoir 72, 1950.

M. Inez Hilger, "Chippewa Child Life and Its Cultural Background," Bureau of American Ethnology, Bull. 146, 1951.

Diamond Jenness, "The Ojibwa Indians of Parry Island, Their Social and Religious Life," Canadian Department of Mines, Bull. 78, 1935.

W. Vernon Kinietz, "Chippewa Village: the Study of Kakikitegon," Cranbrook Institute of Science, Bull. 25. New York: University Publishers, Inc., 1947.

Ruth Landes, "Ojibwa Sociology," *Columbia University Contributions to Anthropology*, Vol. 29, 1937.

ONTONG JAVA Solomon Islands

H. Ian Hogbin, "The Social Organization of Ontong Java," *Oceania*, Vol. 1, 1930–31.

ORASAC Serbia

Joel Martin Halpern, *A Serbian Village*. New York: Columbia University Press, 1958.

PAPAGO Northern Mexico (HRAF)

A. Joseph, R. B. Spicer, and J. Chesky, *The Desert People*. Chicago: University of Chicago Press, 1949.

R. M. Underhill, *Social Organization of the Papago Indians*. New York: Columbia University Press, 1939.

T. R. Williams, "Papago Socialization." Manuscript.

PEYRANE France

Laurence Wylie, *Village in the Vaucluse*. Cambridge: Harvard University Press, 1957.

POKOM-MAYANS Guatemala

S. W. Miles, "The Sixteenth-century Pokom-Maya; a Documentary Analysis of Social Structure and Archaeological Setting," *Transactions of the American Philosophical Society*, New Series, Vol. 47, Part 4, 1957.

PUPAPUKA Polynesia (HRAF)

Ernest and Pearl Beaglehole, "Ethnology of Pukapuka," Bernice P. Bishop Museum, Bull. 150, 1938.

RAJPUTS Hindu India

L. M. Triandis and J. Hitchcock, "The Rajputs of Khalapur" in Beatrice B. Whiting (ed.), *Child Rearing in Six Societies*. New York: John Wiley & Sons, Inc., in press.

SAMOA Polynesia (HRAF)

F. J. H. Grattan, *An Introduction to Samoan Custom*. Apia, Western Samoa: Samoa Printing and Publishing Company, 1948.

Margaret Mead, *Coming of Age in Samoa.* New York: William Morrow & Company, Inc., 1928.

———, "Social Organization of Manua," Bernice P. Biship Museum, Bull. 76, 1930.

SAN PEDRO LA LAGUNA Mayans, Guatemala

Benjamin D. Paul, *Life in a Guatemalan Village.* Chicago: The Delphian Society, 1950.

SIANE New Guinea

Richard F. Salisbury, "Asymmetrical Marriage Systems," *American Anthropologist.* Vol. 58, No. 4, 1956.

SILWA Egypt

Hammed Ammar, *Growing Up in an Egyptian Village.* London: Routledge & Kegan Paul, Ltd., 1954.

SIRIONO Bolivia (HRAF)

Allan R. Holmberg, *Nomads of the Long Bow.* Washington, D.C.: U.S. Government Printing Office, 1950.

SIWAI Solomon Islands

Douglas L. Oliver, *A Solomon Island Society.* Cambridge: Harvard University Press, 1955.

SOMALI East Africa (HRAF)

I. M. Lewis, "Peoples of the Horn of Africa," *Ethnographic Survey of Africa, North Eastern Africa, Part I.* London: International African Institute, 1955.

SUBANUM Philippines (HRAF)

Emerson B. Christie, "The Subanuns of Sindangan Bay," *Bureau of Science Division of Ethnology Publications,* Vol. 6, Part 1. Manila: Bureau of Printing, 1909.

John P. Finley and William Churchill, "The Subanu: Studies of a Sub-Visayan Mountain Folk of Mindanao," Carnegie Institution of Washington, Publication No. 184. Washington, D.C.: 1913.

Charles O. Frake, "The Eastern Subanun of Mindanao" in G. P. Murdock (ed.), *Social Structure in Southeast Asia. Viking Fund Publications in Anthropology,* No. 29, 1960.

———, "Social Organization and Shifting Cultivation among the Sindangan Subanun." Doctoral thesis, Yale University, 1955.

SUYE MURA Japan

John F. Embree, *Suye Mura: A Japanese Village*. Chicago: University of Chicago Press, 1939.

TAITOU China (HRAF)

Martin C. Yang, *A Chinese Village: Taitou, Shantung Province.* New York: Columbia University Press, 1945.

TALLENSI African Sudan (HRAF)

Meyer Fortes, *The Web of Kinship among the Tallensi.* New York: Oxford University Press, 1949.

TANALA Madagascar (HRAF)

Ralph Linton, *The Study of Man.* New York: Appleton-Century-Crofts, 1936.

———, "The Tanala: a Hill Tribe in Madagascar," *Publications of the Field Museum of Natural History. Anthropological Series,* Vol. 22, 1933.

TARAHUMARA Northern Mexico

W. C. Bennett and R. M. Zingg, *The Tarahumara.* Chicago: University of Chicago Press, 1935.

TARONG Philippines

William F. and Corinne Nydegger, "Tarong: an Ilocos Barrio" in B. B. Whiting (ed.), *Child Rearing in Six Societies.* New York: John Wiley & Sons, Inc., in press.

TCHAMBULI New Guinea

Margaret Mead, *Sex and Temperament in Three Primitive Societies.* New York: William Morrow & Company, Inc., 1935.

TEPOZTLAN Mexico

Oscar Lewis, *Five Families.* New York: Basic Books, Inc., 1959.

———, *Life in a Mexican Village: Tepoztlan Revisited.* Urbana, Ill.: University of Illinois Press, 1951.

THONGA South Africa (HRAF)

H. A. Junod, The Life of A South African Tribe. New York: The Macmillan Company, 1927.

TIBET

Sir Charles Bell, *The People of Tibet.* New York: Oxford University Press, 1928.

TIKOPIA Polynesia (HRAF)

Raymond Firth, *We, the Tikopia.* New York: American Book Company, 1936.

EASTERN TIMBIRA Brazil (HRAF)

Curt Nimenaju, "The Eastern Timbira." (tr. by R. H. Lowie) *University of California Publications in American Archaeology and Ethnology,* Vol. 16, 1946.

TIV West Africa (HRAF)

Paul and Laura Bohannan, "The Tiv of Central Nigeria," *Ethnographic Survey of Africa, West Africa, Part VIII.* London: International African Institute, 1953.

E. S. Bowen, *Return to Laughter.* London: Victor Gollancz, Ltd., 1954.

TOBA BATAK Sumatra

Fay-Cooper Cole, *The Peoples of Malaysia.* New York: D. Van Nostrand Company, Inc., 1945.

E. M. Loeb, "Patrilineal and Matrilineal Organization in Sumatra: The Batak and the Minangkabau," *American Anthropologist,* Vol. 35, 1933.

TODA India

W. H. R. Rivers, *The Todas.* New York: The Macmillan Company, 1906.

TONGA Polynesia

Edward Winslow Gifford, "Tongan Society," Bernice P. Bishop Museum, Bull. 61, 1929.

H. Ian Hogbin, *Law and Order in Polynesia.* London: Christophers, 1934.

PLATEAU TONGA Northern Rhodesia

Elizabeth Colson, *Marriage and the Family among the Plateau Tonga of Northern Rhodesia.* Manchester: Manchester University Press, 1958.

———, "Plateau Tonga" in David M. Schneider and Kathleen Gough (eds.), *Matrilineal Kinship.* Berkeley: University of California Press, 1961.

———, "Plateau Tonga." Manuscript, Social Science Research Council Summer Seminar on Kinship, Harvard University. 1954.

TROBRIAND ISLANDERS Melanesia (HRAF)

George H. Fathauer, "Kinship and Social Structure of the Trobriand Islanders." Manuscript, Social Science Research Council Summer Seminar on Kinship, Harvard University, 1954.

Bronislaw Malinowski, *Argonauts of the Western Pacific*. London: Routledge & Kegan Paul, Ltd., 1922.

———, *The Sexual Life of Savages in Northwest Melanesia*. New York: Liveright Publishing Corporation, 1929.

———, *Sex and Repression in Savage Society*. London: Paul, Trench and Trubner, 1927.

———, *Coral Gardens and Their Magic*. London: George Allen & Unwin, Ltd., 1935.

Ellis Silas, *A Primitive Arcadia*. London: T. Fisher Unwin, 1926.

TRUK Micronesia

Anne Fischer, "The Role of the Trukese Mother and its Effect on Child Training." Manuscript, Department of Sociology and Anthropology, Tulane University.

Ward H. Goodenough, "Property, Kin and Community on Truk." *Yale University Publications in Anthropology*, No. 46, 1951.

TURKANA East Africa

Philip H. Gulliver, *The Family Herds*. London: Routledge & Kegan Paul, Ltd., 1955.

UKRAINE

Samuel Koenig, "Marriage and the Family among the Galician Ukrainians" in G. P. Murdock (ed.), *Studies in the Science of Society*. New Haven: Yale University Press, 1937.

ULITHI Micronesia

William A. Lessa, "The Ethnography of Ulithi Atoll." Doctoral thesis, University of California, Los Angeles, 1950.

VALLE CANA Puerto Rico

David Landy, *Tropical Childhood*. Chapel Hill: The University of North Carolina Press, 1959.

WINNEBAGO Wisconsin

Paul Radin, "The Autobiography of a Winnebago Indian," *University of California Publications in American Archaeology and Ethnology*, Vol. 16, No. 7, 1920.

Paul Radin, *Crashing Thunder: The Autobiography of an American Indian.* New York: Appleton-Century-Crofts, Inc., 1926.

WOGEO Melanesia (HRAF)

H. Ian Hogbin, "Sorcery and Administration," *Oceania,* Vol. 6, 1935.

———, "A New Guinea Infancy: from Conception to Weaning in Wogeo," *Oceania,* Vol. 13, 1943.

———, "A New Guinea Childhood: from Weaning till the Eighth Year in Wogeo," *Oceania,* Vol. 16, 1946.

YIR-YIRONT Australia

Richard Lauriston Sharp, "The Social Anthropology of a Totemic System in North Queensland, Australia." Doctoral thesis, Harvard University, 1937.

ZAPOTEC Southern Mexico

Elsie Clews Parsons, *Mitla: Town of Souls.* Chicago: University of Chicago Press, 1936.

ZINACANTAN Southern Mexico

Benjamin N. Colby, "Ethnic Relations in the Highlands of Chiapas, Mexico." Doctoral thesis, Harvard University, 1960.

Index of Ethnographic Cases*

* This index contains all *single references* to ethnographic cases. References that appear in *lists* of cases have not been included here.

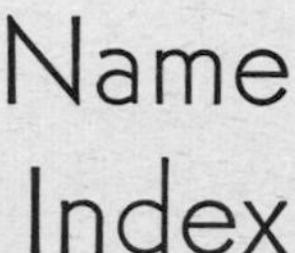

Name Index

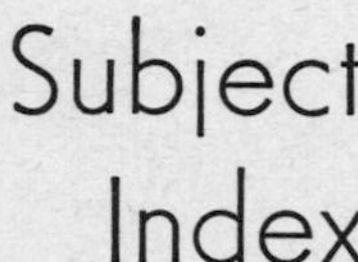

Subject Index